Housing and Family Wealth

This innovative collection provides a multidisciplinary and cross-national perspective on the links between housing, personal wealth and the family in contemporary society. Reasserting the role of the family and informal networks in housing provision, it counteracts a tendency to view housing issues in the narrow terms of market and state provision.

The contributions include analyses from the USA, Japan, Hong Kong, Greece, France, Sweden and Hungary, and this highly international perspective allows the book to address important policy questions and offer new theoretical insights into the way housing is embedded in the wider social structure. By moving away from the more usual, highly ethnocentric discussion of today's housing issues, the book aims to provide a more sociological account of the relationship between housing and wealth, and the social structures within which that relationship is founded.

Ray Forrest is Professor of Urban Studies, University of Bristol. **Alan Murie** is Professor of Urban and Regional Studies, University of Birmingham.

Housing and Family Wealth

Comparative International Perspectives

Edited by Ray Forrest and Alan Murie

London and New York

First published 1995
by Routledge
11 New Fetter Lane, London EC4P 4EE

Simultaneously published in the USA and Canada
by Routledge
29 West 35th Street, New York, NY 10001

Typeset in Palatino by
Florencetype Ltd, Stoodleigh Court, Devon
Printed and bound in Great Britain by
T J Press (Padstow) Ltd, Padstow, Cornwall.

British Library Cataloguing in Publication Data
A catalogue record for this book is available from the British Library
ISBN 0-415-07194-1

Library of Congress Cataloging in Publication Data
Housing and family wealth / edited by Ray Forrest and Alan Murie.
  p. cm
  Includes bibliographical references and index.
  1. Home ownership—Social aspects. 2. Housing. 3. Property.
4. Wealth. 5. Social classes. 6. Family. I. Forrest, Ray.
II. Murie, Alan.
HD7287.8.H683 1995
363.5—dc20   94-20086
                                                            CIP

Contents

Figures

Tables

Contributors

Blair Badcock is Senior Lecturer in Geography, University of Adelaide.

Catherine Bonvalet is a researcher at the Institut National D'Etudes Demographiques in Paris.

Joanna Brownstein is a graduate student in City and Regional Planning, University of North Carolina at Chapel Hill.

Marc Choko is a Professor at the Institut National de la Recherche Scientifique, University of Quebec.

Dimitris Emmanuel is Head of Research in DEPOS, Athens.

Ray Forrest is Professor of Urban Studies at the University of Bristol.

Adrian Franklin is Senior Lecturer in Sociology at the University of Tasmania.

Kazuo Hayakawa is Professor of Engineering at Kobe University.

Yosuke Hirayama is Assistant Researcher in the Faculty of Engineering at Kobe University.

Jim Kemeny is Reader of Social Policy at the University of Plymouth.

Tai-lok Lui is a senior lecturer at the Chinese University of Hong Kong.

Alan Murie is Professor of Urban and Regional Studies at the University of Birmingham.

Michael Stegmen is Cary C. Boshamer Professor of City and Regional Planning, University of North Carolina at Chapel Hill.

Kenneth Temkin is a doctoral candidate in City and Regional Planning at the University of North Carolina at Chapel Hill.

David Thorns is Reader in Sociology at the University of Canterbury, Christchurch.

Antonio Tosi is the Dipartimento di Scienze del Territorio, Milan Polytechnic.

Chapter 1

Housing and family wealth in comparative perspective

Ray Forrest and Alan Murie

The growth of individual home ownership has been a common phenomenon in recent decades across a broad range of developed economies. Its growth has been associated with ideas of extending individual property ownership and with a pervasive privatism and individualism in contemporary society. Home ownership is seen as an essential component of the middle class, or indeed classless, lifestyle and as a key ingredient in ideological constructs such as the American or Australian dream or the British property-owning democracy. In both specialist housing debates and within mainstream discussions in sociology or politics there has been increasing interest in the significance of home ownership in processes of social restratification and political realignment. From a variety of perspectives there is a strong message of societies entering a new and qualitatively distinct period of social change. Whether or not these changes (for example, described as postFordist or postmodern) are indeed occurring on any scale is open to debate. However, whatever the theoretical formulation the spread of individual ownership of dwellings is appropriated as a symptom of such change. And it is the evident and measurable spread of personal wealth in the form of dwellings which is often a principal element of this interest in the social significance of mass home ownership.

This book sets out to examine different elements of the relationship between housing and wealth. Interest in the wealth-generating aspects of housing has been associated with a common experience of increasing levels of home ownership in many countries and its typical status as the majority tenure for households. This development can also be expressed in terms of the *composition* of personal-sector wealth. In the UK, for example, dwellings net of mortgage debt now represent some 36 per cent of total net personal-sector wealth. This compares with 23 per cent in 1971. In France 30 per cent of total assets in 1979 were in the form of owner-occupied dwellings. And in the USA total home equity was two-and-a-half times greater in 1989 than in 1960 and accounted for over a fifth of household-sector assets (see Chapter 5).

The expansion of home ownership has generally occurred initially among younger, mobile households. As home ownership markets have matured, purchasers have aged and with the value of properties being maintained or rising in real terms, personal-sector wealth grew and spread through a wider range of age groups. At the individual household level a lifetime of movement within the home-ownership sector could have produced an extremely valuable asset. The use of these monies has become of considerable interest to social scientists and to policy makers. The differential accumulation of this form of wealth has implications for social stratification for this generation and for the next through intergenerational transfers. And the global amounts involved could have major implications for levels and patterns of consumption.

The accumulative aspects of owner-occupied housing have fuelled a number of debates. The observation that some people can make money out of housing and some cannot has been implicated in more general analyses of a growing polarisation in society – the haves and the have nots, the owners and the renters, the included majority and the excluded minority. The division in housing markets between outright and mortgaged owners and the typically less affluent in the rental tenures has been a key element in references to new social cleavages which may be eclipsing old class divisions derived from work status. The extent to which housing-market processes represent semi-autonomous elements in social stratification or are modifying but epiphenomenal dimensions of social structures which continue to be shaped essentially by class relations has been the subject of considerable debate.

These discussions have been particularly prominent in the UK where periods of rampant house-price inflation over the last two decades have occurred in the context of a highly developed and rapidly expanding owner-occupied market. Particularly in the 1980s, and consistent with the hegemonic discourse of

Thatcherism and privatisation, one of the dominant images in housing was of the nomadic, atomised household pursuing an entrepreneurial path up the housing ladder. It was more speculation than gentrification. In an increasingly deregulated mortgage market, loan finance was freely available and mobility was relatively straightforward. The key attribute of a dwelling was no longer a use value but an exchange value to be traded at the right time in the right place. The fact that such housing entrepreneurs probably constituted a small minority is unimportant. For the majority the message was that housing was something which made money whether you were hypermobile or simply perused the estate agents' adverts in your armchair. The house-price pages were probably monitored more extensively than share prices.

This book does not, however, aim to pursue these debates in a narrow sense. Indeed, the objective is to move away from a highly ethnocentric, if not anglocentric discussion of contemporary housing issues which are increasingly couched in terms of price, affordability and accumulation. Rather it aims to broaden the discussion in a number of ways. First, it aims to provide an international perspective on the relationship between housing and personal-sector wealth. Second, it aims to provide a more sociological account of the relationship between housing as wealth and the social structures within which that relationship is embedded. Third, and related to the above, it aims to help re-establish the connections between the sociology of housing and the sociology of the family, between formal and informal aspects of housing provision.

Mainstream debates in housing have tended to focus on a continuum with state provision at one end and market provision at the other. Issues of access to adequate housing have tended to be seen in terms of the relative size of subsidies to one tenure or another and in terms of the overall shape and incidence of state subsidies. Hence, debates around housing policy have in recent years been preoccupied with an evident general shift away from various forms of direct state provision towards more market-oriented forms and from object to subject subsidies. Within what are generally described as more privatised housing markets, the resources available to individual households have been seen most typically as a combination of earned incomes (bargaining position in the labour market), household structures (multiple-earner/single-earner households) and access to subsidy.

However, within this context, family and other informal resources may take on greater importance. Most directly, this is evident in situations where a substantial deposit may be required to gain a foothold in the home-ownership sector. The family may be the principal source for such financial assistance. These informal elements have always been important in the housing sphere but they have become rather lost in debates where notions of market and/or state provision dominate. Ironically, perhaps, it is the growth of home ownership and the debates around money accumulation and capital gains which lead to a renewed focus on the role of the family and kinship networks in housing. In housing debates in the industrialised societies there has been little reference to informal social relations and the role of social and kinship networks in the attainment of housing goals – at least in what may be regarded as the dominant paradigm. Certainly in the anglo-saxon literature on housing which has been dominated by economists, social-policy analysts and geographers the implicit message is that modern housing markets are fuelled by individual demand related to age, income and employment mediated by modern capitalist institutions (banks, building societies) and state subventions. Other factors concerning the resources which can be mobilised in and around family and friendship networks are regarded as at most peripheral and unimportant and as anachronistic, pre-capitalist remnants. The importance of housing in relation to issues of intergenerational reciprocity, as 'family home' and as a collective emotional and financial project (as opposed to the individual aspiration and achievement of the atomised household) is regarded as anthropologically strange, something relevant to other, typically Third World cultures. Where the role of the family in housing is related to the more industrialised societies it is in relation to the survival of the extended family in, for example, Catholic and southern Mediterreanean societies. And in that context, while the role of the family and family relations is seen to be important in housing provision, it is an element which is seen to have declining significance as more modern institutions take over traditional roles and as urbanisation supplants rural remnants.

There were various influences which led to the production of this book. Initially it was the realisation that the issues around wealth accumulation and transfer through the growth of home ownership had important implications for relations within families. The monetary gains (or losses) through the operation of the owner-occupied market impacted on the overall distribution of personal-sector wealth and raised important issues regarding inequalities between social groups. An understanding of the impact of wealth accumulation in home ownership demanded therefore an analysis of the social structure in which such processes were occurring. It was inadequate to simply extrapolate global sums in an undifferentiated way or to generalise from one society to another. It was also inadequate to focus narrowly on monetary aspects to the neglect of the social relations involved or indeed the impact on the wider political economy. For example, to what extent and in what circumstances were issues of affordability in home ownership requiring a new mobilisation of family resources? Were elder kin being called upon increasingly to assist access to home ownership? Has the focus on intergenerational wealth transfers at death underplayed the significance of lifetime transfers? Does a flow of money from older to younger generations to assist the achievement of independent living imply a reciprocal flow of services in the other direction? What are the implications of the financial importance of individual home ownership for social security in old age and the currently pervasive debates about the viability of existing structures of welfare provision? There was also the simple observation that while household structures were continuing to shift towards smaller units with fewer children and typically no more than two generations, the family was being extended through longevity. In other words, more people than ever have living grandparents and in that sense intergenerational links have greater rather than less significance than previously. These and other questions are addressed in various ways in the papers in this collection.

To avoid creating too broad a backcloth for the discussion it was decided to limit the scope of the book to industrialised (or postindustrialised?) societies. This is interpreted fairly broadly to refer to societies where, intuitively, the ownership of dwellings would have broadly similar meanings and where home and work are generally regarded as separate spheres. A conscious effort was also made to represent a range of disciplines including anthropology, sociology and economics in order to gain a more rounded view of the relationships between housing and wealth.

The contributors to this volume draw on a range of evidence. Some aspects of the debate lend themselves more easily to quantitative measures – where these are available. In other cases, more qualitative studies are used to explore relevant aspects of the nature of housing wealth in culturally specific settings. Some issues can only be explored tentatively as the empirical evidence is lacking.

Chapters 2–6 by Thorns, Badcock, Forrest and Murie, Stegman *et al.* and Lui focus essentially on the distributional impact of accumulation through home ownership. These papers can be seen in general terms as having similar analytical points of departure. The central concern is with the growth of home ownership and the social and spatial implications of differential wealth accumulation. Issues are raised in relation to the class and racial bias in housing wealth accumulation, to cohort effects as regards access to home ownership and monetary gains and the interaction of housing-tenure change and demographic shifts. And the concern with measurable financial gains meshes with a broader appreciation of housing as a family project with intra- and intergenerational implications. These issues are also addressed in the chapters by Emmanuel, Bonvalet, Ladanyi and Hirayama and Hayakawa. However, these papers address the links between housing and wealth from a perspective where the role of the family is more evidently central and issues of family assistance, informal networks, self help and reciprocity are more closely examined. Emmanuel, for example, explores *inter alia* the 'social myth' of family reciprocity in the context of housing provision in Greek society. Ladanyi highlights the role of 'kalaka', the reciprocal exchange of labour, in the growth of individual home ownership in Hungary.

These chapters all situate their discussions in the context of the experiences of one country and focus on home ownership. The chapters by Choko, Franklin and Tosi are intentionally more broadranging. Choko offers a review of the various debates around housing and wealth and is concerned particularly with the political and ideological aspects. In concluding his assessment of the theoretical arguments and empirical evidence from various studies he suggests that the question of differential wealth gains in terms of class, gender or ethnicity is important but may be secondary to the escape from 'tenancy' which home ownership represents for the working class.

Tosi and Franklin explore a variety of aspects of the relationship between housing, family and wealth from sociological and anthropological perspectives. Both pick up many of the issues raised in earlier chapters and both are concerned to represent housing as an 'act' or 'practice' in which family ties, assistance, friendship networks and reciprocity are important elements. Tosi critiques conventional approaches to housing in which analyses are conducted with restrictive social indicators, wealth is conceived of in narrow monetary terms and where processes of self help and informalisation are viewed as anomalous housing practices. The final chapter by Kemeny addresses some of these same issues in the context of Sweden where individual home ownership has been less dominant. Kemeny, like Tosi, offers a different perspective on the nature of wealth and high-lights processes of reciprocity and the mobilisation of informal networks within a housing system which ostensibly operates with bureaucratic rules and procedures. In the concluding chapter we attempt to draw out some of the general lessons and observations from the collection. Some consistent messages emerge but a reading of the various chapters will expose numerous implicit and explicit differences and incompatibilities. These differences are a positive outcome. They expose the way in which housing provision is embedded within specific cultural and social milieux – and of course the immersion of the authors themselves within those milieux.

Chapter 2

Housing wealth and inheritance
The New Zealand experience

D. Thorns

INTRODUCTION

The issue of inheritance has been associated with questions of class reproduction as it is one of the means by which wealth and position are maintained. In the last few decades with the expansion of home ownership, particularly in Britain, the role of housing wealth in patterns of inheritance has attracted increased attention. However, in considering inheritance it is important to appreciate that more than economic issues are involved. The death of a person and the distribution of his or her effects is an important rite of passage which is observed in different ways within families and across cultures. The degree to which the distribution of possessions is organised may well depend on the size of the estate in money terms but this may not be the only determinant. Research into inheritance has attempted to explore the bequeathing process through the wills that people draw up. However, not all people leave wills and then not all wills are primarily about the disposal of economic assets. For example there might be explicit instructions on the nature of the funeral arrangements, who was to be invited, where the bus was to be hired from to take the mourners first to the funeral service and then on to the 'ham' tea, and full details of who would get the memorabilia from the house. In one such case little of this could be effected as at death there was no money for the executors to carry out the wishes of the deceased nor was there likely to be enough mourners to fill the requested coach. In a recent case in New Zealand a dispute arose over the death and burial of a prominent Maori entertainer who was married to a Pakeha (European). Whose rights were paramount, those of the wife or those of the tribe? The Maori iwi (tribe) claimed the body and organised a tangi and then the burial according to their custom on the sacred Taupiri mountain used as the tribal burial ground. The view they held was that the person's prime affiliation was to his tribe and his Whanau (extended family).

What both these illustrations show is that death and the dispersal of possessions both economic and symbolic is a complex social process. To date the debate within the housing-inheritance literature has focused almost entirely upon the wealth-generating aspects and has paid little attention to the symbolic and social. The reason for this is that the current revival of interest and research has been stimulated by recent British experience of house-price escalation during the 1970s and 1980s and the belief which this generated that a major redistribution of wealth was taking place leading to a restratification of the social structure around consumption sectors rather than production. The creation of such housing wealth was seen as exceeding what could be accumulated from other sources, particularly the labour market (Pahl 1975). The nature of the distribution of housing wealth thus became crucial to debates about the nature of inequality and whether or not housing provided a separate or linked form of income and wealth and thus a real material base for collective political and social action.

THEORETICAL DEBATE

The debate over housing inheritance has its origins in the controversy over housing and domestic property classes. The key question here has been the extent to which tenure provides a separate social base and thus impacts upon social stratification and political action. Rex and Moore in their 1967 study of Sparkbrook set the debate in motion through their claim that it was possible to identify housing classes, separate from occupationally defined classes. This dual class structure became the source of much debate and some limited empirical analysis. One critique which developed was that Rex and Moore had misinterpreted Weber in developing their theory and what they were describing was not housing classes but housing status groups (Haddon 1970).

Saunders (1978) picked up on this critique and took the debate a stage further by moving back to Weber's theory and showing the significance of tenure, in particular the ownership of property, which could then be used as a source of return. Domestic property classes then became the focus of attention. This shift allowed the separation of owner occupiers from tenants, especially over the formers' ability to accumulate wealth independently of their labour-market position. Once having established this ability, the next questions were how much was accumulated, from whom was the wealth extracted and redistributed, how was it utilised and finally what happened to this stored wealth on death? The experience of the property booms of the 1970s and 1980s within Britain were crucial for fuelling this debate as the price of property rocketed, increasing the wealth of property owners. As this tenure was steadily expanding over the 1970s and 1980s, did it result in all owners sharing in the bonanza? Saunders emerged as the most strenuous advocate for this view (1984, 1986 and Saunders and Harris 1988). In a series of publications over the 1980s culminating in his *A Nation of Home Owners* (1990), he has argued that owner-occupation has redistributed wealth and led all owners to benefit, creating a new consumption sector of those who gain their services through the market rather than the state, leading to a privatised mode of consumption as the dominant one in British society, replacing the socialised mode which in turn replaced the 'market' mode (Saunders 1986). According to Saunders this shift to the privatised mode gives greater choice and freedom as it transfers property rights to individuals.

Saunder's position however, was originally based upon speculative data and assumptions about the long-term growth of capitalism which seem to underestimate both the extent to which capitalism has cyclical fluctuations and also internal divisions. In his most recent work comparing the experience of 522 households in 450 different houses in three British towns, Slough, Derby and Burnley, he again asserts that all have gained and that in relative terms the gains of those at the lower end of the social scale have been greater than those at the top; hence owner occupation has been redistributive. The difficulty here is that there is a need to look at both the absolute and relative increases as with a considerable range of house prices the results can be quite different (Forrest *et al.* 1990). Saunders also does not give sufficient attention to the variation within the owner-occupier category by ethnicity, gender, location within the country or time of purchase (Pratt 1986a, Edel 1981, Thorns 1981, 1989, 1992,

Dupuis 1991, Hamnett 1989a). Hamnett (1989b), for example, has shown how regional prices within Britain shift in cycles with leading and lagging regions so that it depends on which time period how great the relativities are between the prosperous and declining regions. Saunders also pays insufficient attention to the links between the housing and the labour market – the way in which rather than creating a new independent sector home ownership acts to fragment class relations. For example Forrest, Murie and Williams observe that: 'As home ownership has grown, the fragmentation and differentiation that have emerged have reflected pre-existing variations in local class structures, housing stocks, labour markets and cultural differences' (1990: 126).

A major new dimension to the argument has focused upon housing inheritance. The most comprehensive recent study has been by Hamnett, Harmer and Williams (1991). This study shows that the majority of housing wealth is transferred within the family to the surviving spouse, where they exist, or to the children. Further that housing inheritance tends to reinforce social class position rather than transform it. Finally the impact of inheritance upon individual or household behaviour is lessened by the fact that it normally arrives after the household has been established. The most common use for inheritance was therefore as savings within building societies rather than for either upgrading of housing or other forms of consumption expenditure. This is a very British solution in that building societies play a dominant role in both house-mortgage lending and as savings institutions, which is by no means the case elsewhere. In New Zealand building societies only provide six to seven per cent of all loans, with the major share of the market being supplied by the trading banks (27.8 per cent) and the state Housing Corporation (19 per cent).

The present paper will attempt now to explore some aspects of housing inheritance within the New Zealand context and show that what emerges is a picture of variation and increasing fragmentation within which inheritance tends to exacerbate divisions created in the occupational sphere rather than reduce them.

TENURE STRUCTURE

In considering the New Zealand case it is first necessary to understand the nature of the tenure structure and how this has changed. The time frame for this discussion will be from the 1920s to the present. This period has been chosen as there are reasonably good statistics available and it covers the important periods of the 1930s depression, the post-World War II long boom through to the late 1960s and the marked housing-price rises of the 1970s and 1980s.

In contrast to Britain, New Zealand has had a long period of home ownership as the dominant tenure form. This pattern is not uncommon in colonial immigrant societies where the necessity has been to create a housing stock suitable for the colonial migrants. Government assistance has been provided for the purchase of land and the building of dwellings. The Government in the last decades of the nineteenth century through the Advances to Settlers Act (1894) provided assistance for initially rural and then later in 1899 urban and suburban purchase. With no existing stock it was important for the Colonial Government to support and encourage the building of houses. Also in the nineteenth century a debate took place over tenure structure, whether leasehold or freehold should prevail. This was resolved in the freeholders' favour laying the foundation for the growth of an owner-occupied society.

The linking of home ownership and social stability was quickly established with the politicians of the early decades of the twentieth century seeing this, rather like their British counterparts, as an indicator of reliability, trust and citizenship. For example in the parliamentary debate in 1919 over the Workers Dwelling Act one member commented:

> Home Ownership arouses a better sentiment in the people's pride. Directly you give people a chance of living in a decent house, you render family life a possibility, family discipline possible, and you get an elevating influence working. It will kill discontent and disloyalty, and lead people to be more moral and self denying.
>
> (*NZ Parliamentary Debates*, vol. 185, Oct–Nov 1919: 371)

What, however, these accounts ignore was the existence of a working class of excluded who comprised the rental class, mostly urban dwellers and for whom only limited state assistance was provided. This position was not changed until the arrival of the first Labour Government in the 1930s and the increased building of state houses which was initiated.

The Maori population in the 1920s show up as being over-whelmingly owner occupiers. However, ownership here is communal rather than individual as in European society, and was a reflection of the fact that the Maori population, only numbering some 53,000 (4.5 per cent of the total population) was largely a rural remnant heavily decimated by illness, warfare and land alienation. The actual housing occupied by Maori people was also highly varied and included dwellings of brick, wood, sod, and raupo huts many of which were of poor quality. In the 1920s and 1930s a revival began which was to see their numbers rise. However, in the post-1945 period they also under-went a massive internal migration which turned them from a rural-based people living on their own land to an urban-based and largely tenant people.

The housing crisis which occurred in the 1930s was the result of continuing inadequacies in the quantity and quality of dwellings and the loss of jobs and earnings in the depression. Wages were cut by the Finance Act of 1932 leading to a rapid increase in mortgage foreclosures. Unemployment rose steeply and property prices plummeted leaving those foreclosed with little or no equity. The reduction in state support is shown by the fall in the proportion of new housing loans supplied by the Government from 70 per cent in the mid 1920s to 20 per cent in 1934. The physical condition of the housing stock also was poor. Again this was a continuing problem. In 1919 the Influenza Commission denounced 'the continued habitation of old, dilapi-dated, worm-eaten, vermin infested and in some cases really rotten structures, [and] the economic factors of short supply of houses and excessively high rents' (Crothers 1984: 240). The Housing Survey Act of 1935 also collected considerable evidence of sub-standard housing. Nationally this showed 12 per cent of all dwelling stock was below the minimum laid down (68,405 dwellings). It was in the large cities where much of this sub-standard stock was located. In Auckland, the largest city, of the '10,000 or so inner city residential buildings surveyed, 66% were found to be satisfactory, 26% repairable and 8% so far deteriorated as to be fit only for demolition. About 2000 dwellings were overcrowded' (Chandler 1977: 99).

The Labour Government of 1935 responded to the housing crisis through a broadening of the concept of the welfare state initiated under the Liberals in the 1890s. The welfare state was to

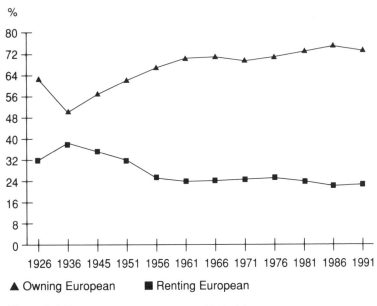

Figure 2.1 European tenure structure 1926–86

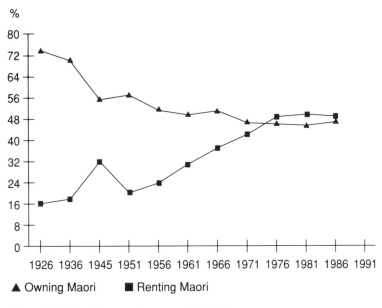

Figure 2.2 Maori tenure structure 1926–86

be constructed around a set of guarantees. These were to provide the citizens with adequate, though never clearly defined, housing, health, employment, education and income. The aim, therefore, was to produce an improved standard of housing for 'ordinary' citizens. The ideology that underpinned the policy was, therefore, universalist. What, however, was the reality?

The Government adopted a strategy which both facilitated house purchase and initiated the construction of public housing on a previously unprecedented scale. However, the balance of activity still favoured the private market and the provision of loans to assist people to buy their own housing. The result was the recovery of the owner-occupation rate which had been depressed by the housing crisis, so that by 1951 the level for European households had recovered to the 1926 level. However, the Maori rate fell steadily as they moved into the cities (see Figures 2.1 and 2.2).

The state facilitated private development through two strategies. One was to take over the development cost of land with the state purchasing land for residential development and carrying out the necessary planning. The actual site development and construction of houses was then left to private capital. The second was the setting up of a new loan scheme through the State Advances Corporation (SAC) in 1936. This was a Government owned and controlled Corporation advancing ordinary loans up to 66 per cent of the value of the security over periods ranging from 25 to 40 years. The Corporation could in addition make special loans where the proportion was greater than 66 per cent. These were intended to assist low-income groups. The SAC provided 3,849 loans during its first three years of existence providing a considerable stimulus to the private house-building industry. The number of houses constructed rapidly recovered under this new system of finance. In 1935 only 2,511 houses were constructed; by 1939 this had been lifted to 5,930 (see Table 2.1). This level was maintained until the pressures of the war on the economy led to a sharp fall in building activity. Production of private housing expanded with the ending of the war and by 1949 had reached 15,200 units per year.

Public housing was also developed by the Labour Government (Mahar 1984). As part of its commitment to providing housing as a right Labour initiated a building programme with the first state house occupied in 1937. The rate of construction increased

Table 2.1   Construction 1926–1970

Year	Completions		Year	Completions	
	State rental	Total dwellings		State rental	Total dwellings
			1946	2,875	
			1947	2,769	
			1948**	3,065	8,253
			1949	3,414	15,200
			1950	3,388	15,800
			1951	3,365	16,400
1926		3,456	1952	2,118	16,300
1927		3,064	1953	2,124	16,100
1928		2,761	1954	2,781	16,600
1929		3,838	1955	2,892	18,500
1930		3,868	1956	2,258	19,200
1931		2,590	1957	2,746	19,200
1932		1,068	1958	1,853	18,600
1933		982	1959	1,647	19,600
1934		1,446	1960	2,128	21,600
1935		2,511	1961	2,148	23,500
1936		3,548	1962	1,972	24,300
1937	22	3,795	1963	1,948	21,100
1938	1,895	4,042	1964	1,562	21,100
1939	3,445	5,930	1965	1,622	23,500
1940	3,870	6,889	1966	1,334	26,000
1941	3,570	6,727	1967	1,469	24,700
1942*	2,605		1968	1,489	23,300
1943	368		1969	1,534	21,800
1944	1,916		1970	1,241	22,300
1945	3,255				

Notes: *   Annual collection of returns from builders and contractors was
          suspended in 1941 and resumed after the War.
       **   1948 figures are unreliable as they do not include flats or the large
          amount of building done by owner builders.

steadily through to 1940, in which year 3,870 houses were built.
The ratio of private to state housing varied over the years of the
Labour Government but in every year private construction far
exceeded that of the state. The actions of the Labour Government
therefore provided some counter to the trend of expansion in
private ownership but it was limited. The proportion of the
population in public housing has never been greater than 9 per
cent of all households and more commonly has been around 6
per cent. The vast majority, even in this time of extensive state

construction, still secured their housing within the private marketplace. The rhetoric of the times may well have been that of universal provision but the reality was closer to that of limited assistance and the underlying commitment was to private housing. It is therefore difficult to see this period as one of a socialised mode of housing provision such as the one Saunders identifies for Britain. If this was not such a period, then New Zealand has never experienced one, as in 1950 the election of a National Government brought a renewed commitment to private provision and the promotion of home ownership (see Dupuis 1989). The New Zealand experience thus raises severe doubts as to the generalisability of Saunders' model of change from market, to state to private modes of consumption.

The new Government moved rapidly to encourage home ownership through a mixture of loans, subsidies for approved home-ownership savings plans and through the capitalisation of family benefits a way of overcoming the deposit problems. New Zealand adopted a set of policies which directly encouraged the production of housing rather than aided the individual purchaser through tax relief on mortgage interest payments as was the case in the British post-war home-ownership expansion. It was arguably rather better targeted assistance as SAC loans were limited to those with a certain level of income buying houses within a given price range. The 1955 Housing Act consolidated previous legislation through establishing a Ministry of Housing introducing a 'fair rents' policy for state housing and encouraging state tenants to buy their properties.

The Government in these policies, however, favoured newly established nuclear families buying their first home. This first home, to attract Government assistance, also had to be a new house, an arrangement which favoured the activities of the larger group builders who produced standardised low-cost housing at a price which fell within the Housing Corporation loan limits. The focus upon new housing reflects the concern within the Government with the size of the housing stock. This remained unchanged until the late 1970s when it was modified to include either a new or existing house.

The result of these policies was a steady increase in housing production from 15,800 in 1950 to 21,600 by 1960 and 26,000 by 1966. Alongside this increase was a rise in the proportion of owner occupiers amongst the European population from 61 per cent in 1951 to 69.7 per cent by 1961. The number has continued to grow and by the 1991 census 73.6 per cent were in this tenure position (see Figure 2.1). This continued increase is despite the onset of a depression within the New Zealand economy which has seen the unemployment rate rise to over 10 per cent of the population, and is an indicator of the limited alternatives available outside of home ownership.

In contrast the Maori rate has continued to decline over the same period. In 1951 54.5 per cent of the Maori population were in owner occupation and 20.4 per cent rental. By the mid 1980s this had changed to 44.9 per cent owner occupied and 49.6 per cent rental (see Figure 2.2). The most significant factor in this change has been the urbanisation of the Maori population. In the 1930s about 70 per cent were rural based whereas by the 1970s 70 per cent were urban based. In the post-1950 expansion of the New Zealand economy labour shortages occurred which were solved through migration from the rural areas by the Maori population and by immigration, from both Europe and the Pacific Islands. In this migration it was into manufacturing, construction and transport services that the Maori and Pacific Island Polynesian were recruited, mostly filling semi-skilled and unskilled manual positions. The result has been the creation of ethnically more diverse and segregated cities.

The tenure structure by the beginning of the 1970s was, therefore, becoming ethnically segregated with a growing difference in the experience of European as against Maori and Pacific Island people. The policies put in place by the state over the 1950s and 1960s had also favoured nuclear households, so single persons especially single women and female-headed households have also been less successful in obtaining ownership due to such problems as raising mortgage finance and their lower wages and less secure employment opportunities and more varied patterns of paid work.

In considering which sections of the population benefited from the explosion in house prices over the next two decades it is important to understand the experience of the cohorts of the 1950s and 1960s. These were groups of people coming into the housing market during very favourable times, probably the most advantageous this century. The economy was growing, there was virtually full employment and there was generous Government support for newly formed nuclear families. These then were the

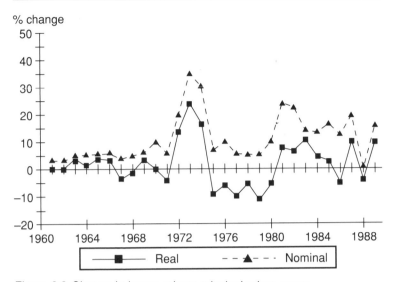

Figure 2.3 Change in house prices: principal urban areas

Source: Data for Figures 2.3–2.5 supplied by Valuation New Zealand and the New Zealand Department of Statistics

beneficiaries. By the 1970s their existing liability had fallen as they had improved their wage levels and their mortgages had been paid back.

The greater instability in the overall economy during the 1970s and 1980s is shown by the succession of booms and busts that occurred in the housing market (see for example Thorns 1992, Roper 1991, Treasury 1984). Figure 2.3 shows clearly the sharp contrast between the 1960s when price variations for the principal urban centres were less than 5 per cent and the 1970s and 1980s when the variations were much greater and the booms and busts much more pronounced.

There have been three distinct boom periods in house prices when they rose much faster than the general rate of price inflation. The first was from 1972–75 when at the height of the boom the prices rose on average over 40 per cent per year in nominal terms (see Figures 2.4a and 2.4b). It is, however, important to appreciate the impact of inflation on these figures. Figures 2.5a and 2.5b show the variations in 'real' terms accounting for inflation. In all four main centres house prices increased by over 20 per cent, with the Christchurch urban region sustaining the

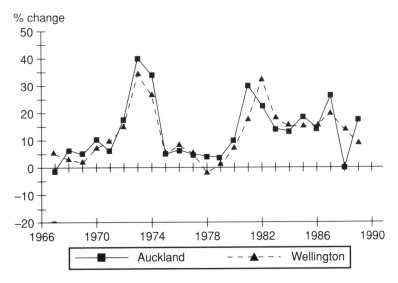

Figure 2.4a Change in nominal house prices: Auckland and Wellington urban areas

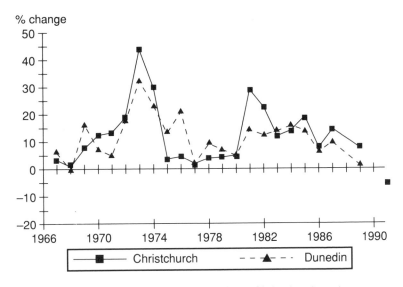

Figure 2.4b Change in nominal house prices: Christchurch and Dunedin urban areas

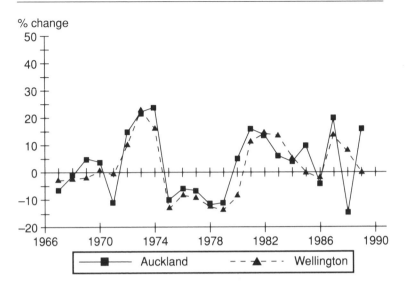

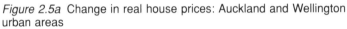

Figure 2.5a Change in real house prices: Auckland and Wellington urban areas

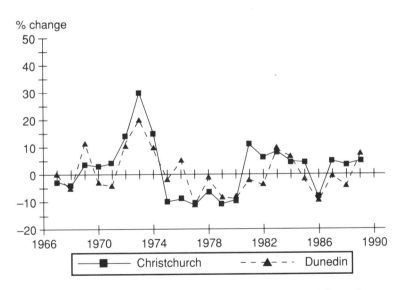

Figure 2.5b Change in real house prices: Christchurch and Dunedin urban areas

greatest increase at over 30 per cent. In 1975 prices slowed and declined in real terms for the next five years in all the main centres with the exception of Wellington. However, the variation was only slight and took the form of some increase in 1976, followed by a steep decline in 1977. The next boom took place in 1980 and lasted through until 1984. By 1985 house prices were again depressed by high interest rates pushing up the cost of access to the housing market. The final period from 1985 to 1990 shows an extremely erratic market with rapid booms and slumps, the recovery in 1986 being short-lived with the stock-market crash of 1987 bringing down house prices, particularly in Auckland (see Figures 2.4a and 2.5a). The losses sustained in Auckland were particularly at the upper end of the market where the impact of the stock-market crash was most acutely felt.

The data show that owners of property during the 1970s and 1980s have generally seen their asset improve faster than the rate of inflation so transferring and storing wealth in their property. The rates of gain vary depending on such factors as when the house and land were bought and sold and both its regional and urban location. A study in the mid 1980s, for example, showed that the annual rates of return from domestic property between 1961 and 1984 averaged 7.9 per cent in real terms (Reserve Bank 1986). The full significance of this is only shown when it is compared with the return from either.the share market or from investment income. The former, over the same period, provided less than a 1 per cent annual rate of return in real terms and the latter a 2 per cent loss. These figures indicate that a cross-subsidisation existed from 'savers' in the various financial institutions to home purchasers, a situation which has been somewhat reversed by the deregulation of the finance market in 1984 and the subsequent level of interest rates which have prevailed for bank deposits and mortgage loans, both now well above the inflation rate. The 1991 rate had fallen to 2–3 per cent per annum whereas interest rates on deposits were still at 8.5–9.75 per cent and mortgage rates for new borrowers were around 11 per cent and still higher for existing borrowers.

The net effect of these changes in house and land values has been to make housing less affordable in the middle years of the 1970s and again in the 1980s, with some improvement in afford-ability towards the end of the 1970s (Snively 1981, National Housing Commission 1988). These shifts impact upon who gains access to housing at these times. It makes it more difficult for single people, single-income families, and single-parent families and those with below average incomes. They are thus compelled to find accommodation within the rental market. This places additional pressures upon both the state rental stock, leading to lengthening waiting lists, and on private-sector stock leading to rising rent levels.

The significance of these variations in general economic conditions for the accumulation ability of different groups is now clear. The 1950s and 1960s provided much more settled and generally easier access to housing. Those reaching retirement age (60) in the 1990s are likely to have benefited both from the easier access of the 1950s and 1960s and the housing booms of the 1970s and 1980s by which time they would have established considerable equity in their property which could then either have been used for further purchase, borrowed against for consumption activity, used as part of a retirement plan or held as part of the 'inheritance' of their children. The changed housing-market experiences of the 1970s and 1980s created a greater awareness of the accumulation potential of housing so that not only is it seen as a form of shelter but also as a source of wealth. New Zealand has no capital gains tax on owner-occupied housing and so its investment potential has continued.

The analysis so far has identified a relatively advantaged 'cohort' whose experience has been shaped from the 1950s to the 1980s. However, it is important to recognise that even within this group substantial variations are found. The most successful were those who have remained married, been in stable employment and have bought and sold in the 'best' locations. Variations within the urban areas and regions have progressively widened under the impact of house-price inflation during the 1970s and 1980s (Thorns 1989, Dupuis 1989, 1991). In the period from 1966 to 1987 regional house-price increases have varied from a fall of 57 per cent in one South Island regional centre to a 98 per cent increase in Auckland, the largest urban centre. Such wide variations make it difficult to generalise about the accumulation experiences of home owners and show the fragmented nature of the market.

The household formation rate has also been dynamic in the 1970s and 1980s, partly as a result of a growing number of dissolutions of marriage. Over the period being considered the rate has risen from 2.95 per 1,000 in 1956 to 11.47 by 1989. This change results in much more complex patterns of inheritance and wealth generation with both more single-person households and blended families.

The final source of variation arises from the fact that some groups have the capacity to exercise choice over their accommodation and thus some capacity to develop a housing career. Research within Christchurch in the late 1970s showed that people moved to enhance their social status and investment opportunities and to acquire increased space (Smith and Thorns 1979). However, the research also showed that the concept of a housing career was only applicable to those who lived and moved in a higher-cost submarket. It was only this group who were able to translate their aspirations into actions.

HOUSING AND PERSONAL WEALTH

The wealth of an individual is acquired through their access to paid work, ability to save and from the capital appreciation of property that they own. There is thus a strong connection between labour-market position and ability to accumulate wealth. In a recent study by the New Zealand Planning Council (NZPC 1990) of wealth distributions based upon estate-duty data it was found that about one third of gross personal wealth was held as real estate, about one fifth as cash and about one eighth as shares. In Table 2.2 the aggregate average asset holdings of private households are shown and the important place within this of owner occupation is demonstrated. In 1985/6 51 per cent of household wealth was derived from this source, making it by far the most significant. By 1987/8 there had been a slight decrease in the importance of owner occupation but only of the order of 3 per cent and it remained by far the most significant source of assets. These figures indicate that housing is a somewhat more important source of personal wealth than in the United Kingdom where residential building, freehold and leasehold accounted for 42 per cent of net wealth in 1974 and 41 per cent in 1984 (Forrest, Murie and Williams 1990).

Variations are found in the assets held at death by the very wealthy and the wealthy. For wealth holders in general, real property including dwellings makes up 35 per cent of gross wealth – about double the value of company shares held by this

Table 2.2 Aggregate and average asset holdings of private households

	Total (NZ$b)		Per household (NZ$000)		Composition (%)	
	1985/6	1987/8	1985/6	1987/8	1985/6	1987/8
Material assets						
Owner-occupied						
housing	39.6	69.3	37.1	61.6	51	48
Contents	15.9	48.2	14.9	42.8	20	33
Vehicles	11.1	14.6	10.5	13.0	14	10
TOTAL	66.6	132.1	62.5	117.4	86	91
Financial assets						
Low-yield	3.2	6.3	3.0	5.6	4	4
High-yield	2.4	4.0	2.2	3.5	3	3
Other interest-						
earning	1.3	1.1	1.2	1.0	2	1
Shares	4.3	2.0	4.0	1.8	5	1
TOTAL	11.2	13.4	10.4	11.9	14	9
Total assets	77.8	145.5	72.9	129.3	100	100

Source: New Zealand Planning Council, *Who Gets What: the Distribution of Income and Wealth in New Zealand*, Wellington, 1990.

group. For the very wealthy (greater than NZ$500,000) this is reversed with over 40 per cent of wealth held in the form of stocks and shares (NZPC 1990). The size of the very wealthy category is however quite small with only 1 per cent of wealth holders (10,000 people) holding about 9.5 per cent of total wealth whereas the wealthy (NZ$200,000–$500,000) comprise 9.9 per cent of all wealth holders (96,000 people) and they own 37 per cent of total wealth. Again these figures reflect a similar pattern to that found in Britain where housing increases as a proportion of wealth in the middle range of wealth holders whereas amongst the top group stocks, shares and land are the most significant (Hamnett *et al.* 1991).

We have now established the importance of housing as a significant contributor to wealth accumulation within New Zealand society. It is now necessary to consider who are the wealthy and how they transmit their wealth to others via property and other forms of gifts and inheritances.

Data from the NZPC study assists us to take the discussion further. In the analysis they provide they look at the area of gifts and inheritances excluding property. The most significant is shown to be cash transfers which comprise 50 per cent with the remainder coming from lump-sum occupational pension payments, life assurance and matrimonial property settlements. The total for all such gifts and inheritances in 1985/6 amounted to NZ$578 per household and in 1987/8 NZ$571. These aggregate figures, however, do not give the full picture as they hide the considerable variations that occur with many households receiving minimal or no gifts and inheritances and others receiving substantial amounts. To explore this further requires more detailed case data.

National aggregate data can also begin to show up variations in wealth distributions by lifecycle, age, gender and ethnicity. Again drawing upon the NZPC data it can be shown that couples with children, except young couples, have the greatest holdings of non-financial assets. Older couples without children have on average more financial assets (see Figure 2.6). In general wealth tends to increase with age up to age 60, when people move into retirement and their assets then tend to decrease. Those with substantial pension funds show a variation to this as they receive a boost to their financial assets at this time. A significant feature of the cohort moving into retirement in the 1980s (60+) is the fact that they are predominantly owner occupiers of freehold property. In the late 1980s 73 per cent of those over 60 had paid off their mortgage and were living in a debt-free house, and a further 14 per cent were still paying a mortgage. This meant that 87 per cent of the over-60s would on death have a substantial asset to be relinquished. The average sale price at the end of the 1980s was NZ$104,800 indicating the size of the potential inheritance. The average figure, however, hides the extent of regional and local variations in asset value. Again to see something of the range we require more detailed data.

Gender is a further significant source of variation in the distribution of wealth. Figures providing data for the wealth holdings of men and women over the 1980s show that the average level of wealth held by women has shown a steady improvement over the decade with women holding 38 per cent of the total by 1988, up from 30 per cent in 1981 (see Figure 2.7). However, one important factor in this is life expectancy which sees women living longer than men. For example, 40 per cent of women's wealth is held by the over-60s, compared with only 25 per cent

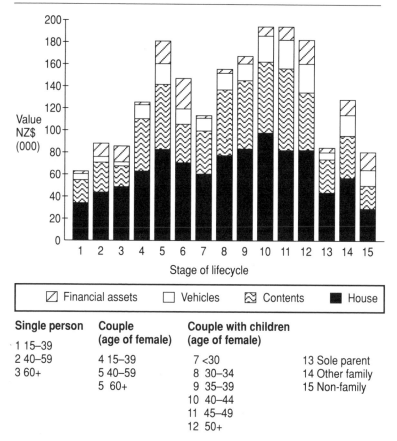

Figure 2.6 Average household wealth-holdings by lifecycle (year ended March 1988)

Source: A. Robins, *Household Distribution of Material and Financial Assets*, New Zealand Planning Council: Wellington, 1990

of that of men. The greater part of housing wealth is initially passed to a spouse on death and then subsequently transferred to children or other relatives. The result is that intergenerational inheritances are generally received in mid life after the receiving household is well established. The increased longevity of the population with more elderly (over 80s) increases the need for lifecare provisions and may well impact upon the size of any inheritance. The family house may well have been sold, with the couple transferring into a smaller unit and then after the death of one partner a final shift to a rest home or lifecare setting may have

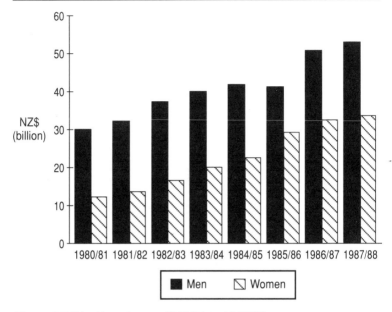

Figure 2.7 Wealth estimates 1980/81 to 1987/88

Source: S. Payne, *Estate Duty Data and FTS Use for Constructing Estimates of Wealth*, New Zealand Planning Council: Wellington, 1990

taken place, thus equity will have been used from the original property and the final size of the inheritance may be much less significant than some have suggested. This is likely to be increasingly the case in New Zealand as the state moves away from a universal superannuation scheme and adopts one targeted around the assets and income of the elderly (Koopman-Boyden 1992).

The probability of inheriting property depends upon the tenure of the previous generation and consequently it is possible to calculate these probabilities given our knowledge of the tenure structure and its changes over time. The results of these calculations are presented in Figures 2.8 and 2.9. The data show how for the population as a whole the probability of parents owning and thus having assets to pass on to the next generation has improved steadily. In 1921 it was likely for 36 per cent of the next generation that both sets of parents would have owned a house; by the 1991 census this was true in 54 per cent of cases (see Figure 2.8). In contrast to this the pattern for Maori households is the reverse, with a declining probability that the succeeding

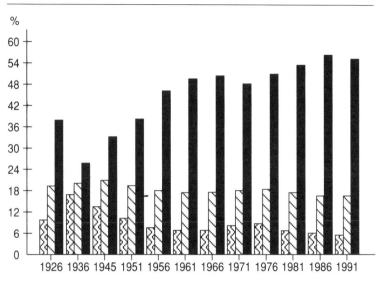

%

Neither set of parents owning   One set of parents owning   Both sets of parents owning

Figure 2.8 European inheritance probabilities

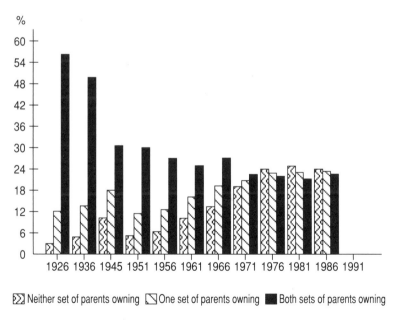

%

Neither set of parents owning   One set of parents owning   Both sets of parents owning

Figure 2.9 Maori inheritance probabilities

generation will be able to become home owners (see Figure 2.9). In 1926 55.2 per cent of establishing households would have come from ones where both sets of parents owned. However, by 1986 this had declined to only 22 per cent. Clearly there has been a marked decline in the potential for inheritance of property amongst Maori households and thus a substantial erosion of their assets. Such a change makes it unlikely that the tenure distribution of the Maori population will change in the foreseeable future. This group will be faced with the high initial costs of raising a deposit in addition to servicing a mortgage and they are unlikely to be able to call upon family wealth to assist. When this is coupled with the recent experience of Maori in the labour market where they form a disproportionately large percentage of the unemployed (for example in 1990 Maori unemployment was 20.6 per cent compared with 7.3 per cent for the total and 5.8 per cent for the European population), it is clear that the potential for wealth creation in the Maori population is substantially lower than within the European.

The tenure distribution of the Pacific Island Polynesian population within New Zealand provides a picture of limited opportunities for owner occupation similar to that for the Maori population. At the 1986 census 42 per cent were in owner occupation and 48 per cent in rental, resulting in only a 17 per cent probability that both parents would be owners of property. Thus as with Maori households there is a much lower probability of inheriting wealth derived from a family-owned house. Again amongst this group unemployment rates (20 per cent) are much higher than for the European population.

The data on housing inheritance probabilities together with that for unemployment indicates the way in which the labour and housing market experiences interconnect to create cumulative disadvantagement and thus the emergence of an 'under' class within New Zealand society.

A further factor shaping wealth accumulation and distribution amongst Maori and Pacific Island households is the size of their families and the nature of their kinship obligations. Data in Table 2.3 show that there is a marked differential between European and Maori and Pacific Island Polynesians in completed family size ranging from 2.5 for Europeans to 3.9 for Pacific Island Polynesians and 4.66 for Maori. In the over-60s group where bequeathing becomes more likely both Maori and Pacific

Table 2.3 Completed family size 1981

Age group	Caucasian	Maori	Pacific Island Polynesian	NZ total
45–54	3.21	5.67	4.93	3.39
55–59	3.04	5.92	5.15	3.18
60+	2.67	6.11	4.96	2.76
Age-standardised all ages rate	2.5	4.66	3.96	2.62

Source: M. Khawaja, 'Trends and differentials in fertility', in *ESCAP Population of New Zealand*, Country Monograph Series, vol. 1, United Nations, New York, 1985.

Island Polynesian families are very much larger than those of Europeans, ranging from 2.67 to 6.11. The greater number of potential inheritors in these families is a significant factor in reducing the likelihood that wealth will accumulate and transfer intergenerationally as a result of owning property.

Christchurch case study

In order to explore some of these issues a little more fully data from a study of housing inheritance within Christchurch will be utilised. The source of the data was the Land Transfer Office through which all transfers of property are recorded on the appropriate Certificate of Title. For a discussion of the role and value of CTs for social and historical research see Hall *et al.* 1982. Where the transfer of property occurs on death this is recorded on a transmission document. Thus by drawing a random sample of transmissions for one selected year it was possible to generate a representative set of cases of property transmission at death. The sample is drawn from property records and as such is biased towards those who own their house, thus the poorest families and those with relatively modest estates are excluded. This same group is also generally excluded in those studies which have approached the analysis of inheritance from wills (see Hamnett *et al.* 1991 or Munroe 1988). The sample rather represents the middle wealth group within which housing contributes the major element (around 50 per cent) of their wealth holding. From the transmission data the general pattern of bequeathing can be determined and some estimates made of the amounts entailed. In addition the data provides a means of identifying other relevant documents for subsequent analysis such as wills, death notices, death certificates and valuation records. For the purposes of the present discussion data from the initial data set only will be used to begin to map the general patterns of property inheritance within Christchurch in the late 1980s.

The British research of Hamnett *et al.* (1991) has demonstrated that inheritance of housing wealth generally occurs when the recipients are in middle life and already established in their own housing careers. Further the work shows that wealth stays within the family. Data from the Christchurch study tends to confirm these findings. Table 2.4 provides data on the gender and age of bequeathers, which shows that the majority are over 50 (62.8 per cent of females and 53 per cent of males). This reflects the pattern of husbands leaving their property to their spouse and the fact that women tend to live longer than men. The discrepancy is particularly marked therefore in those over 80. The longevity of this group together with the increasing costs of care for the dependent elderly is likely to create pressure to sell some or all of the property equity to help finance lifecare. This trend is likely to grow as the state moves increasingly to withdraw financial support for pensions and health services and require individuals to make their own provisions.

Table 2.5 examines the pattern of bequeathing and shows that in the majority of cases the wealth transfers are to a spouse, with 47 per cent going from husband to wife, and a further 17 per cent from the wife to the husband. A further 20 per cent of cases were transfers to children and less than 2 per cent involved intergenerational transfers outside of the immediate family. A final 12 per cent of cases involved the transfer to beneficiaries other than a spouse, children or nephews and nieces. Of the 338 sampled cases just over 50 per cent of the properties were sold to realise capital. The capital generated through sale varied from under NZ$20,000 to over NZ$120,000. Most of the cases realised relatively modest amounts of capital, the median category being NZ$60,000–$79,999. Given the likelihood of multiple inheritors, this means that the additions to the wealth of the recipients are likely to confirm these families as middle wealth owners and provide either additional investment income or a greater capacity to consume.

Table 2.4 Gender and age of bequeathers in Christchurch in the late
1980s

Age	Female		Male		Total	
	No.	%	No.	%	No.	%
20–29	2	1.70	0		2	0.70
30–39	5	4.30	4	2.20	9	3.00
40–49	5	4.30	2	1.10	7	2.40
50–59	8	6.90	16	8.80	24	8.10
60–69	23	19.00	57	31.60	80	27.00
70–79	31	26.70	65	36.10	96	32.40
80–89	30	25.80	29	16.10	59	19.90
90–99	12	10.30	7	3.80	19	6.40
TOTAL	116	100.00	180	100.00	296	100.00

Source: Land Transfer Office: Transmission Records of Property at Death

Table 2.5 Inheritance patterns

Inheritance	Sold		Retained		Total	
	No.	%	No.	%	No.	%
To the spouse						
Husband–wife	55	32.00	104	63.00	159	47.00
Wife–husband	25	14.40	35	21.20	60	17.70
Intergenerational						
To child	52	30.00	18	10.90	70	20.70
To niece/nephew	4	2.30	0		4	1.20
Not sure	1	0.60	1	0.60	2	0.60
Other (i.e. to parent, sibling, friend or executor sale dividing)	36	20.70	7	4.30	43	12.70
TOTAL	173	100.00	165	100.00	338	100.00

Source: Land Transfer Office: Transmission Records of Property at Death

For further investigation of the impact of inheritance upon
recipients it is necessary to have more detailed data which
documents the experience of inheritors. As yet it is not possible
to determine whether the money is mostly invested in banks
and other institutional savings as in the British case, or used for
housing improvements, overseas travel, or other items of
consumption for the recipients or used to assist their family
members enter the housing market, complete their education or

establish a business. In all these cases the access to capital that home ownership provides to middle wealth owners allows them to more successfully reproduce their position within the social structure and maintain their class position.

CONCLUSION

The debate over the impact of housing inheritance upon wealth generation and distribution has been organised around discussion of the rate of return to owner occupiers and has tended to give insufficient attention to the variations amongst such owners. The New Zealand data show that home ownership has grown steadily amongst the European population since the early 1950s and that owners have generally accumulated money through this tenure at a better rate than would have been the case if they had invested in shares or banks. However, the data also show quite clearly that the patterns of accumulation and thus eventually of inheritance vary quite markedly depending upon the time period the market was entered and the region in which the house was situated. Further there are major ethnic and gender differences in housing experience. For Maori households home ownership has declined since the 1950s, reducing their capacity to accumulate wealth through property tenure and thus reinforcing rather than modifying their disadvantaged position within the social structure. In respect to gender both Government policies in the 1950s and 1960s, which favoured single earning nuclear families, and the differential in earning opportunities and employment for women have resulted in couples and single men experiencing the greatest rates of return.

The patterns of capital accumulation thus reflect the class structure of New Zealand society and favour European, 'middle' class, stable family households. For these groups inheritance through housing assists in the reproduction of their social position, it enhances their wealth and allows for the support of their children and close relations who are the principal beneficiaries of this form of inheritance. This ability to support children financially is becoming an increasingly important aspect of class reproduction within New Zealand as the welfare state is restructured away from universal towards heavily targeted benefits and increased 'user pays' within such areas as health and education. In the latter in 1991 a new regime of fees and loans has been introduced which has moved away from a system of universal allowances to one where such allowances are assessed against the household income until the student reaches the age of 25, thus increasing the dependency of most students upon their parents. In households where there is housing inheritance this money can provide a means of supporting the children's tertiary education, funding health user charges and providing capital towards retirement in an environment of increased uncertainty about the level and extent of state support for superannuation.

The study of inheritance needs broadening to move beyond a focus upon housing wealth to look more closely at the impacts, stresses and strains upon household organisation, relations with elderly home-owning parents that result from differential inheritance expectations. It is also important to include in such considerations the non-material aspects of inheritance, the meaning people attach to their house and possessions, the family treasures and the set of obligations. These also vary considerably by gender and across different ethnic groups. The differential ability of households to assist the next generation is not a new phenomenon but is a crucial aspect of how social classes reproduce themselves. It is important that research continues to explore the changing contours of this process as this is vital to increasing our understanding of contemporary patterns of inequality.

Chapter 3

The 'family home' and transfers of wealth in Australia

Blair Badcock

'It is a terrible mistake to let the abuse of capitalist property dis-
credit the idea of family property or to confuse commercial capital
with the home capital which really has opposite possibilities.'
(Stretton 1974, 76)

Home ownership is both a dominant and secure – in the sense
of politically unassailable – element in the Australian housing
system. For these reasons it shares the distinctiveness of those
other societies that are popularly referred to as 'property-owning
democracies' (Daunton 1987). In Australia the term 'family home'
has been used traditionally to evoke complex sentiments
(Richards 1990, 115–43); however, in this essay it will serve as a
term for all manner of households owning or buying their homes,
rather than just the nuclear family. Significantly, although the
level of home ownership has stabilised at about 70 per cent in
Australia, Neutze and Kendig (1991) estimate that almost 90 per
cent of Australian households have been owner-occupiers at
some stage of their housing careers. Indeed, in cultural terms
home ownership represents the very embodiment of the 'Great
Australian Dream'.

The 'family home' fulfils a range of deep-felt needs in an
apparently fragmenting society (Thorns 1992), including shelter
and security, seclusion and respite, self-expression and identity,
and a sense of local belonging. In the minds of buyers, home
purchase avoids the outlay of 'dead' rent money on the one hand,
and the promise of long-term financial security on the other.
But as domestic property, in societies like Britain, the United
States and Canada, as well as in Australia and New Zealand, the
'family home' also represents a potentially significant source of
household wealth and increments to lifetime income (Badcock

1989a; Forrest *et al.* 1990, 127–59; Saunders 1990, 120–203; Yates 1991).

In these societies, where the level of home ownership has stabilised at slightly above two-thirds, owner-occupied housing is the dominant form of private sector wealth and still growing. In Australia, for example, Dilnot (1990) estimates that housing accounted for 59 per cent of aggregate personal wealth in 1986, which compares with 48 per cent for Britain (Hamnett *et al.* 1991, 39), and 41 per cent in the United States in 1984 (Phillips 1990, 183). Other estimates prepared by the Commonwealth Treasury (1990) suggest that dwelling capital has continued to grow as a proportion of private-sector wealth in Australia during the last 20 years: from 50.1 per cent in 1969–70 to 64.9 per cent in 1989–90.

Unremarkably, given the strength of these systemic affinities in English-speaking market economies (Thorns 1992), it has been commonplace until relatively recently to represent the rise of mass home ownership almost wholly in terms of a socially constructed system that helps to sustain the capitalist political economy (Ball 1983). With the one notable exception (Stretton 1974), this is no less true of Australian housing studies (Kemeny 1983; Williams 1984).

That is to say, in Australia after the Second World War a combination of rising real incomes and low real interest rates was fed by a series of Commonwealth housing programmes intentionally designed to assist households to buy their own home. Following his electoral success in 1949, the conservative Prime Minister, Menzies, was astute enough to realise that mass home ownership represented the most effective way of broadening and then securing a base for political support. Thus under Menzies: the financial system was organised to permit the state banks and building societies to advance mortgages at discounted rates; the states were pressured to sell publicly funded homes to tenants on concessional terms; first-home buyers received grants for meeting savings targets. Otherwise, public rental accommodation, which only amounts to a little over 5 per cent of the total housing stock, was provided for the 'deserving poor' under successive Commonwealth-State Housing Agreements since 1945 (Badcock 1989b; Burke *et al.* 1984, 74–112).

Such measures boosted the national level of home ownership from 52.6 per cent in 1947 to about 70 per cent by the beginning of the 1960s. It peaked at 71 per cent in 1966 (Troy 1991), where it has hovered since, suggesting that at least under Australian conditions this is probably close to maximum absorption given the need for a private rental sector for households in transit, and the permanence of a welfare housing sector in the 1990s for the 'non-working poor' (Burke and Hayward 1992).

There is a growing realisation that this preoccupation with the state and market sectors in 'property-owning democracies' has cast a shadow over the role of the family in housing provision. While this emphasis may not have been particularly misplaced as an explanation for the spread of home ownership in countries like Australia during the 1950s and 1960s, since then the changing status of women, the presence of ethnic minorities with quite different housing traditions, and the prospect of a wholesale transfer of housing wealth from one generation of owners to the next *for the first time*, mean that some households are capable of mobilising significant housing resources within the 'family circle'. But how widespread is this phenomenon in Australia? And what of the promise compared with the institutional finance ordinarily available to households in the form of a mortgage or home equity loan, for example? And is there any real prospect of broadening access to home ownership in the next generation (Hamnett 1989c; Kuttner 1987)?

Thus the intention in this chapter is to examine to what degree, if at all, and how these 'family housing resources' actually impinge upon the 'market-driven and policy-driven hierarchy of housing advantage' that already applies under Australian conditions (Cass 1991, 1). This is to say the housing system in Australia confers economic benefits and property rights upon outright home owners, home buyers, public tenants and private tenants, roughly in that order (Kendig *et al.* 1987). The first part of the chapter provides a brief overview of how changes in household demography and the employment status of women are in turn affecting the distribution of housing amongst Australians. Then some of the findings from a survey of Adelaide home owners conducted in 1991 are examined in order to reveal something of the process of accumulation and transfer of housing resources taking place within the family. This evidence forms the basis of a concluding assessment of the contribution of the 'family home' to the distribution of household income and wealth in Australia.

THE CHANGING STRUCTURE OF THE AUSTRALIAN HOUSEHOLD AND ITS IMPACT UPON OCCUPANCY

Table 3.1 characterises the tenure pattern of housing occupied by Australian households in the late 1980s (i.e. at about the same time that the survey of Adelaide home owners was conducted). While the estimates present a static picture, they are the product of demographic, social, and economic processes that are steadily changing the composition of Australian households. In particular, the ageing of the population, the postponement of marriage, and the formation of sole-parent families, have resulted in a significant increase in the proportion of households which are not comprised of a couple, with or without dependants (Cass 1991, 2). About 63 per cent of households were composed of couples in 1988, of whom about one half had dependent children; sole-parent families comprised about 8.5 per cent of households, with about 86 per cent headed by a woman; single people living alone make up a further 28 per cent of households in Table 3.1; and, lastly, multiple families and unrelated individuals living together account for the remainder. Importantly, projections of household formation rates prepared by the National Institute of Economic and Industry Research for the National Housing Strategy forecast that by 2006 the proportion of income units without children in Australia will have increased to around 75 per cent (National Housing Strategy 1991, xii).

The emergence of more varied household types over the last two decades is also bound up with the changing status of women within the Australian economy. According to Neutze and Kendig (1991, 11), only half of women reaching adulthood before the mid-1950s worked full time after marriage, compared with more than 80 per cent in the 1970s. In the case of women with dependent children the labour-force participation rate climbed sharply between 1974 and 1990: for women in two-parent families from 40.7 per cent to 61.4 per cent, and for sole mothers from 45.1 per cent to 52.3 per cent (Cass 1991, 2–3). The increase was most dramatic between 1983 and 1990 when part-time job opportunities were growing disproportionately in those sectors of the economy more likely to be employing women. Moreover, with equal pay legislation and greater access to more highly paid occupations, women's earnings as a proportion of men's rose

Table 3.1 Australian 'families': household composition by nature of occupancy, 1988

Family type	Nature of occupancy												
	Owner: private		Purchaser: public		Renter: other		Renter: rent-free		Renter		Living		Total	
	'000	%	'000	%	'000	%	'000	%	'000	%	'000	%	'000	%
Married couple with no dependents	768.2	55.3	326.4	23.5	180.7	13.0	46.3	3.3	31.6	2.3	35.1	2.5	1,388.3	100
Married couple with children, dependent and non-dependent	882.1	36.8	1,014.0	42.3	268.3	11.2	88.1	3.9	77.1	3.2	66.6	2.8	2,396.2	100
Female sole parent with children, dependent and non-dependent	125.1	28.3	77.3	17.5	93.4	21.1	78.0	17.6	37.1	8.4	31.6	7.1	442.5	100
Male sole parent with children, dependent and non-dependent	26.1	34.8	18.4	24.6	13.2	17.6	7.0	9.4	4.9	6.6	5.2	7.0	74.8	100
Female single person	387.7	43.4	88.9	9.9	229.3	25.7	58.7	6.6	67.5	7.6	61.2	6.9	893.3	100
Male single person	175.0	21.9	104.8	13.1	343.9	43.0	24.2	3.0	101.8	12.7	50.9	6.4	800.6	100
Multiple families and groups	19.8	29.1	6.1	9.0	23.1	34.0	2.3	3.4	7.4	10.9	9.3	13.7	68.0	100
TOTAL	2,384.0	39.3	1,635.9	27.0	1,151.9	19.0	304.6	5.0	327.4	5.4	259.9	4.3	6,063.6	100

Source: Australian Bureau of Statistics, 1990: derived from Household expenditure survey, Australian household characteristics (Catalogue No. 6531.0), Canberra.
Tables prepared for B. Cass, The housing needs of women and children, National Housing Strategy Discussion Paper, AGPS: Canberra, 1991.

from an average of 59 per cent through the 1960s to approximately 75 per cent from the mid-1970s onwards.

The changes in women's access to paid employment and wage rates have had a vital bearing on the kind of housing that they, as individuals or household members, can expect to occupy. For whilst owner-occupancy overwhelmingly remains the preferred housing tenure in Australia, home purchase has steadily declined in affordability since the first years of the 1970s (Neutze and Kendig 1991, 7). Under these circumstances, the purchase of the first home has come to depend not only upon the job security of one of the adult breadwinners, usually the male in the household (Smith 1990), but the additional earnings of the female partner (Wulff 1982). Moreover, Neutze and Kendig (1991, 11) argue that, in the case of first-time home buying, the second income has 'probably helped to push up prices and reduce accessibility for single-income households'. A further implication is that it is less likely that single parents will be able to afford to repurchase should the marriage break down fairly soon after buying for the first time (about 35 per cent of marriages end in divorce (McDonald 1990)).

Thus the combination of these social and economic changes is steadily affecting occupancy patterns in Australia through its impact upon family type. For example, between 1981 and 1986 the rate of increase in outright owners (28 per cent) greatly exceeded the increase in the number of buyers (4 per cent) (Anderton and Lloyd 1991). On the one hand, as the population ages more households discharge the mortgage on their homes; and on the other, as the 'affordability' threshold rises fewer households can buy (Cass 1991, 11).

Table 3.1 reveals how family type ultimately affects rates of home-ownership: in the 1988 survey of household expenditure, families comprising married couples with children had a slightly higher rate of home ownership than couples without dependent children (mainly because more were buying at an earlier stage of the family cycle). The constraint that a single woman's income imposes on access is plain to see when the home ownership rates achieved by male and female sole parents are compared (59.4 per cent and 45.8 per cent respectively). Finally, the differences in ownership levels between single men and women in Table 3.1 reflect two separate stages of the life course: before family formation; and later in life, following separation and divorce, or

the death of a marriage partner (Coleman and Watson 1987).
However, while a widow would normally remain in her family
home, this prospect is much more remote after the property has
been distributed following separation and divorce (McDonald
1986).

This survey of the dimensions of housing occupancy in
Australia according to household and family type provides a
backdrop to the section that follows. In it I briefly outline the
main background features of a study of home ownership in
Adelaide from which the evidence on wealth transfers within the
Australian family is drawn.

SURVEYING HOUSING WEALTH IN ADELAIDE

Adelaide, the state capital of South Australia, had a population
of a little over one million in 1990. The metropolitan area is very
linear in form, stretching more than 80 kilometres from north to
south. The data and case studies reported in this essay are drawn
from a survey of households that sold their homes in one of eight
hand-picked suburbs of Adelaide during 1988–9 (Table 3.2).
Significantly, the survey coincided with a twenty-year peak in
Adelaide house prices, and a very sharp rise in mortgage interest
rates that crippled many home buyers in Australia (up from 14
per cent in 1987 to 17 per cent in 1989 (Reserve Bank 1990)).

The eight suburbs were mainly chosen to represent the
upper and lower segments of the 'family home' submarket; that
is, they were all freestanding dwellings occupied by a single
household. Each suburb is reasonably homogeneous with respect
to demography and class and has a common development
history including the date of subdivision (see Table 3.3), predominant house type, and private or public sector provenance.
Accordingly, some are located in nineteenth-century areas closer
to the centre of Adelaide (North Adelaide, Birkenhead-Exeter),
while others typify the outlying southernmost or northern-
most suburbs built by either private developers (Hallett Cove),
or South Australia's public housing agency, the Housing
Trust (Elizabeth Park-Elizabeth Downs, Christies Beach). In 1990
the average house price – in Australian dollars – recorded for
each suburb was as follows: North Adelaide, AUS$282,610;
Burnside, AUS$227,032; West Lakes, AUS$225,032; Flinders
Park, AUS$98,561; Hallett Cove, AUS$96,730; Christies Beach,

Table 3.2 'Eight suburb' survey of Adelaide dwellings owned in 1988–89

Suburb		'Target' home owners*						Survey response				
		1988/89 address T	Traced to T+1,2,3	Untraceable	have left T+1	Refusal	No response	Responded: promptly	to 1st reminder 13 June	to 2nd reminder 20 June	after callback 13–14 July	Response rate†
Birkenhead–Exeter	n	67	40	1	26	8	10	13	4	5	0	22
	%		60	1	39							55
Burnside	n	92	65	8	19	14	24	20	2	3	2	28
	%		71	9	21							43
Christies Beach	n	86	49	3	34	12	16	18	1	1	1	20
	%		57	4	39							41
Elizabeth Park/Downs	n	100	56	9	35	13	12	20	8	2	1	31
	%		56	9	35							55
Flinders Park	n	63	47	0	16	13	11	14	1	6	2	23
	%		75	0	25							49
Hallett Cove	n	100	63	5	32	10	17	29	3	2	2	36
	%		63	5	32							57
North Adelaide	n	51	19	9	23	5	4	7	3	0	0	10
	%		37	18	45							53
West Lakes	n	110	74	12	24	15	23	25	5	5	1	36
	%		67	11	22							49
Total	n	669	413	47	209	90	117	146	27	24	9	206
	%		62	7	31	22	28					50

Source: Home ownership survey, 1991

Notes:
* T = target dwelling in 1988–89
T−1, −2, −3, −n Dwellings owned prior to the 'target residence'
T+1, +2, +3 Dwellings occupied (i.e. not all were owner-occupied) after selling the 'target residence'
† Proportion of 'target' home owners that could be traced.

Table 3.3 Relationship between returns, dwelling age, home improvements and household income (in 1990 prices)

Suburb	n	Average household income	Average age of dwelling (years)	n	*a* Average value of 'adds + alts' (Council records)	Net returns n	Annual return x	SD	Percentage yield p.a. x	SD
Birkenhead-Exeter	19	28,860	73.6	21	6,442	18	2,205	3,104	5.2	6.5
Burnside	26	48,920	24.9	51	25,904	41	7,546	12,969	4.3	7.4
Christies Beach	17	27,710	25.8	38	6,412	29	−441	2,354	−0.2	3.2
Elizabeth Park/Downs	28	26,100	24.3	48	7,140	42	−503	1,503	−0.5	2.3
Flinders Park	16	30,200	35.3	30	13,657	23	−671	2,466	−0.5	2.3
Hallett Cove	25	39,920	8.5	54	8,871	49	−465	3,589	−0.1	3.2
North Adelaide	8	51,320	79.0	17	28,577	14	7,165	12,369	3.2	6.2
West Lakes	31	53,280	7.8	61	9,659	49	9,083	15,240	4.1	6.3
	170	33,270				265	2,169	9,082	1.0	4.8

Source: Home ownership survey; Council Building Applications

AUS\$67,655; Birkenhead-Exeter, AUS\$65,559; Elizabeth Park/
Downs AUS\$55,490. Only two suburbs had average house prices
approaching the metropolitan mean i.e. AUS\$99,800 in 1990
(South Australian Department of Lands, n.d.).

Accurate records of the prices paid and realised for housing
sold by owner-occupiers living in these suburbs were matched to
survey information gathered about the prior housing experience
of those same households. The house price data, upon which
the estimates of returns to investment and annual yields are
based, were extracted from an integrated property ownership
and valuation database managed by the South Australian
Department of Lands called LOTS (Land Ownership and Tenure
System). All prices reported in this essay have been adjusted by
the Consumer Price Index 'All Groups Series' for Adelaide so
that the estimates can be expressed in constant terms (i.e. 1990
Australian dollars).

In broad terms, the survey schedule was designed to yield
information about the housing and employment histories of
the adult members of the household, and to generate estimates
of household wealth. As well as that, some attempt was made
to determine what sources of financial assistance, including
within the family, were made available to home buyers and
details of the expected pattern of inheritance in the future.
Because of the purposive approach to the selection of suburbs
this is not a 'sample' in the strict sense of the term, so the analysis
does not purport to represent patterns of home ownership for the
population at large.

Table 3.2 gives some indication of the process whereby the
'Eight suburb' home owners were traced to a new, and sometimes second, or third place of address for interviewing. The
study began with 669 'target' home owners but naturally some
families had dissolved due to the death of a spouse or incompat-
ibility; some households had sold up to move back into the rental
sector – perhaps a Housing Trust cottage flat – or gone into a
nursing home (see Table 3.4); others had moved to the South
Australian countryside, interstate, or overseas. All told, a total
of 413, or 62 per cent, of the original owners were traced by
searching sources such as the LOTS ownership list, the State
Electoral Rolls, the 1990 telephone directory, and the South
Australian Register of Births, Deaths, and Marriages. Table 3.2
reveals a response rate of just on 50 per cent of the traceable

Table 3.4 'Family' type × household income, average age of adult members, current tenure, 'equity-release' (dwelling sold in 1988–89)

Household type	n	%	n	Household income	n	Average age of adult members (years)	n	Current tenure (%)					'Equity-release'	
								Fully own	Mortg.	Rent	Nurs. home	n	Amount	%
Single person	27	13.1	19	$19,630	26	37	25	28	28	12	32	16	+$22,394	+18.5
Couple, no children ever	31	15.0	28	$34,890	31	42	30	33	47	7	13	22	+$11,054	+9.0
Couple, grown-up children no longer at home	48	23.3	33	$26,640	48	58	48	52	16	15	17	35	+$24,329	+15.7
Couple, 1 child	23	11.2	22	$47,730	23	41	23	30	43	2	–	17	–$1,755	–1.4
Couple, 2–4 children	62	30.1	54	$37,610	62	40	62	21	61	18	–	53	–$5,649	–3.7
One parent, 1–4 children	11	5.3	10	$24,800	11	27	11	27	45	27	–	6	–$1,207	–2.3
Multiple families and groups	4	1.9	4	$24,500	4	42	4	50	50	–	–	2	–$6,295	–11.8
Total	206		170		205		203					151		

Source: Home ownership survey, 1991

households, despite two telephone 'reminders' and a 'callback' by fieldworkers. The refusal rate (22 per cent) reflects the sensitive nature of some of the information sought on household finances and housing investment decisions; none the less, the checks made by the fieldworkers together with the survey findings provide no reason for suspecting that any serious response bias has occurred.

It is not possible to elaborate at any length on the technical assumptions that lie behind the estimates of capital gain/loss within the household (Table 3.3). But in view of the considerable difference of opinion over what should be included in the calculation of returns to investment and yields (Beer 1989; Dupuis 1991; Hamnett *et al.* 1991, 31–3; Forrest *et al.* 1990, 136–40; Saunders 1990, 123–41), after taking advice it was decided to keep the method simple. Consequently, the net returns to home owners reported in the tables are just the average difference between the *actual* purchase and sale price of each dwelling, minus the value of the improvements. The data on home improvement activity were extracted from Local Government records of building applications and approvals. All the estimates in the tables are standardised, or expressed as yearly values, to remove the effect of different periods of ownership.

Though it is not the primary concern of this chapter, it is none the less worth noting that no clear-cut relationship emerges between the 'class position' of home owners, as measured by household income, and capital gains when net returns and yields per annum are grouped by suburb (Table 3.3). The standard deviations confirm that there is a high degree of variability in the gains or losses flowing to sellers, regardless of area of residence. Returns to investment are mediated by a combination of home improvement activity, the timing of house purchase and disposal in relation to the property cycle, and the externality effects of public and private (dis)investment within the general vicinity. Of course, the age of a suburb's housing stock, together with the disposable income of the occupants, governs both the need for and likelihood of home improvement activity (Table 3.3).

Perhaps the most distinctive feature about the pattern of capital gains and losses according to suburb, if one sets aside the middle distance suburb of Flinders Park, is the metropolitan-wide contrast between inner area gains and outer area losses during the lifetime of these 'Eight suburb' dwellings sold in

1988–9 (Table 3.3). It has been suggested elsewhere that this general pattern of redistribution within the residential property market can be attributed to the processes of urban restructuring under Australian conditions during the last two decades or so (Badcock 1989a; Badcock 1992).

'FAMILIES' AND THEIR HOUSING IN ADELAIDE

Table 3.4 profiles the respondent households in the Adelaide case study bearing in mind that they were *all* home owners prior to 1988–9 whatever their present housing situation. When the breakdown of home owners by 'family' type in Table 3.4 is compared with the corresponding household groupings in Table 3.1 for 'owners' plus 'purchasers', it is apparent that the Adelaide survey overrepresents 'childless couples' and underrepresents married couples with children in the Australian population. With that one proviso, Table 3.4 reveals significant differences in the life course and circumstances of households. For example, the variations in household income and current tenure according to 'family' type are a direct reflection of social and economic changes occurring within the labour market and impinging upon the housing situation of households. In terms of paid employment, 47.8 per cent of households possessed one full-time earner on wages or salary, or self-employed. Where both parents or partners were employed outside the home, in 43.3 per cent of cases both worked full-time; and in 5.5 per cent of cases full-time earnings were supplemented with part-time work. The remainder of home owners received a statutory income of some kind.

Table 3.4 reveals that amongst these home owners, couples with one child, at an average age of 41 years, had the highest household incomes ($47,730) followed by couples with 2–4 children ($37,610), and couples that have never had children ($34,890). Of course, once these differences are adjusted for household size the real income of 'childless couples' greatly improves. For similar reasons, 'one parent households with dependants' ($24,800) are much more susceptible to financial stress than individuals living alone ($19,630), or couples approaching retirement with grown-up families ($26,640).

The table also presents estimates of the average equity released in the process of selling one home and buying another; or alternatively, moving into rental or nursing-home accommodation. This provides a measure of the extent to which particular households have extracted some of the equity built up over the years in their home by 'trading down'. There is a clear demarcation between households with and without children which is a life-course phenomenon, suggesting that on average households without children traded down, while those with children and expanding family needs mostly traded up in the process of changing residence; except, that is, in those cases where families had to 'sell up' as part of a divorce settlement or to reduce the burden of mortgage repayments.

Of the eleven one-parent families surveyed, five were actually forced to move in 1988–9 as part of a property settlement. The families of these divorcees – six males, five females – all ended up in less favourable housing. Only five had sufficient funds after settlement to remortgage even a home unit, while another three had to rent.

Other – as yet unpublished – data from the survey indicate that investment-related reasons for moving house such as 'tax benefits' are overshadowed by the restructuring of financial commitments in response to the stress of high interest rates, job redundancies, and business failure in the late 1980s. About one in five households stated that they were obliged to sell their homes in 1988–9, whilst another 9 per cent used resale as an opportunity to extract some of the equity from their housing upon retirement. Appropriately, some of the latter households were lower income families from suburbs like Christies Beach, Elizabeth Park/ Downs, and Birkenhead-Exeter. By moving to a country location, at least some were able to purchase cheaper housing and reduce their levels of indebtedness and other living costs. For example, in the six cases where mortgage defaulting was precipitated by business failure, families approached the Housing Trust for housing assistance, moved to a caravan park, or converted an old State Transport Authority bus!

Couples with grown-up children no longer at home and people living alone, in particular, were able to extract significant portions of their equity ($24,329 or 15.7 per cent, and $22,394 or 18.5 per cent) in the process of trading down. Because of the effect of the 'empty nesters' syndrome a greater proportion of these households were moving to smaller homes, townhouses or home units which they were able to buy outright. With an average age of

58 years, couples with grown-up children were clearly in a good position in 1988–9 to capitalise on surging house prices by selling the 'family home' and switching to a house type that was presumably smaller with modern appointments. An illustration is provided by a retired couple in their mid-sixties with an adult daughter: they bought their first home in 1952 for $57,000 in real terms, traded it in 1980 for a new home in West Lakes ($114,500) on which they realised $365,000 in 1988. They are now renting in order to free up some capital for retirement and 'help the family'.

Many of the people moving into nursing homes or retirement villages in their 'twilight' years also took the opportunity provided by the inflated house prices in the late 1980s to convert their equity in the 'family home' (Table 3.4). Others simply sold in 1988–9 due to a change in their domestic situation or health, and profited from the fortunate timing (especially if they had purchased somewhere near the trough of the property cycle in earlier years). For many this marks the completion of their tenure as home owners, and the closing of a rich chapter in their lives with the move from the 'family home'.

The housing autobiography reprinted in the Appendix of an 84-year-old pensioner stands as a testimony to the complex role that home ownership performs in the domestic sphere in the course of a lifetime. It describes close interdependence and cooperation between family members in the management of housing resources to their mutual benefit: not only did brothers help rehouse a sister after her husband died, but a son and his family moved interstate to live with an ageing father. This leads on to a questioning of the extent to which the family circle actually is a source of housing resources apart from those provided through the usual institutional channels by the state and the market.

FINANCIAL OR 'IN-KIND' FAMILY ASSISTANCE FOR HOME BUYERS

From the introductory remarks it is apparent that the state has actively promoted home purchase in Australia since the early 1950s. Financial assistance for home buyers has been channelled directly through a series of government schemes (for example, in the 1980s the Commonwealth's First Home Owner Scheme [FHOS] grant, and the South Australian Government's Home

Ownership Made Easier [HOME] supplement), and indirectly through private-sector institutions like savings banks and building societies. The Commonwealth has made cheaper mortgage finance available at concessional rates to assist 'marginal' applicants into ownership; and prior to 1986, when the financial system was deregulated, 'capped' mortgage finance a couple of points below the prime rate set by the Reserve Bank.

This is to say that in Australia housing provision became so institutionalised that the postwar generation automatically expected to mortgage their homes through the banking system. And in those enviable cases where 'young couples' in the 1950s and 1960s received help from their parents or an employer, it seldom amounted to much more than a deposit, or down-payment on a block of land. Of the 206 Adelaide households surveyed in 1988–9: 9.2 per cent and 6.8 per cent received gifts or loans respectively from parents and relatives towards the 'setting-up' costs of their first house; only 4.4 per cent were in the position to put all or part of an inheritance towards its purchase; 3 per cent were eligible for War Service loans, which averaged about 15–25 per cent of purchase price; 3 per cent received a supplementary loan from an employer; 3.4 per cent purchased their first home from the Housing Trust under the Rental-purchase scheme; 15 per cent qualified for either the FHOS or HOME grants.

A few couples obtained their home finance from a variety of sources including from within the family circle: a first home bought for $35,000 in 1982 by two insurance clerks was acquired with a $1,000 gift, together with a $5,000 loan, from the parents; another built by a supermarket manager and a departmental supervisor in 1984 was underwritten by a $7,000 gift from their parents, and a $2,500 FHOS grant.

Typically, gifts or loans from parents and/or relatives ranged between about 10 per cent and 25 per cent of the purchase price of the first home, whereas the nine bequests constituted as little as 12 per cent and as much as 135 per cent of the purchase price. In one case the parents advanced the full amount of the asking price to help their son and daughter-in-law to make a successful adjustment to city life in 1984; they could not, so sold in 1989 to move back to the family farm. Another survey respondent, a retired weighbridge operator and widower in his late seventies, inherited the family home at Birkenhead which his father had built in 1911. However, partly because he was too frail to continue the upkeep of the property it had deteriorated so much that he only realised $63,000 at auction before moving to a nursing home.

Since all but 17 of these 206 'first homes' (8.3 per cent) were bought after the Second World War, it can be said that inheritance has not been an important determinant of access to home ownership for the immediate postwar generation of 'Eight suburb' home owners. Nor have family savings: in the majority of cases the monetary gifts and loans made by parents or other relatives to the postwar generation of home buyers might have helped secure a block of land or the 'right' house, but the burden of the mortgage repayments fell to the next generation. And for the remaining 55 per cent of 'first time' home buyers, having saved the deposit, the whole of the mortgage had to be borrowed from a bank.

Significantly, by contrast almost half of the 206 households that owned, or were paying off their homes in 1988–9 expected to receive bequests in the future. The estimates of the size of the estate to be inherited at some time in the future are based in large part upon the value of property owned by parents and the 'in-laws' (Table 3.5). Consequently, in the space of little more than a generation the transfer of housing wealth from parents to their children will grow from a point where not more than 5 per cent of 'Eight suburb' home owners were beneficiaries, to potentially effect a majority of Australian home owners. Some of the evidence for this emerging phenomenon – the intergenerational transfer of housing wealth – and its implications for Australian society are considered in the concluding section of the paper.

THE TRANSFER OF HOUSING WEALTH BETWEEN THE GENERATIONS

The existence for the first time of a generation of home owning retirees raises a series of interesting questions about the significance of the phenomenon in societies like the United Kingdom (Hamnett *et al.* 1991; Hamnett 1992; Leather 1990; Munro 1988) and the United States (Kuttner 1987, Phillips 1990). In Australia, a journalist writing in the *Business Review Weekly* claimed that, 'Australia's middle-aged generation will get a stupendous windfall of inherited wealth in the next decade. Bequests will

Table 3.5 The estimated private wealth of 'Eight-suburb' households by value of bequest

Estimated private wealth (AUS$)	Estimated value of bequest (AUS$, 1990 prices)				
	0	<25,000	25–75,000	>75,000	Total
0–49,000	27	6	4	2	39
50,000–99,000	17	10	4	3	34
100,000–249,000	32	10	16	12	70
>250,000	16	7	5	6	34
TOTAL	92	33	29	23	177

Source: Home ownership survey

turn thousands of already comfortably established 40–55 year olds into "common or garden millionaires"' (Thomas 1990, 45). Another explained,

> As the baby-boomers' parents age and die over the next two decades, they will be bequeathing to the children a wealth of assets – assets built up in a bygone era of stable employment, high inflation and real estate booms. And the baby-boomers, who will have reached at least their mid-50s by then, will inherit that windfall at an age when most are already 'comfortably' well-off with a home and other assets of their own ... What is this wealth? The cornerstone is the family home which, if it was bought in Sydney around 1950, was worth 165 times its purchase price in 1989.
>
> (Bagwell 1993, 12)

An actuarial study based upon mortality and home ownership figures at the 1986 Census has forecast that 94,000 homes will be passed on to dependants in 1996, rising to 168,000 dwellings in 2031 (Mitchell 1993). In aggregate this represents a potential transfer from one generation to the next of about $157 billion. And because family size is declining the estate will invariably be divided between only two dependants at most.

Whilst Sydney house prices are significantly higher than those paid for similar dwellings in Adelaide, Table 3.5 suggests that the popular impression being fuelled by the financial press in Australia is out by an order of magnitude. Table 3.5 relates expectations about a future bequest to the estimated private wealth of the 'Eight suburb' households in Adelaide.

Private household wealth was broadly defined in the question-naire to cover assets and investments such as equity in the home, other real estate, vehicles (including boats), savings, stocks and shares, art and antiques. Exactly 75 per cent of the 'Eight suburb' home owners said they could estimate their total household wealth and were prepared to disclose a figure within five broad bands. Significantly, three in four households set their total private wealth at a level above $50,000 (with 39.6 per cent lying within the modal class of $100,000–$249,000) (Table 3.5), compared with the 18.7 per cent of 'Eight suburb' home owners that said they expected to inherit more than $50,000.

While these sums are not going to create any 'common or garden millionaires in Adelaide', the table does suggest that the pattern of inheritance will act to further concentrate private wealth within Australian society. On the one hand, almost 70 per cent of the households with only very modest assets ($49,000) have no prospect of inheriting; on the other, there is an impres-sive increase in the proportion of 'Eight suburb' households that stand to receive a bequest from the parental estate. Therefore, if the slender evidence in Table 3.5 is anything to go by, every second household already owning their own home in Australia stands to inherit the 'family home' or its cashed-up value. Although some of that bequested wealth is expected to disperse downwards amongst the 'Eight suburb' households with lower incomes and limited personal wealth, much more in absolute terms will flow to those higher income households already in possession of considerable private wealth.

IMPLICATIONS OF THE TRANSFER OF HOUSING WEALTH

The elaborate system of subsidies to home owners that grew up throughout the postwar period has entrenched the 'family home' as the single most important form of private wealth in Australia. Beyond working towards their own financial security in retire-ment, the eventual aim of many parents, as home buyers, is to make some provision for their children's future. What are the broader implications of the transfer of housing wealth from one generation to the next within the family 'circle'?

Writers like Bagwell (1993, 12) posit that such a wealth transfer is capable of accelerating consumer spending sufficiently to pull

Australia out of the recession which appears to have stalled the economy in the first half of the 1990s. But this is premised on a number of questionable assumptions: first, that housing necessarily increases its real value in the long run; second, that the costs of residential care and nursing will not significantly deplete the savings of ageing parents; third, that 'baby-boomers' will spend the 'inheritance dividend' on consumer items, or extra leisure and services, rather than helping their own children to finance a home.

This last option would remove the dependence of at least some young home buyers upon the banking system for a mortgage, yet give the parents some form of income in their retirement. If this course becomes a popular one over the next two or three decades, it could reduce the demand for mortgage finance amongst the young middle class and free up more housing funds for 'marginal' borrowers who might otherwise fail to qualify for a home loan.

Finally, because beneficiaries tend to sell the 'family home' in the process of settling an estate, it may be subject to capital gains tax under the Australian provisions. As an alternative to losing anything between 20 and 30 per cent of the value of an estate to capital gains tax, more beneficiaries with places of their own may choose to hold on to the 'family home' and thereby expand the supply of private rental accommodation. Either way, part of the domestic capital created from family property would flow back into the social economy to be deployed as Hugh Stretton envisaged in his Boyer Lectures in a socially constructive way (Stretton 1974).

ACKNOWLEDGEMENTS

The survey that this chapter is based upon was funded by the Australian Research Council and the Commonwealth Department of Health, Housing and Community Services. The survey was administered by a social research group, INFODEC, under the direction of Dr Dorothy Cloher.

I am indebted to the Director-General of Lands in South Australia at the time, Mr John Darley, and his staff, for access to the LOTS database and providing technical advice. However the other person with a commitment to the project that more than matched my own is Ms Lisel O'Dwyer who was employed as a

Research Officer during its lifetime. Mr Errol Bamford, the departmental programming officer, solved many analytical problems along the way. Special thanks are due to all these people.

APPENDIX

Letter provided by an 84-year-old pensioner in lieu of completing a questionnaire

Woodville,
May 31, 1991

Dr Blair Badcock
University Adelaide

Dear Sir,

Have moved around a fair bit due to work commitment and other reasons. The first home I owned was at Grants Patch on the Kalgoorie Goldfields in 1938. I built it all myself. I obtained 3 blocks of Crown Land just off the mining lease. For 2 boarding houses . . . 1 for an uncle and aunt and 1 for my mother and brother and we built a residence shops and post office. The one I built all myself was for my future wife and myself. I was married in 1939 and before my first son was born had to move in to Kalgoorie as my wife was ordered to use a diet of white meat.

I ask you (th)is was impossible as petrol was rationed. 4 gallons a month and we were 42 miles from Kalgoorie. So I pulled the house down sold the iron and sawn timber and rented a house in Kalgoorie and landed a job at the South Kalcurli mine. There 12 months my son was only a baby when came back to Adelaide. Got one of the houses at Salisbury Munitions staff. And when war ended bought a house and shop at George St. Thebarton from SA Ancient Orders of Foresters and had to raise a mortgage thru the Manchester Unity (of) which I was a prominent member. Lived there till the Highways bought the land for the proposed new South Road scheme. The Highways paid $10,000 and I bought 3 flats at Port Noarlunga/Christies.

When my sister's husband died my brother and myself bought the house off her as she went to Watervale to live with my brother. She had to finally go into a nursing home and later to a hospital where she still is. My brother sold me his share so she would have plenty of cash and no financial worries. That meant I had to look after the Flinders Park residence and Port Noarlunga flats. I was no longer young so I sold the flats and moved into the Flinders Park house.

Quite a lot of upkeep and I was well over 60 so sold the Flinders Park home and bought the unit at Grange. My wife . . . was injured in a car accident and I found it hard at that stage to manage by myself so my youngest son and his wife and daughter came over from Queensland to help. But the flat was not large enough for all of us and we had to sell and raise a mortgage and buy the residence at James Street.

My wife . . . passed away on 26 October at her residence James St, Woodville.

The property at 46 George St Thebarton was purchased for seven hundred and fifty pounds. The Highways bought for $10,000. The flats at Port Noarlunga bought for $15,000 . . . sold for $31,500. Increased in value, repaired and sewered. Had to shift bathroom and toilet and turn 2 shower rooms into laundry.

Trusting this will help you, best I can do.

Thanking you.

Chapter 4

Accumulating evidence
Housing and family wealth in Britain

Ray Forrest and Alan Murie

Since the late 1970s there has been increasing analysis of the role of housing as a source and store of wealth in Britain. In this emerging literature the preoccupation has been with home ownership and its role in wealth accumulation and considerable attention has been given to issues of equity release and inheritance.

The importance of accumulation through home ownership has related to debates about social inequality and the importance of differences in housing tenure relative to more traditional social class differences. And as debate around this issue has developed the importance of intergenerational and interfamilial transfers has also aroused attention.

There is now a body of evidence related to the scale and nature of transfers through inheritance of housing-related wealth. Links into a broader literature on the sociology of the family remain, however, relatively undeveloped. In this chapter the basic elements identified in the British literature are summarised. The chapter updates and develops debate and considers the wider role of housing-wealth transfers within the family.

BACKGROUND

The growth of home ownership in Britain during the twentieth century has been dramatic. At the turn of the century probably fewer than 1 in 10 households were home owners. With the decline of rentier landlordism speculative building had switched its attention to building for individual home owners. Links with building societies and the provision of public subsidy for some 400,000 dwellings for home owners facilitated this development. By 1945 there were 3 million home owners in Britain representing

1 in 4 households. By 1970 the proportion had reached 50 per cent and by 1990, 66 per cent. The financial advantages associated with home ownership became more apparent after the 1970s with the value of tax reliefs for home owners increasing rapidly (for a more detailed discussion see Forrest *et al.* 1990).

In the early years of the growth of the tenure most home owners had outstanding mortgages and rates of house-price inflation were low. A change in these two factors affected the debate over the significance of home ownership. First, as the early cohorts of home owners aged and paid off their mortgages a substantial number of outright owners emerged. For this group the house was now an asset unencumbered by debt and this began to show in data on wealth. The value of this wealth was affected by a second factor – the rate at which house prices rose was faster than for other assets.

When housing was predominantly owned by private landlords it formed part of individual and company assets and in this sense the emergence of housing as an important element in wealth is nothing new. Its association with individual home ownership and a majority tenure is, however, a new development. The potential sociological significance of this process was referred to by Pahl in 1975 when he claimed that 'The maintenance of property values and the possibility of making appreciable capital gains has become a dominant value.' And he continued, 'A family may gain more from the housing market in a few years than would be possible in savings from a lifetime of earnings' (p. 291).

Initially observations about home ownership and wealth came from two different sources. First, a literature developed which emphasised accumulation through home ownership as a major factor affecting the interests of households. Dunleavy (1980, 1986) and Saunders (1986, 1990) focused on the accumulative potential of home ownership as a key distinction between owners and renters of housing and a central component of a broader emerging division between those households which operated in the market sector and those dependent on public, collective forms of provision. These emergent-consumption sector cleavages were, it was argued, part of a process weakening employment as the primary force of class structuration and social inequality.

At this stage the debate about housing wealth included little empirical data and rested largely on observations about the growth of home ownership and a debate about interests, power and politics. A second and separate focus emerged from new data available in the 1970s. Murie and Forrest (1980a, 1980b; Murie 1983) drew on the evidence provided by the Royal Commission on the Distribution of Income and Wealth to identify new elements in social inequalities and a widening gap between renters and owners. These papers provided data about housing wealth and other aspects of housing inequality. They made little reference to the consumption-sector debate and were principally concerned with debates about social polarisation, the residualisation of council housing and the role of housing tenure in exacerbating other inequalities. These contributions also identified inheritance as a significant element in the role of home ownership in inequality.

The importance of housing as a source and store of wealth had increasingly been recognised by government. Within the Conservative party the term 'property-owning democracy' tended to be most strongly linked with home ownership. Margaret Thatcher as Prime Minister following electoral victory in 1979, referring to the policy to give all council tenants the right to buy their houses, stated: 'It will give more of our people that freedom and mobility and that prospect of handing something on to their children and grandchildren.' In the housing debate two days later, the Secretary of State for the Environment stated:

> I believe that, in a way and on a scale that was quite unpredictable, ownership of property has brought financial gain of immense value to millions of our citizens. As house prices rose, the longer one had owned, the larger the gain became. The average-priced new house in the early 1950s was worth about £2,000. Anyone who bought it now has an asset worth approximately £16,000. Simply to have bought a house a year ago meant that the purchaser has seen the value of that house increase by 25 per cent in a year. It is not my purpose to argue whether the rate of gain has exceeded the rate of inflation or whether people have simply preserved their own original asset in real terms. What it is my purpose to argue is that this dramatic change in property values has opened up a division in the nation between those who own their own homes and those who do not.
>
> (Heseltine, 1979)

HOUSING AS AN INVESTMENT

In considering these statements it is important to acknowledge that people buy houses not only for use but also as an investment to increase their personal assets. The idea that 'bricks and mortar' is one of the most secure areas in which to invest personal savings is a long-standing axiom. Housing choice and decisions to change dwellings are not just decisions about consumption and use, or about adjusting the dwellings to changing family structure and size; they involve decisions about investment, about using income available once essential needs have been met, about maximising net income and about returns on savings.

This element in housing decisions is not always easily separable from other elements. Surveys concerned with decisions to move tend to group diverse reasons under 'housing' or 'job' reasons. Nevertheless such surveys generally identify housing reasons as dominant. For example, reasons such as 'wanted better dwellings, better area, garden, present house too small or too few rooms', accounted for some 40 per cent of moves between owner-occupied properties in 1973 (Department of the Environment (DOE) 1977a). In reality, however, many of these moves derive from investment decisions. In the British Market Research Bureau (BMRB) Housing Consumer Survey published in 1976, 27 per cent of owner-occupiers identified 'a saving/investment' as an advantage of owner occupancy, and other positive advantages (feeling of security 16 per cent; can use as collateral 3 per cent; cheaper in the long run 7 per cent; can leave it to children 5 per cent) are also linked to this (BMRB 1976). For households with a rising real income net of tax, housing was a strong competitor for investment.

More recent data present a similar picture. For example, a study of households buying new dwellings in the South and East of England in 1988/9 indicated that 24 per cent of purchasers gave as their reasons for moving factors relating to ownership, investment or financial stake (Forrest and Murie, 1993). These are a mixture of financial/investment and independence/control factors and it is difficult to disentangle these from social survey data. There are important differences in the reasons for moving given by newly formed and existing (continuing) households. In this survey new households mainly referred to obtaining a home of their own, buying their own home or to marriage or moving in with their partner. For continuing households there was much more reference to work-related moves, and moves designed to change housing or neighbourhood factors were very important. In many of these decisions about improving housing there is likely to be a significant investment calculation. Other data for 1991 indicate that continuing households moving between dwellings in the home-ownership sector gave very different reasons for moving than other households. Of home owners buying with a mortgage, 18 per cent gave their main reason for moving as a change of job/nearer to job; 37 per cent gave their main reason for moving as wanted larger house or flat; and 16 per cent wanted to move to a better area or neighbourhood. The comparable figures for continuing households moving to all other destinations were 13 per cent, 12 per cent and 9 per cent respectively (DOE, 1993).

Data of this type cannot, however, reveal how many people move house for financial or investment reasons. The design of questionnaires, the problems of coding answers on reasons for moving, the large residual (other reasons) category which emerges and the problems of analysing data do not enable adequate empirical information to emerge. Furthermore, the way that people make decisions about household movement involve considering a range of factors and probably seeking to satisfy various items in a package rather than optimise on any one (see, e.g., Murie 1974). In-depth interviews with households enabling them to express their housing strategies provide important complementary data to that obtained through large-scale social survey. These data indicate *inter alia* that among households buying expensive housing, decisions to move and what to buy are often triggered by job factors and give priority to satisfying requirements in relation to the use and location of the dwelling (see, e.g., Forrest and Murie 1987, 1991). It is easy to confuse consequence with cause in this context and to assume that a strong investment orientation is necessarily what has fuelled an individual housing history characterised by numerous moves and a position at the top end of the housing market.

Saunders' (1990) attempt to challenge this view by manipulation of his own more limited survey data is out of step with the body of research evidence on this issue in Britain. His attempt to deduce a dominant influence of investment considerations is as unconvincing as his implication that other commentaries deny that investment considerations are present in housing moves. What is at issue is not whether such investment considerations exist but how far they trigger moves and determine choices or they represent one of a number of interlinked elements in decisions. Saunders' one-dimensional person preoccupied with accumulation and organising their life's events around opportunities to accumulate wealth through housing is inconsistent with the more general evidence on housing behaviour in Britain and its polemical basis appears extraordinarily crude in the light of developments in home ownership in Britain between 1989 and 1993.

Without accepting exaggerated images, the various data on housing mobility and home ownership establish that, in Britain, the considerations surrounding household movement, search behaviour and choice include direct investment and financial considerations and more general judgements about quality and desirability of house and area. Considerations about asset appreciation may not be explicit in these judgements but will often form part of them.

The British home owner, at least in the period since the 1960s, has been influenced by periods of rapid house-price inflation, came to expect property to retain its value over the long term and hoped for a higher rate of increase. The owner-occupier who traded up benefited from tax reliefs while purchasing, and the tax relief broadly increased in value with income and size of loan. Annual increases in property value and their realisation on sale are not subject to tax. In this environment many households traded up, increasing their asset holdings, possibly freeing some resources for other purposes and benefiting from advantages in terms of access to credit. There were relatively few obvious competitors for savings, especially for households with sufficient cash to have, say, reached the maximum savings with tax advantages (e.g., deposits with building societies), as well as having the full range of household consumer durables. In all of these ways the growth of home ownership was inextricably bound up with aspects of saving, investment and wealth accumulation. The experience of the 1980s has demonstrated this further. Changes in tax-relief arrangements are widely regarded as having encouraged residential movement and increased borrowing in 1989 and to have contributed to the boom and slump affecting the sector in the late 1980s. The subsequent fall in house prices is also widely regarded to have inhibited movement as households were unwilling to sell at prices below those which they had begun to expect. Not surprisingly, households which found that house-price falls left their property with a value less than the outstanding mortgage on it (negative equity) were also influenced in their decisions to move (Forrest, Kennet and Leather 1994).

HOUSING AND THE DISTRIBUTION OF WEALTH

Alongside this evidence of households' awareness of housing wealth and asset appreciation there have been various studies indicating the association between the distribution of wealth and the growth of owner occupation. For example, Atkinson (1975, 448), argued that the increase in owner occupation had led to a definite reduction in the degree of concentration of wealth, and Atkinson and Harrison (1978) explained the decline in the share of all wealth held by the top group of wealth owners by the spread of 'popular wealth' – the value of owner-occupied housing plus the value of consumer durables.

The Royal Commission on the Distribution of Income and Wealth (1977, 142) referred to the 'considerable and growing importance of housing in the statistics of wealth'. Estimates made by the Commission indicated that the percentage of total personal net wealth accounted for by dwellings (net of mortgages) more than doubled from 17 per cent to 37 per cent between 1960 and 1975. This was largely due to the growth in owner occupation and increase in the net value of dwellings in relation to other asset prices. Persons in the bottom range of wealth owners (less than £5,000) had below average holdings of dwellings and land. For those in the middle range (£5,000–£20,000) dwellings accounted for more than 50 per cent of assets. These developments were of considerable social and economic significance. Policies which had principally been expressed as housing policies, and as policies designed to solve housing problems and provide housing choice, had facilitated a considerable growth of individual wealth. The way housing was taxed and subsidised had been critical in this.

In view of the dominance of house property in the assets of households with assets valued at between £5,000 and £50,000, it is evident that few households who did not own dwellings could accumulate wealth on a scale comparable with the house owner.

At the same time trends in asset prices had meant that the house owner had narrowed the gap in wealth relative to more wealthy groups whose assets were more varied (Murie and Forrest 1980).

There were a number of dimensions to this question. Housing policies, and particularly the structure of housing finance, had reduced inequalities in wealth in certain areas. The decline of the private rented sector, the breakup of property portfolios held by landlords, and the relative improvement in the position of the dwelling owner compared with holders of other assets related to the taxation treatment of housing. These changes led to a reduction in wealth inequality but only up to a point where the existence of non-owners of dwellings and the increasing inequality between tenants and owners of dwellings was reached. While the growth of direct public provision of housing was a major factor in the decline of private renting, tenants had no claim on the wealth stored in these dwellings. It is possible to argue that access to non-marketed assets including rights to subsidised housing constitute a real capital value (see Harbury and Hitchens 1979). But the capital value associated with tenants' rights cannot be realised legally, transferred or borrowed against. These differences mean that tenants' rights do not register in the wealth statistics. Those who must rent in the public and private sectors do not benefit in terms of wealth accumulation and it is only those who buy who accumulate wealth through housing. The consequence of this situation was that while direct public intervention through provision of council housing had significantly altered patterns of access, reduced problems of housing shortage and house condition and reduced the association between social class or income and the quality of housing, it had been accompanied by increased inequalities in wealth associated with ownership, tenure status and income. The structure of housing taxation and subsidy had helped solve one dimension of inequality while it had generated another.

The growth of housing wealth up to 1975 was the product of a particular set of circumstances – expansion of home ownership, increases in house prices and trends in the value of other assets – and did not itself represent a trend. Analyses of housing wealth in the subsequent period have sought to assess changes in the significance of housing wealth and have focused on differential accumulation (Forrest and Murie 1989; Hamnett 1992). The Royal

Commission's calculations of the growth in the importance of dwellings in personal wealth reflected a growth in the number of households who were home owners but also reflected the high levels of house-price inflation between 1970 and 1974. Calculations from Inland Revenue data since 1975 do not show a steady continuing rise. Between 1974 and 1986 residential buildings as a percentage of the net wealth of individuals fluctuated between 40 per cent and 47 per cent reflecting changes in the prices of different assets. The environment was not so favourable for the growth of housing wealth in this period. An analysis in 1985 (Building Societies Association (BSA) 1985) noted that housing had grown steadily as a proportion of wealth held as physical assets – from 60 per cent in 1957 to 71 per cent in 1983. Until 1980 the proportion of net wealth invested in physical assets grew strongly but since that date the trends have changed. Prior to 1980 high inflation and negative real interest rates encouraged individuals to favour physical assets, especially housing, which could be expected to maintain or increase value.

This situation changed markedly after 1980. The report by the Building Societies Association commented that:

> the rate of inflation has fallen and positive real rates of interest have again become available on many financial assets. Moreover regulatory changes have meant that housing has lost its special attractions. The mortgage interest tax relief limit has been raised only marginally compared to the increase in house prices while new financial assets (particularly index linked gilts and national savings certificates) have become available that offer the same inflation-protecting benefits as housing but without the transaction and maintenance costs. In addition the virtual abolition of capital gains tax has removed housing's special position in this respect.
>
> (BSA 1985, 17)

In a similar vein a report by Credit Suisse First Boston (1987) drew on a number of calculations to suggest that 'owner occupation represented an attractive financial proposition during the 1960s and 1970s but not during the 1980s' (p. 9). And commentary in *Social Trends* (Central Statistical Office (CSO) 1988) showed the sharp increase in the value of dwellings (net of mortgage debt) in the early 1970s, their relative decline in value until 1978 when they rose again until 1980. After that they declined again and by

1984 were below the overall figure for 1974. This situation changed dramatically after 1985 with a period of rapid house-price inflation. By 1988 the proportion of net personal wealth accounted for by dwellings had risen to 52 per cent (Inland Revenue, 1990). In 1989, reflecting peak prices, the proportion almost certainly increased but subsequently it will have fallen significantly along with house prices. Data are not yet available to demonstrate the subsequent changes.

These fluctuations in value not only affect the overall composition of personal-sector wealth but the relative holdings of different groups in the population. The original data presented by the Royal Commission showed that housing wealth dominated the wealth holdings of those in middle ranges but was less significant for top wealth holders whose wealth was mainly held in stocks, shares and land. In periods of high house-price inflation, especially if share values are stable or fall, middle-range wealth holders increase their share of all wealth at the expense of others.

Two other factors merit reference in this. First, government's privatisation policies in the 1980s have had an impact on personal wealth holdings. The sale of over 1.5 million houses through the right to buy and related policies have boosted wealth held in the form of dwellings especially because the substantial discounts (up to 70 per cent of value) involved lower rates of mortgage indebtedness. Against this the mechanisms for sales of shares in former nationalised industries encouraged share ownership and resulted in high rates of appreciation of share holdings. While many original purchasers of shares sold after a relatively short period, higher rates of share ownership remain with consequences for the importance of housing in asset values. Second, while the boom in house prices between 1986 and 1989 increased the value of housing relative to other assets, the fall in prices between 1989 and 1993 significantly eroded the value of housing assets. By 1993 house prices had fallen in real terms to their 1984 levels and the implications of this are that there would be no growth in the value of housing assets in that period except for that attributable to the growth of the tenure as a whole. In that same period other assets have increased in value.

What emerges from this discussion is that the new importance attached to home ownership in the picture of personal wealth holdings remains but has not developed. There has not been a steady growth in the importance of home ownership in wealth. Against this background issues of spatial variation, equity release and inheritance have had considerable importance. At the same time it is important to recognise that neither the growth of home ownership nor other privatisation policies have resulted in dramatic redistributions of wealth. In 1976 the wealthiest 1 per cent owned 21 per cent of wealth, the top 5 per cent 38 per cent, the top 10 per cent 50 per cent and the top 50 per cent 92 per cent. In 1990 the comparable figures for marketable wealth were 18 per cent, 37 per cent, 51 per cent and 93 per cent (CSO 1993).

SPATIAL VARIATIONS

Unlike most other forms of personal-sector wealth the particular location of a dwelling is fundamentally important for the rate of return. The uneven distribution of housing wealth is a product of different levels of home ownership and differences in house prices. As the differences between regional house prices have varied considerably over the past 20 years spatial variations in housing wealth are sensitive to the years referred to. Broad estimates by Forrest and Murie (1989) indicated that in 1986 some 56 per cent of the total housing wealth of elderly home owners was in the south east and south west of England. More recent calculations by Lloyds Bank (1993) have come to similar conclusions regarding the spatial distribution of residential property inheritance and indicates that the south east of England will benefit disproportionately. However, interregional flows will produce net benefits for the regions with younger populations. These include Wales, the Midlands and the northern regions.

Hamnett (1992) calculated that for 1989, London and the south east accounted for 31.6 per cent of the owner-occupied housing stock but 42.5 per cent of national gross value excluding housing debt. Average gross capital appreciation in London was almost twice the level of that in the north of England. Hamnett states (p. 312):

> The original purchase price was, of course, considerably higher in London, and buyers generally have larger mortgages and higher mortgage/income ratios. Precise calculations of relative rates of gain should also take into account the opportunity costs forgone. But it is clear that absolute wealth appreciation

from the housing market is much higher in the high price regions than in others, even though it may reflect some degree of enforced saving via higher mortgages.

EQUITY RELEASE

The value of housing wealth in Britain reflects the growth of home ownership and movement in asset values. In assessing future levels of wealth and the inequalities resulting considerable attention has been given to equity release. Those who have accumulated wealth through housing draw on it during their life-time. The security provided by ownership of a high-value housing asset may change savings and consumption activity. However, there are three more direct forms of equity release: when moving house deciding not to reinvest the full proceeds of the sale of the previous house and, instead, taking out a larger mortgage to release a block of equity; achieving the same effect by trading down to a cheaper house; remortgaging or taking out a new mortgage without moving house. These forms of equity release can be seen as ways in which households reschedule their housing expenditures. Higher expenditures on house purchase in early years may mean very low costs in later years. While this represents a good protection against falling income in older age it may not represent the desirable profile. These judgements will also be affected by the availability of tax relief on mortgage interest and by consumption preferences.

The general view is that in Britain equity release grew considerably after 1970 (Holmans 1991). Gross equity withdrawal (including inheritance) rose from £914 million in 1970 to £27,637 million in 1990. Adjusted for inflation at 1985 prices gross equity withdrawal rose from £4,458 million in 1970 to £26,216 million in 1988. This almost sixfold increase does not take into account the money injected into the housing market for improvements and new building.

Holmans' calculations suggest that equity release related to overmortgaging and remortgaging rose between 1970 and 1988. While overmortgaging rose from 15 per cent of equity release in 1970 it accounted for 41 per cent in 1988. Holmans' estimates of equity release through remortgaging show major fluctuations but rose from around 10 per cent in 1970 to over 40 per cent in 1990. The growth and volatility of these forms of equity release reflect the growth of financial advice, new financial packages and the operation of financial institutions following financial deregulation in 1986. With houses regarded as a low-risk security and with building societies and banks competing to find borrowers, opportunities to extend mortgages and extract equity grew. The attractiveness of this was seriously damaged initially by high rates of interest in 1989–91 and then by falling property values. In this context the role of formal equity-release schemes directed at older people should also be acknowledged. Mullings (1992) and Hamnett (1992) estimate that only some 12,200 elderly persons entered these equity-release schemes in 1989. This represented approximately 1 per cent of home owners over 75 years of age. However, loans and sales under equity-release schemes had grown significantly between 1976 and 1989. The low house-price inflation following 1989 affected the ability of these schemes to provide a secure income and as a result the use of schemes declined.

INHERITANCE

It is the implications of the growth of home ownership on patterns of inheritance which has attracted the greatest attention. At death, estates which include housing wealth pass to other individuals who may or may not sell these assets and convert them for other uses. Because inheritance often involves transfers within family networks it raises different links in the role of housing and housing inequality in society. It has been identified as a process which could sustain social inequalities between generations – or alternatively smooth out existing wealth inequalities. The possible effects of housing inheritance in Britain were set out in 1980.

First, the cohort of first-generation owners whose purchase of housing between the wars marked the first significant growth of owner occupation were by then ageing outright owners. The number of estates containing a large element of house property being inherited had increased and would continue to increase. This was evident from forecasts in the Housing Policy Review which indicated an increasing number of dwellings coming on to the market through the dissolution of elderly households (DOE 1977b, 18). It was shown by the steady increase in the proportion of outright owners where the head of household was aged 60 or over: from 62 per cent in 1972 to over 65 per cent in 1977 (Office of Population Censuses and Surveys (OPCS) 1978). It was clear that an increasing number of households would become substantial beneficiaries as a result of trends in housing.

Second, inheritance was likely to occur at a stage when beneficiaries were already well into their housing careers – they may have already benefited through gifts or loans from parental property ownership. Inheritance was less likely to affect new households but could encourage trading up and house-price inflation. As a result, households without the advantage of access to cash through inheritance or loans and gifts associated with ownership may find that the price (deposit) obstacles on gaining entry to owner occupation, or trading up beyond a limited level, become greater and greater. In this sense the likelihood of being trapped in the rental sector or at particular points in the owner-occupied sector could increase for households without the benefits of inheritance, or the access to funds associated with ownership by parents or relatives. While inheritance could increase the mobility of existing owners and encourage trading up, it could contribute to reduce mobility and choice for those who lack any equivalent asset – whether they are owners or renters.

Against this background we outlined a number of possible effects in an earlier paper (Murie and Forrest 1980b).

- Inheritance could encourage trading up in the housing market and contribute to house-price inflation.
- It could increase the importance of personal or private loans, especially between generations. Sharp distinctions might develop in the competitive positions of first-time buyers (and others) according to whether they had access to such loans as well as to the institutional sources of borrowing. In this way the effects could leap-frog one generation (who do not wish to change their housing situation) and benefit a younger generation embarking on their housing careers.
- Inheritance could encourage multiple house ownership. Rather than sell an inherited dwelling beneficiaries might prefer to maintain the investment in its secure form as housing. Whilst the growth of home ownership has been a major factor in the erosion of the private rented sector, the inheritance of owner-occupied properties could, paradoxically, act to sustain some level of private renting. Alternatively, an inherited property

might be used as a second home, or indeed kept vacant if rental income was regarded as marginal and the costs of letting too great.

- Inherited properties might be sold and the proceeds saved in institutions (most obviously building societies) which will channel these funds back into the housing sector.
- Finally, inheritance might be used neither directly nor indirectly for housing but for increased consumption expenditure or savings.

This is not an exhaustive list of possible effects, and factors such as the tendency for estates to be split up and the need to sell properties to meet taxation demands are important.

The assessment of housing inheritance relates initially to different cohorts of owners. The patterns of inheritance observed in the 1980s reflect the social structure of home ownership some 50 years earlier. Thus the level and nature of inheritance reflects past patterns of access and accumulation. Later cohorts of owners are larger and may have a different social profile and different wealth holdings. Thus, for example, Munro's work in Glasgow showed that it was the more expensive houses which were being inherited. This may have reflected the relatively privileged nature of home ownership in Scotland in the immediate postwar period (Munro 1988). The general point is that there will be waves of housing inheritance which may vary qualitatively and quantitatively reflecting both the different cohorts in the past growth of home ownership and current differences in the relative values of different assets. Some cohorts may contain, for example, disproportionately large numbers of households who bought as sitting private tenants. In other (subsequent) periods council-house purchasers may figure more prominently. Indeed this is a significant factor in the calculations made by Lloyds Bank (1993) on the future regional distribution of property inheritance. All this cautions against erecting too simplistic a model of future housing inheritance from the present position.

THE PATTERN OF RESIDENTIAL PROPERTY INHERITANCE

The source of statistics on inheritance in Britain is the Inland Revenue's analysis of 'estates passing at death' which require a formal grant of representation or grant of probate. The statistics cover almost all house property not passing between spouses (Hamnett 1992). The number of estates containing residential property did not increase significantly over 20 years from the late 1960s but is projected to double by 2025 (Hamnett, Harmer and Williams 1991).

Although the number of estates containing residential property had not risen very much, the value of housing inheritance rose from £465 million in 1968–9 to £5,000 million in 1987–8, reflecting increasing house prices. Thus in 1968–9 the average value of residential property in estates was £3,700. By 1987–8 it was £48,000. The data suggest that about 1 per cent of adult individuals and 2 per cent of households can expect to inherit house property each year and that the majority of beneficiaries receive less than £16,000 from housing inheritance (Hamnett 1992).

The proportion of estates containing residential property varied from 55 per cent in Wales and 50 per cent in England to 38 per cent in Scotland and 36 per cent in Northern Ireland and these figures are respectively 46 per cent, 44 per cent, 33 per cent and 28 per cent when residential property is expressed as a proportion of the total capital value of estates.

Survey data on the characteristics of beneficiaries is available from 1989 and 1991. The great majority of beneficiaries of housing inheritance are aged over 40 years when they inherit and the median age at inheritance is 50 years. A quarter of professional- and managerial-headed households had inherited house property at some stage in their lives compared with 15 per cent of junior nonmanual-headed households, 10 per cent of skilled manual households, 7 per cent of semi and unskilled workers, and 5 per cent of economically inactive. Some 17 per cent of home owners had inherited compared with 3 per cent of council tenants. The proportion of households inheriting property was 12 per cent in Great Britain but figures ranged from 19 per cent in the south west and 17 per cent in the south east and Wales, to 9 per cent in the north west and in Greater London and 7 per cent in Scotland. The regional differences in the value of inheritance received are very considerable and largely reflect differences in house prices. The sum inherited nationally averaged £22,000 but ranged from £48,500 in London to £13,400 in Yorkshire and Humberside. Hamnett concludes from all of these data that the location of parents and other benefactors influences both the incidence and value of inheritance. Housing wealth accumulates disproportionately in more buoyant and affluent areas and most transfers are intraregional. Thus, housing wealth accumulates fastest in the south east of England and most of it remains there.

A more recent analysis by Froszteg and Holmans (1994) using Inland Revenue data and additional data from the General Household Survey has largely confirmed the general picture which has been established of the pattern and significance of housing inheritance. They estimate that in 1989–90 about half of the £11.3 billion bequeathed was attributable to dwellings. The median age at inheritance was 47, and among those whose inheritance primarily consisted of a dwelling the mean value was £68,974. Inheritors were typically sons or daughters and the money was most typically invested or saved. Froszteg and Holmans reinforce the view that those who inherit are 'a generation already well established in their housing'. Significantly, they point out that the middle generation benefits from the proceeds of selling inherited dwellings to the debt-financed 'young'. And they conclude that because the amount transferred in any one year represents only 1 per cent of marketable wealth, the impact of the growth of residential property inheritance will be a gradual process. Their general conclusion is that the overall effect of mass home ownership on the distribution of wealth will be significant but not transformative – a larger minority of those with substantial holdings.

The growth of home ownership with its implications for a more pervasive experience of inheritance among families has begun to attract the attention of sociologists with a more general interest in the sociology of the family (Finch 1994; Finch and Hayes 1994). Among other things this research shows that housing wealth is generally shared equally among beneficiary children, remains within the family and that, consistent with previous assessments, inheritance is an event which generally occurs late in the family lifecycle. The notion of 'children' inheriting conveys a rather distorted view of the effects in practice since the majority of these children are likely to be ageing adults whose own children have long since departed. This means that the impact of housing inheritance will be dissipated through its subdivision according to the number of children involved (as opposed to the impact on the principle of primogeniture) and because it will occur when the pattern of life chances is already established. Drawing on the work of Andersen (1985), Finch remarks that

> Children born as late as 1891, in a family which was statistically typical, could expect both parents to be dead by the time the average child was aged 37. The corresponding figure for children born in 1921 was age 47. But for children born in 1946, in a statistically typical family, the children could expect to be aged 56 before both parents would be dead.
>
> (Finch 1994, 6)

Finch goes on to point out that 'for generations born since the war, few can expect to inherit from parents until they themselves are contemplating retirement' (ibid., 12). This is consistent with the evidence from Froszteg and Holmans: of those inheriting from parents (the vast majority) well over half were aged 45 and over. And the size of the inheritance tended to increase with age. In other words, younger people for whom a significant bequest could make a major difference to their housing trajectory and general life chances, tended to inherit relatively small amounts.

These observations about the stage at which inheritance occurs have important implications for the potential impact of housing-related wealth on social inequalities. Stated simply, working lives will continue to be shaped primarily by occupational and labour-market factors: it is in retirement or near retirement that the general contours of social inequalities will be modified by inheritance swollen by the growth of home ownership.

INTER VIVOS TRANSFERS

The assumptions about the impact of wealth accumulation associated with the growth of home ownership have tended to focus on equity release (to augment incomes and lifestyles of the households releasing the equity) and inheritance. The extent and pattern of transfers *inter vivos* complicates the picture. Evidence in this area is, however, patchy. There is an extensive, general literature on intergenerational exchange (see, for example, Hogan *et al.* 1993; Rossi and Rossi 1990) which focuses on issues such as reciprocity, instrumental altruism (Becker 1984) and intergenerational assistance in the care of elderly people. Specific research on lifetime gifts or assistance in the form of financial assistance for housing – say deposits for house purchase for children – is limited and inconclusive in the British context. And the extent to which there is a trickle-down effect from children to grandchildren associated with property inheritance is an important area for further research.

Survey evidence on, for example, the source of deposits for house purchase among new entrants to the housing market shows limited direct assistance from parents or relatives. For example, in a recent survey of home owners in Britain, some 4 per cent had received assistance with the initial deposit from relatives (Maclennan *et al.* 1994). Saunders (1990), however, found that 8 per cent of his respondents had received cash for a deposit from family sources – and 24 per cent of respondents in all housing tenures had received some form of financial help with housing costs. There are differences in the age of respondents and the tenure compositions of the samples which complicate comparisons. And a more general problem is that gifts or loans from such sources may have become absorbed into general savings and not appear as lifetime transfers between generations. Froszteg and Holmans' analysis shows *inter alia* that among inheriting existing owners, 2 per cent mainly used the bequest to help others buy or improve a dwelling. More than half of those existing owners invested or saved the money and 19 per cent improved their own accommodation. From a different perspective, Finch (1994) refers to the lack of a 'strategic dimension' among the new generation of property inheritors. By this she means the apparent absence of any attempt to build 'fortunes' or to develop a broader family strategy in the use of property inheritance. The new inherited wealth is most typically used to 'enhance comforts in old age' rather than passed directly or indirectly to the grandchild generation. Some is passed on but chaotically. Finch describes the process rather neatly as wealth trickling down to the younger generation but 'not the kind of trickle which comes from a dripping tap, which flows from a single source to an identifiable exit. The more appropriate imagery is that of the mountain stream which, as it descends, divides and redivides, over rocks and underground, beginning from a single source but flowing through many exits, which could only be traced with great difficulty' (p. 12).

A study by Pickvance and Pickvance (1993) explored family help in the housing decisions of young people in the south east of England in the late 1980s. This is a region with a high level of home ownership, relatively high house-price inflation and the core region of the British space economy. The context for the study was that the middle generation of home owners in the south east had accumulated significant amounts of equity: the younger generation, however, faced major affordability problems in a period of rampant house-price inflation in the late 1980s. There was thus a younger generation of potential home owners in need of financial assistance and a middle generation well placed to provide it. Pickvance and Pickvance in fact found a relatively low level of financial assistance in these circumstances – some 7 per cent of their respondents had received financial help from family for housing purposes. And among those who had received financial assistance the amounts were small relative to the cost of buying a house. Pickvance and Pickvance offer various explanations for the apparently low level of financial assistance in such circumstances. Part of the explanation, they suggest, lies in the extension of home ownership to lower income households with relatively more parents less able to help their children financially. However, attitudes towards the receipt of financial assistance with housing costs are also complex. Pickvance and Pickvance found that almost half of their young respondents thought their parents could afford to help them but only 20 per cent supported the idea that their parents should provide financial assistance. They comment, 'The low level of financial help would thus seem to be due both to the circumstance that only half of parents can provide financial help, and to the attitudes of young people to receiving such help' (p. 31).

The wealth tied up in a parental home can also be mobilised indirectly to assist offspring. The fall in house prices in real and nominal terms in many parts of the UK since 1989 has placed significant numbers of younger purchasers in situations of negative equity. Family growth or change of employment may necessitate a move for many households in this more mobile section of the population. Some lending agencies have developed schemes whereby the positive equity in a parental home can provide temporary security to offspring needing to finance a house move.

HOUSING AND SOCIAL CLASS

Much of the above discussion in the British context has been linked to a broader debate about the class dimensions of these processes of wealth transfers associated with the growth of home ownership and the impact on social inequality. Saunders (1990) has gone to great pains to seek to establish that wealth accumulation through housing bears little relation to occupational class. Accumulation through housing, he argued, can exceed remuneration through work and the pattern of benefit from it bears little relation to the work process. Gains made through home ownership cut across conventional class divisions and form part of the process through which these divisions have ceased to be key social divisions. This position has been generally accepted by Lowe (1992). However the basis of Saunders' original calculation is open to serious challenge. His calculation does not relate to absolute returns but to the rate of return (see also Chapter 7 in this volume). Moreover the rate of return was not calculated according to the purchase price, i.e. the rate of price increase, but according to the original deposit. This is a wholly artificial calculation. Some households purchased properties without a deposit; some benefit from discounts which affect initial purchase price; the level of deposit is often largely arbitrary reflecting lenders' practice (and the state of the market when the loan was taken up), decisions about overmortgaging and other issues, and no account is taken of transaction costs.

Leaving aside problems with the data acknowledged by Saunders his calculations can result in high rates of return involving low absolute gains and the converse. Because the base for calculation is deposit, the key to rate of return is whether a large or small deposit was paid. Not surprisingly this produces the pattern of returns Saunders sought – one which shows no clear association with income or class. The highest gains are generally achieved by those who have been in home ownership longest. Even this conclusion is questionable because of the way council-house sales cases and those paying no deposit are treated.

In our view Saunders' attempt to construct a measure of return to owner occupation is at worst spurious and at best seriously flawed. The picture it presents is heavily affected by when the survey was carried out, and a recalculation to take account of the fall in house prices since 1989 would yield very different but equally misleading results.

In terms of life chances, realisable wealth, and people's own perceptions of wealth accumulation it is more appropriate to refer to absolute values of property. The distribution of owner-occupied dwellings shows a clear relationship between value of property and occupational class (see Figure 4.1). And a recent survey of house conditions in England shows that certain social groups – lone parents, ethnic minorities and low income owners generally – are more likely to be living in lower-value properties which are more likely to be in the worst condition (Department of the Environment 1993). The implications of this are that where house-price fluctuations do enable working-class households in particular housing situations to do better than higher income households in different housing situations these relative gains are likely to be temporary. They are not sustained over lifetimes, and differences in income, the likelihood of trading up and the ability to afford more expensive housing (which in absolute terms appreciates in value to the greatest extent) re-establish the association between social class and housing wealth. This general relationship between income, occupational class and housing wealth is not surprising and is evident in other countries. Quercia and Rohe (1992), for example, referring to official government data, comment that in the USA there is a positive correlation between household income and the amount of housing equity.

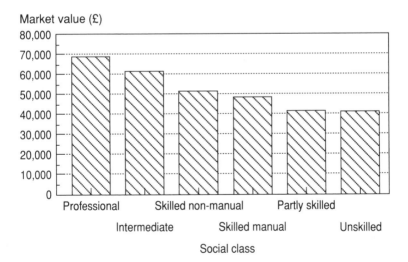

Figure 4.1 Average market value of dwelling by social class (owners only, 1989)

Source: Joseph Rowntree Foundation Housing Finance Study. Market values based on Hedonic estimation. Sample number 4148.

The degree of crosscutting is exaggerated by snapshot surveys which show short-term gains associated with the volatility of the housing market or accidents of when people moved house. The picture emerging from data on inheritance or from lifetime patterns will not support a crosscutting element except in relation to region. Even here the situation should not be overstated. Hamnett's analysis shows that while regional house prices differ, the rate of appreciation of house prices in different regions has not differed significantly over the period 1969 to 1991. House prices in London and the south east lead any boom in prices but over the long term London and the south east do not have rates of house-price inflation significantly higher than other regions. Because home owners in the south east tend to pay more for houses, the application of a common rate of house-price increase will yield larger returns but these returns are offset by higher borrowing and expenditure and opportunity costs and are less significant than would apply if rates of inflation differed.

A longer-term or lifetime perspective, rather than Saunders' short-term extrapolation, is consistent with a range of evidence. It explains the consistent strong association between occupational class and position in the home-ownership market. The Royal Commission on the Distribution of Income and Wealth demonstrated a clear link between household income and value of dwelling occupied and a range of other data have referred to the links between class and tenure (Murie and Forrest 1980a, 1980b; Murie 1983; Hamnett 1984; Bentham 1986).

One final element of the debate about housing wealth and social class relates to inheritance. The discussions above indicate that the value of housing wealth relates to social class. It is also true that the size and age of families varies by social class. As Salt and Coleman (1992) show, the 'norm' for middle-class households in Britain is a two-child family. Families above three children and less than two are more frequent in the manual social class. In 1971 41 per cent of wives of manual workers married in 1955–60 had 4 or more children compared to 29 per cent in the non-manual group. While numbers of children were in decline for successive cohorts in the interwar period, class differences remained. The general point is that the estates of manual workers are likely to be smaller and to be divided among a larger number of beneficiaries.

COHORTS OF HOME OWNERS

The debate on housing wealth in Britain as outlined above has referred initially to the amount of personal wealth held in the form of housing and then to the distribution of this wealth in spatial and social terms. A prime interest has been in the extent to which the generation of housing wealth or its transfer through inheritance have cut across inequalities relating to incomes or class or have weakened the class basis of inequality. The importance of housing wealth and inheritance in affecting access and price in home ownership and in cutting across economic inequality has also received considerable attention. However, some of the confusions in the debate derive from a tendency to want to refer to wealth and inheritance as intrinsic attributes of home ownership rather than attributes associated with particular cohorts of households in home ownership. Some of the most important qualifications to the empirical data which have emerged relate to how far they reflect the position of a particular cohort and the extent to which results can be generalised. Thus, for example, Munro's findings on housing inheritance in Glasgow relate to the nature and social composition of early home owners in that city. More generally, later home owners will have different lifetime experience and this will affect the size of estates. Later cohorts of home owners will include more manual-worker households, more households with low incomes during their working lives, with experience of periods of unemployment, and with dependence on state benefit in old age. They are also likely to have smaller sibling families and smaller numbers of children. These factors not only affect the pattern of inheritance but also affect decisions about housing in later life.

Much has been made in the British literature of people's desire to have 'something to leave to the children' and of the extent to which this has influenced people's housing decisions. However there is no reason to regard this as a cultural attitude unaffected by other developments. In the postwar period in which home ownership careers have mainly been embarked upon the context for home ownership included two key elements which tend to be neglected. The first was an effective redistributive welfare state which was founded on full employment and provided universal social insurance and health provision. While benefits were not high relative to average earnings the home owner who was generally in secure non-manual employment had little recourse to long-term dependency until retirement and even then was likely to be able to supplement the state pension from occupational pensions or savings. The front loading of mortgage payments had itself enabled savings and house repair for all but the poorest home owners. This cohort of home owners was affected by a second factor – family networks. Although middle-class families were smaller than their working-class counterparts this cohort of home owners was more likely to have a family-based support network than later cohorts. This involved mutual assistance with the older generation assisting with child care and housing of their children and grandchildren. In the latter respect gifts and loans to assist with house purchase have been important elements in some households.

These two elements – the family and the welfare state – provided a secure framework for what was a generally affluent cohort of home owners. In older age, incentive and opportunity to move to alternative housing was limited and the family home was only left with ill health or at death. This family home had appreciated enormously in value with the house-price inflation of the 1960s and 1980s and other family resources were sufficient to add to this in inherited wealth. For more recent cohorts and for those entering home ownership since the 1970s there are a number of differences. These can be summarised as follows:

(i) a greater range of occupational groups with more low income and manual workers

(ii) a greater experience of redundancy, unemployment and interrupted earnings with economic restructuring and higher unemployment

(iii) an erosion of state benefits and welfare-state support

(iv) a wider experience of separation and divorce with division of housing assets forming an important part of family settlements

(v) smaller families and family support networks even where geographical mobility has not affected these

(vi) an increased number of lower-value properties with the development of sitting-tenant purchase for public tenants, converted properties and low price, low-standard housing built for sale.

The much larger later cohort of home owners is more differentiated even when controlling for age differences. It no doubt still
includes a group comparable to that which dominated the earlier
cohort. But this group no longer typifies the cohort. Changes
in the housing market, the economy, the welfare state and the
family have had an uneven impact spatially and socially. At
one extreme there is the affluent home owner with a second (or
third) home, substantial private pension and other assets. At
the other extreme is the owner of one home at the bottom of the
market and with little or no savings or income except from
the state. The former group and many other owners of properties
with substantial asset values may decide to trade down, to
reduce the work and costs associated with a large property.
Modern lower-price housing is an attractive alternative and there
is evidence of significant trading down among older home
owners (Forrest and Murie 1993). This implies changing asset
portfolios but not necessarily reducing them. Home equity
schemes and other ways of releasing assets held in housing to
supplement income have been attractive to an asset-rich/income-
poor group and have meant reducing asset holdings (and leaving
less for children). The experience with some of these schemes was
disastrous in the 1980s and led to new regulations. Nevertheless
the expectation must be that more home owners will trade down
or otherwise reduce their housing wealth. The reasons that
they are doing this relate to their lifetime experience and to
specific circumstances relating to the family and the welfare state.
For this group housing is being recycled as social security. The
final group of older home owners have property which is not of
sufficient value to trade down and may increasingly emerge as an
asset-poor/income-poor group. Their housing status does not
offset the adverse effects of changes in the welfare state, and low
income and perhaps lack of family support will increasingly
be apparent in problems of disrepair of housing and application
for subsidised or residential accommodation outside the home-
ownership sector.

One of the key perspectives on housing wealth which emerges
from this is how housing-tenure decisions relate to the schedul-
ing of housing costs. A strong example is provided by decisions
of tenants to take advantage of opportunities to buy. As well
as referring to having something to pass on to children these
purchasers refer to avoiding constantly rising rents and to having

completed housing payments by retirement (Murie 1975). While it may involve a misjudgement about repair and maintenance costs it reflects a concern to reschedule lifetime housing costs and influence claims on resources in older age.

Decisions to trade down and increase resources available for everyday expenditure represent a similar step. Saving through housing does not occur in a vacuum but relates to broader household strategies. Inevitably these strategies are adjusted in the light of different circumstances and resources outside the narrow sphere of housing. The way that home owners develop their strategies will vary according to these circumstances. Job history, social class, housing history and family networks will all be important dimensions of this. And the significance of cohort membership will be evident in what rights and resources are associated with these dimensions. The cohort of households entering home ownership in the 1980s have been variously affected by economic recession and unemployment, by house-price collapse, negative equity and repossession. How far adverse experience is offset by subsequent events is of crucial importance for this group. For households in well-paid, career occupations steady growth of employment income will form a stability which enables them to cope with volatility in the housing sector. For other households recovery from adverse circumstances is likely to be much more dependent on the vicissitudes of the housing market.

CONCLUSIONS

The importance of housing wealth and inheritance in Britain is now well established and issues around inheritance and social class have aroused considerable debate. In this debate a number of important issues have emerged. The first is that the marked expansion of housing wealth by the mid 1970s has not been sustained. The statistics on the volume of housing wealth are likely to show some increase because of the continuing expansion of home ownership. However the most important influence will be the movement of house prices. The decline in house prices in Britain between 1989 and 1993 was previously regarded by some as inconceivable and some accounts of home ownership and wealth are defective because of this. Some accounts are also misleading because of a tendency to exaggerate the extent to which processes in home ownership produce patterns of gain which cut across other patterns of inequality. Such crosscutting effects have not been established empirically and the most reasonable interpretation of available data is that the crosscutting effects which occur in periods of house-price inflation are largely temporary, are eroded in subsequent periods and that other sources of inequalities reassert themselves.

Thus, for occupational class categories, or those with similar lifetime work experience, housing experience will be effective in determining relative resources. But where class, lifetime work experience and income differ significantly it will be usual to find that housing histories also differ and in a way which reinforces rather than cuts across other differences. Households whose jobs involve moving house and command rising and high incomes are likely to have different housing histories more compatible with maximising gains through housing. Even if this was not true and they did not move any more often, higher income groups tend to buy higher-priced housing and over their lifetime their housing wealth reflects the larger absolute gains arising from this.

Within this perspective two other factors are important. First, because house prices and housing markets differ regionally and widely, the geography of housing histories is of great importance. Second, the existing literature has tended to neglect cohort effects and the importance of the context in which home ownership operates. In the context of Britain in the 1990s the differentials and uncertainties about what home ownership means and what opportunities it provides are particularly striking. The British accounts of home ownership have not anticipated house-price decline, low rates of mobility and exchange, negative equity, repossession, trading down by necessity or by choice, and low asset low income owners with limited room to manoeuvre. As it has expanded home ownership has changed. While it still represents a source and store of wealth for most owners it does not for a substantial number. Even if subsequent housing market developments re-establish this relationship the importance of differential accumulation and of cohort differences provides the essential framework for assessing the significance of housing-related wealth for social inequality and for intergenerational transfers.

Chapter 5

Home ownership and family wealth in the United States

Michael A. Stegman, with Joanna Brownstein and Kenneth Temkin

INTRODUCTION

The presumed rights and privileges of home ownership are embedded in the American consciousness. Based in Jeffersonian democratic ideals, the concept of private property is as fundamental to the structure of the United States as the belief in individual rights. The intense national desire for ownership of real property means that more resources (tax incentives) are used to encourage that goal, and less resources (tax outlays) are committed to the social housing sector. And at around five per cent, the size of the US social housing sector is considerably smaller than in most West European countries. More than 90 per cent of the US housing stock is privately owned and part of the market economy. This abundant supply makes it relatively easier for American families to adjust their housing circumstances to changes in needs than is true of most European countries with larger social housing sectors. Between 1985 and 1989 almost half of all of American households moved into their present homes, and approximately 18 per cent moved during 1989 alone. While renters were more than four times as likely to move as home owners, approximately 8 per cent of all owner-occupiers moved during 1989 (US Bureau of the Census 1991, 17, 20). While mobility and choice are maximised when such a large fraction of the US inventory is priced and allocated by the market mechanism, this also contributes to severe housing-cost burdens for large numbers of low-income families, and exacerbates the problem of homelessness.

According to the US Bureau of the Census, changes in either family status or housing needs motivated 56 per cent of all renter moves and 47 per cent of all moves by owners. More than a fifth of all owner-occupiers who moved achieved their goal and became home owners in 1989, while job-related factors caused more than 20 per cent of renters and almost 16 per cent of home-owners to move (Table 5.1).

This essay on home ownership and family wealth is written at a time of transition in the United States. The demand for quality owner-occupied housing is expected to remain strong into the next century, with the total US population projected to increase by 29 million just between 1985 and 2010 (Horowitz 1990, 5). But its financial benefits are diminishing. If the latter half of the 1980s is any measure of what to expect during the 1990s, the prominent role that home ownership has played in the accumulation of family wealth could be changing; especially for young, newly-established, single-person and minority households. And for many elderly, their family homes that once were passed along to heirs are now being sold to secure long-term institutional care.

In the next five sections we describe some disturbing social out-comes of the economic turmoil of the 1980s, including a further skewing in the distribution of national income and a decline in the home ownership rate. That is followed by a discussion of the historical role home ownership has played in the accumulation of family wealth. Section four reviews the significant ways that federal policies promote the institution of home ownership, and why the Bush Administration proposed to extend home ownership opportunities to the nation's poor. Changing demand patterns and the growing conflict between the home ownership aspirations of younger Americans and their inability to afford a home are covered. We conclude with suggestions for further economic and social research.

HOME OWNERSHIP IN THE UNITED STATES IN THE 1980S

The 1980s was a decade of economic turmoil in the United States. An unprecedented period of sustained economic growth ended in the latter quarter of the decade, and was followed by a reces-sion that has lasted into the early 1990s. The overall distribution of income became more unequal through the 1980s as the richest 1 per cent of all families received 60 per cent of the after-tax income gain. Families in the top 2–5 per cent also did very

Table 5.1 Main reasons for move and choices of present home and neighbourhood by tenure, 1989 (respondent moved during previous twelve months)

	Owner-occupied (%)	Renter-occupied (%)
Main reasons for move		
Job-related	15.6	24.9
Family status	20.8	28.2
Housing needs	26.0	28.0
Tenure change	20.9	1.3
Other	16.7	17.6
TOTAL	100.0	100.0
Main reasons for choice of home		
Financial	34.1	32.1
Physical attributes	34.7	22.6
Only one available	2.1	12.4
Other	29.1	32.9
TOTAL	100.0	100.0
Main reasons for choice of neighbourhood		
Job-related	8.9	18.6
Good schools	5.1	3.9
Home choice	27.5	18.6
Convenient location	10.7	13.3
Physical attributes	16.3	9.7
Other	31.5	35.8
TOTAL	100.0	100.0

Source: US Bureau of the Census, 'Housing Characteristics of Recent Movers: 1989', *Current Housing Reports*, Series H121/91–2, Washington, DC, 1991, p. 11.

well, receiving 14 per cent of all income gains. Those in the top 6 per cent through 20 per cent received 20 per cent of all income gains, while collectively, families with incomes below the top 20 per cent received just 6 per cent of all income gain. The US middle class, most commonly defined along income line, shrank in size from 68 per cent of all households to 63 per cent (Table 5.2). (This essay bases its definition of middle class on a US Bureau of the Census study of changes in the income distribution of American families.) Also during the 1980s, the real incomes of families in the bottom fifth of the income distribution fell

Table 5.2 Per cent of persons with high, middle and low relative incomes, United States, selected years

Year	High income (%)	Middle income (%)	Low income (%)
1969	10.9	71.2	17.9
1974	11.0	70.3	18.7
1979	11.9	68.0	20.0
1984	14.1	64.0	21.8
1989	14.7	63.3	22.1

Source: US Bureau of the Census, 'Trends in Relative Income: 1964–1989', *Current Population Reports, Consumer Income*, Series P-60, No. 177, Washington, DC, 1991.

Note: Middle income is defined as a relative income of between half and two-times the income of the median individual. The relative-income measure of an individual is the distance from the median of an income distribution that contains adjustments for differences in family size. A person with a relative income of .50 has only one-half the income of a person in the middle of the income distribution and a person with a relative income of 2.0 has twice the income of a person in the middle, or at the median. High relative income is defined as a person with an income of 2.0 or higher, and low relative income is defined as an income of .50 or lower. See US Bureau of the Census, 'Trends in Relative Income: 1964–1989', 1991 for details of the measurement technique.

by 9 per cent adjusted for inflation (Nasar 1992, A-1). Slower economic growth in the latter half of the decade dampened sales prices for owner-occupied housing. While in many markets nominal prices actually fell, this did little to overcome the price-boosting inflationary surge of the 1970s and early 1980s.

The income dynamics of the 1980s also have serious implications for the future of the US rental market. Large numbers of higher income families left the rental sector to buy a house during the 1970s and 1980s, while those remaining as renters experienced little or no real income growth. This has resulted in the impoverishment of the rental sector and there is little effective demand for new rental housing construction. Also, owners of the existing rental stock are finding it increasingly difficult to maintain the quality of their older inventories due to low tenant incomes (Joint Center for Housing Studies 1991, 25–6).

The home ownership rate in the US remained relatively stable at around 30 per cent of all households from 1900 through 1940. Between 1940 and 1980, it doubled to around 60 per cent. The surge in home ownership is thus a post-World War II phenomenon. During this period home ownership was spurred by rapid economic growth, increasing headship rates among home owning-oriented cohorts, and home ownership-boosting federal policies and programs, including the introduction of federal mortgage insurance (Chevan 1989, 252). Over the past ten years, however, American families – especially young families, and families with children, and low-to-moderate incomes families who have rented for most of their adult lives – have lost substantial ground in their struggle to buy a home. While it has been widely published that the home ownership rate in the US fell during the 1980s for the first time in more than 40 years, the overall decline was just 1.5 percentage points, from 65.6 per cent to 64.1 per cent, and has since stabilised (US Bureau of the Census, 1992). Far more significant than this marginal decline, however, is its uneven impact across the population. While middle-age families (age 45–54) held their own, and older households actually increased their ownership rates from the early 1970s to 1990, home ownership rates fell for the 25–34 age group from 51 per cent to 44 per cent, and from 23 per cent to 15 per cent for those under age 25 (Table 5.3). And the picture is the same for families with children across all income groups. While home ownership rates for families with children fell from 70 per cent to 64 per cent between 1978 and 1989, the drop was more precipitous for those at the lower end of the income spectrum (Table 5.4).

The recent recession, combined with liberalised monetary policies that significantly lowered interest rates in 1992, made housing more affordable than it has been in some time. But lower borrowing costs alone are not likely to enhance home ownership opportunities for low- and moderate-income families in the US. Many aspiring home owners have too little savings for a downpayment and are overburdened with consumer debts for automobiles and household furnishings, which further reduces their capacity to carry a mortgage. In 1988, two-thirds of all renters in the US were unable to afford a modestly-priced house in their region for reasons other than high mortgage payments alone (Table 5.5).

HOME OWNERSHIP AND WEALTH

To an extraordinary degree, Americans equate having a home of their own with 'having it made' and an overall sense of

Table 5.3 Home ownership rates by age of head, United States, 1973–90

Age of head	1973 (%)	1976 (%)	1980 (%)	1983 (%)	1987 (%)	1990 (%)
Under 25	23.4	21.0	21.3	19.3	16.1	15.3
25–34	51.4	52.2	52.3	47.0	45.1	44.3
35–44	70.7	71.4	72.3	69.6	66.9	66.5
45–64	75.9	77.3	78:5	78.8	78.2	78.1
65 and over	69.8	70.6	72.3	74.8	75.1	75.5
Total households	64.4	64.8	65.6	64.9	64.0	64.1

Source: Joint Center for Housing Studies of Harvard University, *The State of the Nations' Housing*, Cambridge, Mass., 1991, p. 33.

Table 5.4 Home ownership rates by household type and relative income, United States, 1978 and 1989

	Families with children		Families without children		Elderly		All Households	
	1978 (%)	1989 (%)	1978 (%)	1989 (%)	1978 (%)	1989 (%)	1978 (%)	1989 (%)
Very low income	37	29	52	47	62	65	47	44
Low income	63	52	58	56	80	82	60	56
Middle income	78	70	65	67	83	85	69	65
Upper income	90	88	82	84	85	92	81	81
TOTAL	70	64	73	74	72	77	65	64

Source: Kathryn P. Nelson and Jill Khadduri, 'To whom shall limited housing resources be directed?', *Housing Policy Debate*, 2(2), 1992, Table 5.3.

Table 5.5 Factors preventing the purchase of a modestly-priced home, United States, 1989

Debt level too high	8.5%
Can't afford monthly payments	22.3%
Can't afford down payment	4.1%
More than one of above reasons	65.1%
TOTAL	100.0%

Source: US Bureau of the Census, 'Who can afford to buy a house?', *Current Housing Reports*, H121/91-1, Washington, DC, 1991, pp. 20, 34.

Note: Modestly-priced house is equal to 75 per cent of the price of the median-priced house. Payments calculated on basis of FHA-insured, fixed-rate, 30-year mortgage at prevailing interest rates.

well-being. In a 1978 Survey on the Quality of Community Life, Louis Harris Associates reported that regardless of their present housing circumstances, 75 per cent of all Americans would prefer to own a single-family house. This was true for rich and poor; white, black and Hispanic; and families in all-white, racially-mixed or all-minority neighbourhoods (cited in Stegman 1991, 29–30). This core value was reaffirmed in a 1992 national survey which found that by a 3 to 1 margin, American families would rather own a home than retire 10 years early, and they would rather own a home than take a better job in a city where they could only afford to rent. Further, home ownership was considered one of life's most important goals by 60 per cent of those in the lowest income brackets and by only 31 per cent of those in the highest, reflecting that what the more affluent take for granted the poor can only hope for (Federal National Mortgage Association 1992, 2, 6).

As in other western cultures with market economies, home ownership in the United States implies a degree of financial security that is not normally associated with rental occupancy. For most of the past 40 years, home ownership has not only been a symbol of wealth, but also the most important actual wealth most American families accumulated. A 1983 Survey of Consumer Finance found that house value represented an average of 89 per cent of total assets for families with an income of under US$5,000; 75 per cent for those with incomes between US$20,000 and $30,000; and a smaller but still significant 52 per cent of total assets for families with an income of US$50,000 or more (Shear, Wachter and Weicher n.d., 33). As Irving Welfeld, a HUD policy analyst, put it,

> During the post-war period . . . young couples with almost no money to their name bought houses with a minimal down payment, and over the years, with the steady buildup of equity and a little inflation, before they knew it they were rich. The value of owner-occupied homes at the end of 1986 was $3.758 trillion and the net equity was $2.113 trillion – an average owner had an equity of over $50,000.
>
> (Welfeld 1988, 9)

For a variety of reasons (including racial discrimination), home ownership rates are substantially lower among minorities – poor and nonpoor alike – than they are for whites. In 1990 some 42 per cent of all black households, 41 per cent of all Hispanic households, and 68 per cent of all white households were home owners (Joint Center for Housing Studies 1991, 10). In fact, the proportion of poor white households that own their homes – 46 per cent – is greater than the proportion either of all black or Hispanic-owner households. A 1991 report from the US Department of Housing and Urban Development indicates that the incidence of racial discrimination in US housing markets continues unabated. According to the study, despite two decades of fair housing enforcement, blacks and Hispanics are still denied information about available housing and credit (US Department of Housing and Urban Development 1991, 13, 20).

William C. Apgar argues that 'the lack of homeownership opportunities for blacks has undermined their ability to accumulate wealth.' In 1989, equity in a house accounted for more than 55 per cent of the average home owner's net wealth (Table 5.6). And this percentage was stable across all age groups, but varied dramatically by race and ethnicity. Though both net wealth and home equity were lower among black owners, home equity accounted for fully 80 per cent of their net wealth. Among Hispanics, home equity represented 98 per cent, or virtually all of the household's wealth. The fact that minority families who do manage to become homeowners accumulate substantial equity, according to Apgar, underscores 'the penalty paid by [minority] households locked out of homebuying entirely by the lack of income or wealth, or by discriminatory practices' (Joint Center for Housing Studies 1991, 14).

The reliance on home equity for future wealth accumulation is also evident in the proportion of household savings accrued in the appreciation of home values. The savings rate of American families more than doubled, from 4.7 per cent to 10 per cent, when unrealised capital gains were added to more liquid savings instruments like stocks, bonds and certificates of deposit (Ibbotson and Siegel 1984, 224).

From 1960 to 1989, total household-sector wealth increased by 167 per cent, from around $6 trillion to $16 trillion (in 1982 US dollars) (Table 5.7). The value of financial assets held by households (i.e. checking and savings deposits, credit market instruments, corporate equity shares, life insurance and pension reserves) during this period increased from $4.1 trillion to around $10.5 trillion, or by 155 per cent. In contrast, the value of

Table 5.6 Household income, wealth and net equity of home owners
by age and race, United States, 1986 (in 1989 US dollars)

	Median net wealth ($)	Median home equity ($)	Home equity as percentage of net wealth
Total	86,626	47,542	54.9
By age			
25–34	40,561	22,090	54.4
35–64	102,736	56,268	54.8
65 and over	89,782	50,912	56.6
By race			
White	94,484	50,912	53.9
Black	38,348	30,621	79.9
Hispanic	69,137	67,458	97.6

Source: Joint Center for Housing Studies of Harvard University, *The State of the Nation's Housing*, Cambridge, Mass., 1989, pp. 10 and 13.

Note: Owing to small sample size, there is no separate category for Hispanics

owner-occupied real estate held by households grew by a more rapid 216 per cent, from $1.1 trillion to $3.6 trillion. Thus, the relative importance of homeownership in the asset mix of American households grew from 18.9 per cent of total assets at the beginning of the period, to 22.5 per cent at the end.

Although owner-occupied real estate's share of total household assets increased over the entire period, 1980–89 produced a relative decline in net worth as a result of a taming of the high inflation rates of the 1970s and the onset of the economic recession. This phenomenon is reflected in Table 5.8 which incorporates household debt, including outstanding home mortgage debt, into a picture of changing household-sector net worth over the 1960–89 period. According to Holloway, because owner-occupied housing is a leveraged asset and home mortgages do not automatically increase with inflation, increases in home equity rise more rapidly than the inflation rate.

Home equity as a share of net worth tends to increase during periods of accelerating inflation, and generally decrease during periods of decelerating inflation (Holloway 1991, 40). Thus, while home equity's share of total household-sector net worth increased from 13.5 per cent in 1960 to 18.2 per cent in 1980, the slowing of inflation during the 1980s pushed it all the way back

Table 5.7 Household-sector assets (billions of 1982 US dollars)

Year	Total	Per cent	Owner-occupied real estate	Per cent	Financial	Per cent	Other tangible	Per cent
1960	5,982.1	100.0	1,133.4	18.9	4,122.5	69.0	726.1	12.1
1970	8,520.0	100.0	1,608.2	18.9	5,798.4	68.0	1,113.3	13.1
1980	12,027.4	100.0	2,966.4	24.6	7,553.0	62.9	1,508.1	12.5
1989	15,967.2	100.0	3,591.8	22.5	10,539.3	66.0	1,836.1	11.5

Source: Thomas M. Holloway, 'The role of homeownership and home price appreciation in the accumulation and distribution of household-sector wealth,' *Business Economics*, April 1991, p. 39.

Table 5.8 Household-sector net worth (billions of 1982 US dollars)

Year	Total	Per cent	Home equity	Per cent	Other	Per cent
1960	5,297.9	100.0	716.1	13.5	4,581.8	86.5
1970	7,371.6	100.0	932.2	12.6	6,439.4	87.4
1980	10,308.3	100.0	1,878.2	18.2	8,430.1	81.8
1989	12,235.3	100.0	1,791.1	13.5	11,444.2	86.5

Source: Thomas M. Holloway, 'The role of homeownership and home price appreciation in the accumulation and distribution of household-sector wealth,' *Business Economics*, April 1991, p. 39.

to its 1960 level by the end of 1989. However, it is important to note that while the relative contribution of home equity to total household wealth was the same in 1989 as it was 30 years earlier, total home equity (in constant dollars) was two and a half times greater at the end of the same period.

Viewed from a rate of return standpoint, home ownership has also proven to be a competitive investment. Ibbotson and Siegel show that from 1947 to 1982, an index of residential-property capital appreciation showed an annual compound rate of return of 7.4 per cent. This was lower than the return on common stocks (11.0 per cent), but just about equal to the market composite (7.5 per cent), and higher than the returns on US Government securities (3.98 per cent). Returns on residential capital averaged a higher 10.3 per cent per year for the period 1974–82 (Ibbotson and Siegel 1984, 239).

There is also empirical evidence that price-appreciation rates of lower-priced homes mirror those of higher-priced properties. For four out of five metropolitan areas sampled by Pollakowski, Stegman and Rohe, lower-valued dwellings appreciated at least as much as did the higher-valued ones during the period 1974–83. In Baltimore, the lower-valued dwellings appreciated more considerably (12.6 per cent per year versus 9.2 per cent, respectively), while in Boston, Minneapolis–St. Paul, and Washington, DC, the lower-valued appreciation rates were only slightly greater than the higher-valued houses. In Dallas–Fort Worth, lower-valued houses appreciated at slightly lower rates than higher-valued ones. These results suggest that modest owner-occupied housing may represent as good an investment as more expensive homes. This is good news for lower-income, younger and minority families because, as suggested earlier, home equity is a larger percentage of total assets among these groups.[1]

Racial barriers and other market failures notwithstanding, the literature indicates that widespread home ownership acts as a leavener. It makes the distribution of national wealth in the United States more equal than it would otherwise be. As recently as 1983, next to automobiles, owner-occupied housing was more equitably distributed than any other capital asset (Holloway 1991, 41). Holloway also points out that the 'degree of wealth concentration of total assets, net worth, and owner-occupied housing increased from 1962 to 1983 . . . but housing still remained significantly less concentrated than most other types of assets'

(Holloway 1991, 41). Indeed, 'even in the lowest two income quintiles, nearly half of all households owned homes' (ibid., 40) and, while homeownership rates have since declined among lower-income households, a significant share of them still own their own homes.

Despite the collapse of the American savings and loan industry, and inadequate reserves in the federal government's principal mortgage insurance fund (Federal Housing Administration) due to high rates of foreclosures on low downpayment loans originated in the early 1980s, federal policies favourable to home ownership are likely to continue into the future. This probability is underscored by the extent to which federal preferences for home ownership are built into the American tax system, and the fact that both major political parties seem to favour home ownership by lower-income families.

FEDERAL SUPPORT OF HOME OWNERSHIP

When it comes to supporting the ideal of home ownership, the federal government uses a very complicated tax system that puts its money where its mouth is. The initial federal home ownership subsidy was enacted more than one hundred years ago in the Homestead Act, and the deductibility of mortgage interest became US policy in 1913. In 1992 alone, 'the estimated cost of selected credit supports and projected direct outlays for more than 30 federal housing programs ranging from homeowner writeoffs to public housing operating expenses totaled more than $113 billion.' Of this amount, nearly $78 billion, or 69 per cent, will go to people who already own homes. 'Homeowner tax deductions – that permit homeowners to write off from their federal tax bill the interest they pay on mortgages, property taxes and capital gains realized when selling a house – will cost the federal treasury an estimated $78 billion in lost revenues (Table 5.9). That total is almost twice as much as the government will spend on programs for would-be homebuyers, the homeless, low-income and elderly renters and public housing tenants combined' (Steinbach 1991, 1615).

Of course, these tax benefits to home owners are rarely viewed as subsidies – in direct contrast to low-income housing assistance – and as such do not carry the stigma that is often associated with the low-income housing programs. This policy myopia is

Table 5.9 Federal subsidies to housing in the United States (projected 1992 outlays, including credit programmes)

	Amount (US$)
Subsidies to home owners	
Mortgage interest deductions	40,545,000,000
Deferral of capital gains on home sales	13,925,000,000
State and local property tax deductions	11,575,000,000
Capital gains exclusion on home sales (elderly)	4,395,000,000
Rural housing credits	2,652,000,000
Other	4,802,000,000
Total home owner subsidies	77,894,000,000
Subsidies to non-home owners	
Subsidised housing	14,244,000,000
Tax deductions for apartment owners	10,645,000,000
Community development block grants	3,097,000,000
Public housing operating subsidies	2,150,000,000
Section 8 assistance renewals	1,499,000,000
Elderly housing credits	741,000,000
Other	3,107,000,000
Total non-homeowner subsidies	35,483,000,000
TOTAL HOUSING SUBSIDIES	113,377,000,000

Source: Carol F. Steinbach, 'Housing the haves', *National Journal*, June 29 1991, p. 1619.

reflected in a recent speech by a senior federal government housing official who made the point that 'the budgeteers in Washington use the term "tax expenditures" to mean money that is not collected and, therefore, lost to the government. I see deductions for mortgage interest and property taxes as legitimate tax breaks for the little guy' (DelliBovi 1991, 5). This, despite the fact that a third of the benefit from mortgage interest and property tax deductions, a congressional study indicates, goes to households with taxable earnings above $100,000, and 12 per cent goes to families with earnings above $200,000 (Steinbach 1991, 1615).

Until recently, federal law established no limit on the size of the mortgage interest deduction. In 1987, the Congress imposed a maximum of $1.1 million as the total amount of mortgage debt on which individuals could deduct interest (Woodward and Weicher 1989, 301). Continual assault by low-income housing advocates who argue its lack of equity, and a growing chorus of concern by influential policy-makers that regressive subsidies can no longer be justified or afforded hasn't shifted the high-income bias of US housing policies.[2]

This preference for home ownership was extended to low-income housing policy by the Bush Administration. In 1990, the administration announced a goal to create one million new low-income home owners by the end of 1992 (*Builder Magazine* 1990, 60), and to give 'all public housing residents in America a chance ... to manage and control and ultimately own public housing units within three to four years' (cited in Stegman 1991, 57). Neither of these goals has been achieved.

From a policy perspective, what is more interesting and important than keeping a scorecard on the administration's progress in meeting these goals, is understanding the complicated, interdependent mix of philosophical, social/psychological and financial considerations that motivated it. With regard to philosophy, Housing and Urban Development Secretary Jack Kemp's determination to put assets in the hands of the poor is based on his belief that 'owning something changes behavior in ways that no amount of preaching middle class values ever could' (quoted in Raspberry 1990), and that 'making a home-owner out of a renter is a way of giving people a stake in the system and making them more responsible for their future and that of their children' (quoted in *Boston Globe*, 1989). In social terms, 'broadening ownership of private property will improve maintenance and upkeep of housing, increase pride of ownership, and give low-income people more reasons to save, invest, and plan for the future' (US Department of Housing and Urban Development, 1989). Home ownership also would enable families to gain financial equity in an asset. This could be especially important to low-income minorities because equity in a house represents a very large portion of that household's net wealth. And, according to Apgar *et al.*, 'the equity buildup associated with homeownership appears to magnify differences in income into larger disparities in wealth' (Joint Center for Housing Studies 1990, 10).

The value of the asset, however, is not a sure bet in this equation. Despite empirical evidence that lower-priced, private-market houses experienced similar patterns of price appreciation to those of higher-priced properties during 1974–83 (Pollakowski *et al.* 1991, 422), this may not be true for privatised public housing properties. The location and condition of many of these properties sold in HUD's national public housing home ownership demonstration are testament to market limitations.

Another impediment is the severe resale restriction imposed by a Congress that was reluctant to approve a large-scale sell-off of the social housing stock. Under HUD rules, housing authorities were required to adopt prohibitions against windfall profits from resale for a minimum of five years and were permitted to extend them further if local market conditions so justified. These restrictions could severely slow equity buildup and have an adverse impact on wealth accumulation. The unanswered question is, of course, given a low- or zero-probability of capital gain, whether achieving home ownership *per se* is a sufficient motivation to change the behaviour of the poor and disenfranchised in socially desirable ways.

CHANGING PATTERNS OF DEMAND FOR HOME OWNERSHIP IN THE 1990S

We previously indicated that the demand for bigger and better owner-occupied housing will remain strong through the 1990s thanks to the ageing of baby-boom households (aged 35–54 years). At the same time, however, the 1990s will witness an acceleration of the racial, cultural and social diversification of American households, which could dampen the effective demand for owner-occupied housing. For example, 'at the turn of the [previous] century, only one out of twenty American households consisted of a person living alone. By 1990, one out of four households consisted of a single person. And single person households will be a dominant growth sector in the 1990s' (Hughes 1991, 1227). Similarly, the past 30 years has witnessed a steady decline in the relative size of the cohort of married couples with children – the group with the highest propensity to own a home.

> In 1960, married couples still accounted for more than three-quarters (76.1 percent) of all households in the U.S. This share fell to 60.8 percent by 1980 and continued to fall during the ensuing decade. By 1990, married couples with children under age 18 represented only 27.3 percent of all households. Thus, the classic American family of Mom and Pop with two-point

something children represent barely one out of four households in the U.S. as the 1990s unfold. Spouse-absent families account for more than one out of seven.

(Hughes 1991, 1227)

During the 1990s, too, 'the population of African Americans will grow at a rate nearly double that of the overall population. And America's Hispanic community will grow at a rate about double that of the African American community' (ibid., 1226). It is not that these minority populations have lower home ownership preferences than the majority. Rather, their lower levels of effective demand for owner-occupancy can be attributed to their lower levels of expected household income, and the fact that a substantial portion of household growth among the black and Hispanic populations will be in family configurations with lower historical home ownership rates.

> For example, 58.6 percent of white households are made up of married couples, while this is true for 35.8 percent of black households. And the household share held by black spouse-absent families (35.5 percent) is almost triple that held by white spouse-absent families (12 percent), and is nearly equal to the share held by black married couples. . . . Minorities are underrepresented in higher-income, higher homeownership family sectors and overrepresented in lower-income, lower homeownership ones.
>
> (ibid., 1228)

While the above data address anticipated home ownership impacts of expected changes in the composition of the American population through the 1990s, they do not deal with the more personal aspirations of individual Americans to own their own homes. Even HUD's national public housing home ownership demonstration was too limited in scope and too recently completed to collect and evaluate significant behavioural data (Rohe and Stegman 1990). However, to determine why public housing residents bought their units under the demonstration, HUD's evaluators asked each buyer a series of multiple-choice questions concerning their motivations to become home owners. The three most frequently cited reasons for wanting to own their home were (1) to be able to fix up the house or yard the way they wanted; (2) to have something to leave to their children; and

(3) to have a good financial investment. But when the new home owners were asked to identify the single most important reason for buying, a different pattern emerged. At the top of the list was to have a good financial investment (cited in Stegman 1991, 66).

Besides financial benefit, home ownership impacts a family's perception of self. Richard Easterlin found, for example, that children form expectations about their future standard of living based on the living standards they experienced as adolescents living in their parents' homes (Henretta 1984, 132). Thus, according to Henretta, 'parental ownership and home value might influence a child's housing decisions as the child strives to emulate his or her parents' housing level' (Henretta 1984, 132). Given the fact that a large percentage of existing home owners could not afford to buy the house they currently own, the homeowning aspirations of their children are likely to be frustrated as they try to enter the home buying market for the first time.

While we could not find any empirical literature dealing with the above dilemma, Hohm carried out a survey of American college students to determine their housing preferences and willingness to sacrifice to achieve their goals. According to Hohm, 54 per cent of the respondents definitely expected to become home owners, while 40 per cent felt that home ownership was a possibility for them. Eighty-eight per cent felt it was quite important or very important to own a home (Hohm 1984, 357). Students expected to purchase homes costing about $100,000 in 1980 US dollars (more than $140,000 in 1991 dollars). To afford the houses they described – assuming a housing-expense-to-income ratio of 25 per cent – would have required an income of $53,000, which was more than double the average family income in the US at the time the study was conducted (Hohm 1985, 54).

Recognising the disparity between expectations and economic realities, Hohm explored students' views about how they might go about adjusting their housing circumstances to their needs. Citing the previous work of Morris and Winter, Hohm identified three possible behavioural responses to an existing housing deficit. The first is to move to a different house. In the introduction to this essay, we highlighted the importance of residential mobility in the US housing market. A second response is to adapt one's existing residential unit to meet changed needs. Indeed, throughout the 1980s a large number of American families invested heavily in renovation and remodelling of their current homes as a way of accommodating their living environment. The third and final behavioural response is what Hohm refers to as family adaptation, which 'include actions having to do with childbearing and the entrance into and departure from the household of other members' (Hohm 1984, 351).

To test the importance of family adaptation as a means of resolving the home ownership conflict, Hohm asked the college students whether they would consider limiting the number of children they would have in order to have more money available to pay for a home. The interpretation of the survey responses is not straightforward. First, the number of siblings a student had turned out to be the best predictor of desired family size. Second, students with stronger home ownership aspirations also desired to have larger families. However, these students tended to indicate that they would consider having fewer children if it meant the difference between being able to afford a home and not being able to afford one. In general, however, these respondents were not willing to forego having any children at all in order to buy a house. However, he also found among these respondents that the expected timing of birth of a first child and purchase of a first home were often linked. One was often delayed to achieve the other.

Students whose parents owned a home were more willing to limit family size in order to buy a house, and the higher the value of their parents' house the more they were willing to consider limiting family size and even to forego having any children. Desired family size, Hohm found, was affected not by absolute levels of economic well-being but by the level of well-being to which a student cohort had become accustomed.

Another indication of family adaptation to the current housing-cost squeeze is for adult children to remain living in their parents' home for a longer period before establishing an independent household; or to return to their parents' home after being on their own or attending college. Empirical studies indicate that the 'back-to-the-parents' home' trend is not limited to recent college graduates.

Glick and Sung-ling Lin analysed the living patterns of 18-to-34-year-olds between 1940 and 1984 (1986, 107–12). Of separated or divorced adults, they found the proportion of men living with their parents to be significantly higher than for women through-out the study period, although over time the proportion climbed for both sexes. In 1990, more than half (52.8 per cent) of all young adults between the ages of 18 and 24 lived with their parents, compared to 48 per cent in 1980 and 43 per cent in 1960 (Table 5.10). The proportion of 25–34-year-olds living with their parents also increased after 1960, from 9.1 to 11.5 per cent. Among males, the percentage gain was nearly 50 per cent (from 10.9 per cent to 15.0 per cent), while among women it was much smaller: from 7.4 per cent to 8.1 per cent.

Table 5.10 Young adults living with their parents, by age, United States, 1960, 1970, 1980 and 1990

| | Total (thousands)* | | Percentage | |
	18–24	25–34	18–24	25–34
Total				
1960	6,333	2,038	43.0	9.1
1970	10,582	1,958	47.3	8.0
1980	14,091	3,194	48.4	8.7
1990	13,367	4,986	52.8	11.5
Men				
1960	3,583	1,185	52.4	10.9
1970	5,641	1,129	54.3	9.5
1980	7,755	1,894	54.3	10.5
1990	7,232	3,213	58.1	15.0
Women				
1960	2,750	853	34.9	7.4
1970	4,941	829	41.3	6.6
1980	6,336	1,300	42.7	7.0
1990	6,135	1,774	47.7	8.1

Source: US Bureau of the Census, 'Marital status and living arrangements: 1990', Current Population Reports, Series P-60, No. 450, Washington, DC, 1990.
Note: *Includes unmarried college students living in dormitories

The data documents the reality of longer periods before young people achieve residential independence, but opinion surveys suggest that they are not happy about living with their parents. A 1987 study of 210 college undergraduates found that 53 per cent of the respondents said they would not consider moving back home, or would consider doing so only as a last resort (Pats 1987, 249). Students who felt closer to their families were more willing than others to consider moving back home; and students who owned cars, perhaps a measure of greater social and financial independence, anticipated greater difficulties with having to move back in with their parents.

Finally, the most significant adaptation that American families have made to achieve home ownership is the entry of wives into the labour market. This was especially prevalent during the 1980s. Myers carried out extensive analyses of 1970–83 Census data to determine whether 'wives' increasing employment could explain why, despite escalating costs of home ownership and falling real incomes of young men, the home ownership rate of young married couples continued to rise' (Myers 1985, 320). His analysis of the experiences of 4,800 married couples with wives between the ages of 25 and 30, found that not only did wives' financial contributions have a strong effect on home ownership, but that the importance of wives' earnings increased substantially between 1974 and 1980 as a determinant of home purchase. In 1980, couples allocated larger portions of both the husband's and wife's earnings to housing expenses than at the beginning of the study period. Wives' earnings also increased the likelihood that young families would purchase single-family homes.

CONCLUSIONS

This essay confirms the historical importance that home owner-ship has had in American society, and in the creation of family wealth and democratisation of capital accumulation. Racial barriers to the achievement of home ownership are believed to be an important cause of wealth and income disparities among the black and Hispanic populations. These beliefs underscore the importance of eliminating all racial and ethnic impediments to the achievement of home ownership in the 1990s.

The 1980s witnessed the advent of the two-wage-earner family, which seems to have been an important factor in sustaining home ownership levels among young families during a period of economic stagnation for male wage-earners. But by the end of the decade, this trend has played itself out. That is, labour-force participation rates among wives in husband–wife families are about as high as they are likely to go. We should not expect any additional boost in the demand for home ownership from the incremental earnings of wives during the 1990s.

Among the older population, the homes they inherited, or purchased, may not be transferred to the next generation. It is apparent that economic realities are forcing more of the aged to sell their properties to pay for institutional care. How the elimination of the housing asset ultimately impacts upon the intergenerational transfer of wealth remains to be seen. This is a future area of study.

While few social scientists have focused on this issue, it does not seem to us that young people have fully adjusted to the new economic realities of home ownership. Because the housing expectations and aspirations of young people are based on their experiences growing up, they are only now coming to realise the sacrifices they might have to make in order to become home owners like their parents. The kinds of trade-offs they are prepared to make to buy a home are not clear, but the literature suggests that postponing their first child and having fewer children than they wish, are two possible responses to the housing-cost dilemma. Clearly, this is a fruitful area of potential research for the social-science community.

So, too, is the relationship between the social and economic benefits of home ownership, especially among low-income families. The proposition underlying the home ownership bias of the Bush Administration's low-income housing policies was that, other things being equal, home owners are better citizens than renters; more active in their communities; more responsible for their children; and, that they are more entrepreneurial, more dedicated to becoming financially self-sufficient, and therefore are more likely to exhibit a stronger work ethic than renters. These are all testable propositions. Indeed, from our review of the international literature, these policy presumptions seem to be near universal, thus laying the stage for some interesting and provocative cross-cultural policy research in the 1990s.

NOTES

1   Seward, Delaney and Smith (1992, 204) report different results. Their study of house-price appreciation rates in St. Petersburg, Florida over the period 1970–85 found high-price properties to have a higher rate of appreciation than either medium or low-priced properties. However, they also found that higher-price housing appreciated at a greater rate during periods of expansion, but exhibited no statistical differences during periods of contraction. However, a study of

Houston house prices had slightly different results. From 1970 to 1985, the real average price of high-quality houses in Houston increased 27 per cent compared to 14 per cent for low quality houses. But during the more recent market downturn the decline was greatest in high quality units (Smith and Teserak 1991, 411).

2 The current policy is not without academic support. Economists Susan Woodward and John Weicher argue that both the housing consumption and revenue effects of limiting deductibility for high income taxpayers would not be so great since many wealthy home owners would simply sell other interest-bearing assets to pay off their mortgages. While this would reduce the value of federal tax expenditures, it would also lower federal revenues because interest income is generally taxable (Woodward and Weicher 1989, pp. 301, 311).

Chapter 6

Coping strategies in a booming market
Family wealth and housing in Hong Kong

Tai-lok Lui

INTRODUCTION

From the mid-1980s, property prices in major East Asian cities started to appreciate rapidly. Within a short period of time they have skyrocketed. The magnitude of the increase in real estate prices in these cities is phenomenal. In the case of Taipei, both office and residential prices have soared 350 per cent in the two years 1988–9 (Wieman 1990, 11), and real-estate prices are catching up with the highest in the world. Hong Kong has also experienced rapid increases in property prices since 1984. In 1991 residential property prices rose by 52 per cent (Hong Kong Bank 1992, 1). The condition of Hong Kong's property market has become alarming and the colonial government, which is renowned for its image of being non-interventionist in economic affairs, has recently introduced measures to control real-estate speculations. In short, the performance of the property markets in the East Asian cities has been spectacular and such escalations of real-estate prices have significant implications for the structuring of housing inequalities in the region.

This essay is an attempt to probe the significance of home ownership in the context of a buoyant real-estate market. Here Hong Kong's residential property market in the 1980s is taken as a case to illustrate the effects of housing-market conditions on the significance of domestic property for the distribution of wealth and the structuring of life chances in a capitalist economy. In particular, we shall dwell upon how a booming residential property market, be it short-term speculative buoyancy or long-term restructuring of the housing market, would shape the housing strategies of the population, which, in turn, reinforce existing inequalities in a capitalist housing market.

The main theme of this paper is the experience of a booming residential property market. Our theoretical concern is related to the key questions of a sociological analysis of domestic property. How is access to the domestic-property market related to positions in the class structure? Does home ownership really constitute an important and enduring source of wealth accumulation? How is wealth accumulated as a consequence of home ownership transferred intergenerationally? These are the basic questions which continue to inform the debate developed out of the 'housing class' thesis (see, for example, Rex and Moore 1967; Saunders 1984 and 1990; Badcock 1989a; Thorns 1981 and 1989; Forrest, Murie and Williams 1990, 78–97). These controversial, and yet fundamental, questions constitute the basic analytical constructs for further investigations of the connections among housing tenures, social consciousness and political alignment. Without ruling out the contributions of current research on these topics, it is my contention that the existing literature tends to understate the importance of market experiences in the structuring of life chances in the housing market. Upswings and downswings in the property market, even short-term ones, are always real enough to have significant impacts on individuals' access and mobility in their housing careers. The case of contemporary Hong Kong, and perhaps property markets in East Asian capitalist societies in general, represents the situation wherein the property market has become a 'casino economy' and basic housing needs and property buyers' investment concerns are tightly interweaved. There home ownership is always more than an item of consumption. It is an important form of economic asset. And in this context, the family plays an important part both as a resource network for financing home ownership and as an agent for the transference of familial property.

HOME OWNERSHIP IN HONG KONG

In terms of its home ownership rate (42.6 per cent in 1991), the performance of Hong Kong is by no means impressive. However, in terms of the speed with which the tenurial system in the colony has been changed, the achievement is remarkable (see Table 6.1). In a period of 30 years the percentage of owner-occupier households has doubled from 20.1 per cent in 1961 to 42.6 per cent in 1991. However, this is an understatement of the

Table 6.1 Domestic households* in percentages by tenure: 1961–91

Tenure	1961	1971	1981	1991
Owner-occupier	20.1	18.1	27.9	42.6
Sole tenant		45.5	44.0	45.6
Main tenant		5.9	3.9	0.8
Sub-tenant	73.7	20.2	11.7	2.6
Co-tenant		4.1	5.6	4.0
Rent free	6.2	6.2	2.5	1.1
Provided or subsidised by employer	NA	NA	4.4	3.3

Sources: Census and Statistics Department, *Hong Kong Population and Housing Census 1971* Main Report, Hong Kong: Government Printer, 1972; *Hong Kong 1986* By-Census Main Report: vol. 1, Hong Kong: Government Printer, 1988.

Notes: * Excluding households in the Marine district
NA Not available

pace of the growth of home ownership. The plain fact is that the official statistics on housing tenure can be deceiving. What is critical is that they do not tell us the kinds of housing associated with each type of tenure. In the context of developing countries, tenurial status does not necessarily reflect the true housing conditions of the inhabitants. For instance, the slight drop of owner-occupancy in 1971 (18.1 per cent from 20.1 per cent in 1961) is largely due to the clearance of squatters (Census and Statistics Department 1972, 174). In other words, the rate of owner-occupancy in 1961 is an inflated figure (by the inclusion of a sizeable squatter population) and thus, when taken as a benchmark for subsequent comparisons, tends to deflate the magnitude of increase in the ownership of self-contained private flats in the 1970s and 1980s. Table 6.2 shows the distribution of households of different housing tenures by housing types in 1986. It is evident that the majority of owner-occupiers are found in private self-contained housing blocks, government home ownership estates and private houses. In other words, the rapid growth of home ownership in the past two decades is the result of changes in the tenurial system as well as the improvement in housing quality.

The dramatic growth of home ownership in the postwar era is closely related to changes in the class structure of contemporary Hong Kong.[1] As has been noted earlier, the meaning of tenure varies in accordance with the associated type of housing and this

Table 6.2 Domestic households in percentages by type of housing and tenure, 1986

	Owner-occupier	Sole tenant	Tenants (others)	Rent free	Provided or subsidised by employer
Public and aided housing	NA	76.2	4.8	3.6	3.8
Government home ownership estates	11.0	—	—	0.2	1.4
Private housing blocks (self-contained)	67.2	13.9	88.6	33.4	43.2
Private housing blocks (non-self-contained)	0.1	0.1	0.8	0.3	—
Houses	5.1	1.4	1.5	5.0	3.9
Simple stone structure	6.3	1.5	1.9	12.5	1.3
Institutions and other permanent housing	0.2	0.4	0.2	8.9	44.6
Temporary housing, roof-top structures	10.1	6.5	2.2	36.1	1.8
TOTAL	100.0	100.0	100.0	100.0	100.0

Source: Census and Statistics Department, *Hong Kong 1986* By-Census Main Report: vol. 2, Hong Kong: Government Printer, p. 150.

Notes: NA not applicable
— zero or value negligible
Tenants (others) include main tenants, sub-tenants and co-tenants

creates difficulties in discerning the connection between housing tenure and social class. However, that said, it is still reasonable to argue that changes in the class structure (see Wong and Lui 1992b for a study of Hong Kong's class structure and social mobility) have facilitated the increase in owner-occupancy. That there have been expansions of the service class, technicians and supervisors and routine non-manual workers, and growing affluence of the working class is contributive to the spread of home ownership down the class structure. Table 6.3 describes the association between social class and housing tenure in 1976 and 1986. It shows that owner-occupancy has been growing across all classes, with the capitalist, the service class and supervisors and technicians faring particularly well in becoming home owners.

Table 6.3 also shows that there is an association between class position and home ownership, with the capitalist, the service

Table 6.3 Social class and housing tenure, 1976 and 1986

	Capitalist	New middle class	Routine non-manual workers	Petty bourgeoisie	Supervisor/ technicians	Routine manual workers
Owner-occupier (%)	66.4 (47.7)	54.3 (33.8)	41.8 (24.1)	43.1 (37.0)	36.9 (9.1)	25.5 (13.4)
Sole tenant (%)	26.6 (36.0)	23.2 (39.0)	42.3 (44.7)	43.8 (36.3)	37.1 (72.7)	49.8 (47.5)
Main, sub- and co-tenant (%)	3.7 (11.5)	4.2 (11.6)	10.6 (25.5)	9.1 (21.6)	6.1 (18.2)	20.1 (32.6)
Rent free (%)	1.0 (4.0)	1.0 (1.5)	1.6 (3.5)	3.1 (4.2)	0.6 (0.0)	2.2 (3.8)
Provided or subsidised by employer (%)	2.3 (0.8)	17.4 (14.2)	3.6 (2.2)	0.9 (0.9)	19.4 (0.0)	2.5 (2.7)

Source: based upon a reanalysis of a 1 per cent random sample of the land-population of the 1976 and 1986 Hong Kong By-Census data set.
Note: 1976 figures in brackets

class, the petty bourgeoisie and routine non-manual workers more likely to be home owners. However, as is repeatedly pointed out in current research on housing tenure, the connection between class and tenurial status is by no means straightforward. Nor is it reasonable to assume that there is a necessary relation between class and home ownership, with the former determining one's acquisition of domestic property. Of course, the point here is not to deny the effects of class position on one's situation in the housing market. Rather, it is to argue for the complexity of the class–tenure relations. For instance, both the service class and the technicians and supervisors have sizeable proportions of their members living in accommodation provided or subsidised by their employers (17.4 per cent and 19.4 per cent respectively) (see Table 6.3). This reflects how differences in work and market situations in employment affect one's tenurial status. For the service class and technicians and supervisors, employers' provision of housing (which can be in the forms of staff quarters or subsidies for private accommodation) is part of their employment package. Moreover, compared with other employees, these two classes are relatively privileged not only in obtaining housing provision through their employers, but also in living in higher-quality accommodation or receiving more generous housing allowances.

What is more pertinent to our discussion here is that there are class differences in the propensity to become home owners (see Table 6.3). The capitalist, the service class, the petty bourgeoisie and the routine non-manual workers stand out as those classes scoring higher rates in owner-occupancy. This, in a sense, is hardly a surprise. Given that class position is closely connected with the possession of economic resources (be it wealth, income or marketable skills), there would be variations in the affordability of home ownership and the access to housing mortgages among people of different class backgrounds.

SOARING PROPERTY PRICES IN THE 1980s

That tenurial status is embedded in class differences has significant implications for our understanding of how home ownership (and non-ownership), in turn, structures the reproduction of class inequalities. But before we go into the discussion of how class differences affect the responses to the opportunities opened up by a booming property market, it would be helpful to review the development of the housing market in the 1980s.

The rise and fall of property prices in the 1980s are shown in Table 6.4. It is clear that Hong Kong's domestic property market is currently in the phase of upswing of a new cycle beginning from 1984. Prior to the current upswing, Hong Kong had already experienced two completed cycles since 1967. 'The first cycle saw residential prices rise by around 440% during the period 1967–74 and drop by about 10% in 1975. In the following cycle, prices increased by approximately 310% in the up-phase (1975–81) and then plunged by about one-third in the following two years' (Hang Seng Bank 1992, 3). The dramatic property downswing in the early 1980s was triggered off by political uncertainty prevalent during the Sino–British negotiations over the future of the colony. However, as we can also observe from the statistics of Table 6.5, the crisis of the property market in 1982 has its deeper roots in surging prices and an uncomfortably high affordability ratio (181 per cent in the second quarter of 1981). In other words, in the early 1980s, residential property prices had risen to a level which was beyond the reach of the majority of the local population. The eventual downswing was, in a sense, a consequence of the structural problems of such a property market.

Since 1984, domestic property prices have been soaring and the pace of increase has accelerated. Between 1985 and 1991, the price has tripled. There are various reasons for such buoyancy in the domestic real-estate market. Speculations inevitably play a very significant role in the structuring of such a buoyant market.[2] However, it is also important to note that, apart from speculation, there are structural conditions supporting such marked increases in property prices. First, those who were born in the postwar baby-boom era of the 1950s and 1960s are now forming new households. Unlike the young couples of the 1960s and early 1970s, who, for economic reasons and/or familial obligations, were likely to live with their parents after marriage, this is the generation whose ideal is to form their own nuclear family, instead of sharing their homes with their parents or other kin. No doubt, such demographic changes constitute a significant factor in increasing housing demand (Wallace and Faure 1991, 18–20). Second, continuing economic growth with a tight labour market in the mid-1980s has driven up wage levels. This, coinciding with

Table 6.4 Domestic property price index, percentage increase in consumer price and wages of all employees, 1981–91

Year	Domestic property price index (1989=100)	Percentage increase in consumer index (B)	Percentage increase in wage of all employees
1981	61	14.8	NA
1982	53	10.6	NA
1983	45	9.9	7.5
1984	43	8.5	8.3
1985	48	3.5	6.5
1986	53	3.5	6.2
1987	65	5.3	9.4
1988	79	7.4	10.0
1989	100	9.7	12.2
1990	111	9.7	12.5
1991	151	11.7	10.6*

Sources: Census and Statistics Department, *Annual Digest of Statistics 1991; Monthly Digest of Statistics* (various years); Rating and Valuation Department, *Property Review: 1992.*
Note: * Calculated on the basis of the statistics for the third quarter of 1991

a reduction of interest rates (see Table 6.5) for mortgage finance has contributed to making home ownership more affordable than in the early 1980s (ibid., 21–3). But then, within a few years' time, as property prices escalated at a frightening speed, affordability again deteriorated and it has become increasingly difficult for potential homebuyers to purchase their own residential properties.

Whether or not the current buoyant conditions of the domestic-property market continue is not the central concern of this paper. What I wish to emphasise from the above discussion is that, while it is crucial to note the cyclical development of the residential real-estate market and thus the fact that monetary gains from an upswinging market may be just illusory, surging prices have continued for nine years and there is still no sign of an imminent collapse.[3] The point is that the past nine years (1984–92), during which property prices escalated rapidly, constitute a critical period which is sufficiently long to have an impact on an individual's life chances in the housing market.

This raises two particular issues for sociological analysis of home ownership. In the first place, it is about the potential of

Table 6.5 Changing affordability for an average household

	Average price* of private domestic flats (up to 39.9 sq. metres) (HK$ per m)	Median household income	Mortgage rate (% p.a. end period)	Monthly repayment† (HK$)	Affordability ratio‡ (%)	Downpayment (as number of months of income)
1981 Q2	10,433	2,955	18.00	5,363	181	28
Q4	10,233	3,345	17.00	5,027	150	24
1982 Q4	8,411	3,848	12.00	3,222	84	17
1984 Q4	7,491	4,561	12.50	2,947	65	13
1990 Q4	19,898	9,824	11.25	7,319	75	16
1991 Q2	23,577	10,490	11.75	8,911	85	18
Q4	30,432	10,985	10.25	9,265	84	33
1992	34,084§	12,117//	10.25	10,376	86	34

Source: Adapted from Hong Kong Bank, 'The Hong Kong property market', *Hong Kong Economic Report*, May 1992, p. 2.

Notes:
* Average of all districts
† Assuming an 80 per cent mortgage for 15 years up to 1991 Q3; since 1991 Q4 the mortgage ceiling has been reduced to 70 per cent
‡ Affordability ratio = monthly repayment/median household income
§ A 12 per cent increase over 1991 Q4 has been assumed
// An 11 per cent year-on-year increase over 1991 Q1 has been assumed

wealth accumulation in housing. Given the magnitude of the increase in property prices within the period, there are possibilities for home owners to make significant monetary gains in such a buoyant market. Table 6.4 shows that the rate of increase of property prices, especially since 1986, is higher than the inflation rate and the rate of wage increases in the same period. One may argue that for those who bought in 1984 and then sold their residential flats towards the end of the period, they would have made significant monetary gains from their property sale. Of course, whether one can thus conclude that housing has the potential for capital accumulation is still arguable. The fact that there are significant differences between buying and selling prices, even after adjustments for inflation, is not sufficient to show that there are real capital gains from the transaction. Other expenses involved, such as those on maintenance, legal fees and stamp duties in the process of purchase, are, no doubt, also essential for the calculation of the accumulative potential of home ownership. It is not my intention to go into such detailed calculations and, indeed, I shall argue that such calculations are unnecessary for demonstrating the economic significance of the ownership of domestic property. Suffice here to say that, given the significant increase in property prices in the period 1984–91, property owners are able to make some gains by 'buying cheap and selling dear'.

Second, even if we can discount the accumulative potential of housing, it is still important to recognise the economic implications of home ownership for the production and reproduction of inequalities. The point is that wealth accumulation is only one, and not necessarily the most important, aspect of the economic significance of home ownership. Furthermore, why should we give primacy to wealth accumulation in our analysis of home ownership? Indeed, the overemphasis on the accumulative potential of property ownership is a misplaced theoretical and empirical exercise for discerning the economic implications of home ownership. Some of the criticisms of the accumulation thesis are relevant here. It is, for example, difficult to compute capital gains from home ownership, especially in the long term (adjustments after upswings and downswings). Also critical is the oft-cited comment that capital gains from home ownership are unrealisable – most home owners have to acquire new homes after selling their properties and, therefore, they cannot really turn their assets into cash (see, for example, Kemeny 1981, 36–7). However, relevant as they are, these comments only emphasise the complexities in analysing the process of wealth accumulation through home ownership and cannot disconnect property ownership from other economic implications. What is missing in debates evolving from the accumulation argument is the Weberian notion of 'housing class'. The key issue is an individual's market position in the housing market, and not the quality of the property *per se*. Indeed, the point is that what really matters is the structuring processes of the housing market. The significance of property cannot be abstracted from the market conditions of housing. Whether commodified housing is equivalent to other commodity productions in that it has the potential for value creation does not trouble us here. Opportunities and constraints in the housing market are real enough to make a significant impact on an individual's position in the competition for housing. In other words, the issue at stake is not the potential for capital accumulation of commodified housing, but how one can utilise economic resources as well as assets in the housing market to improve one's market situation in the competition for housing. To dwell upon the question of capital gains and accumulation is like approaching a Weberian problematic with a Marxist orientation – asking the question of valorisation when actually analysing changes in market situation. While the Marxist is posing the question of the creation of value, the Weberian is looking at the socio-economic processes wherein one's position in the housing market is structured. The former approach does not require an analysis of the structuring of the housing market, whereas the latter takes competition in the market arena seriously.

The important and yet often neglected issue in the discussion of home ownership is one's experience and *fate* in the housing market. In other words, current discussions often fail to take the notion of housing market situation seriously.[4] And as a consequence of this neglect of market dynamics in the structuring of one's chances in the property market, the focus of the discussion has been placed on the process of capital accumulation of the assets, and not on individuals' fate and mobility in the housing market. Relating this question to the case of Hong Kong, I would argue that irrespective of whether there are real capital gains or otherwise, the prolonged buoyancy of the domestic property market and drastic increase in property prices are adequate to restructure the life chances of home owners *and* non-owners and to reproduce economic inequalities and class differences in the realm of housing.

As shown earlier (see Tables 6.4 and 6.5), buoyancy in the domestic property market in the period 1984–91 brought about an upsurge in property prices and changes in the affordability ratio. Such market conditions make it very difficult for end-users, and especially first-time owners, to gain access to home owner-ship. Potential home owners have to possess a relatively large amount of savings to cover the downpayment. According to the Hong Kong Bank's estimation, for a 40 square-metre residential flat (see Table 6.5), the amount required for downpayment has gone up to the equivalent of 18 months' median household income in the second quarter of 1991. Due to subsequent changes in bank mortgage policy (with typical percentage of loans falling from 80 per cent or higher to 70 per cent), the level went up to that of 34 months' median household income in April 1992. Obviously, this is a level of downpayment requirement beyond the capabilities of many potential home buyers.

Furthermore, soaring prices have brought about a deteriora-tion of the affordability ratio, i.e. new home buyers have to set aside an increasingly large share of their earnings for mortgage loan repayment. In the second quarter of 1991, monthly mortgage repayment went up to 85 per cent of the median household income (see Table 6.5). Another way to gauge the affordability of home ownership is to see the percentage of households that can afford to take out a new mortgage for purchasing their properties. As estimated by the Hang Seng Bank in May 1992 (p. 2):

> The current practice for banks is that they would not extend mortgage loans to households if the monthly repayment accounts for more than half of their income. On this basis, it is estimated that at the present price level, only the top 15% of households would be eligible to purchase a 400 sq.ft. unit with 90% mortgage financing. This level is also the lowest in recent years.

In brief, buoyancy in the housing market has actually kept the majority of the local population out of home purchase. Surging prices not only mean more expensive residential flats for home buyers, but also make home ownership less affordable in the sense that the buyers have to pay higher downpayments and mortgage repayments and the number of households eligible for bank financing is reduced accordingly.

So, the economic implications of home ownership are not confined to the question of capital gains. More often, they are concerned with the fact that home ownership and non-ownership make a big difference in the context of a booming property market. Market processes and experiences really matter at this critical point. Whether the property has gained real value in the up-phase of a domestic property cycle or otherwise is not really pertinent here. More important is that, as shown in the above paragraph, non-ownership as such, namely the status of being a first-time homebuyer, would put one in a deteriorating market position as prices continue to escalate. This is not to argue that home ownership *per se* is adequate to distinguish who can and who cannot gain access to home purchase. There are, no doubt, differential potentials of price increase according to types of housing. In the case of Hong Kong, large privately developed housing estates (for example, Taikoo Shing, Whampao Garden, and Kornhill in the highly urbanised districts, City One Garden in the New Territories) are very popular among the middle class and have been particularly successful in securing a higher-than-average rate of increase in property prices (Bartlett 1990). Such differences notwithstanding, given the pace of increase in property prices in the period, on average most owners would find their properties significantly inflated in value. While it is not the case that home ownership is a zero-sum game wherein home owners secure their gains at the expense of non-owners, it is nevertheless true to say that non-owners, as property prices continue to surge, have been placed in an increasingly difficult market position for purchasing their own properties.

In other words, what home owners have gained from a buoyant housing market is not necessarily values in cash. The realisation of such gains can take many different forms. As expressed by Donnison and Ungerson (1982, quoted in Saunders 1990, 163), home owners

> can raise further mortgages on their houses (to buy a car or a country cottage perhaps), or they can sell their houses and use the proceeds as down payments on bigger and better houses, or they can purchase annuities when they retire if they move to smaller and cheaper houses at that stage in their lives.

Home owners are not necessarily free to make use of their gains from their properties. For instance, the possibility of remortgaging depends heavily upon bank policy in financing property purchase. However, it is still important to note the monetary gains which can be realised for various usages. One important function of the proceeds obtained from selling the property is for making the downpayment for a larger or better unit. This has increasingly become the popular housing strategy among the Hong Kong people. It is a strategy of 'buying dear and selling dearer'. In those large private-housing estates (which have experienced an 'above average' rate of property price increase), it is commonplace to find, 'after a few years, couples who have managed to buy a small apartment in this category then "trade up" by buying a larger unit, usually in the same development' (Bartlett 1990, 8). High resale value of a property comes to constitute one of the most important concerns when deciding home purchase. Flexibility in terms of the relatively liquid secondary market of certain housing types is an important factor behind the success of large-scale private-housing estates in the urban area, which are 'considered the blue chip developments of the mass residential sector, and their strong price performance will have a domino effect on nearby developments' (Wallace and Faure, 1991: 33). Hedging is the key word of this housing strategy.

The hedging consideration need not be restricted to the owners of properties of high resale value. In a housing market of prolonged buoyancy, most domestic properties would carry some hedging potential as reflected in their varying scale of price escalation. But the popularity of large private-housing estates reminds us that, first, there are differences in such hedging potentials in accord with types of housing (and perhaps also locations). This relates back to earlier remarks that housing inequalities are embedded in class differences. Apparently, the (broadly defined) middle class is in an advantageous position in responding to property-price escalation. That they can afford to purchase higher-price flats in private-housing estates before and during the upswing of the property market actually helps strengthen their position in the housing market. They can make use of the proceeds from selling their properties for 'upward mobility' in the housing market, i.e. 'trading up' to better and larger flats.

Second, the popularity of large private-housing estates reflects the growing concern of hedging and high resale value among homebuyers. In Hong Kong, there is no tax concession for home ownership. The motivations for home purchase come from the aspiration of owning one's home and the estimation of property-market conditions. Home purchase comes to constitute an investment strategy in the defensive sense of the term. Stated differently, home buyers are increasingly aware of the threat of their earnings and savings being eroded by soaring property prices. A significant proportion of home buyers, therefore, decide to purchase their properties more on the grounds of protecting themselves from being further jeopardised by market buoyancy than that of a search for 'ontological security'. The hedging strategy implies that home buyers have a stronger investment orientation and are concerned more with potential price increases and resale values than housing qualities as such. It is security mainly in the economic sense of the term.

Values on paper are real enough therefore in assisting mobility in the housing market. As noted above, it is the economically resourceful classes which gain most from a booming market environment. However, while it is true that class differences matter in structuring the mobility opportunities in a buoyant real-estate market, it is also important to recognise that the polarisation between home owners and non-owners is not entirely class-determined. Generational differences are critical here. Young lower-middle-class families have been badly hit by soaring property prices since the mid-1980s. Indeed, they are the group of people who experience the erosion of their earnings and savings by the buoyant property market most bitterly (*South China Morning Post*, 15 May 1992, 13). Their grievances have recently been taken care of by the government's establishment of a working committee for handling the housing problems of the so-called 'sandwich class' (families in the monthly income bracket of HK$18,000–40,000) and have attracted the attention of local political parties as an issue for mobilisation.[5] The point is that the polarisation between the home owners and non-owners is an outcome of the interplay of class and demographic factors. While lower-middle-class families may still hope to participate in the competition for home ownership at the lower end of the housing market, lower income groups have been almost totally excluded from the game and the possibility of purchasing their own residential flats has been more or less confined to the option of the home ownership scheme established by the government.

To recapitulate, a buoyant property market has significantly restructured the processes of mobility in the housing market, with the economically resourceful classes capitalising on the opportunities opened up in the up-phase of the market cycle and the non-owners being placed in a deteriorating market position.

HOME OWNERSHIP AS A FORM OF INVESTMENT

An important consequence of soaring property prices and the concomitant deteriorating affordability ratio is that the achievement of home ownership has increasingly become a family project. Increases in the amount required for downpayment and the costs of repaying mortgages have turned home purchase into a collective familial effort. And, as stressed earlier, as a consequence of surging property prices, only those in the top income-bracket can secure bank financing and afford the mortgage repayments. In this context, family and kinship ties constitute an economic resource network for home ownership.

Generally speaking, there is a strong desire to own one's home among the Hong Kong Chinese. The findings of the 1988 Social Indicators Survey show that 75.6 per cent of the respondents aspire to the ownership of their own private residential flats and 13.6 per cent have a desire for their own flats in the Government Home Ownership Scheme (Lee 1991, 69). In other words, an overwhelming majority (almost 90 per cent) of the respondents aspire to home ownership. This, however, is largely a new phenomenon. As stated by Topley in her discussion of the concepts of wealth in the 1960s,

> the demand for housing does not usually come as high on the list of preference goods of the Chinese as on that of the westerner. The Chinese home does not provide the same opportunities for prestige as does that of the westerner and in Hong Kong this fact can be of importance. Chinese entertainment of guests is usually in the form of costly and elaborate banquets which need complicated preparation and organization. For this reason, Chinese social life is carried on largely in restaurants.
>
> (Topley 1969, 195)

In the 1960s, when Chinese families in Hong Kong were asked about their preferred housing type, 69 per cent of the respondents wanted to move to public-sector housing (Mitchell 1969, 428). The contrasts between responses in the 1960s and 1980s, perhaps, sum up the differences in the housing and tenurial conditions of the population in the two decades. However, beneath such differences in housing aspirations, there is the common conception of housing as a form of investment. As observed, again, by Topley, 'real estate, particularly blocks of flats, is a popular form of investment for Chinese of various income levels. Sometimes an attraction of investment in property is that it can be used partly to accommodate relatives towards whom some obligation is felt. They in turn can act as caretakers and help protect the property' (1969, 196). In a study of Mei Foo Sun Chuen, the first large private-housing estate in Hong Kong, it was found that

> Flats in Mei Foo Sun Chuen are currently considered excellent investments, and sources in the sales office there noted that, as of the end of 1973, 30% of all purchasers were investors with no intention to live in the flats they had purchased. . . . Sixty per cent of the buyers actually do move into the Estate, and it is estimated that another ten per cent move in but also 'part-let' one or two rooms of their apartment.
>
> (Rosen 1976, 48)

Economic concerns constitute an important part of the decision for home purchase. In a way, one can argue that the emphasis on economic returns and the hedging effect of buying property at the right moment by home purchasers in the current buoyant property market is consistent with the folk concept of housing among the local population. Home purchase has long been perceived in terms of economic calculations. To buy or not to buy one's home? Hong Kong people make their decisions on the basis of their housing aspirations as well as their assessment of the purchase as an investment opportunity.

Investment in housing is often a collective project of the family. Here it is pertinent to note the emphasis placed on familial ownership and economic exchanges among kinsmen by the Chinese family. In a study of the Hong Kong Chinese family in the 1960s, it was found that, 'consistently, more than 70 per cent of our respondents say that the item (whether it is a car, typewriter, radio or magazine) belongs to the whole family irrespective of the person who buys it. It also shows that if the items are bought by their parents, familial ownership is almost the unanimous pattern' (Hong 1970, 123). In his comparative study of families in Hong Kong and some Southeast Asian societies, Mitchell (1971, 40) points out that 'the Chinese in general and the Hong Kong population in particular tend to have the lowest levels of social involvement with kin, but these populations have the highest level of economic interchange among kinsmen'. Children's economic contribution to the family budget is part of the familial obligations (see Hong 1970; Salaff 1981). As home purchase is a major project of the family, members are expected to pool their economic resources for financing the investment.

Research on the Hong Kong Chinese family in the 1970s has shown that familial ownership of property and economic exchanges among kins are closely connected. In her study of the working daughters of Hong Kong, Salaff notes that in the process of economic development, some of the better-off families she had interviewed

> were preparing moves to new apartments. Whereas the working-class families hoped to transfer from resettlement estates to low-income housing units, middle-income families expected to move from tenements to private apartments in newly built quarters. This whole complex of expenditures was undertaken only because the working daughters augmented the family budget from 30% to 70%.
>
> (Salaff 1981, 263)

In one of Salaff's ethnographic interviews, Ju-chen, a teacher, took charge of the decision of buying a flat in Mei Foo Sun Chuen: 'As a chief breadwinner, Ju-chen selected the Leung's housing and furnishing and committed her salary to pay for them. She made most of the arrangements to purchase the flat.' In another study of the Mei Foo Sun Chuen neighbourhood, Rosen remarks:

> (t)here are, however, several discernible new trends in the living patterns of the Mei Foo couples and their extended families. Most notable is the tendency for shared residence to be a phenomenon of certain periods of the young family's life

cycle. Especially for sons lower in the birth order, living with the parents after marriage provides an opportunity for the new pair to save their money and prepare for the day when they will move out and into their own apartment. Like the residents of East London described by Young and Willmott, they face housing shortages in the market; but unlike the situation in London, the problem is also one of extremely high rents and purchase prices as well as lack of available units. In this increasingly common solution to the problem, young newlyweds live with the husband's parents and family in what is usually the family's home.

(Rosen 1976, 182)

Among the middle-class families of Mei Foo there are almost equal amounts of reciprocal aid and financial aid. It is no accident that there seem to be no loan companies in Hong Kong, for financial aid is still an important part of family interaction. This help may take the form of ongoing participation in rent or mortgage payments, or it may come as regular monthly subsidies to old, infirm, or otherwise needy relatives. . . . The Chaos were living in an apartment owned by the husband's parents, and the Cheungs received help from the husband's older brother in making the monthly payments on their own new flat. In an example of truly 'mutual' aid, two brothers-in-law, husbands of sisters, were co-purchasers and co-residents of their tiny Mei Foo apartment.

(ibid., 196–7)

Apparently, there are different forms of familial assistance in connection with home purchase. Without going further into the details of the economic function of the Hong Kong Chinese family, suffice here to say that the family assumes the central position in the facilitation of home ownership.

There is, unfortunately, a paucity of information about the role of the family in home purchase in the 1980s. In a study of social mobility in contemporary Hong Kong (Wong and Lui, 1992a), the respondents were asked the hypothetical question 'If you encountered the problem of not having enough money to pay for the down payment for a flat, what would you do?' (see Table 6.6). Given that the question was not designed for probing housing strategies and the actual practice of financing home ownership, the data should be interpreted with caution. Indeed,

Table 6.6 Coping strategies for home purchase by class

Class (according to the Goldthorpe scheme)	Network (borrow from family, relatives or friends) (%)	Market (borrow from bank, finance company) (%)	Public (complain, criticise government) (%)	Individual (save, and postpone plan) (%)
I	18	32	0	50
II	18	28	0	54
III	14	36	0	50
IV	11	21	0	68
V	15	31	0	54
VI	12	26	0	62
VIII	15	16	1	68

Source: T.W.P. Wong and T.L. Lui, 'From one brand of politics to one brand of political culture', Occasional Paper No. 10, Hong Kong Institute of Asia-Pacific Studies, 1992, p. 32.

the relevance of Table 6.6 to the current discussion lies more in its information about the respondents' inclination towards drawing upon resources provided by kinship and social ties than in how local people actually handle the financing of home purchase. While more than half of the respondents show some signs of resignation and choose to postpone their plans, between 11 and 18 per cent of them would turn to their kinship network for assistance. However, more interesting are the observations that nowadays the market mechanism (for example, bank loans) constitutes the most important source for financing home purchase and there are class differences in coping with the problem posed. Compared with family strategies for financing home ownership in the 1970s, Table 6.6 shows some signs of greater reliance on the market for financial assistance. This is not to suggest that family is, therefore, no longer a resource network. Rather, it reflects changes in people's access to bank loans and their attitudes towards borrowing. Moreover, as property prices continue to escalate, assistance from kin can hardly be the only source of money for financing home purchase. Indeed, as we can observe from Table 6.6, the service class, routine non-manual workers and technicians and supervisors are more likely to use the market mechanism as well as social networks to raise money for paying the downpayment. This illustrates class differences in the access to the market mechanism for loans. More importantly, it also shows that the relevance of familial assistance for costly projects like home purchase depends on the economic resources which can be provided by the social network. In the issue of financing home purchase, class differences are clearly pertinent.

So far we have discussed the role of the family in the facilitation of home ownership. None of the local research on urban families and housing has examined the inheritance of domestic property.[6] However, the question of inheritance is important to our understanding of housing inequalities (cf. Murie and Forrest 1980b). This is especially true in the context of soaring property prices. One way whereby the accumulated values of housing can be realised is to transfer the wealth across generations. People who have the opportunity of inheriting properties from their families will have the advantage of starting with home-owner status in a buoyant market. And they can make use of their inherited properties for 'trading up' to better housing or sell them for more immediate returns. Like other inherited assets, housing constitutes a form of wealth inequality. Class differences in home ownership in the earlier generation will reinforce housing inequalities in the present generation. However, since Hong Kong has only experienced significant increases in owner-occupancy since the 1970s, how housing inequalities are transferred across generations is still an under-researched topic.

Given the dearth of available information on housing inheritance, I shall not attempt to make any conjectural statement on the issue. That said, three observations are worth noting here. First, the connection between family and housing should be understood in the light of the developmental process of the domestic group. As noted by Rosen (1976, 183), 'as the life cycle progresses and the wealthy and formerly supportive parents become the needy recipients of family assistance, Eldest Brother is the one who is then obliged to offer his home to his parents'. There is clearly some expectation of reciprocity in the arrangement of family assistance and economic exchanges. More interestingly, the succession of domestic property does not necessarily have to wait until the death of the family head. The parents may leave or sell their property and move to live with their eldest son before they die. Second, under the traditional inheritance practice, the family head's estate is divided more or less equally between all his sons (Baker 1979). Whether this is still the practice of urban Chinese families in Hong Kong or otherwise requires further investigation. But it is reasonable to assume that although daughters may have made significant contributions to the familial project of home purchase, the sons receive the largest, if not all, shares of family wealth. Thus, the inheritance of family wealth is essentially structured by gender inequalities.

Third, inherited wealth will, no doubt, make a difference to one's position in the housing market. However, the realisation of inherited wealth does not necessarily come at the right moment when cash is most needed for home purchase. The timing of wealth realisation is especially critical in a buoyant market where prices can shoot up in a short span of time. The expectation of inherited property does not guarantee the right timing for selling the property and reinvesting in real estate. But then, that said, it does not need one to make the best of a booming housing market in order to recognise how inherited property can bring material benefits. Inherited wealth will provide people with the much-needed resources, such as money for downpayments, for enhancing one's capability in the competition for housing.

CONCLUSIONS

The case of Hong Kong serves to illustrate the empirical and theoretical significance of the effects of market conditions on the structuring of life chance and fate in the housing market. It shows that to ask whether the monetary gains from transactions in a booming real-estate market are 'paper money' or real gains in value is to miss the point of the Weberian notion of 'housing class'. A buoyant property market allows people to realise their gains in cash. More important is that soaring property prices intensify differentiation in the housing market and widen the gap between home owners and non-owners. While home owners, especially those in the service class background, can capitalise on the opportunities opened up in a buoyant real-estate market for making monetary gains from their transactions or 'trading up' for better housing, non-owners experience a rapid erosion of their savings and earnings and are either pushed toward the lower end of the housing market or simply kept out of the home-purchase sector. Such impacts on an individual's life chance in the housing market are real and significant. To look into these matters, we need to rethink the adequacy of the analysis of domestic property in terms of accumulative potential and to take market experiences seriously in our understanding of the structuring of life chances in the housing market.

Surging prices in the real-estate market also have a significant impact on homebuyers' strategies for financing their purchase. In Hong Kong, housing has always been perceived as a form of familial investment and the family plays an important part in pooling resources for the project of home ownership. Here class differences are again pertinent. Class-based differences in economic resources affect one's access to home ownership in terms of the availability of economic support and differential family wealth. However, since the pattern of owner-occupancy is not strictly class determined and home ownership in a buoyant market has independent effects on one's chance and fate in the property market, housing inequalities are outcomes of the inter-actions between class and tenurial differences. In the booming property market of Hong Kong, the timing of home purchase can make a substantial difference to individuals' careers in housing. In other words, property-market cycles hit at certain cohorts of some social classes. At present, it is the newly formed lower-middle-class families which are adversely affected by the housing market. They experience an erosion of their earnings. Also, they see how their chances in home ownership have been structured by flux and fluctuations in the housing market. Their grievances are becoming important political issues for mobilisa-tion. How the state would respond to them and whether there will be further politicisation of such grievances remain to be seen. However, it is quite clear that the question of home ownership has brought the lower-middle-class families to the arena of urban politics. Their grievances will constitute an important source of urban conflicts in the coming years.

ACKNOWLEDGEMENTS

I would like to thank Professor Rance P.L. Lee and Professor Yue-man Yeung for their support of the idea of carrying out research on social class and housing inequalities. In the process of data collection and analysis, S.M. Hsu, Terence Poon and Irene Leung have been most helpful and their assistance is gratefully acknowledged. I would also like to thank Ray Forrest and Thomas Wong for their critical and insightful comments. I have benefited particularly from the comments of Ray Forrest who read every line of an earlier version of this paper. I am most grateful for his encouragement and comments in writing this paper. Finally, the research is supported by a small grant from the Hong Kong Institute of Asia-Pacific Studies.

NOTES

1 In the following discussion, the analysis of social class is based on a re-analysis of a 1 per cent sample of the land population of Hong Kong in 1976 and 1986. I rely mainly on the schema developed by John Goldthorpe for the classification of class. However, due to the limitations of the census data set, those of employer status in employment are separately classified as the capitalist. The service class here primarily refers to professionals, administrators and managers of the employment status of employee. The coding scheme for classifying social classes with the 1976 and 1986 census data is available from the author.

2 The vacancy rate of newly-completed buildings rose from 42.7 per cent to 54 per cent during 1986–90. While this may reflect the time-lag between completion and actual occupation, it can also be taken as a sign of speculative activities. 'Compared with the potential capital gain, the opportunity costs of holding onto vacant units are relatively small at the current low level of interest rates. Speculators may also be cushioned to some extent by profits accumulated from previous transactions. Thus, property owners seem to be in no hurry to unload their holding' (Hang Seng Bank 1992, 2).

3 It was noted in *Hong Kong Property Review* 1993 that 'taking the year as whole, prices in 1992 were 42 per cent higher than in 1991. Quarterly indices show, however, that prices for small units fell moderately in the second half of the year' (Rating and Valuation Department 1993, 5).

4 Here it is worth quoting Weber's remark on class situation:

> We may speak of a 'class' when (1) a number of people have in common a specific causal component of their life chances, in so far as (2) this component is represented exclusively by economic interests in the possession of goods and opportunities for income, and (3) is represented under the conditions of the commodity of labour markets. . . . It is the most elemental economic fact that the way in which the disposition over material property is distributed among a plurality of people, meeting competitively in the market for the purpose of exchange, in itself creates specific life chances. According to the law of marginal utility this mode of distribution excludes the non-owners and, in fact, gives to them a monopoly to acquire such goods.
>
> (quoted from Gerth and Mills (eds) 1948, 181)

Apparently, in Weber's conception, what is determinant of one's class situation is not so much the quality of the goods possessed but the market value of such goods. There is no point in talking of the possession of property or skills as abstracted from the market context in which their prices of exchange are determined.

5   There are signs showing the politicisation of the issue of home ownership in East Asia. On urban protests provoked by soaring property prices in Taipei, see Lin *et al.* 1989. In Hong Kong, actions had also been organised, mimicking the styles and symbols of those protests in Taipei.

6   Most of the research on Chinese families in Hong Kong was carried out in the 1960s and 1970s. The research focus is placed on family formation and the phases of extension and completed extension. In those years, inheritance, in a way, was a non-issue for urban Chinese families.

Chapter 7

Home owners
Richer or not – is that the real question?

Marc H. Choko

INTRODUCTION

All through the nineteenth century and until World War II, to be wealthy, to be a man of property, to own real estate, did not mean that one owned a very large luxurious house or apartment in which one lived. For example, in Paris in 1897, many landlords, some of whom owned fifteen or more apartment buildings, rented their own living premises, either near their properties or in another neighbourhood, at a more prestigious address. The data I am presently gathering show that owner-occupancy at that time was as low as 1.8 per cent. Daumard (1987, 106–7, 110), although she does not quantify this phenomenon, does mention it: 'Most Parisian bourgeois occupied a rented flat, even if they owned buildings in the capital . . . and they often moved.'* In all the European capitals of the time, the bourgeois invested in the real-estate market as they did in the stock market or other instruments. They saw housing as both a convenience that could be adapted to the household's changing needs or means and as an investment. By the mid-nineteenth century, property had become a major form of investment, to the extent that half of all owners had no other employment. To own or to rent did not in itself mean anything; the significance was in what one owned or rented. Status was attached to an address – its size and attributes, the qualities and services it offered, the number of servants, and so on – not to the tenure. If a man could afford all these things, no matter how, he had to be wealthy.

In Europe, up to World War II, statistics did not count owner-occupiers (except for partial data in Great Britain); the term as

---

* French quotations have been translated by the author.

such was not meaningful. What was counted, more often, were the buildings that corresponded to plot divisions. The counting of owner-occupiers and housing units appeared with the advent of urban sprawl, the rapid rise of home ownership, and, much later, the condominium phenomenon. In the United States, on the other hand, censuses introduced the category of owner-occupancy by the end of the nineteenth century. Canada did not do so until 1921; most European countries looked at this category only after World War II. Through time, the meaning of ownership has changed and taken on different connotations. The house became the home (Harris and Weaver 1994). The idea arose that the owner of the house could be the 'master of his home'. Owners began to believe that their home reflected their success and that home ownership could be a means of accumulating assets for their children. Eventually, the home came to be considered an investment among others: with a little cash down, one could make big money (Dubois 1989). After a period during which home ownership, though cherished, meant savings, efforts, and sacrifices to most – 'renting is as opposed to buying as enjoyment is to sacrifice' (Haumont 1976, 42) – it became associated with the joys of consumption and indebtedness (another way to become happier and richer). 'To be a debtor – a social taboo in the nineteenth century – became, by the mid-twentieth century, a virtual social necessity for enjoying home-ownership, the pinnacle of full citizenship' (Hancock 1980, 157). To become an owner was no longer perceived as the accomplishment of a lifetime, the crowning of a hard life of labour, but as the beginning of a process of social mobility (Peraldi and Spinousa 1990). 'Owners, to the contrary, have invested themselves in their houses through debt and obtained the social esteem and "freedom" from landlords that renters cannot acquire' (Agnew 1982, 75). In short, to a dominant ideological concern was added an ever-increasing economic concern. By believing, or making the majority believe, that owner-occupiers become 'rich', that almost anyone who wants to can acquire a home, governments had discovered a magical solution to the social issue of housing.

After a flurry of research on behavioural changes among new home owners in the late 1960s and 1970s, the new trend in the literature has been toward discussing their enrichment. This chapter briefly reviews the roots of the ideological debate, discusses the economic issues introduced in the literature, and raises questions for further consideration.

THE ROOTS OF THE IDEOLOGICAL DEBATE

For a long time, the dominant rhetoric endowed home owners with all the same desirable qualities, 'moderation, frugality, order, honesty, and a due sense of independence, liberty, and justice' as those evoked during the debates about tenant suffrage in New York in 1821 (Heskin 1981, 184). This was used to justify exclusion of the masses: 'Men who possess nothing are not held by any link to society' (d'Holbach 1773, quoted in Guerrand 1967, 17).

After a period during which industrialists had no regard for their workers, simply replacing them as they 'wore out', exploitation in industrialised countries became more rational. It was thought that workers in better physical and mental condition could produce more. The workplace – modern industry – was improving. The housing milieu, however, was not; it thus became the target of the reformist movement. Epidemics, loose morals, alcoholism, and the spread of revolutionary ideas among workers were all said to be the fault of poor housing conditions. 'If family life does not exist among the working classes, it is usually because of crowded and dirty housing. The cabaret is thus the place for meeting and leisure: there, workers become envious, greedy, revolutionary, and cynical, finally communist' (Leroy-Beaulieu 1872, quoted in Houdeville 1969, 56).

The solution: good housing and, above all, home ownership. Armand de Meulun, a member of a commission on the working class in France under the Third Republic, praised industrialists who had promoted home ownership among their workers, for it 'has valuable qualities: it makes its owner steadier; he works harder; it keeps him from harmful distractions by keeping him home, with his family, and it keeps him busy with useful activities during his leisure time' (*Journal officiel* 1875, quoted in Guerrand 1967, 177). The campaign promoting home ownership for the working class in Quebec in the 1920s borrowed directly from all of these French authors (see Choko 1980).

It became obvious that home ownership for workers could be accomplished much more easily outside of large cities. Frederic LePlay (1864) and other influential writers did not hesitate to promote the transfer of industries to the countryside in order to solve the housing problems of the working class. To these thinkers, it was a matter of salvation of societal values, central among which was individual private property.

Engels had discussed the issue of workers acquiring houses next to their place of work as early as 1887 (after receiving a letter from Eleanor Marx-Aveling, the daughter of Karl Marx, who lived in Kansas City and told him about this new issue there), and was of the opinion that it made workers even more dependent on their employers. Shackled to their homes, burdened with heavy debts, they had no choice but to accept the working conditions they were offered:

> Thus, to house themselves, workers had to take on heavy mortgage debts, and they were more than ever the slaves of their bosses; they were tied to their house, they could not leave it, and were constrained to accept any work conditions that were provided to them.
>
> (note in 1887 edition, in Engels 1975, 32)

Engels argued against the ideas and followers of Proudhon, who saw home ownership as a promotion for workers. To Engels, this was a step backward. He saw collective housing as being linked to collective industrial work, just as individual housing had been the norm for artisanal production.

Engels was basing his comments upon very little evidence, as few workers actually owned a house at that time. Also, he must have been influenced by the prevailing situation (workers' houses were built by the company, the workers were more or less tied to their job) and the prevailing political and ideological battles (proletarians had to own nothing that could attach them to the capitalist system) of his time. His opponents felt exactly the same, but reversed the arguments:

> Home-ownership completely changes a working man . . . With a little house and a garden he becomes a real family head, which means morality and providence, a feeling that he has roots and authority over his own people . . . Soon it is his house that 'possesses' him: it makes him a moral, settled, transformed man.
>
> (Cheysson 1881, quoted in Guerrand 1967, 267)

This debate, at first theoretical – home ownership among the European working class being very low – was, of course, revived once the issue became more and more real. Many contemporary authors borrowed from Engels and Marx the concept of 'an army of small owner-occupiers' serving as a bulwark for the ruling classes against the proletariat to argue for or against home ownership.

Regarding the belief that owners would have something to lose if left-wing parties came to power, see, for example, Houdeville (1969, 211–12; 217–18) and Trout (1979, 17). 'Communism can never win in a nation of homeowners', declares Hoyt (1966). To Harvey (1978), a mortgaged worker is a pillar of social stability. 'In a certain way, home-ownership leads to turning more toward family life – one feels a greater desire to remain at home' (Pinçon 1988, 112). But the direct link between tenure status and changes in political behaviour has not been satisfactorily proven. Vitt (1990, 9; 1992, 5) notes that among workers who became owners, although the link between ownership and general satisfaction is very strong, there is no correlation with 'feeling middle-class' (see also Pratt 1986a, 1986b; Williams 1988). On the contrary 'Hugh Stretton, a leftist Australian historian ... argues that participation in collective life may be dependent upon people feeling secure in the private sphere of home life and relates this view closely to the importance of home-ownership' (Kilmartin 1988, 15–16).

The idea that workers who own homes become traitors to their class, that if they make money through owning property (and not only through productive work) they even become exploiters, has sometimes caused neo-Marxist authors to misjudge this phenomenon and to minimise some of the real advantages that accompany home ownership for most workers (see Edel 1981 for a general theoretical discussion of this issue). Saunders and Harris (1988, 21) also argue that 'this means that owners ... have a very real stake in the system', and they are right – but no more or less than do tenant workers who own a few shares of a company (whether purchased or given as a bonus). The problem is not the stake itself, but, of course, how much 'stake' one gets, and under what conditions. A quick glance at American literature on disparities between black and white home owners provides very convincing proof of this (see, for example, Long and Caudill 1992).

THE ECONOMIC ASPECTS OF HOME OWNERSHIP

A great deal of literature exists on this subject, and a detailed review is beyond the scope of this chapter. Again, there are two basically antagonistic approaches. The first, issuing from a Marxist viewpoint, argues that home ownership does not change much for workers in economic terms – that they do not benefit from it, or that their situation even worsens. The second refutes these ideas and assembles data to prove that through ownership workers do accumulate assets or, even better, shrink the gap between themselves and the well-to-do.

Thorns's (1981, 28) statement that 'Gains from the job and housing markets are in fact closely related and to some extent mutually re-inforcing' is a classic opinion, echoed in the writings of authors such as Forrest (1983), Short (1982), and Doling, Karn and Stafford (1986). Thorns (1981, quoted in Forrest *et al.* 1990, 89) goes on to say:

> The housing market functions to create a growing differen-tiation amongst owner occupiers. This growing differentiation means that wealth accrues to some, more rapidly than it does to others. The evidence further suggests that this process of accumulation transfers wealth to those who already have substantial assets, thus reinforcing rather than reducing existing social inequalities.

The role of the state is also presented as discriminatory. Divay and Richard (1981, 52) show that in Quebec during the 1970s mortgage-interest rebates and tax deductions of all kinds cost governments between $1.8 billion and $4.8 billion, and they conclude, 'The wealthiest groups of taxpayers benefit more: more of them own, the value of their dwellings is higher, and so is their rate of taxation.' Forrest, Murie and Williams (1990, 108–12) illustrate the same situation in the United Kingdom, and Wood (1990, 819–20) does so for Denmark, the United States, and the United Kingdom (see also Harris and Hamnett 1987, 174). It seems that it is also more or less true for the home-ownership boom in Japan (Hayakawa and Hirayama 1990).

To authors who question the advantages of home ownership, this type of tenure also usually means more trouble for workers. First, it represents an increased financial burden. Vervaeke (1990, 7) notes that 'home-ownership has been made possible for more and more groups with modest means . . . but they are facing the problem of an extremely high cost-to-income ratio'. This may in part explain why signs of increasing (although still marginal) numbers of foreclosures are detected here and there. Kaufmann (1985) and Potter and Drevermann (1988) discuss this issue for Germany, and Saunders and Harris (1988) and Forrest *et al.* (1990) do so for the United Kingdom. Of course, extreme situations are observed in specific locations, such as resource or single-industry towns in which the company or subsidiary collapses (see, for example, Bradbury 1990). Among the low-income households that benefited from the special home-ownership program in Canada during the 1970s, 11 per cent had defaulted by 1985 (Steele 1988, 10). Doling and Lehtinen (1992) state that with the ongoing economic depression, numbers of households in arrears in Britain and Finland are growing. In Britain, households over two months late with payments were estimated at 9 per cent to 10 per cent of all mortgaged owners.

The very rapid rise of interest rates in 1981–2 and the incapacity of many households to face much higher monthly payments when their mortgages came up for renewal caused much turmoil in Canada and the United States. However, Godbout and Blais (1983, 95–6) show that although home owners had to pay more for their housing than did tenants (and this applied to new units as well as to existing ones), their actual cost-to-income ratio was lower.

Another line of argument is the 'housing rich, cash poor' concept. This borrows from Engels's (1975) demonstration that the money invested in the workers' houses is not capital – it needs to be there to be usable. The problem is that nowadays owners can use their house both to live in and as capital (at least, to a certain extent). Refinancing or 'reverse' mortgages (accumulated-equity-release programs) serve this purpose to a point, whatever the criticisms that can can be made of such practices or their limited potential to workers (see, for example, Forrest and Murie 1989; Hamnett *et al.* 1989; Mullings 1992).

Opposed to this viewpoint are a whole series of authors who trumpet the overwhelming advantages of ownership. Kemeny (1981b, 156) summed it up this way:

> Ask any householder what the advantages of owner-occupation are and answers will be forthcoming with little effort: house

prices are always rising yet one continues to pay mortgage repayments based on the price when the house was bought; one makes a 'capital gain'; one has security of tenure, and so on.

In its most recent report on this matter, Clayton Research Associates (1992(i)) takes an extreme position:

> Home-ownership has generally been an excellent investment for Canadians over the past thirty years. The combination of increased house prices plus the lower shelter costs for home-owners after they have owned their home for some period has led to a large advantage for owners compared to renters over the long-term.

The report goes on to argue that if renters had put their money in guaranteed investment certificates or the Toronto stock market over the same period, it would not have done as well as if they had invested it in a home.

In a more classic argument, Bianchi, Reynolds and Daphney (1982, 40) declare, 'Home-ownership is an important form of asset accumulation for many families. Investment in real estate provides both a hedge against inflation and a modicum of security, independence, and privacy for a family.' Saunders (1977) and Saunders and Harris (1988) claim that over the last 20 years, the value of housing has greatly outstripped inflation in the United Kingdom. In Paris, the *Bulletin d'informations et d'expertise notariales* (September 1992) states that value per square metre has doubled over the last ten years, despite a recent drop. Gaboriault (1989) and Pastor (1992) show that this is not always the case for Canada. Pastor's data indicate that location (urban or rural, size of the city, etc.) plays an important role. Dupuis (1991) comments on the impact of location and time period on gains.

From my own work on the evolution of the value of typical single-family houses in suburbs of Montreal over the last 15 years (1976–91) it appears that, in general, the value of homes rises more quickly than inflation. However, this is not true in all locations, among them some well-to-do and some working-class suburbs. This may show that Munro and Maclennan's (1987) results for Glasgow, where increases were proportionally higher in low-price areas, cannot apply as a rule. Of course, as Doling and Lehtinen (1992) clearly show for Britain and Finland, the current economic depression has a major impact, as some areas and types of housing suffer more than others.

It should also be noted that in Canada, on average, home owners occupy better-quality, larger, and thus higher-value units than renters. Topalov (1981) showed the same for France, but he also demonstrated that there was a very large gap between outright owners and mortgage-holders (Topalov 1987; see also Bourdieu and Saint-Martin 1990). Forrest *et al.* (1990) illustrated a similar situation of great disparities among home owners in the United Kingdom (see also Murie 1991). Regarding Athens, Maloutas (1990a, 1) noted that 'there is not a great social distinction between owners and tenants. However, home-ownership is more common among the wealthiest, but also among the poorest.'

It thus became of some interest to take a closer look at these gaps and their evolution through time. Edel, Sklar and Luria (1984, 107) declared home ownership to be a less remunerative investment than those 'open to large-scale investors'. Discussing the evolution of the distribution of household wealth in France, Gotman (1988, 172) states, 'Although the household assets remain more unequal than incomes, it must be noted that among the various elements of these assets, home-ownership is the one most shared.' In a way, this must be interpreted as home owner-ship being a less discriminatory factor than possession of bonds, stocks, and shares.

Hulchanski (1988) illustrates a rather contrasting situation for Canada, where home ownership is increasingly concentrated in the upper-income groups, as it dropped dramatically for lower-income groups during the 1970s. After noting the same trend for the following decade in the United States, Schwartz, Ferlauto, and Hoffman (1988, 7) provide a partial explanation for this phenomenon, which no doubt applies to Canada as well: 'Part of the reason for the decline in home-ownership in the 1980s is, of course, the skyrocketing cost of buying and maintaining a home.' (See also ibid., 13.)

Saunders and Harris (1988, 29) plainly argue for homogenisa-tion. 'The spread of home-ownership thus reduces the relative inequality of wealth between more and less affluent groups, although the absolute gains between them is widened.' To reach this conclusion, they argue that to calculate the variation of economic gains among owners, one should take into account not only absolute gains but also rates of return, and that the latter should be based on the original investment made by the purchaser. Forrest *et al.* (1990, 138) challenge this, but perhaps their position needs more ammunition, since, in theory, Saunders and Harris's argument withstands their attack. Saunders and Harris posit that even though the absolute-gain differential widens, the rate of return to the poorest home-owners can be higher (even against their will, as the main problem for the cash-poor less affluent in buying a dwelling is obtaining the down-payment, which is thus always as low as possible, forcing their rate of return up). But these authors forget that even though housing may be increasingly seen as an investment, it cannot be bought and sold every day, so that better rates of return on smaller amounts could not actually enable the poorest owners to catch up with the wealthiest. And this does not take into account transaction and moving costs, which consume most, if not all, of the smaller returns.

It must also be noted that Saunders and Harris's formula does not hold up mathematically, as it means that an owner who does not invest any cash at all to acquire a house would 'gain infinitely'. The fact that they did not take this into account only reinforces the invalidity of their way of calculating returns. Saunders (1990) himself refined his former proposal and tried to take into account more variables, but Murie (1991) shows that the problems remain pretty much the same.

Dupuis (1991) attempted a very detailed analysis of gains including rates of return and provided some clarification. But are all these questions the central ones? When 'everybody' owns, it is not being a home owner in itself that establishes status and some guarantee of wealth. It is, rather, what you own, where, under what conditions, and so on.

SOME QUESTIONS FOR FURTHER CONSIDERATION

The term *home owner*, as it is generally used in English-language literature, disguises the reality of ownership. In France, the differentiation between outright and mortgaged home ownership is always present and reveals two very distinct portraits of owners. In the first category there has tended to be a concentration of older, less educated, and less wealthy households, living in smaller, inferior-quality, lower-valued units; the second category generally presents the opposite characteristics. Not taking this into account can lead to curious misinterpretations, for example, when analysing real-estate assets. One could very well end up with equal net assets, by averaging much lower values totally paid off and much higher ones heavily mortgaged.

It is not a huge surprise that average mortgages are generally higher for home owners with higher incomes and more wealth. However, Stimson (1988, 23) shows that the proportion of income allocated to home ownership is much higher among lower-income groups. An interesting calculation would be a per-household ratio of debt to income, analogous to the debt-to-GDP ratio utilised for governments, which could provide a much better idea of the real latitude to make choices – especially if Minc (1991) is right. In an article about the new economic context, Minc argues that there has been a shift such that 'from now on one who goes into debt grows poorer and one who owns without debt gets richer'. This would mean that the capacity to 'play' with indebtedness and, if needed or desired, to pay off a mortgage will also discriminate against lower classes.

But this is not the only important cleavage in the home-ownership market. First-time buyers are also in a very different situation vis-à-vis other buyers, especially as the 'first step' for entry into the market becomes higher and higher. Since the 1980s, during the period of boom and inflated prices, downpayments followed the trend. Now, with the economic slump, down-payments have continued to rise, as financial institutions, lacking confidence, ask for higher cash-to-mortgage ratios in order to minimise their risk.

Of course, less wealthy households are also discriminated against in their ability to raise financing. Financial institutions consider not only level of income, but also other assets and debts, establishing a 'net worth' portrait of the borrower and his capacity to pay off the mortgage, thus fixing a maximum potential loan. They also estimate the proportion of downpayment that the borrower offers to pay, and thus their own risk, in view of the current and future value of the house to be bought.

In Paris, the occupational profile of all owner-occupiers is much more 'democratic' than that of new purchasers, among whom employees and blue-collar workers account for only 10 per cent (Taffin 1987, 6; see also Massot 1990, 84). Taffin (1987) also stresses that among mortgaged owners there are very large disparities according to when the dwelling was bought. For France as a whole, Bourdieu and Saint-Martin (1990, 57) note that levels of ownership are not correlated to income levels, but that income levels determine the decision to purchase (to go into debt) or not. Thus the portrait of all owners is totally different from that of recent purchasers (three years and less) alone. Linneman and Wachter (1989, 389) note that wealth has a greater impact than income constraints on home ownership decisions.

The rules used by lending institutions tend to limit the choices of a majority of households to the more standardised segments of the market (among them those in which repayment is government insured) or simply to exclude them from home ownership. In part, zoning and construction by-laws must be considered a guarantee to lenders of the product being financed and they have contributed in a major way to the homogenisation of post-World War II developments by setting thresholds (costs of minimum basic lots and structures) that excluded entire classes of society from specific locations. Walden (1987) showed that home-ownership rates were lower in suburbs that had adopted more restrictive zoning and construction by-laws. Before these were enacted, the freedom to build (or self-build) step by step, the ability to enlarge and finish when money was available, and the option of renting out part of the house when additional income was needed allowed lower classes to gain access to ownership (see, for example, Doucet and Weaver 1991, 171). It must be noted that to buy a new or an old house and to have it finished and decorated before entering the premises is very different from living in a 'building site or construction zone' for a while and spending most of one's leisure time working on it.

Another aspect that should not be overlooked is the discriminatory effect of access to information. Level of education and wealth are important factors, as is belonging to a group in which most others are experienced home owners. An interesting avenue for research may be that there seems to be a 'culture of property' created among home owners, with children of owners more likely to become owners than others. One study on condominiums in old, renovated housing in downtown Montreal (Choko and Dansereau 1987, 93–4) shows that most owners (63.8 per cent) spent their childhood in a house that their parents owned.

All of these limitations do not call into dispute the fact that even the poorest owners do accumulate some wealth that otherwise (if they remained tenants) they would not. However, there has not been much discussion of the issue of 'compelled accumulation' in which one must 'invest' time and money in one's property for restoration or to meet monthly payments and cut back on other vital expenses. Thus, when debating wealth accumulation among different groups of owners, one should always remember to ask 'Under what hidden conditions?' for each group.

Krohn and Duff (1971), in a pioneer study on the Portuguese in central Montreal, have explained how, despite their very low incomes, this group presents some of the highest home-ownership ratios. In this case, community assistance, mutual aid, working parties, self-renovation, cohabitation for some length of time, and multiplying the number of wage-earners under the same roof were determining factors. Cuturello and Godard (1982), after a thorough analysis of how working classes in the south of France gain access to and maintain home ownership, found that three aspects should be considered as explanations: wages; financial supports and transfers from family; and self-help (see also Blöss 1986, and Cuturello 1988).

Forrest et al. (1990, 145 and *passim*) argue that inheritance is a very important aspect, in that it helps some to acquire a house; because inheritances are a growing phenomenon, ownership through inheritance may be on the rise. Forrest et al. refer to Hamnett et al. (1989, 148), who show that 9.2 per cent of inheri-tances included residential property; this figure is very close to the figure of 9.0 per cent of new owners who inherited their property cited by Taffin (1987, 6), who argues that inheritances are declining. Of course, a distinction should be made between those who inherited and kept their property, the percentage of whom may be declining, and those who inherited a property and sold it, using the money to help them buy another one (thus one that is not directly inherited).

Cuturello and Godard have shown that although these aspects – wages, transfers from relatives, and self-help – are important, and more easily quantifiable than others, they provide only a partial accounting. Home ownership for the working class had far-reaching effects. The whole life of the household was changed, in terms of consumption, leisure time devoted to the house, postponement of vacations, and so on (see also Raymond et al. 1966, and Spinousa 1991). However, Maison (1992) reminds us that home ownership does not mean simply constraints and effort to the working class; it also encourages autonomy and creative ways to overcome the risks, unpredictability, and complexity of such an undertaking. Whatever the difficulties encountered, the fact is that the vast majority of owners will withstand most problems, even drastic rises in monthly payments due to interest-rate hikes, municipal-tax increases, or loss of jobs; the one they will not withstand in most cases is the breakup of the couple.

Home ownership has been associated with the creation of a family – having children (Bonvalet 1992). Ironically, today, because of economic constraints, home ownership may play 'against the family', as women may postpone childbearing to remain in the labour force (Rudel 1987; Schellenberg 1987). In developed countries, the home-ownership boom has been linked to the growing proportion of double-income households and their much higher level of real income. (Roistacher and Young (1979, 230) note that the greatest increase in working wives has occurred in households in which the husband's income was above average.) What if more and more households, because of deep societal transformations, are single-income ones and thus are excluded from the dream? For home ownership is a dream; when Doucet and Weaver (1991, 172) ask, 'If home ownership has constituted . . . an unwise investment for common folk . . . why have North Americans committed themselves to this dream?', one must agree that there is a part that is irrational.

In his philosophical essay on ownership, Attali (1988, 12–13) claims that 'to have and to be are nearly always merged', that 'what property hides is the fear of death'. Ownership is one way 'to be, to last, to delay death'. In ancient Greece and Rome, the dead were buried in the house under the 'foyer' (the fireplace – in French, the word also means 'home'); they protected the house and its grounds, thus closely associating sacred matters with the family house and property. The 'will to possess' described by Doucet and Weaver (1991) and the 'ontological preference for home-ownership' in Saunders (1990) are but the same 'theme with variations'.

But if the irrational does play a role in home ownership, it is impossible to ignore another plausible answer to Doucet and Weaver's question: Maybe people do not know whether it is a good investment or not. The issue is a complex one, as revealed in this article and in the literature in general. Perhaps, since they do not have much of a choice, most purchasers simply gamble. Also, as Berry comments, 'the major cause of the massive switch in tenure patterns (not necessarily tenure preferences) is that buying is so often the only way to get a house at all' (Berry 1974, 129). But it is Verret who may have a more contextualised answer: 'To be an owner, or, rather, to become an owner . . . is above all not to be a tenant anymore. The working class has all the reasons in the world not to want to remain tenants' (Verret 1979, 105–6).

ACKNOWLEDGEMENTS

I would like to thank Käthe Roth, who carefully edited my original text and turned it into real English. The support of the Social Sciences and Humanities Research Council of Canada is gratefully acknowledged.

Chapter 8

The extended family and housing in France

Catherine Bonvalet

INTRODUCTION

In France, as in most industrialised countries, owner-occupation has expanded considerably since the 1950s; it now accounts for 54 per cent of all housing, less than in parts of Southern Europe, where the levels are particularly high (75 per cent in Spain) and more than in parts of Northern Europe (43 per cent in Sweden). With growing prosperity, more and more households were able to invest in property, thus reviving the rural tradition of home ownership.

In the late twentieth century, housing is an important element in our lives. Unlike other possessions, homes are both consumer goods, and durables to be handed down, representing a large part of French family wealth (53 per cent of household wealth) (Babeau 1988). Thus, their symbolic and emotional value is substantial. Housing policy aimed at developing home ownership responded to a national desire. The housing loans introduced from 1953 onwards enabled many French families to fulfil their dream without having to wait for an inheritance, which consequently weakened the role of the extended family. This was in keeping with the ideology of the time: the extension of social systems and education reinforced the nuclear-family model, and the family was increasingly stripped of its former functions of solidarity and intergenerational reciprocity. The young no longer learnt their trade at their father's (or mother's) knee, and were no longer responsible for their parents in their old age. During the 1950s–1960s, the family fell into the background. The young couple, with its borrowing and consumer capacity, came to the fore. Housing studies focused on households. The fact that these were not isolated, but belonged to larger family groups, was neglected. The present economic crisis, as well as the crisis of the welfare state, has revealed the subterranean role played by the family in the industrialised world. Despite the upheavals of the past century, the family remains intact. Longer life expectancy means longer life as a couple, and families of three or four generations are becoming frequent. Greater purchasing power means that pensioners can ease their grandchildren's entry into adult life and help their middle-aged children through a bad patch. Reciprocally, children continue to provide support and affection for their elderly parents.

It is against the present backcloth of economic and housing crisis that we propose to analyse the relationship between family and housing in France.

HOME OWNERSHIP AND FAMILY CHANGES

The diffusion of home ownership is one of the most striking features of late-twentieth-century urban history. In 1988, 55 per cent of households were owner occupied, against 35 per cent in 1954. At the same time, privately rented housing fell from 33 per cent in 1961 to 18 per cent in 1988 (see Table 8.1). Compared with many other European countries, the pattern of housing tenure is somewhat dualistic in France with, on the one hand, owner-occupiers, and on the other, the public or local authority rented sector. This situation is the result of successive housing policies: state intervention was massive after the Second World War and there was extensive public-sector construction to answer the dire shortage of dwellings. Then the role of the state was gradually reduced and personal savings were encouraged, resulting in a rise in owner-occupied households with mortgages (from 5 per cent in 1954 to 27 per cent in 1990) and a fall in investment in privately rented housing. Finally, state intervention has grown again in recent years to assist the most needy segments of society.

These successive housing policies have produced differences in the diffusion of home ownership, depending on period, social class and generation.

HOME OWNERSHIP AND THE LIFECYCLE

Most young people start out as tenants, generally in the private sector. In 1988, 84 per cent of household heads aged under 25

Table 8.1 Housing stock in France 1961–88 (principal residences)

	1961	%	1970	%	1978	%	1984	%	1988	%
Owner-occupied	5699	39.4	7332	44.8	8796	47.2	10280	51.2	11233	54.2
Rented	5589	38.6	6572	40.2	7652	41.0	7723	38.4	7625	36.8
privately	4805	33.2	4744	29.0	4829	25.9	4460	22.2	4085	19.7
from local authority	784	5.4	1828	11.2	2823	15.1	3263	16.2	3540	17.1
Other	1093	7.6	665	4.1	537	2.9	2090	10.4	1841	8.9
Total (main homes)	14466	100	16368	100	18641	100	20093	100	20700	100
Total housing stock	16103		19099		22236		24249		25007	

Sources: Household surveys 1961, 1970, 1978, 1984 and 1988, INSEE

lived in rented housing (two-thirds in the private sector). It is only around the age of 30–35, when the need for more room is most acute, that the step into owner-occupation is made. State-subsidised low-interest loans and a variety of housing allowances have lowered the age of first-time buyers, particularly since the Housing Reform of 1977. Age-specific tenure patterns show that only 5 per cent of household heads aged under 25 own their homes; this proportion rises to 70 per cent at ages 55–65, then starts to fall (Table 8.2). This reduction reflects a cohort effect. People born before the First World War were too old to be concerned with the new housing loans, having set up home long before they were introduced. They are also those who enjoy the advantages of rents 'frozen' between the two world wars, which remain particularly low.

Because of population ageing, this age-wise increase in the proportion of home owners will in the years to come lead to a rise in owner-occupation and a fall in the demand for rented housing, when the smaller cohorts enter the housing market in 1995–2000. But in the meantime, young people encounter great difficulties in finding a home of their own. The changing structure of the housing stock, with fewer privately rented dwellings, the disappearance of lodging houses and maids' rooms, has enhanced these difficulties. In addition, unemployment and temporary employment mean that more and more young people are practically obliged to stay on with their parents until they have found a steady job: in 1982, 53 per cent of men aged 20–24 were still living with their parents; in 1988, the proportion was over 60 per

Table 8.2 Tenure by age and type of household

	Owner-occupied (%)	Rented (%)	Housed free of charge (%)	Total (%)
Age				
Under 25	4.5	84.0	11.5	100
25–34	32.2	60.5	7.3	100
35–44	57.8	35.8	6.4	100
45–54	64.2	29.4	4.0	100
55–64	70.4	23.9	5.7	100
65 and over	60.5	28.7	10.8	100
Type of household				
One person, male	36.7	52.3	11.0	100
One person, female	40.8	47.2	12.0	100
Lone parent family:				
father	43.3	50.5	6.2	100
mother	29.4	64.9	5.7	100
Couple				
with child(ren)	61.5	32.5	6.0	100
with no children	62.3	31.4	6.4	100
Other	49.5	38.3	12.2	100
TOTAL	54.3	38.0	7.7	100

Source: Household survey 1988, INSEE

cent. Thus, young people set up home later and with greater difficulty because of the economic crisis and housing shortage.

The elderly, on the other hand, tend to have larger dwellings, often in better areas. This contrast between the young have-nots, with neither a job nor a home, and the elderly haves, may in the long run create intergenerational conflicts and problems of distribution of national wealth.

In fact, these age differences in tenure patterns are linked to the family lifecycle. Age is important, but marriage is the key stage. The spread of home ownership has principally concerned couples, and houses more than flats. Owner-occupation and the intention to have or increase a family are strongly linked, as reflected in the correlations observed between numbers of marriages and housing investment, or between fertility level and tenure. The close link between family and home ownership is a historical constant, which has been encouraged by government policies: low-interest loans from the Credit Financier, savings accounts with government premiums and lower-rate government mortgages introduced with the 1977 Housing Reform. To buy the roof over one's head means security and family wealth. France was urbanised relatively late and rural influences are still strong; these may underlie the nationwide attachment to 'solid' property. All the Household Surveys conducted by INSEE report the same concern: to have 'a home of one's own'. In 1988, 61 per cent of couples with children owned their home, and more than 70 per cent when the household head is aged 35–44. In accordance with the ideas of the nineteenth-century reformers, home ownership seems to have become a family value.

Recent marriage trends are somewhat upsetting this applecart. The process of acquiring one's home is based on the stability of the couple. The extension of unmarried cohabitation, the growing number of unions in the lifecycle, are in complete opposition to the traditional family model of the 1960s. Young people tend increasingly to live first on their own, then in a more or less stable union, which may lead to another period of living alone if the union breaks down. At first, those who turned their backs on marriage as an institution also rejected home ownership. Since cohabitation has become more commonplace, some unmarried couples do become owner-occupiers when they have reached the stage of more long-term commitment. However, home-ownership levels are much lower among unmarried cohabitees than among married couples, whatever the family size. Informal union often means staying on in rented housing and postponing the decision to buy a home. It also means a different demand for housing. In contrast with the married couples who prefer a house in the suburbs, they prefer the city-centre life.

Divorce is another disrupting factor in the traditional family and residential lifecourse, which consists first of rented housing, followed some time after marriage and the birth of children by home ownership. Divorces, currently around 100,000 per year, account for over half of lone-parent families and a growing number of separated men living on their own. But, like the periods of living alone, these lone-parent periods are often transitional stages between two periods of living in a couple. Four years after their divorce, almost 60 per cent of women have formed another union (Festy 1991). The family lifecycle has thus become in some cases (but not yet the majority) a succession of different stages: living alone; living in a couple; living alone with or without children; living in a new union. This more complex cycle has considerable impact on residential patterns. Marriage dissolution goes hand in hand with a return to rented housing, particularly in the public sector. A recent survey by IN-ED reported that out of 1,300 women who divorced between 1970 and 1982, roughly 30 per cent were owner-occupiers at the time of the separation and over half were expected to sell. Of those who moved out at the time of the separation, twice as many went into local authority as into owner-occupied housing (Festy 1990). The 1988 Housing Survey reported that 65 per cent of women living alone with their children were tenants (69 per cent when they were divorcees). This type of mobility is shackled by the inflexibility of the housing stock, the shortage of privately rented dwellings and the difficulties of access to local-authority housing.

The changing structure of the housing stock, with fewer rented dwellings, limited residential mobility and the reduction of the role of the state means that we are, and will continue to be, faced with serious problems of imbalance between housing supply and demand.

HOME OWNERSHIP AND SOCIAL CLASS

Home ownership has evolved differently in the various strata of society. Some periods have been more favourable than others for the working classes (Topalov 1987). In the mid-1950s, there was an upsurge of owner-occupation among managers, but also among employees and manual workers. The movement then slowed down in 1963, particularly in the lower classes. This continued until the 1970s, when owner-occupation once more gained ground in all social classes, although less rapidly than in the 1950s. In 1988, owner-occupation ranged from 75 per cent of farmers to 33 per cent of employees in the private sector. Table 8.3 shows two main divisions. First, between self-employed and salaried workers: for the former, property is linked to work, which explains the particularly high rates for farmers, craftsmen and tradesmen. Second, among salaried workers, between the public sector (civil servants, local authority personnel) and the private sector (companies, banks). In the private sector (excepting employees), there are more owner-occupiers than in

Table 8.3 Proportion of owner occupiers by type of household and social class

	Total (%)	One person, male (%)	One person, female (%)	Lone parent family (%)	Couple with child(ren) (%)	Couple without children (%)
Farmers, craftsmen	75	79	87	80	71	78
Company, directors	68	60	64	47	70	70
Senior managers (public sector)	55	35	28	42	64	57
Professional, senior managers (private sector)	63	37	30	43	71	51
Middle-level professions (public sector)	49	14	26	38	65	25
Middle-level professions (private sector)	57	29	32	20	68	52
Employees (public sector)	42	31	27	28	54	38
Employees (private sector)	34	12	23	27	51	34
Skilled manual workers	50	24	38	27	57	40
Unskilled manual workers	38	15	25	23	45	34
TOTAL	54	37	41	29	61	62

the public sector. Wages are higher in the private sector, and in some cases there are incentives to buy, while civil servants or local-authority personnel have easier access to low-rent state-subsidised dwellings (HLM) and are more frequently housed free of charge (almost 10 per cent of public-sector personnel).

The housing problems related to changing family patterns, which we mentioned above, are more acute in some social classes than in others. Divorce does not always mean moving out. In the upper classes in particular, the family home may be kept: over 40 per cent of female 'senior managers' ('cadres', a somewhat heterogeneous French category which includes higher-level education) are owner-occupiers, compared with 20 per cent of employees in the private sector.

Finally, whatever the socio-occupational group (with the exception of unskilled manual workers), couples with child(ren) are mostly owner-occupiers: the proportion exceeds 70 per cent among independent workers and managers. Thus, owner-occupation is becoming the general rule in France for families with children.

But a particular aspect of French society should be borne in mind. Owner-occupiers are not the only home owners, and tenants or those housed free of charge may also own property. When they have little or no rent to pay, some of them invest in property other than their principal residence. Compared with other industrialised countries, France has a relatively high number of second homes. If we include these, the proportion of home owners in France rises from 54 per cent to roughly two-thirds. In addition to economic reasons for investing in a second home rather than in the main residence, there are more personal ones. 'Home is where the heart is' . . . and some people prefer to buy where they feel at home, and have their roots. This is often the case of provincials living in Paris and foreign residents who prefer to buy something 'back home' (Bonvalet 1991).

THE EXTENDED FAMILY AND FAMILY WEALTH

With urbanisation and industrialisation, composite households have gradually given way to the nuclear family. Census data and national Housing Survey data concern households (that is, people who live together), and provide no information on the relationship which the household may maintain with other family members, in particular as regards housing. Yet recent studies have shown the necessity of interpreting household data in a broader family context (Bonvalet *et al.* 1991). The division of the family into smaller households and the weakening of the family as an institution have not led to the disappearance of the family network but are the sign of a fundamental reorganisation of the family economy and of the bonds of solidarity between its different members.

Housing is above all a 'family affair'. The present-day family is very different from that of eighteenth-century France. It is less extended in terms of brothers and sisters, but more in terms of parents and grandparents because of the ever-longer life-span. This transformation of the extended family has considerably modified intergenerational transfers such as inheritance, donations, and access to family wealth.

Inheritance, donations and financial assistance

One of the reasons why the French are so attached to owning their home is that it represents property which can be handed down from one generation to the next. French inheritance law is based on the lineage system, that is, legacies go first to the deceased's children. The diffusion of home ownership increases the number of potential heirs. It is true that because of longer life expectancy they inherit later (at age 42 on average), but two-thirds of the French will inherit at least once and a dwelling will constitute half their legacy. In 1990, 20 per cent of households had inherited a dwelling (40 per cent of those aged 60+); but, once more, social inequalities exist. Farmers, tradesmen and craftsmen are twice as likely to inherit a dwelling as employees and manual workers. A senior manager or independent worker leaves a legacy of around 1,000,000 francs, compared with 200,000 francs for an employee. When this legacy comprises a dwelling, the differences persist: on average, the value of the property left by a senior manager is three times that of an employee (Marpasat 1991).

In 1988, 14 per cent of owner occupiers (7 per cent of all households) had inherited their home. Among over-65s, the proportion was 15 per cent. However, with urbanisation and industrialisation, fewer and fewer people will live in the home handed down by their parents. Some will keep it as a second home, but most will be obliged to sell, particularly when there are several brothers and sisters. The proceeds of the sale will often be used to purchase a main home or other dwelling.

The gains in life expectancy have transformed intergenerational transfers. To avoid conflicts between generations, the family has adapted by anticipating inheritance through donations and financial assistance when young couples wish to buy their home.

Cuturello and Godard (1982) were the first to bring to light the mobilisation of family resources involved in the process of buying a home. They reintroduced the intergenerational dimension into an area where hitherto only the household had been considered. The economic lifecycle theories had accustomed us to considering individuals as perfectly rational beings, who weigh up the advantages and disadvantages of renting or buying their homes, of immediate consumption in the former case and deferred consumption in the latter. However, an individual is not isolated, but belongs to a family group (two if he/she is married), which may have a marked impact on housing strategies. Family assistance, being economically invisible, distorts calculations of solvency and debt ratios, since elements other than cost of housing and household's financial resources are involved. The burden for the household may be considerably lightened by the various forms of assistance and donations from the family group.

The purchase of a home offers a unique opportunity for the extended family to demonstrate its solidarity, by contributing to the capital required to raise a mortgage. The beneficiaries are mostly young family members, who are thus helped to achieve residential stability, a form of security which is all the more important as the present crisis does not favour their professional stability. The decision to buy a home is a major one, since this will represent a large proportion of family wealth and the mortgage raised will imply substantial payments over many years. Such a decision means a long-term commitment, in which the young people's families play a role. Eight per cent of recent home buyers aged under 30 had been helped by means of a donation (Table 8.4), which represented on average over a quarter of the total price. In the less urbanised areas, the contribution is often the land on which a house can be built. The most privileged young people had received an advance on their inheritance, or a combination of inheritance and loans from the family.

As we saw for inheritances, social inequalities are enhanced by the family's participation in buying a home, which is most common among the upper classes (Table 8.5). But since their housing is more upmarket, it is in the middle classes that the family's contribution is largest in terms of proportion of total cost (Marpasat 1991). Furthermore, differences are observed not only in volume, but also in effect: in the upper classes, family assistance means being able to buy earlier, while in the middle and working classes, it sometimes means being able to buy.

However, these figures should be considered with caution. In a recent survey of the Paris Region, semi-structured interviews conducted on a sample of respondents revealed discrepancies with the survey responses (Bonvalet 1991). In half of cases, the family assistance mentioned in the semi-structured interviews did

Table 8.4 Family gifts to the young

Age of home owner	Proportion of recent home buyers having received a gift (%)	Proportion of total cost represented by this gift (%)
Under 30	7.9	26.8
30–39	7.4	14.9
40–49	5.9	18.3
50–64	3.4	19.7
65 plus	4.7	1.4
TOTAL	6.4	16.9

Source: INSEE, Housing survey 1988
Base: Households having bought their home between 1985 and 1988

Table 8.5 Family assistance and occupational class

Owner's occupational class	Proportion of recent home buyers having received a gift (%)	Proportion of total cost represented by gift (%)
Farmers	4.9	4.6
Craftsmen, tradesmen, employers	8.4	15.2
Senior managers and intellectual professions	8.4	17.0
Middle-level professions	6.5	21.0
Employees	7.1	17.6
Manual workers	6.4	19.4
Retired	2.9	2.6
Other inactive	1.4	6.2
TOTAL	6.4	16.9

Source: INSEE, Housing survey 1988
Base: Households having bought their home between 1985 and 1988

not appear in the survey responses, but was included in 'savings'. Thus, family contributions in the form of loans and donations were 'concealed' to some extent, in contrast with inheritances, which were reported in both cases.

The mobilisation of family resources varies from one family and one social background to another. Different ethics and moral values are involved. In some cases, the participation of the family is deemed 'natural': it functions as a bank in which money circulates among the different members of the family when and where it is needed. For these families, it is important to pass on the status of home owner. In other cases, family assistance is considered an 'extra'. What counts most is to provide education capital and see the children into a good job; a housing capital is not a 'due' and they are expected to buy their homes themselves.

When family assistance in housing is considered only in terms of financial contribution, manual workers and employees seem to participate much less frequently than the upper classes. But in reality, this reflects differences in the forms of assistance practised. Having fewer financial resources, manual workers and artisans help in constructing and finishing the home. Brothers, sisters, in-laws, all give a helping hand. One out of three manual workers and craftsmen–tradesmen receive this kind of help (Table 8.6). Without it, many workers and employees would not own their home (Cuturello 1990).

The role of the family is observed throughout the process of purchasing a home, in advice and information, incentives such as giving children access to home-savings accounts or to the lower-interest rates they offer.

The access to family wealth

The donation of a dwelling or a cash gift to young couples to buy their home means that the older generations agree to sacrifice some of their capital for their descendants and thereby deprive themselves of the security that capital represents. The fact that people are living longer may reduce such practices. Thus, certain households prefer a solution which does not mortgage their future: to give access to family property, either free of charge or rented, to the member who needs it.

In 1988, 4 per cent of households were housed free of charge by their family and in a survey of the extended family conducted in 1990, 20 per cent of respondents reported that they had lived at some point in a dwelling belonging to their family or in-laws. The young and the elderly are those who most frequently benefit from access to family property. With the housing crisis and the problems young people have in finding a rented flat, parents who have enough money often buy a flat which they lend to their

Table 8.6 Proportion of persons having received some form of family assistance in housing, by occupation group

Occupation group	Inheritance, gift, free accommodation (%)	Information, acting as guarantor (%)	Construction, finishing (%)	Total (%)
Farmers	75.7	43.9	19.2	78.1
Craftsmen, tradesmen	51.5	38.3	34.1	69.9
Senior manager	50.9	53.9	25.8	72.3
Middle-level profession	41.1	46.2	29.9	68.8
Employees	32.5	40.9	28.6	60.5
Manual workers	29.9	35.4	32.6	62.2
TOTAL	39.8	42.4	29.1	66.0

children. This is far from negligible in Paris: in 1988, two-thirds of owned dwellings were occupied by their owners and 14 per cent by a member of the owner's family – generally someone young, but also elderly parents who had come to be near their children (Massot 1989). Buying a home thus fulfils two aims: to build up capital which appreciates quite rapidly, particularly in the city centre, and to solve the housing problems of one of the family.

Between being housed free of charge by a member of the family and renting from a private landlord outside the family circle, there are many, often complex, situations. The landlord may be one of the family – parents, in-laws, an uncle or a cousin who accepts to rent a dwelling at a below-market price – though this is not always the case. When the property is joint-owned or mortgaged for a life income, the situation becomes more complicated. In the 1988 Housing Survey, 10 per cent of tenants, in particular elderly persons, reported that their landlord was a member of the family.

In fact, the family has become a sort of owner-lessor and its role in the housing market is far from negligible, since, in all, 16 per cent of French households owe their home to the family (4 per cent housed free of charge, 5 per cent renting from a relative and 7 per cent living in a home they have inherited). If we add the family's financial assistance to members buying a home, we reach a figure of one household in four housed directly or indirectly through the family (1988 Housing Survey).

In addition to the main home, the family may also provide access to other family properties. Holidays are the opportunity to reconstitute the extended family which was predominant in the last century. The family home, a feature of French life, becomes the nest where grandparents, parents and children can gather together again. This desire for family gatherings is one of the reasons for the purchase of second homes or for keeping those which have been inherited. Grandparents and grandchildren spend all the more time together as the mother goes out to work (47 per cent of working mothers ask the grandparents to help out during the school holidays, 29 per cent of children go to stay with their grandparents, and 27 per cent of grandparents come to stay with their grandchildren) (Toulemon and Villeneuve-Gokalp 1988). Women more readily ask mother than mother-in-law to look after the children during the holidays (42 per cent and 27 per cent respectively).

These practices are common to all social classes, but with variations. Manual workers and retirees more frequently go to stay in the main home of a relative living in the country, while senior managers and professionals more often borrow a second home at the seaside or in the mountains. Young Parisians with small dwellings are those who benefit most by this form of housing provision (Marpasat 1991).

When we add together all the different contributions, financial (inheritance, donation, loans for capital deposits) and in-kind (lending a dwelling), 40 per cent of French households have at some point in their lifecycle received housing assistance from the family ('Proches et Parents' Survey 1990). Farmers are those who gain most, since they generally inherit the family farm, followed by craftsmen–tradesmen and senior managers.

THE FAMILY SUPPORT

The role of the family is not merely an economic one. Services, information, exchanges, also circulate through the family, forming a network which bridges the gap between the individual and society. The kin group offers a variety of solutions to the housing problems of its members, such as keeping older children on at home, taking in the elderly, serving as intermediary by acting as guarantor. These are all part of the extensive support system provided by the family.

Cohabitation of different generations

When older children continue to live with their parents, this is in fact the first form of housing assistance provided by the family. It may be the result of unemployment or unstable employment, the wish to have a comfortable background for studying, or the problems of finding a relatively cheap dwelling. This cohabitation may continue when the son or daughter forms a couple. In 1990, 15 per cent of respondents in the 'Proches et Parents' Survey had lived as a couple at their parents' or in-laws' home. The early 1990s are similar to the postwar years in that many young couples live with their parents because of the housing crisis. This solidarity is discreet and has attracted little attention. But if it did not exist, the present situation would be practically unbearable for many young people faced with employment and housing problems to which society offers little solution.

In some cases, children leave the parental home, then return a few months or years later to 're-cohabit'. Such cases are by no means rare: in a survey conducted in Marseilles, 14 per cent of young women had re-cohabited by the age of 27, in particular daughters of managers. A large proportion had separated or divorced, circumstances which bring many young people 'back to the fold'. This was also shown in another survey conducted by IN-ED on 2,300 women who had experienced a separation over the past twenty years. The return to the parental home was most common at the time of the split. Seventy per cent of those who left the marital home when they separated went back to their parents' home, and in all, 19 per cent had done so at some point during the first five years after the separation (Festy 1990).

Thus, the family is a haven to which one can turn when things go wrong in one's professional or personal life, an anchor, and a bridge over troubled waters.

Finally, family solidarity is also expressed towards the elderly. Cohabitation of several generations is considered marginal today, yet it concerns 1.5 million elderly households in France. Above age 75, a single retired person is twice as likely to live with his/her family (30 per cent) as in an institution (15 per cent) (Cribier 1989). According to a recent survey the standard of living of older persons living in an extended family is on average 17 per cent higher than it would be if they lived alone (Canceil 1990).

Although this type of cohabitation is related to specific ways of life (farming families), and to the transmission of working capital (craftsmen, tradesmen), as well as to low incomes, it is generally more than a one-way young-take-care-of-old relationship. The exchange of services is often reciprocal, with the elderly helping young adults in a difficult situation (for instance unemployment, single mothers).

Although the French housing model is characterised by a large degree of autonomy between generations, cohabitation is often the answer to a need for mutual assistance, produced by an event such as unemployment, divorce, illness or loss of self-sufficiency. The child–parent relationship is often more complex than it might seem at first, and intergenerational exchange is in most cases reciprocal. If the form of solidarity represented by cohabitation did not exist, many young and elderly people would find themselves in a completely different situation which might modify the priorities defined as regards the redistribution of national wealth.

Access to housing

Parental influence does not stop when children leave home. Many studies have shown that exchanges and assistance continue afterwards (Roussel and Bourguignon 1976; Pitrou 1976; Gokalp 1978). Housing is, with employment, one of the spheres in which family intervention is most pronounced. Thus, in the present housing shortage, the family has become a sort of estate agent, using its relations to scout round for dwellings, acting as guarantor, or directly renting flats which will be used by members of the family.

This mediating role was revealed in a survey conducted by IN-ED in 1990. Twenty-one per cent of respondents, and a third of those aged under 35, had found their dwelling through the family, mainly through parents or parents-in-law. But there again, differences are observed by social group (Table 8.6). It is easier for senior managers than for manual workers to pull strings, either by knowing the landlord or by being informed when a room is about to become available in the neighbourhood. When dwellings are rare, this role of informer or go-between is cardinal. Another, more direct, form of support consists of acting as guarantor. With rising unemployment, young people are looked upon with suspicion by landlords who have to chase after their rent, or look mournfully at a growing list of defaulting tenants. They are therefore required to provide more and more guarantees, and parents frequently stand guarantor for their offspring to enable them to become tenants (Table 8.7). This was the case for 28 per cent of respondents, and 48 per cent of those aged under 35. Resorting to the family is thus becoming the general rule for finding a home of one's own.

Table 8.7 Proportion of persons having received some form of family assistance in housing, by age group

Age group	Inheritance, donation, free housing (%)	Information, acting as guarantor (%)	Construction, finishing (%)	Total (%)
Under 35	30.9	63.1	31.1	76.0
35–49	33.9	42.8	37.8	69.8
50–64	47.0	33.4	27.8	64.1
65 and over	50.3	26.3	16.7	50.7
TOTAL	39.8	42.4	29.1	66.0

In the private rented sector, there is a strong tendency to select tenants by the security they offer and thus by social background. The person who acts as guarantor must be capable of covering the rent if the young person defaults and this naturally biases selection of tenants. In Lyons, for instance, a study of applications for privately rented flats showed this clearly. Of the potential tenants, two-thirds of those accepted had a close relative (generally father or mother) who stood guarantor, while 70 per cent of those refused offered no such guarantee. The role of the family is even more direct when the parents become the fictitious tenants of a dwelling inhabited by their child (Grafmeyer 1990).

Such practices are also observed in the public or social rented sector, despite the regulations which govern the allocation of such dwellings. The existence of family networks within the same council estate (HLM: low-rent dwellings) shows the extraordinary capacity of the family to 'successfully brave the institutional allocation procedure' (Anselme 1988a). The family plays such an effective role that it is more or less implicitly acknowledged by the HLM offices, private landlords and banks. HLM officials have been surprised by the extent of family networks in housing estates which are very different socially or ethnically. Very often, several generations of French or immigrant families live, or have lived, on the same estate. If the HLM officials now take family ties into account when allocating dwellings, it is because this constitutes a 'guarantee' and a means of control: young would-be tenants must come from a family of 'good tenants' (Blöss 1989). The 'settling' of families in certain HLM estates sometimes makes them act like 'owners', and strategies emerge whereby children 'inherit' the council dwelling of their parents (Anselme 1988a).

Thus, when they have no property to hand down, certain households hand down instead the use of dwellings which they do not own. The semi-structured interviews revealed that dwellings were sometimes rented for years, even decades, to the same family, with children taking over the lease of their grand-mother or uncle. Tenancy strategies are elaborated to keep the dwelling in the family, so that it is available when required by one of the members. Many dwellings in which rents were 'frozen' by the Law of 1948 were occupied for years by the same family, taking it over in turns. The only solution for the owner was to eventually sell it to the occupying tenant.

The family's role is not confined to access to a dwelling. In certain circumstances, the intervention of a parent, brother or sister is necessary, to keep one's home and avoid being evicted or seized. There is evidence that such 'helping hands', or financial bailing-out, is far from negligible (Pitrou 1978). Difficult professional situations (unemployment or temporary employment) or conjugal situations (divorce, separation) often make it necessary to turn to the family. It is difficult to estimate the volume of such aid, and the figures we have only cover part of reality. In the 'Proches et Parents' Survey, 10 per cent of respondents reported that they had received help at some time to pay rent or an installment.

CONCLUSION

A fine-level analysis of this kind challenges the housing-market analysis in terms of stocks, where the relationship between supply and demand is studied on the basis of 'screening' of demand by solvency, in the private sector, and by allocation procedures in the public or local authority sector (Vervaeke 1990). Individuals are defined not only by age, income and socio-occupational group, but also by family membership, or rather by the existence of a family network and its capacity for housing mobilisation. They are considered less in terms of social class and more in terms of local, family, professional and associative networks. The extent of this mobilisation is such that two-thirds of respondents stated that they had received some form of housing assistance, and three-quarters of the young. It concerns all social strata, but with variations. Farmers, craftsmen and tradesmen more often inherit a home along with the family concern. Senior managers benefit from inheritance, financial aid and family connections. Employees and manual workers receive material aid, which often consists of help in building the home (one case out of three).

Family assistance in housing also reinforces inequalities between those who have a very extended family and can use its relations, those who have a family but which cannot help (and may even become a handicap), and those who are isolated. When the labour and housing markets are running smoothly, the chances of finding work or a home are more evenly distributed and depend more on personal qualities. But when there is a shortage of both, and growing tensions, the role of intermediary which the family comes to play accentuates differences between individuals.

The housing market is therefore governed not only by an economic logic, but also by a family one. Invisible at the macro-economic level, this family logic, or rather, these family logics, are necessary to understand a population's housing behaviour. Having considerable influence, relational and financial resources, the family acts in the background at all the different stages in the lifecycle, and more particularly at the beginning. It is a sort of 'invisible' economic actor on the housing market, successively estate agent, lessor, constructor. It is the family which, by acting as guarantor for the young, gives them access to both public and private sector housing. And which, by 'mobilising its financial and material resources', participates in reality in the home-ownership market.

The family acts as an insurance, a kind of safety net. It constitutes a 'housing capital' to which its members can resort at any time: holidays, unemployment, divorce, loss of self-sufficiency. Family intervention has become so widespread that it is henceforth impossible to analyse the housing market without taking into account this economic factor.

Chapter 9

On the structure of housing accumulation and the role of family wealth transfers in the Greek housing system

Dimitris Emmanuel

INTRODUCTION

Consider this puzzle: Greek households have an income level that is much lower than the average of the European Community and at the same time enjoy better than average housing conditions as well as one of the highest rates of owner-occupation. Moreover, this tenure structure is mainly based on outright ownership – very few people live in mortgaged properties and even in these cases debt represents but a small share of their dwelling's value. In fact, mortgage credit, the main avenue to owner-occupation in developed economies, has a limited role in housing finance and is very costly. Thus, in terms of simple economics it appears nearly impossible to achieve respectable owner-occupation by means of saving and borrowing. Nevertheless, most people do manage and, to add to the puzzle, this wide access to home ownership is not differentiated along class lines: the percentage of owner-occupation is essentially similar in the different occupational and income groups.

Accounting for this state of affairs has been a permanent fixture of discussions on the Greek housing system and one can certainly collate a list of reasonable-sounding explanatory factors though the issue is far from settled. It is not my purpose in this paper to tackle the whole dubious matter of universal housing 'overinvestment' among Greeks though I will not resist some comments. What is of interest here is that one of the most prominent factors in all accounts, is that to a very great extent Greek households save a lot and invest most of their wealth in housing because they want to provide housing assistance and bequests to their offspring. Conversely, and as a result, quite a lot of the achievement of owner-occupation and improved housing conditions is due to this universal norm of family assistance and family wealth transfers. This alleged fact seems to form the backbone of most official policies as well and helps explain the common complacent attitude that the housing problem gets solved in Greece by independent means, so to say. Most of what follows will examine the extent, structure and social distribution and implications of this pattern. To anticipate some of the conclusions, we will show that family assistance is indeed very extensive and crucial, in fact much more so than is currently believed, while, on the other hand, its force as a cultural norm in saving and wealth accumulation practices is much less strong than is thought and is quite probably on the decline.

Part of the argument will be concerned with the broader problem of understanding the structure of household wealth formation in general and housing accumulation in particular. This is mainly a matter of logical necessity. Both the reasons and processes by which people accumulate and transfer wealth to family members and the impacts of these transfers on the living conditions and behaviour of recipients will vary significantly depending on the prevalent model of household behaviour vis-à-vis consumption, saving and wealth accumulation in general and the place housing wealth has in such a model. Moreover, differentials across social classes and tenure groups will also largely depend on the structure of the prevailing model. Lastly, family transfers and their impacts offer an excellent opportunity for *testing* the validity of the major alternative models of household behaviour and the formation and distribution of personal wealth. This is an additional good reason for digressing somewhat into wider theoretical territory.

Perhaps there is a more important puzzle to consider. What happens to those unlucky ones who are not recipients of assistance or wealth transfers? Given the harsh reality of limited incomes, absence of public support and extremely high credit costs, we would expect major differences, in terms of housing conditions, living standards and, more generally, lifetime achievements, between those that have to devote most efforts and resources in the project of entering owner-occupation status and those that have the benefit of substantial family support or inherited wealth. Such a broad and far-reaching division between major sections of the population raises a number of crucial issues about the role of housing status in the more general pattern of class divisions and socio-economic stratification. These questions have been raised in the literature in connection with the role of tenure and the public/private sector division in the formation of class consciousness and class behaviour in a rather superficial and simplistic way. I will argue that, in the face of the evidence, we may have in the matter of differentials in family wealth transfers and more generally in the availability of family wealth, a much more significant factor than tenure or sectoral status. This factor may be less recognised in its more modest manifestations on the level of ideological and class-related political 'superstructure', but it is certainly much more crucial in wider terms of social inequality in the life chances of households.

THE CASE OF THE GREEK HOUSING SYSTEM

Greek households during the postwar period showed saving propensities that were well above the EEC average. About a quarter to one-third of these personal savings, augmented by the substantial inflow of funds from Greeks repatriating or working abroad and in the merchant marine, financed similarly high rates of residential building. While the proportion of savings out of disposable income started, as in most of Europe, from well below 5 per cent in the early 1950s, it has quickly risen to more than 20 per cent in the 1970s (average 1974–9: 20.4 per cent). During the last decade the propensity to save has levelled off and showed signs of decline (average 1980–9: 19.1 per cent, EEC average: 11.8 per cent). Housing-capital formation peaked by the end of the 1970s at truly exceptional levels, and then entered a period of relative decline and fluctuation around more modest levels. While the percentage of residential construction in the GDP has fluctuated throughout the 1960–89 period around levels just above the EEC average (6.2 per cent and 6.0 per cent respectively) the actual physical volume of housing-capital accumulation per capita was certainly much higher compared to EEC averages given the well-known underestimation of its value in Greek National Accounts (certainly higher than 30 per cent). Thus, in the light of these figures and the fact that the state and bank financing play a very limited role in housing finance, Greek households not only save by a substantially higher rate than the European average but place a higher share of their savings directly into residential construction and the acquisition of housing capital.[1]

Econometric studies of the saving behaviour of Greek households have arrived at the conclusion that the predominant factors involved belong to a class of non-neoclassical models that differ from the more influential 'lifecycle' hypothesis (Modigliani, Ando, Brumberg) and Friedman's related 'permanent income' hypothesis, in that they are essentially 'sociological' ones: they are mainly derived from Houthakker and Taylor's 'habit persistence' hypothesis (the protection of accustomed levels of consumption and the occurrence of increased saving when income rises faster than expected), and Dusenberry's 'relative income' hypothesis (the protection of consumption standards with reference to those above and below the group in the social status hierarchy) and factors such as age, the nature of one's occupation, and the size of the family.[2] Thus, the high savings propensity in Greece during the postwar period has been the product, on the one hand, of high rates of income growth over an extended period and, on the other, of such social factors as the high percentage of farmers and petty proprietors in the urban sector (who are by nature high savers), the skewed income distribution (given higher savings propensity in higher labour and property incomes), the relatively large size of families, and, lastly, the relatively young age of the population up to the 1970s (given that after retirement the saving propensity falls substantially) (Koutsouveli 1985; Baltas and Drougas 1980). These same factors may also explain the levelling-off and partial decline of saving after the mid-1970s.

These explanations are essentially the product of 1950s theories or, more generally (to include the neomarxists and neokeynesians), of theories that were aware of hard times as well as conscious of the difficulties that most working people face in the effort to save and accumulate some modest wealth (or more appropriately and pressingly, to protect and improve their consumption).[3] Nowadays, after more than a decade of generalised economic insecurity coupled with high inflation and, for large segments of the population in Greece, stagnant or declining real incomes, I have much greater appreciation of these approaches and find their mode of analysis very relevant indeed. As it happens, my own work, mainly formed during the end of the 1970s (at the end of a long period of near-solid growth) and much more heavily influenced by the role of housing-wealth accumulation, has been more inclined towards the opposite camp of neoclassical 'lifecycle' models with an added emphasis on wealth as a utility argument in maximising behaviour.[4] Suspending for the moment any critical reconsideration, I would formulate that alternative quasi-neoclassical model in the following manner.[5] First, Greek households seem to save in quite a purposeful and planned manner according to a lifecycle plan in order to achieve social status, secure their old age and plan for contingencies, support their offspring and leave sufficient bequests. Second, the achievement of owner-occupation plus the ownership, if means permit, of some additional land and housing property which, in order of priority, will satisfy the needs for housing the next generation and provide a second, vacation house, are major goals of the lifetime plans for a household's savings. Third, for each socioeconomic class (with a structurally determined level of lifetime resources), there is an 'equilibrium' (desired/planned) level of wealth achieved at a certain stage in the lifecycle (thus representing the class as a whole) and a particular equilibrium (desired) composition of wealth in terms of housing wealth and non-housing wealth. Lastly, the relationships between income, consumption, saving and wealth apply to both the dynamic dimension and the cross-sectional class dimension; there is an essential homogeneity of the population vis-à-vis the behavioural parameters determining consumption, saving and wealth accumulation (including, most importantly, housing).

Abstracting from short-term influences, such a model postulates that households save and accumulate wealth according to a mechanism that at some nodal point for each socioeconomic class approximates a certain balance of consumption and wealth assets and within the latter, a balance of housing assets and other forms of wealth. We have in a most simple mathematical formulation:

$$(1) \quad C = a\,W^b \qquad (2) \quad W_h = c\,W^d$$

where C is consumption, W is the total of a household's assets and W_h is housing wealth. It should be stressed again that this model is definitely one of medium and long-term dynamic equilibrium. It abstracts from fluctuations during the short term and during the lifecycle of the household. It assumes, however, that household behaviour during short-term changes is tending towards the equilibrium point represented by (1) and (2) and that the lifecycle curve of saving and consumption is, for each economic class ('lifetime resources' class), patterned around a nodal equilibrium point representative of the class. Moreover, there is an essential uniformity in the structure underlying both cross-sectional and time-series variation and the variation among economic classes.

Owner-occupied housing is, of course, only a part of household wealth but is certainly the most important one. Moreover, it is the part of household assets that is most influenced by planning over one's lifetime and most close to the concept of a 'desired' level of wealth postulated in the model described above. We should therefore expect our model emphasising the role of an 'equilibrium' level of planned wealth around which lifecycle, class and time patterns are structured, to apply in the case of owner-occupied housing in an even more pronounced manner. The data on the extent and social differentiation of the rate of owner-occupation in Greece seem to support this. Table 9.1 shows the rate of owner-occupation at various times during roughly the last 20 years (1974–88) by urban and non-urban areas and by major groups of households according to the occupational class of the head of household and its stage in the lifecycle measured by the age of the head. It should be noted that the percentage of owner-occupiers includes those having a dwelling free of charge – a substantial group in Greece, about 4 per cent, mostly cases where the dwelling is owned by the immediate family.

Let us comment first on the broad picture described by Table 9.1. While the rate of owner-occupation for the country as a whole is certainly very high by European standards, especially if we take into account the fact that most of this stock is owned outright, this high rate is to a very large extent due to the 93 per cent rate found in non-urban areas. Urban areas show a much smaller rate of 68 per cent and for Athens 66.5 per cent. These rates, nevertheless, should still be considered quite remarkable given the extremely limited role of mortgage financing. Moreover, the extent of owner occupation has been steadily increasing during the 1974–88 period in all urban areas with a most notable increase in Athens – from 56.4 per cent to 66.5 per cent. This increase is not the continuation of any long-term trend of expanding access to ownership during the postwar period, as anyone familiar with the current European literature will hasten to assume. On the contrary, it is a reversal of trends: between 1957/8 and 1974 the rate of owner occupation in urban areas *fell* from 67 per cent to 60 per cent.[6]

Table 9.1 Consumption level (C) and per cent owner-occupiers

Area/social group	1987/8 monthly C ('000 drs)	% owner-occupiers		
		1974	1981/2	1987/8
COUNTRY TOTAL	159.1	73.1	74.7	76.8
Greater Athens	179.9	56.4	60.0	66.5
Rest of urban areas	164.5	64.8	67.5	70.1
Non-urban areas	133.7	91.7	93.1	92.7
URBAN AREAS, ALL GROUPS: BY A) OCCUPATIONAL CLASS OF HOUSEHOLD HEAD:	173.0	60.0	63.3	68.1
Higher administrative and managerial	272.4	55.8	69.0	71.2
Professions, technical and related	245.3	58.1	59.1	55.4
Tradesmen and sales workers	214.0	64.2	68.0	73.7
Clerical occupations	206.6	54.6	57.3	65.9
Personal services	183.9	55.2	50.0	52.7
Craftsmen and workers in industry, transport and construction	169.8	56.1	59.1	61.6
Farming and related	172.7	82.5	81.7	74.5
Non-gainfully employed, etc.	132.8	64.7	70.0	77.6
B) AGE OF HOUSEHOLD HEAD:				
Under 35	173.6	31.4	38.3	42.4
35–44 years	205.4	61.7	60.6	60.2
45–54 years	205.0	69.1	72.7	73.6
55–64 years	169.4	67.2	75.5	81.3
Over 64	115.0	71.8	75.0	82.4

For anyone versed in the modern literature on the sociology of home ownership, the two most striking facts in Table 9.1 are surely the relationship between urban rates of owner-occupation, socioeconomic class and stage in the lifecycle of the household. In the beginning of the period, the mid-1970s, occupational class differences in the rate of home ownership were virtually non-existent, with the exception of a somewhat higher rate in the case of tradesmen and sales workers and, of course, farmers. The non-gainfully employed had a much higher rate, naturally, being mostly pensioners. It should be added that before 1974, things were even more equitable with urban industrial workers having in 1958 and 1963 higher than average rates and certainly higher ones than those of the two top social groups of managerial and professional occupations. During the 1980s class differences seem to have widened to a significant extent, despite an avowedly socialist government and an observed decrease in income inequalities. This is most probably an indication of the inherent class bias of the relative expansion of mortgage credit during this time.[7] The creditworthy groups, i.e. managerial, trades and clerical occupations (the latter mainly public employees), have increased their rate of home ownership by as much as 10–15 percentage points, while the increase among industrial workers is only five percentage points, and the professions and technical and service workers have shown an absolute decrease in their rates. Still, the social differentials between major socioeconomic groups are very limited compared to the strongly class-divided pattern observed in some advanced economies – most notably in the case of Britain, which the relevant literature has made so familiar.[8] Aside from the relatively 'democratic' distribution of access to property, the data in Table 9.1, seen from another angle, reveal two equally important points: first, the great importance of housing-wealth accumulation even among lower incomes obviously pressed by other equally or even more important needs; second, the essential uniformity in the rate of home owner- ship among different classes despite the substantial variations in economic resources shown by the monthly levels in consumption expenditure (a spread of 1 to 1.7 per cent between households headed by industrial workers (including own-account) and those headed by managerial occupations).

The data on the relationship between the age of the head of the household, measuring the stage in the 'lifecycle', and the rate of home ownership are similarly crucial for understanding the workings of the Greek system. There is a clear and quite sharp step-by-step increase in home ownership as the stage in the life- cycle progresses, starting from about 40 per cent for the group with a head below 35 and reaching a plateau of double this rate after the age of 55. It could be noted that before the 1980s, both age differentials and a low absolute rate for younger households were much more noticeable. This clear-cut mechanism of gradual accumulation of assets and increasing rates of access to owner- ship seems to be the natural corollary of a lifecycle model of saving with wealth (housing in this case) valued as such (since it is not liquidated in old age) under conditions of limited credit availability. On the other hand, it could also be the result of a simple model of constant saving coupled with increasing income as the lifecycle progresses. The data on consumption levels in Table 9.1 do not show the increase in household income up to retirement, which from the little available evidence seems to follow, in the 1970s at least, a quite steep curve (Emmanuel 1979). What is important is that in the Greek housing system the stage in the lifecycle is clearly the most important determinant of the rate of home ownership, clearly more so than social class.[9]

We have already noted that the lifecycle patterning of owner-occupation rates provides certain *prima facie* support for a theory that emphasises the planning of household wealth accumulation towards some desired 'equilibrium' stage. We have also added a caveat, however, that such crude data are susceptible to alternative simpler models. The data on the social class pattern – namely its essential uniformity up to the 1980s – seem to offer additional substantial corroboration for the 'equilibrium' model. It should immediately be said, however, that the data on ownership rates indicate the strong probability of the operation of a lifecycle equilibrium model for *housing* wealth, and a *part* of it at that, rather than total household wealth. Thus, we have no direct support for the broader lifecycle model of saving or for the special formulation advanced in equations (1) and (2) above. Let us for the moment postpone judgement on this issue. It is evident from Table 9.1 that both young households and low-income ones have a surprisingly high rate of access to property given Greek conditions. Aside from the fact of limited credit availability and its high cost, the cost of housing is quite high compared to real incomes. It has been estimated that for any household in a particular socioeconomic class the cost of acquiring a dwelling of socially equivalent average standards, requires much more than five times its annual disposable income (DEPOS 1989). The data in Table 9.1, therefore, indicate the presence of an extensive inflow of outside resources which is, of course, transfers and help from the family. After the previous somewhat lengthy preliminaries we are ready to examine the role of these factors in some detail in what follows. To what extent is the relatively high rate of access to ownership in the various social classes due to family assistance and wealth transfers? Moreover, to what extent is housing wealth accumulated for the purpose of providing such assistance and bequests? Lastly and more importantly, what are the impacts of family assistance and transfers in view of the saving and consumption patterns predominant among Greek households? It is in relation to this later point that the issue of which model represents the underlying structure of behaviour of households in the housing system will be crucial. If households strive towards a socially determined standard of wealth that includes owning a house of certain material characteristics (which are stratified by class-specific income and 'lifetime' resources), family transfers will have limited impact on the housing conditions of owners at the 'equilibrium' point. Family transfers will simply help households get to the desired level of wealth faster than those without the benefit of such help. By implication, consumption and saving by households that differ with regard to transfers at each particular age group, will also differ substantially. With regard to the size and value of the owner-occupied dwelling we may have different effects depending on the relationship of housing to the value of accumulated total wealth at each stage in the life of a household. In one case, we may have a direct and 'elastic' relationship to wealth in which housing conditions among owners before the 'equilibrium' point will vary substantially with the presence or absence of transfers. In another, more realistic alternative, housing will simply be a basic priority item in a household's 'portfolio' and will vary little among home owners of the same class regardless of different circumstances with respect to family help. If, however, the wealth transfer is quite substantial the receiving household will move to a clearly different class of lifetime resources and may shift the desired amount of housing wealth to a level much higher than that of its social class.

In the context of the non-neoclassical 'disequilibrium' model, households, especially those with middle and lower incomes, save not according to plan but to the extent they can, and accumulate significantly only in favourable times, mostly living under the pressure of more immediate needs for consumption, security, education etc. and the sustenance of a socially acceptable standard of living. To the extent that such a model applies, the incidence of family-wealth transfers will make a major difference in their capacity to save and achieve ownership and better housing conditions. In a certain variant of this mechanism, more appropriate perhaps to situations of limited economic development, housing conditions among home owners will differ to a very large extent depending on the circumstances and the presence of windfalls such as family transfers. In more developed situations with better-established living standards, home ownership will be associated with certain socially acceptable conditions and housing will be more in the nature of necessary consumption (a basic-needs item). Thus, under certain conditions, we may again have a certain uniformity of conditions within a class and an orderly patterning between classes and stages in the lifecycle. In a way, this introduces some elements of planning towards a desired level of assets akin to the 'equilibrium' lifecycle model, but specifically for owner-occupied housing. Other assets and wealth as a whole, in contrast, will vary much more in the 'disequilibrium' model while, again in contrast to the former model, consumption will vary little regardless of the presence or absence of windfalls or differences in accumulated wealth. The rationale for this is that in the 'disequilibrium' model, it is consumption in the sense of satisfying basic needs that is the relatively 'inelastic' factor: savings will fluctuate depending on the presence of a steady growth in income or windfalls which, aside from transfers, result from good phases in a household's life such as those with many working members, periods of fast income increase or working abroad for a period.

FORMS, EXTENT AND SOCIAL DISTRIBUTION OF FAMILY ASSISTANCE AND HOUSING WEALTH TRANSFERS

Despite its widely recognised importance, it is only recently that the role of family assistance and wealth transfers in the achievement of home ownership has received some attention from housing research. This has been limited to the role of inheritance and the common practice of cash help in the downpayment towards a loan.[10] In the Greek context the more important form is neither of these but rather the direct transfer of a dwelling or a land plot to the offspring of a family – most often well before the parents reach old age. These practices have commonly been associated with the institution of the dowry. They have been, however, much more general in nature and the reform of civil law in the beginning of the 1980s has rightly ruled that they be treated as 'parental gifts' in general with no distinction as to the gender of the recipient. In fact, we can distinguish a whole

complex spectrum of forms of family assistance and wealth transfers. On the basis of the DEPOS 1988/89 survey of households in
the eight larger Greek cities we identified the following major
forms with the corresponding percentages of owner-occupiers
that received such help in the process of acquiring their present
home:

(1) Inheritance of dwelling: 5.1 per cent

(2) Inheritance of land plot: 3.9 per cent

(3) Parental gift of dwelling: 14.8 per cent

(4) Parental gift of land plot: 7.5 per cent

(5) Substantial cash contribution
    in buying/building a dwelling: 4.9 per cent
    _____

    Total (1) – (5):   36.2 per cent
    _____

To these we may justifiably add two other major forms of
'outside' assistance in securing home ownership. First, the
process of 'antiparochi', i.e. the exchange arrangements between
owners of land and developers whereby the owner receives in
place of the land price a part of the product and uses the whole
or part of it for owner occupation. This form, given the fact
that properties bought at a certain time 'mature' for intensive
(small-scale) speculative development at a much later stage, is
essentially based on inheritance and family gifts. Second, the
occupation of a dwelling free of charge. Most of these cases are,
obviously, based on the use of family properties though there
might be some limited over-reporting of this category due to
cases of genuine renters making tax-avoiding agreements with
the owners. Let us add these types to the previous ones:

(6) Real gains ('antiparochi'):   5.3 per cent

(7) Free use: 7.8 per cent
    _____

    Total (1) – (7):   49.3 per cent
    _____

To these cases we may also add the better part of the large
group of people who have financed the acquisition of their
dwelling by the sale of some other piece of real estate. This is
a very substantial category, nearly an additional 10 per cent

(9.3 per cent) of home owners (DEPOS 1989, Tables 9.3 and 9.10). Arguably most of these cases were based on properties transferred from the family. However, since the ownership of some piece of real estate may be part of the process of wealth accumulation of the household we cannot be sure of the extent of direct family transfers in this case. Nevertheless, certainly a large part is immediately relevant to our argument. In combination with the above cases (1) to (7), it justifies the general estimate that *more than 50 per cent of owner occupiers have received substantial wealth transfers from their family.*[11] In contrast, only 20 per cent of owners have had the benefit of a mortgage loan in the process of acquiring or building a dwelling (DEPOS 1989, Tables 9.3, 9.10).

This high incidence of family assistance and wealth transfers is to a very large extent similar across the socioeconomic class spectrum; there is also, however, a noticeable inverse relationship of the role of family transfers with class position. In Table 9.2, we have a broad division of households in Athens according to the occupation of the head. In both wealth gifts (cases 3 to 5) and inheritance (1 and 2) the share of owner-occupiers receiving such help increases as we move from the more comfortable middle class to the lower middle class and the working class. In all cases we have included the respective pensioner category in order to abstract from the lifecycle factor. Category 4 in Table 9.2 is a special case composed mainly by a mixed group of households headed by students and non-employed women. Here the role of family help is markedly lower. The exception to the rule is 'Real Gains', the third column in the table showing properties acquired through 'antiparochi'. This is strongly associated with more central areas of better value and middle class population.

As in the case of home ownership in general, there is a much stronger differentiation in the extent of family assistance and transfers when we examine the pattern along the lifecycle axis (Table 9.3). In the case of wealth gifts there is a clear-cut downward curve of the share of owners who received such help from a high 43 per cent in younger households with heads below 35, to 12 per cent in those with heads over 64. Inheritance also shows a significant negative relationship with age but a less steep one since the probability of inheriting increases with age. Lastly, the role of real gains from the development of property ('antiparochi') acts in the opposite direction again, increasing

Table 9.2 Extent of family assistance by household class, Athens 1988

Occupational class	Wealth gifts (%)	Bequests (%)	R. gains (%)	Total (%)
Professional, managerial, middle-level services, higher-level sales, pensioners of same categories (20.6 %)*	20.3	7.6	5.5	33.5
Clerical, middle-level sales, foremen and senior craftsmen, pensioners of same categories (20.7 %)	22.1	8.1	5.0	35.3
Lower-level sales and services, skilled workers and craftsmen, unskilled workers, farmers, pensioners of same categories (40.3 %)	25.8	9.2	3.8	38.9
Other non-gainfully employed (18.4 %)	15.7	6.8	3.7	26.3
TOTAL (100.0 %)	22.0	8.3	4.4	34.7

Note: * In parentheses, the per cent share of the group in the total of owner-occupiers.
'R. gains' refers to dwellings aquired through the 'antiparochi' system of land development.

with the age of the head. The sum total of these patterns, taking also into account the other forms not presented in Table 9.3, is that family transfers are the basis of most of home ownership among young households, between half and two-thirds of those in the 35–44 group, nearly half of those in the 'mature' ages 45–64, and more than one-third of those in retirement age.

It is clear from the data presented in Table 9.3 that by the time households pass the 'mature' stage of their lifecycle, the predominant means by which most have achieved home ownership is personal savings. Envisaging a process where all households save and accumulate through their lifecycle towards the state achieved by the vast majority of people in retirement age, some succeed in reaching this desired state much earlier than others. It is quite evident that the most important factor in this difference in timing is family transfers. Seen from another point, these transfers

Table 9.3 Extent of family assistance by lifecycle stage, Athens 1988

Age of household head	Wealth gifts (%)	Bequests (%)	Gains (%)	Total (%)
Up to 34 years (10.4%)*	42.7	11.9	2.1	56.7
35–44 years (18.6%)	28.5	9.5	3.5	41.5
45–54 years (22.7%)	21.6	7.5	3.4	32.6
55–64 years (25.5%)	18.1	7.8	4.5	30.5
65 and over (22.7%)	12.1	6.8	7.0	25.9
TOTAL (100.0 %)	22.0	8.3	4.4	34.7

Note: * In parentheses, the per cent share of the group in all owner-occupiers.

introduce a major force of social differentiation among younger households which, in contrast, is not present in the class structure. In fact, it seems to favour lower-income classes, in numbers at least if not in terms of value of assets transferred.

It is also clear in Tables 9.2 and 9.3 that the main form of the transfer of resources from the family to the household is 'gifts' or what the Greek legal system considers 'parental subventions'. When not a money transfer, these are a special category of real-estate transfer (to which dowries have been subsumed) treated in a particular and favourable way by tax law. Such 'subventions' are especially prevalent in the earlier stages in the lifecycle. The role of inheritance is clearly important but certainly more limited in the numbers involved. This raises the question of the source of these transfers and their role in the behaviour of the parents' household vis-à-vis saving and accumulation. It is obvious that the provision of substantial help to offspring is a major factor in the saving and accumulation plans of a great number of households. We are certainly justified in considering it a widespread social norm. On the other hand, however, the actual role of intentional saving for the purpose of transferring wealth to the next generation during its early and middle stages in the lifecycle must be judged much more limited than current Greek folklore would have us believe. While parental gifts are predominant among the newly formed households (up to 34 years in Table 9.3), they reach relatively few people given the small share of owner-occupiers in this group. Among households in middle stages in the lifecycle where the bulk of home ownership is formed, substantial parental gifts benefit fewer than one in four.

Moreover, only a part of these, certainly less than 50 per cent, is based on a savings effort. Most, we could safely say, are based on inherited or transferred real-estate wealth.[12] Thus, the role of planned saving under constrained resources in order to provide for the housing of the next generation is very limited when this is most needed. Its role is much more important as a constant underlying objective of the general saving behaviour throughout a household's lifetime.

Given the cost and value of home ownership, these dramatic differences in the first stages of the lifecycle between the lucky ones who achieve ownership early and the unfortunate ones who have to struggle paying rent *and* save for additional extensive periods, must surely be reflected in the outcome: in the final housing conditions achieved as well as in the more broader set of assets that the household has accumulated or failed to. This aspect of the matter has not, to my knowledge, been raised or examined in the literature, though it has an obvious relevance. Let us then examine the impacts and implications of being among the haves and the have-nots in the process of family assistance in the form of wealth transfers. We will proceed in two stages: first, we will examine the differences among owner-occupiers and, second, the differences between owners and renters in otherwise similar groups. The main object of interest will be the material conditions of households and their assets and resources in a broad sense with a view to covering major aspects of wealth as well as consumption. In a later section we will examine some broader impacts and implications for the housing system and Greek society more generally.

IMPACTS OF FAMILY TRANSFERS: DIFFERENCES IN CONDITIONS AND HOUSEHOLD ASSETS AMONG HOME OWNERS

What aspects should we include in a comparison between home owners who had the benefit of family wealth transfers and those who did not? I think we should take a broad view, including everything that requires a major long-term saving and invest-ment effort, and the possession of which is near-universally valued – that is, everything from major consumer durables to the means of raising children and giving them a good education. The list must obviously take into account local conditions in terms of costs as well as in terms of social value: a good private car should be a major item in this list in the Greek context because of its cost; a second house in the country should also be included because of its high valuation by people in Greek cities but also because of its high cost. Conversely, we should also compare differences in the opposite of saving and investment – namely, current consumption expenditures. In this analysis I have examined the following items using data from the DEPOS 1988/1989 survey:

1 Housing floorspace (square meters) per household member
2 Value of the occupied dwelling (as estimated by the owners themselves)
3 Ownership of a second or vacation home
4 Ownership of a private car
5 Available financial resources. This is in response to a question about the amount that the household would be prepared to advance for buying a better house if conditions were attractive. Obviously, a rather problematic variable, but, nevertheless, it may represent major differences in money wealth.
6 Monthly consumption expenditures ('cost of living for the household')
7 Number of children
8 Number of children in higher education (including those in technical colleges)

I have compared the average value or incidence of these variables for home owners with and without family assistance of any form (cases 1 to 7 above) for each group in a five by four matrix constructed by a combination of five major occupational classes and four lifecycle stages of the household according to the occupation and age of the head. Thankfully, we do not have the space or the time here to present all the tedious statistical material involved, and the results must, as a matter of necessity, be summary as well as largely qualitative.[13]

The main, and in my view quite surprising, result of the analysis is that *in all of these variables* there is no significant difference between owner-occupiers with family help and those without. There were some minor exceptions to this rule but there were also exceptions in the opposite direction. The most important result, from the point of view of this analysis, is that material housing conditions measured by housing floorspace per capita show no significant differences among owners that are in very different circumstances with respect to family-wealth transfers. The only group that seems to benefit directly by such transfers in terms of significantly improved conditions (by less than 20 per cent however) are the younger working-class households (age of head less than 35). In the case of lower-middle-class households there is also a slight benefit in terms of space in the lifecycle stages up to maturity but this is balanced in the aggregates by the fact that households living in inherited dwellings have much lower space amenities than average. More generally, comparing the various forms of family assistance and transfer of wealth, inheritance is associated with somewhat worse present housing conditions of the recipients while real capital gains in the form of 'antiparochi' are in the majority of cases associated with better conditions. All other forms show no significant effects either way. Moreover, in terms of the perceived capital value of the occupied property, those that *have not received family help* of any kind seem to be living in significantly better-valued properties on the whole.

With respect to the other variables examined, be they consumption items or more important aspects of a family's life, there are no significant differences save for the fact that in some aspects those without the benefit of family help seem to have achieved *more* than average. Thus, aside from the value of dwellings mentioned above, home owners in the middle and lower middle class have a somewhat higher average of financial resources available for new housing while the households in the lower middle class and the working class have a relatively better average of students in higher and technical education compared with households that had the benefit of family help and are, presumably, at an advantage in terms of the opportunity to accumulate resources for these purposes. These more lucky households show slightly improved indices in one respect, namely the average number of children per household unit.

Equally importantly, home-owner households in the two groups differing with respect to family assistance and wealth transfers show no significant inequalities in the level of current monthly consumption expenditures. It could be argued that the influence of family help would be more significant *before* the achievement of home ownership rather than after. If this were true it should be reflected in the housing conditions at least of the two categories of households. In fact, the housing conditions of owners with some family help before the move to owner-occupation were essentially similar to the prior conditions of owners without any help.

The pattern observed in the comparison between the recipients of family help and wealth transfers and the non-recipients is illustrated in Figure 9.1, constructed with data for Athens. Social groups are arranged along the x-axis as combinations of the occupational class and lifecycle stages of the head of the household in a ranked order from class 1 to 5 and lifecycle stages 1 to 4. Thus, group 2.3, for example, is class 2 (lower-middle) and age 45–64 following the categories in Table 9.1. Occupational classes have been expanded to 5 by separating the numerous and distinctly low-income category of pensioners of class 4 (working-class) in a group on its own. The diagram compares the average for each group of owning a private car, owning a second house for vacations or weekends and the average amount of financial assets available for buying a new house in the two cases of recipients of help and transfers and the non-recipients in each class/lifecycle group. The base of comparison are the non-recipients: their situation is represented by the horizontal line at point 1.0 in the y-axis. The averages for the recipients have been transformed into indices representing deviations from those of the non-recipients, to facilitate comparisons. Index values above 1 represent higher levels of asset ownership while those lower than 1.0 worse conditions. Missing parts of the line diagrams are due to insufficient data.

It is obvious that the overall pattern is one of seemingly random fluctuations around the horizontal line representing non-recipients. There are certain sharp deviations in particular groups but these do not have any coherent structure. Group 2.4 (lower middle class, age 65+) shows lower values in all three indices, especially in available financial resources. This is not so in groups 1.4 and 3.4 where, in fact, we have relatively better conditions. Category 5 (non-employed heads) which does not fit well in a class-related ranking order, presents some extreme variations but these are mainly due to the small statistical values of the indices. Thus, we may justifiably say that within the owner-occupation category no systematically better conditions can be observed for the beneficiaries of help and transfers. As we noted, this pattern is repeated in all the other indices with limited exceptions that are arguably special cases. In effect, then, abstracting from class and lifecycle influences and exceptionally large wealth transfers

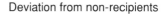

Deviation from non-recipients

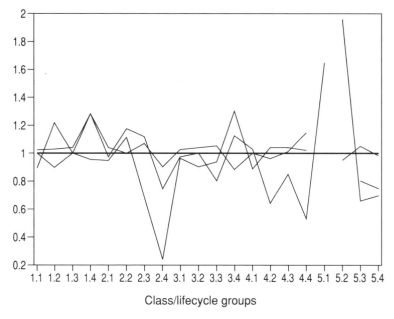

Class/lifecycle groups

Figure 9.1 Variation in assets by occupational class/lifecycle group

(such as 'antiparochi'), both categories of home owners seem to follow essentially similar trajectories in terms of consumption and achieved levels of wealth, in most important aspects at least, and tend to live in relatively similar conditions. This is true for housing, both main and secondary residence, but also for other major items of lifetime investment such as securing higher education for children.

These results can hardly be reconciled with the neoclassical 'equilibrium' lifecycle model of wealth accumulation represented by relationships (1) and (2) in our theoretical preliminaries. In a strict version of such a model, similar housing wealth at the equilibrium stage implies similar *total* wealth. Thus, we must assume that the presence of family-wealth transfers makes no difference in terms of total wealth among home owners. This is, obviously, not very credible. Even for the cases that might be considered as *tending* towards the equilibrium stage, there must be some significant observable differences in consumption and other wealth items. Again, the results do not show any such systematic differences. Lastly, even if we assume that owner-occupied housing as well as the other items reviewed here are not directly determined by total wealth but are formed as first priorities, there must have been, according to such a 'weak' equilibrium model, important differences in saving and therefore in consumption which, as we have seen, is not the case. We must conclude, then, that the evidence on the impact of transfers leans towards the alternative 'disequilibrium' model of saving and consumption, though to its less radical versions that incorporate certain elements of planned saving for housing. Clearly, if housing and the accumulation of basic wealth items were the result of whatever savings and windfalls remained after striving to sustain a level of consumption, conditions among owners would show much greater differences. If, however, owned housing and the other items reviewed are basic priorities akin to socially necessary consumption given available resources, we may have both the uniformity observed in these items and current consumption as well as differences in total wealth as implied by the presence of transfers.

IMPACTS: THE CONDITION OF RENTERS

Thus, the surprising uniformity among home owners despite radically different life histories in terms of having the benefit of substantial family help or other wealth transfers, points to some far-reaching theoretical implications. We will turn to these shortly. In a very simple and socially resonant way, however, the empirical evidence and its corollaries imply that the non-recipients of help among home owners have been in some way equally successful or lucky in a manner that is equivalent to or compensates for the lack of family assistance or inherited wealth. It follows that home owners as a whole enjoy the benefits of improved access to wealth not by virtue of the (tautological) fact that they are home owners, but due to advantageous prior conditions that lead to higher levels of wealth in more forms than simple owner-occupation which is but a part, albeit a major one, of household wealth. If this is so, it also follows, given the universal norm of owner-occupation in the Greek context, that renters are the relevant group to compare in the matter of wealth accumulation and that, abstracting from lifecycle factors, renters are most probably households that are systematically handicapped vis-à-vis access to or success in accumulating wealth in general including, of course, housing.

The evidence seems to bear this out. We repeated the previous comparisons of possession of various items of wealth, living conditions and achievements such as having children in higher education, this time for home owners and renters. In almost all items and most class and lifecycle groups, renters showed worse indices. In some respects the differences involved were limited. In some other major aspects, however, the differences were substantial and strongly supportive of a hypothesis of significant underlying inequalities in access to wealth.

Figure 9.2 shows some of the most important differences between the tenure groups. The horizontal line at point 1.0 on the y-axis in Figure 9.2 represents in this case the average values for renters. The fluctuating lines represent the deviation from this base line of averages for owner-occupiers as a whole for every class and lifecycle group. The latter are arranged hierarchically along the x-axis. In this case we only included the three main class groups 1–3 in Table 9.2 with pensioners incorporated in the group from which they originated. Three 'asset' items are compared: ownership of a car, ownership of a second house and the average number of children in higher education.[14] The latter are represented by the broken line since only values for age groups 3 and 4 are, obviously, significant.

In contrast to the comparison between the two sub-groups of home owners in Figure 9.1, in this case the lines of deviation from the level of renters are mostly above the base line showing in most cases substantial inequalities in favour of owners with differences that often reach extreme levels in the order of 50 per cent or 100 per cent. These, most significantly, are more pronounced in the groups belonging to classes 2 and 3 (lower middle and working class) where inequalities in access to wealth between the two tenure forms seem to have a major negative impact on chances for succeeding in such universally valued lifetime projects as giving higher education to your offspring or having a vacation house and a car. Ownership of a private car shows the most consistent inequalities – the respective line is above the renters' level and seems to follow an upward trend as we move down the class hierarchy and upwards to older-age households. Differences in the possession of second, vacation housing appear more erratic with most owners in the more

Deviation from renters

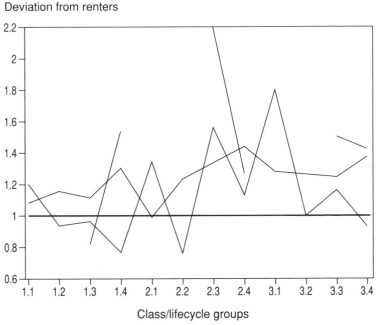

Figure 9.2 Variation in assets by tenure and class/lifecycle group

comfortable middle class having lower levels of ownership, albeit to a small extent. Home owners in age groups 2 to 4 (35+) in the working class similarly show essentially equal average levels with renters. It is lifecycle groups 3 and 4 (45–64, 65+) of the lower middle class (groups 2.3, 2.4 in Figure 9.2) and all class groups of 'young' households (heads up to 34) that show a substantial advantage of home owners in the possession of a second house. These cases shift the overall balance towards a pattern of inequality favouring home owners.

I find the inequalities between home owners and renters in Figure 9.2 in the average number of students in higher education the most significant and the most telling. Arguably the most talked-about issue in modern Greek sociology is the significance of higher education in both the social and political structure.[15] Two aspects of this larger issue are crucial here: first, the fact that achieving entrance into higher education for one's offspring is a goal of major significance in Greek society in that it secures both a certain social status and enhanced opportunities for secure

employment, mainly in the state; second, that this goal is important for all social classes and opportunities for its realisation
are relatively widespread. Thus, even among working-class
and farmer households, a lifetime 'investment' aiming at securing
higher education for their children is a major priority. This is
certainly more so for the lower middle class which is largely
dependent on opportunities for public-sector employment. Conversely, any substantial inequalities in terms of access to higher
education signify a major disadvantage in the context of the
Greek social structure. In the light of these wider ramifications,
the differences between home owners and renters in the averages
of children in higher education shown in Figure 9.2 indicate
major inequalities in lifetime resources. With the exception of
one case (group 1.3), home owners show radically higher rates
of achievement in this respect – typically more than 40 per cent
above the rates achieved by renters in the same class and age
group. In the case of lower-middle-class households in the
'mature' 45–64 age group, the difference in rate is more than 100
per cent.

In terms of living conditions and consumption levels, renters
show limited differences from the home owners in the same
class/age group. Nevertheless, these differences are always in the
direction that favours the owner-occupiers indicating a consistent
negative pressure in the everyday financial situation of renters.
We do not have enough space to examine the material in any
detail but a few major points are necessary.

First, renter groups have consistently less housing floorspace
per household member than the similar owner groups despite
the fact that it is relatively easier financially to improve space
standards by an equivalent rent increase than to accumulate the
equivalent capital for owning more space (given, of course, that
few people receive loans). Home owners enjoy more space by
percentages that vary between 3 per cent and 20 per cent in the
various groups with a simple numerical average of +12 per cent
for class 1, +6 per cent for class 2 and +9 per cent for class 3. In
the last case, working-class households, the worst conditions are
found in renters in the 65+ lifecycle group, a difference of +20 per
cent in favour of owners. These inequalities in conditions are in
point of fact somewhat larger: home owners have in all groups
larger average numbers of household members by about 5 per
cent to 10 per cent. Given the well-known economies of scale that

apply in the relationship between housing space and household size, their conditions per capita should have been slightly worse, other things being equal.

Second, this difference in household size, though small, is also indicative of negative economic pressures. More importantly, it is due to a reduced average number of children in the case of renters. Again the differences are small but consistent. Home owners showed higher numbers of children in ten of the twelve class/age sub-groups in the three social classes.

Lastly, the average levels of monthly consumption expenditures in the various sub-groups were essentially similar in both owners and renters with the exception of the last age group (65+) in classes 1 and 3 where owners enjoyed levels of consumption higher by about 30 per cent.[16] The differences in the older age group are understandable: home owners at that stage need not keep saving as in previous stages in the lifecycle. The similarity of expenditure levels between renters and owners in the other age groups is perplexing at first glance. It is a fact, however, that is quite understandable in the context of the 'disequilibrium' model of consumption where saving is essentially residual and the preservation of necessary consumption expenditures is paramount. If the planned equilibrium wealth model applied we would have much higher saving and greatly reduced consumption expenditures. From another viewpoint, of course, we do have substantial differences in *real consumption* between tenures. For an economic comparison to be valid we must either add to the consumption level of owners an amount equal to the imputed rent of their dwelling or, alternatively, we must deduct paid rent from the consumption of renters. Given that according to the data of the 1988 DEPOS survey, rent covered about 20–25 per cent of the declared total of household expenditures, we have a similar gap in the consumption levels of the two tenures. This is not balanced by mortgage payments on the part of owners since less than 15 per cent have received a loan. This major gap implies that consumption of other items – mainly essentials – is reduced in the case of renters by an equivalent amount. Moreover, to the extent that renters try to keep their living standards in line with those of the majority of the socially similar, their capacity to save towards owner-occupation or other lifetime projects is greatly handicapped. It is these strong negative pressures that account, of course, for the inequalities in various indices of wealth and social achievement we have been examining. For those who remain renters by the time they reach 65+ (who, presumably, by a process of selection are the least economically successful within their class), the inequalities in living conditions in comparison to owners if we deduct rent payments from consumption, are striking: in sub-groups 1.4 (middle class, 65+) and 3.4 (working class, 65+) there is a gap in consumption expenditures of more than 50 per cent.[17]

CONCLUDING POINTS: THE SOCIOECONOMIC SIGNIFICANCE OF THE FAMILY ASSISTANCE SYSTEM

It is evident that, in the Greek case, nearly one in two home owners have the benefit of some form of substantial family help in wealth transfers in money or real property. I include in this most cases of having a dwelling free of rent as well as most cases of financing the acquisition of a house through the sale of other property. For households in the earlier stages of the lifecycle the beneficiaries are the large majority. Obviously, there is a very strong social norm dictating that families accumulate wealth and at some moment transfer a large part of it to their offspring while these, in turn, do the same for the next generation. Is this norm and the associated values and obligations *binding* to the extent that households will shape their behaviour accordingly?[18] While we have no direct evidence, the implication of the economic model that seems more appropriate to the data suggests that this is not the case. Families, it seems, are prepared to offer help to the extent that their own priority objectives have been reached and favourable economic circumstances permit the accumulation of wealth beyond this level. Moreover, if the provision of some minimal help (though adequate for housing acquisition) was a binding norm, we would observe significantly worse living standards due to a higher savings effort among those home owners with no benefit of wealth transfers themselves. Renters in middle and older ages would have even more restricted consumption budgets if they were to comply with a strong version of this norm. To put it simply, it is true that Greek households save and accumulate in order to help their descendants and leave bequests, but in a weaker and less deter-minant and constraining sense than the social myth implies.

It may be objected that we are making too fine a point that has no significant bearing on the overall pattern. On the contrary: this is essential for understanding both the forces that shaped the pattern in the last decades and the current trends and prospects. From the point of view of our analysis, the prevailing structure and incidence of family assistance and transfers is, in the last instance, not only a result of a social norm but also, to a very great extent, the result of the favourable economic trends in the postwar period. It is the fact of continuous economic growth and widespread capital gains on land and property that permitted the extensive household accumulation on which the help system was based. Greek society has a lot of characteristics that predispose for a strong norm for saving, namely the small-holding peasant economy from which most urban dwellers originate, the high share of small proprietors and businesses in the urban sector, and the economic uncertainties resulting from an underdeveloped social security and insurance system. However, the simple facts of very high income growth rates in the 1960s and 1970s and the land value gains due to urbanisation, economic growth and tourism can easily account for high savings rates in the context of a 'disequilibrium' model with no particular reliance on a hypothesis of strong cultural norms for saving. The much weaker norm according to which windfalls and excess income relative to current consumption are for the most part put into savings, is quite enough.

For the same reasons, we should expect both savings and family assistance to decrease in adverse economic conditions. There are indications that this was already happening in the 1980s. Our simple alternative model, in contrast to the 'equilibrium' wealth model, suggests that the savings rate will not decline as higher levels of wealth are attained. It also suggests that under conditions of economic stability people will keep on saving at a similar rate unless their accustomed or socially expected standard of living is threatened. These implications explain quite sufficiently the pattern of the 1980s when growth was minimal while for certain periods there were decreases in real incomes. During this time we saw a tendency for the persistence of the high savings rates achieved after continuous increases in the previous two decades. We also saw, however, decreases in the saving rate when real incomes fell. More significantly, we observed during the 1980s a major shift away from the investment of household savings in real property assets towards newly introduced forms of high-yield and high-security assets such as high-interest bonds and debentures backed by the state (Emmanuel 1990). This again indicates that the norm of accumulating housing property for the sustenance of the extended family system is not only susceptible to pressures from adverse economic conditions but, also, to pressures from strong income-producing alternatives.

The latter point deserves some further comments. It can be very plausibly argued that the postwar system of family assistance and wealth transfers in the field of housing was based, aside from favourable economic trends, on the prevailing tendency among households to place their savings in real property, mainly housing and land as opposed to other assets. These real assets were added to household wealth that was already predominantly based on such real holdings, be they in urban areas or the countryside. We found occasion in the beginning of this paper to mention the widespread influence of theories of housing 'overinvestment' in the Greek context and the important role assigned to motives for family assistance in these theories. I would not dispute the fact that there is some value in this line of argument. I have used it often myself. It is worth insisting, however, that in a wider perspective the line of determination goes the other way as well: were it not for the economic and institutional conditions that made for the predominant role of housing and land in the investment plans of households, due to an important extent to the absence of antagonistic alternatives for most of the postwar period, the system of family help would not have been as extensive and important.[19] It is equally important to note that were it not for the near-permanent background of public policies that encouraged the investment of small family savings, though not always of business capital, in housing assets and the realisation of capital gains from land development, the family-help system would, again, not be as extensive.

There has also been, of course, substantial direct support of the family-help system by state policies in the field of housing and urban development. Aside from the common legal forms of inherited wealth, gifts and donations, the Greek legal and tax systems offer special treatment to family-wealth transfers aimed at helping the next generation to form a household. Up to the early 1980s this meant dowries. The reform of family law towards equal rights regardless of sex, introduced the wider institution of parental gifts or subventions which are taxed much more favourably than property transfers from inheritance. Thus, there are strong incentives to transfer wealth to one's descendants well before old age. Moreover, town-planning law and practice is suffused with the concept that individual land plots are for housing an extended family rather than a single household: land development controls and building regulations are structured accordingly. In addition to this set of direct or indirect public subsidies the new home owner has the benefit of the considerable general tax and credit subsidies offered to those acquiring a dwelling for the first time. By liquidating the real wealth that a family intends for its offspring in order to finance the acquisition or building of a new dwelling, the beneficiaries can secure access to the full range of state supports and subsidies. Needless to say, these add up to very substantial amounts that are disproportionately higher than the limited tax subsidies provided for renters.[20]

Thus, postwar economic growth, fast urbanisation and the resultant land development gains and highly favourable public policies have been major factors in the expansion and successful reproduction of the family-help system. It can hardly be denied, of course, that the system has deep roots in Greek social structure and that it involves a complex web of social relationships, norms and habits that are equally crucial determinants. We do not have the space in this paper to examine the other side of the family-help system, namely the housing behaviour and housing problems of young and newly formed households as well as the dependency on and obligations towards parents that are either results or essential elements of the system. These structures may have many problem-ridden aspects[21] but they also help sustain the social prevalence of the family-help system. I would insist, however, on the importance of the 'material' preconditions and determinants suggested by the foregoing analysis as a corrective of reification and overblown functionalistic accounts of the structural significance of the family system that view it as an overarching major determinant not only of the housing system but of the Greek class structure and political system as well. More importantly, the results of our analysis of the impacts of family assistance and wealth transfers among home owners and between owners and renters have shown that from the point of view of housing conditions and opportunities, the more important dividing line is between those with some access to wealth, family-provided or otherwise, and those without. The quasi-ideological insistence on the role of the family system with its value-ridden and myth-suffused associations hinders the recognition of this more important fact and a more realistic and thorough critique of prevailing housing policies.

More broadly, our analysis suggests that housing theory should not only place more emphasis on the role of family help and wealth transfers but go a step further and give a prominent role to wealth differentials in general and most especially in relation to tenure structures and their effects on the shaping of households' lives. There has been a lot of spurious discussion, most prominently among British sociologists, about the role of tenure as such in shaping social and political behaviour along distinct sectoral divisions. It has rightly been suggested that tenure divisions are essentially reducible to more important income and class differences.[22] This approach may be relatively adequate for economies and housing systems with developed, modern mortgage-credit structures – economies, that is, where wages and salaries are the near-exclusive base for a household's lifetime resources and household sectors that, largely as a result, depend on credit as the main avenue to home ownership. However, even in such societies the role of differentials in access to wealth are much more important than is currently recognised. In less 'pure' capitalist formations, where ownership of capital is more diffused and underdeveloped credit structures or permanently high inflation are present, the role of wealth differentials should certainly be a major preoccupation of housing research.

NOTES

1 For the comparative statistics in this section see OECD 1991. See also Ministry of Housing (Netherlands), *Statistics on Housing in the European Community*, 1991. It should be noted that personal savings flow directly into the housing sector in Greece in more than one sense. Aside from the limited role of financial institutions in the buying of dwellings, business and institutional finance play an even less important role in housing production itself. For one thing, about a third of urban housing is owner-built; moreover, speculative builders are very small with limited capital and no access to bank finance; thus, production is mostly financed by advance sales of the unfinished properties i.e. by the savings of the final users.

2 It makes no sense to go over the vast literature on household consumption and saving at this point. I have mainly consulted Bruce Johnson (1971), Marglin (1984) and Koutsouveli (1985). Marglin's 'disequilibrium' model of saving also belongs to this group of non-neoclassical theories and is similar to the 'habit-persistence' model though in a rather more radical form deriving from the neo-marxian and neokeynesian emphasis on the limited saving capacity of workers.

3 In contrast, lifecycle models of rational maximisation of the utility derived from consumption and wealth with good foreknowledge of lifetime prospects, are a product of more prosperous and optimistic times or, perhaps, as someone (Marglin) said, a generalisation of the economic experiences of tenured academics.

4 Emmanuel, 1979, 1981. It should be added, however, that these works were exclusively based on medium and long-term econometric analyses of empirical data which are, of course, very susceptible to alternative interpretations, especially so for periods of continuous growth. An econometric analysis attempted at a later time with full consideration of short-term factors (Emmanuel, 1987a) showed quite a strong resistance to accommodate the formalism derived from the previous models which determined housing investment by current savings. I found that simple lagged disposable income was a much more appropriate determinant. This is not conclusive either way but suggests a much greater importance of short-term behaviour and economic constraints.

5 My 1979 and 1981 formulations follow in essence Bruce Johnson's 'endogenous income' hypothesis (1971) where both consumption and wealth enter a utility function optimised (planned) over the house-hold's lifetime. Bruce Johnson advances two versions of this model: a simple one and a more complex one with income-producing wealth (hence the 'endogenous income' term). I have abstracted from this factor which was not relevant for the bulk of Greek households in the 1970s.

6 See Emmanuel 1979, Table D.4. The positive trend in the second half of the 1970s and the 1980s comes as a bit of a surprise given the much worse economic record of these years compared to 1958–74. Housing policy during the last 15 years was favourable to owner-occupation but it can certainly not be the responsible factor except in a small way by mainly permitting and encouraging a modest expansion of mortgage credit. This is not the place to attempt a systematic explanation of these trends but I would venture the opinion that the main cause has been a negative one: the lack of urban growth in comparison to the previous years. Stable or slightly declining urban population after the mid-1970s permitted for the first time the steady accumulation of household wealth without the pressure imposed by the needs of incoming people. It was for the same reason that housing standards improved during the 1980s despite stagnant incomes per capita. For policies and trends during the 1980s, see Emmanuel 1990.

7 The decrease in the role of the owner-built housing sector which in

the past has greatly helped the reproduction of high rates of land and housing ownership by lower incomes may have also been important. For this argument see Maloutas 1990.

8   See among others, Ball 1983, Kemeny 1981, Saunders 1990. To show the extent of the differences: by 1985 in Britain, about 88 per cent of professionals, employers and managers owned their home (10–17 per cent outright); in the case of semi-skilled manual and service workers we had 46 per cent were owners and in the case of the unskilled, 33 per cent.

9   Given the extensive availability of mortgage credit to young households in advanced economies, this aspect has received scant attention, to the benefit of class and (of all things) spatial factors. I find this a sign of bad and biased analysis and certainly a sign of bad economics and bad sociology. The lifecycle model of saving is by far the most well-known and debated theory in household economics. Nevertheless, in more than 400 pages devoted to home ownership, Peter Saunders does not devote even one table to this crucial relationship. Judging from official British statistics (Ball 1983, 275), there is quite a significant increase in ownership up to the 35–44 group and then a gradual decrease. More importantly, the extent of outright ownership and more generally the burden of debt shows a dramatic near-exponential decrease with age. Why these matters deserve so little attention is beyond my grasp and must have to do with the peculiarities of modern urban sociology.

10 Forrest and Murie 1989 and the material and review of available literature for Britain in Saunders 1990, 158–61. While these issues have received much more attention in Greece, there has been little systematic data and analysis. This has been substantially rectified by reports from two large-scale surveys undertaken in 1986 by the National Centre for Social Research and in the end of 1988 by DEPOS, the Greek Public Corporation for Urban Development and Housing. Some of the relevant material is presented in Maloutas 1990 and DEPOS 1989, 1990. I would like to mention that while I was the Project Manager for the DEPOS research, the chapters on the forms and means of housing acquisition and financing have been written by Efie Strousopoulou. I have consulted her material quite extensively in the initial stages of preparing this paper. The tables and diagrams presented here, however, are based on my calculations from the DEPOS database.

11 Essentially similar results have been reported by the 1986 Sample Survey by the National Centre for Social Research. In the case of Athens, 23 per cent of home owners have acquired their dwelling as inheritance or gift and 12.5 per cent had the extended family finance the acquisition either as a gift (10.1 per cent) or as a loan (2.4 per cent) (Maloutas 1990, Tables 2.5.1 and 2.6.2). These major forms of assistance or transfer add up to 35.5 per cent. If we add the more indirect or more limited in size forms registered in the DEPOS survey, the overall extent of help/transfers should approach 50 per cent.

12 Having a piece of real-estate wealth in addition to one's house is

quite widespread in Greece. Unfortunately, we have nearly no systematic information on this important facet of the system. A mid-1970s survey in a large provincial town found that 84 per cent of households owned some real property. More than 40 per cent of owners of apartments owned at least an additional unit. In the case of owners of houses, on the other hand, who were the majority, only 9 per cent owned additional units. It is well known, however, that additions to houses are a major way of providing for the extended family. In their case the ownership of land and legal or *de facto* development rights is in essence additional wealth (Tsoughiopoulos 1981, 139). The 1986 NCSR housing survey found that 26.8 per cent of households in the eight larger cities owned at least an additional dwelling unit with an average of 1.53 units per household. More than 40 per cent of these units, however, were vacation homes (Kouveli and Kotzamanis 1988, 88).

13 The basic tables examined had 80 cells (20 groups for each case of assistance or no assistance). In some cases, the cells were 160 – when all particular forms of family help (or lack thereof) were considered. Given that the factors involved were mostly non-linear in form, the application of quantitative methods was something I was not prepared to contemplate. Moreover, I strongly believe that statistical multivariate analyses of non-parametric data, such as component or factor analysis, are equivalent to abandoning rational thinking. In contrast, the inspection of multiple-entry tables is a time-honoured technique in sociology that demands clear prior expectations of causal relationships. Unfortunately, the results are, quantitatively speaking, impressionistic. I can live with this. In such complex cases only the very strong effects should be considered valid. These are, by definition, obvious even in simple inspections of complex multiple-entry tables.

14 The third item in Figure 9.1, the amount that households have available for buying a new dwelling as a proxy for financial solvency, has not been included in Figure 9.2. This item is influenced, obviously, not only by the available financial resources but also by the need for acquiring a new unit. In the case of renters this involves the need to change tenure status. Thus, this item is not comparable across tenures. As expected, renters showed substantially higher scores in this variable.

15 Mainly, of course, due to the numerous works of K. Tsoukalas. See, *inter alia*, his *Social Development and State*, Athens, 1981 (in Greek).

16 Incidentally, in this last age group there was also a significant difference in expenditures between recipients and non-recipients of family assistance and transfers. Surprisingly, the recipients of help in these older households show in all classes much lower levels of consumption.

17 It could be said, of course, that this argument concerns very few people. Renters in the 55+ age group are roughly 5 per cent of all households. For the 65+ age group the share is only 2.5 per cent. A substantial number of this group, moreover, are renters by choice.

Thus, those facing the structural disadvantages we describe in the long-run are a tiny minority in Greece. This does not erase the problem but helps explain its limited political and social significance. As I see it, this is socially accepted wretchedness on a grand scale. People are or are supposed to be satisfied with struggling for something between 20 and 40 years for the benefit of being with near-certainty successful in their housing project after 60 with the added pleasure that they can leave something to their children. This is not the time to tackle this issue, but, in my opinion, what we have here is a pure case of ideology in the classic sense of a set of ideas that help reproduce an irrational and unjust social order.

18 I have often criticised theories of Greek housing 'overinvestment' based on the lack of 'alternatives' (cf. Emmanuel 1981, ch. 5) and thus I feel a bit uncomfortable with this argument. However, such theories have essentially been based on a form of counterfactual evidence derived from the experience of developed capitalist countries where 'proper' industrial investment alternatives were presumably present. This is scarcely relevant, of course, for the behaviour of most households as well as historically inaccurate. The presence of a developed market of bonds, securities or debentures (and insurance policies, I would add) is a different story. I used to think that this will not be important for the Greek situation. The experience of the 1980s shows that a reconsideration on my part is in order.

19 In the 1993 Planning Law this has reached absurd levels by introducing a special 'family floorspace coefficient' that legally violates the planning rules in a particular area in order that on even the smallest plot (often originating in an illegal subdivision) one can build at least two standard dwellings, one of them supposedly for the benefit of children.

20 For an analysis of the subsidies system in the 1980s, see Emmanuel 1990.

21 Suffice it to say that Greece most probably has the highest rate in the EEC of young people in their late twenties and early thirties living with their parents and one of the highest averages for the marriage age of men. Equally significant are the extremely low rates, in comparative terms, of cohabitation or single-person households (aside from students) for people in their twenties and thirties and the divorce rate in these ages. Whatever the influence of social values, these statistics clearly indicate limited opportunities for autonomy and household formation in the existing housing system. For these matters, see Emmanuel 1987b.

22 See for example Forrest and Murie 1987, among others.

Chapter 10

Market, state and informal networks in the growth of private housing in Hungary

J. Ladányi

INTRODUCTION

In Hungary housing and other private property increased in importance over the postwar period. This growth occurred despite a policy environment which was initially antagonistic. If we did not know that Soviet-type regimes failed in Albania, Bulgaria, Romania and the Soviet Union itself, where private property had a significantly smaller role than in Hungary or Poland, we would be tempted to reverse the famous words of Karl Marx to read: Communism produced its own enemy, the bourgeois with private property, in its own body. Nevertheless we can still hypothesise that where the bourgeoisie with private property is strongest in a post-communist country, the chances of the revival of any form of communist system are smallest.

THE ROLE OF PRIVATE HOUSING CONSTRUCTION IN THE HOUSING STOCK

The patterns of population growth and tenure change between 1949 and 1989 are outlined in Table 10.1. During the 40 years between 1949 and 1989 the number of flats per 1000 inhabitants increased from 268 to 373 in Hungary. This fairly moderate (40 per cent) increase occurred alongside a very low (15 per cent) increase in the population. The 60 per cent increase in the housing stock was coupled with a 25 per cent decrease in flats rented from the state. The housing stock increased most rapidly between 1970 and 1980 when the housing stock rented from the state had started to decrease. It is this phenomenon which deserves special attention (Farkas and Vajda 1990). Central planning and

Table 10.1 Changes in the housing stock in Hungary 1949–89

	Population in thousands	Annual rate of growth	Housing units in thousands	Annual rate of growth	Housing units per 1000 capita	Rented from state (%)
1949	9205	−0.15	2467	0.3	268	38
1960	9961	0.73	2758	1.1	277	38
1970	10322	0.33	3122	1.2	302	34
1980	10710	0.34	3542	1.2	331	30
1984	10657	−0.10	3774	1.3	354	26
1989	10590	0.14	3951	0.9	373	19

Source: E. János Farkas and Zsuzsa Vajda, 'Housing conditions: state and private housing', in Rudolf Andorka *et al.* (eds), *Social Report*, Budapest, 1990.

redistribution had lost control over a fairly significant part of housing and the most important element of family budgets. This significantly modified ownership relations, changed family budgets and shook fundamental ideological taboos.

In order to cast light on this phenomenon, let me relate a personal experience. At the very end of the 1960s in the middle of the reform processes that swept over all Eastern Europe but advanced farthest in Hungary I wrote one of my essays at Karl Marx University of Economics as a student of housing. I must have asked very inconvenient questions because my professor, a famous financial expert, evidently in order to make me feel a part of the realities of 'existing socialism', sent me to one of the chief officials of the National Planning Office to get more information. When listening to my misconceived questions the 'authorised comrade' burst out in the following way:

> Look, we have been planning a considerable amount of private housing construction since 1956. In each planning period, we plan the share of private housing construction to be one-third, and that of state housing construction to be two-thirds. These proportions become true, by and large, but the other way round. Irrespective of our efforts, two-thirds of new flats are always constructed from private resources, and one-third is constructed by the state. But do not worry – he said – these will be the planned ratios next year!

As we shall see later 'spontaneous trends' were consistently stronger than the 'centrally scientifically planned' ones. The plans had to be changed often, and to a fairly considerable extent. The proportion of total housing construction which was private housing construction exceeded the 'magic two-thirds' for the first time in the early 1970s. But by the early 1980s it exceeded 80 per cent and by the end of the decade it was well over 90 per cent.

In this period not only did the volume and proportion of private housing construction change but also its quality. The vast majority of flats constructed by the state were built in the cities as multi-storey, new housing estates constructed from pre-fabricated elements. In contrast the houses built privately were mostly in the villages, in dispersed settlements using far more traditional technology. These houses did not reach the standards of the new state flats in respect of water supply, sewerage and heating. However, private housing construction exceeded the state in respect of all the other quality indicators. For example, in 1970 12.4 per cent of state-owned flats and 9.1 per cent of private housing consisted of more than two and a half rooms. By 1984 these proportions had changed to 13.6 per cent and 33.4 per cent respectively. The share of private construction companies was (and still is) very small. In 1987 most of private housing construction and reconstruction was carried out by private individuals. State (OTP) loans for private housing construction were basically the same irrespective of whether they were built by private individuals or by small private construction companies. Private companies did not sell dwellings which were constructed by them but only carried out the construction work.

Data showing the number of working hours spent in housing construction and reconstruction indicate the importance of private housing very well. In 1987 17 per cent of total working hours spent in housing construction and reconstruction were worked by workers in state construction companies, 9 per cent by those in small private construction companies, and 74 per cent by private individuals (Farkas and Vajda 1990).

PRIVATE HOUSING CONSTRUCTION AND CENTRALISED REDISTRIBUTION

At the end of the 1940s the Soviet Union forced Hungary to apply the so-called central-planning model of economic management. The basic principle of this system was the separation of ownership of goods and services from the production units, their centralisation, and the redistribution of these centralised goods and services. The living-standard policy that accompanied this system was basically characterised by very low wages, and the centralisation of a part of the real costs of labour into the state budget. This element was used, in principle, to subsidize low wages in different forms. To a great extent the above measures can be explained in terms of social aims – above all the aim of the state to guarantee for all the families a certain part of those goods and services produced which were considered to be basic to equal social chances. The consumer price system developed in this period was in conformity with these objectives (Ladányi 1975). This system separated relative prices from real costs, gave great subsidies to 'basic food' and levied high turnover taxes on clothing, durable consumer goods and other goods considered to be 'non-basic'. In this way a certain minimum standard of living was intended to be guaranteed. At the same time the system of social benefits (mostly benefits in kind) meant that very low charges were payable for public transport, health care and education. The aim of the system was again to grant equal chances of access to certain services for all people, independent of their place in the social hierarchy and their income differences.

By the end of the 1940s the redistributive system embodied in income policy became inseparable from the redistributive system interweaving the whole economy. This is apparent not only from its consequences but also in view of the conditions of its birth. The redistributive system in the economy, through the separation of goods and services from the basic units of the economy, their centralisation and redistribution, served the purposes of forced extensive industrial growth and the preparation of the country for the Third World War, which was considered to be inevitable by the leaders of the country. After the late 1940s and early 1950s against this economic background and in spite of the very limited resources available, the most privileged social groups began to obtain different economic and social advantages for themselves (e.g., hospitalisation under far better conditions than the average, highly subsidised recreation, use of state-owned cars, special supply of certain shortage goods) through the secondary and often hidden redistribution of goods and services. Though no appropriate data are available about the size of advantages obtained this way by the privileged elite it is very likely that the inequalities thus created under the highly egalitarian income conditions and low living standards of the 1950s were similar to, if not greater than those at any time during the period of 'existing socialism'. Thus the extensive social inequalities in the distribution of social benefits cannot be considered to be the consequences of reform communism, and we can in no way speak about their increase as a consequence of the different forms of the economic mechanism. What we are faced with is the phenomenon that before the period of reform, privileges and disadvantages emanated from position in the political hierarchy. Subsequent reform of the economic mechanism mixed this with the logic of economic rationality, and made part of the hitherto hidden differences visible (Ladányi 1976).

This general pattern also applied in housing. Apartment houses and bigger villas were nationalised in the second half of the 1940s. However, single-family houses remained private property because the communists wanted to indicate that small-scale private property was not to be disturbed. The rents of flats in state property were highly subsidised. Consequently the rent paid and the location, size and quality of a rented flat could be completely independent of the income of the family renting the apartment.

What emerged was that where goods were in short supply those social groups which had greater influence on the social process of centralised redistribution were more likely to receive the goods and services. However, where these people were regarded as 'more important members of the society' their status was also expressed by the amount of their salaries and wages (Szelényi 1972). Here we are faced with the redistribution of a part of the national income which results in granting better chances to higher-status and higher-income people through higher state subsidies.

In addition to this, as capital investments into the sphere of production were practically impossible in Hungary until the end of the 1960s and were very difficult (and insecure because of the unpredictable political attitudes towards private investment) until the very end of the communist period, housing was by far the most important among private commodities. However, it is important to mention that for these reasons, and because travelling to 'capitalist' countries was restricted, a very high share (probably the highest in the world) of Hungarian families bought a second home or built one themselves. This second home was often as big as, if not bigger than, the first one. This is quite surprising given the very bad housing conditions characterising main homes in Hungary, but was a rational response to the situation of Hungarian families. We could also say that such irrational investments can only take place in a centrally planned economy.

Private apartments and houses could always be sold and inherited. In the earlier period this involved many restrictions, and from the late 1960s fewer. There was little tax if somebody inherited or sold housing commodity. Characteristically, some private apartments constructed by the OTP from the beginning of the 1960s were called 'apartment for ever' to express family ownership for ever. There was always a strong secondhand housing market, not only for privately owned houses but also for state owned ones. These have been sold and bought illegally or semi-legally. The black-market price of a state apartment was traditionally one half of that for an equivalent privately owned apartment.

The share of private housing ownership has dramatically increased during the late 1980s and early 1990s. State houses/apartments have been sold at a very low price to sitting tenants. There is a strong trend for dwellings in higher-status neighbourhoods and for the better apartments/houses to be sold sooner. As a result, it is often the worst housing stock which has remained the property of the new local councils, and high status families which enjoyed the privileges of housing subsidies have gained another advantage through purchasing their home.

THE INFLUENCE OF PRIVATE HOUSING ON THE EXISTING SYSTEM OF SOCIAL INEQUALITIES

What effect did massive private housing construction have on the pattern of social inequalities developed under the system of centralised redistribution? Who were the people who tried to make their living and operate outside the centralised system of state housing construction and centralised distribution?

As we have already stated, the fact that an increasing number of families tries to solve their housing problems outside the care of the omnipotent state shook fundamental taboos. A Hungarian joke which gives a very good description of the redistributive state consists of two words which in Hungarian are almost the same (with only one letter difference between them: 'osztogato – fosztogato') but which mean 'dispensing' and 'looting' respectively. This questioning of the real nature of the state was very important, especially in the field of the most expensive durable consumer goods.

The ethnographic description of the pioneers of private housing construction was expressed by writers and sociographers well before social researchers who were successfully limited by the social taboos could come to the scene. Essentially this picture was not different at all from that subsequently drawn by more in-depth research and by work which was more embedded in the system of social relations.

A simplified summary of this work indicates that the typical actor of early private housing construction is the young, married 'post-peasant' or 'pre-worker' who, because of the enforced collectivisation of agriculture, either had to stay in the village and commute to the neighbouring city, or, more typically, move to the city. The concept of 'post-peasants' was elaborated by István Márkus (Márkus 1991) in the early 1970s and with this concept he tried to describe the social consequences of Hungarian-type collectivisation, industrialisation and urbanisation, the relative stability of the transitional position between peasantry and the working class and the survival of subsistence farming as a part of household economy.

This very special interpretation of the 'new working class' was worded also in the early 1970s by István Kemény (Kemény 1972). Kemény, when speaking about the 'East-European new working class' referred to the phenomenon that, due to the characteristic features of the Soviet-type economies, the tendencies of changes taking place in the composition of the working class were fundamentally different from the changes taking place in Western Europe at that time, and being disputed by several experts as the issue of the 'new working class' (Mallet 1963; Gorz 1967). Kemény interpreted the individuals and families becoming workers both in geographical and in structural terms as a 'mass on the road', and being on the road is not free from drawbacks and lasting tendencies either.

György Konrád and Iván Szelényi (1971) introduced the concept of 'delayed urbanization'. With this term they tried to explain the systematic delayedness of urbanisation by central planning,

the withdrawal of urban and of general 'non-productive' investments and the redistribution of financial means into the industry
(and the 'productive sphere'). The main losers in this strategy,
the workers living in the countryside were forced to undertake
industrial work in the cities.

'Delayed urbanization' is characteristic of the whole period,
which resulted in an exceptionally high proportion of those who
moved or commuted to the towns from the villages (Ladányi
1977), and in the especially severe housing problems of 'post-
peasants' and 'pre-workers' (Szelényi 1983). As a result of all this,
the key figure of our story sooner or later realised that he would
either never, or only several decades later, obtain any kind of
housing through the channels of central redistribution, and he
started to build his own house. From his very low salary he could
only buy a plot at a faraway place which had no public utilities
and had been used for agricultural purposes earlier. Later
he 'gets' (buys, steals or buys stolen) steel or cement and brick
(according to very moderate estimations, at least one-third of the
houses built this way were built from construction material
stolen from state companies) and a small building (one room, or
one room plus kitchen) without any utilities is soon completed.
In spite of the numerous problems with this building it is possible
to live in it, there is no need to commute long distances, and
there is no need either to pay the extremely high sum required
for renting a room. Our hero does a lot of overtime (at that time
it was the most important, if not the only way for workers to
increase their salaries), spends all weekends and paid holidays
working for several years (Kemény and Kozák 1971) and fighting
with the calculator of norms constantly, he tries to exceed the
norm (Héthy and Makó 1972; Haraszti 1989). In the meantime, he
spends very little, usually eats what he gets 'from home' (from
the village) and restricts all his demands. As a result, if nothing
adverse (illness, divorce, accident or, especially, serious period of
alcoholism) happens, he can again 'get' some more construction
material. The foundations of the 'final house' are dug, the walls
are slowly built and, sooner or later, there will be a roof on the
house as well. However, due to constant lack of cash or loan
finance the construction proceeds very slowly. In the beginning,
no loan at all could be obtained for the construction of one-family
houses. Later, in the 1970s, the loan that could be obtained for
this purpose was much smaller and had much worse terms and

conditions than the loans available for housing construction subsidised by the state and used by higher-status people. Consequently, the one-family houses built by the pioneers were usually built on what were then the least valuable lands. Usually there was no public utility supply and the dwellings were small and of very low standard and took a long time to build. The external plastering was often completed only after between 8 and 10 years, the 'bathroom' had been used as a pantry for a long time and the obligatory balcony still has no fence or railing.

RECIPROCITY

We can summarise this by saying that those who built their family houses in the 'heroic era' spent more on their poorer-quality houses than was the case for higher-status families who obtained free, or almost free state-owned flats through the different, though limited channels of centralised redistribution (Szelényi 1972). This was possible not only because of the high proportion of 'own-labour content' and of the materials 'got', but also because the vast majority of these houses were built by reciprocal exchange of labour ('kaláka'). Kaláka is a widespread form of labour network based on reciprocity. Within this framework it was mainly households rather than individuals who were in contact with each other and the aim was to give and get roughly equal amounts of labour for and from each member of the labour-exchange network over a relatively long period of time (Sik 1988). The new workers forced to build one-family houses brought the traditions of kaláka into the cities and were successful in minimising the money expenditures on the construction of their houses through the application of this type of cooperation. Kaláka made possible the application of highly labour-intensive technologies because in the majority of cases outdated concrete mixers were the closest to high-technology equipment and the main purpose was to minimise cash expenditures and not so much labour in selecting construction materials. However, as the repayment of this type of work is strictly regulated by traditions, the time spent at work by those new workers who did overtime, built their houses for years and did black work as well, was further increased with the repayment of kaláka done for them earlier.

How did all this influence the existing system of social inequalities? Several contradictory theories exist. According to orthodox

Marxists, the centralised redistribution of housing benefits operated as a part of the centrally planned economy and resulted in decreasing inequalities. All the contradictory facts are individual exceptions and are caused by corrupt officials. It is needless to say that this theory has not yet been sustained empirically. In contrast to this Konrád and Szelényi (1971) not only proved that higher-status social groups have systematically better chances to get subsidised state housing, but also that it clearly stems from the logic of centralised redistribution. Their argument was that where services are free (or almost free) an unlimited demand develops. However, as state-owned flats are still limited in number (or more precisely they are limited in number especially due to the fact that they have no real price) they can in no way meet unlimited demand. Consequently, the implementation of a new principle of distribution is unavoidable: the flats are not distributed by need, but by 'social usefulness' and 'merits' of applicants. However, society also tries to remunerate its 'worthy members' with higher salaries. Consequently, central redistribution of housing benefits does not decrease but rather increases social inequalities (Szelényi 1972). Similar tendencies could be detected when analysing the entire redistribution system of social benefits (Ladányi 1975, 1976).

Later, after generalising the above findings, Szelényi came to the theoretical conclusion that redistribution results in the increase, and market mechanisms in the decrease, of social inequalities. As a result, not only will the economy become more effective due to market conditions gaining more ground in Eastern Europe, but the decrease of social inequalities can also be expected. Later, as a consequence of further empirical evidence, Szelényi changed his model again and argued that in every society it is the fundamental system of integration that generates primary inequalities, while the additional scheme of integration corrects the system of inequalities developed in this way. Under conditions of socialism, where redistribution is the 'fundamental scheme' of integration, inequalities are produced by redistribution and the market equalises these inequalities. At the same time, in market economies, exactly the opposite takes place (Szelényi and Manchin 1986). Without trying to criticise the above theories in detail (see Ferge 1986 on this) we examine only the initial theory in this paper. What was the consequence of the appearance, and later the spread of private housing construction for the system of social inequalities developed in the Soviet-type societies?

It is important to clarify the extent to which housing construction activities performed mostly by post-peasants or pre-workers in the period examined can be considered market activities. It is true, on the one hand, that the heroes of our story found the cracks in the redistributive system and they tried to widen these cracks, and in this way they developed the rules of an activity which is fundamentally different from the system of centralised redistribution. On the other hand, it is also true that the houses constructed from stolen or taken materials with kaláka can be considered the products of the market only with great limitations, as the actors in this activity are much more in reciprocal than in market relations with each other.

The theory that existing social inequalities undoubtedly decreased due to early private housing construction in state socialism also has to be specified. The majority of early private house constructors belonged to social groups whose members could not count on getting (within a reasonable period of time) subsidised flats within the framework of centralised state housing distribution. In the end these social groups 'made an advantage of their disadvantage' (Szelényi 1972) and helped themselves to better housing than many of the privileged ones. However, we also note that this way of solving housing problems was, then and since, impossible for those at the very bottom of the social hierarchy. These people were not only the losers in centralised redistribution of housing benefits, but could not make a profit in the housing market either.

OTHER FORMS OF PRIVATE CONSTRUCTION

At the same time, almost parallel with the spread of private housing construction of post-peasants or pre-workers, other forms of private housing construction also appeared. Among them the so-called Savings-Bank (OTP) constructions deserve attention due to the number of flats constructed and privileges obtained this way. The National Savings Bank (which was the only bank at that time and during the whole communist era dealing with housing construction in Hungary) not only monopolised the legal market of new flats, but granted loans on highly favourable terms for the purchase of flats constructed by the Bank.

OTP loans were highly restricted. From the mid-1980s this limit only applied to cheap, subsidised loans. A 'bank loan', with normal bank conditions, could be obtained without limitations. A 'housing need' (which depended on the family size and composition) was identified and theoretically no loan could be given to fulfil higher needs. However, this rule was often violated by high-status families. There was also a maximum limit of OTP loans, and (again only theoretically) one family could only enjoy an OTP loan once 'to fulfil its housing need' in a lifetime. A second OTP loan could only be given if the previous apartment was smaller than the number of rooms 'required' by the size and composition of the family. This rule was also often violated by higher-status families. Characteristically enough professionals could argue that they needed a separate room as a study-room, but the argument of workers working in 3 shifts (that their 'housing need' included a need for a separate room because they must sleep during the day) was not accepted. Most families used more than one loan. OTP loans were often combined with different sorts of state subsidies and loans provided by the company. The number of subsidies and loans was strongly correlated with the social status of the families.

In practice these loans were hidden subsidies as the percentage of interest payable did not depend on demand and supply in the market but on central decisions. While there were a great many families capable of paying the whole purchase price in cash and waiting for the chance to do so, flats were given to families at the top of the bureaucratic hierarchy. These families paid a small fraction of the purchase price in advance and obtained loans on favourable terms. In certain periods favourable loans were coupled with other forms of subsidies (non-repayable grants) which were not permitted for the construction of one-family houses. Later on, highly subsidised flats could be sold or exchanged on the market very profitably. Needless to say, the above tendencies did not decrease the inequalities developed by the bureaucratic hierarchy. Since the end of the 1970s the elite of the post-Stalinist regime was very efficient in changing their bureaucratic privileges into market ones. By then the unsustainability of the equalising effects of market mechanisms became evident.

CONCLUDING COMMENTS

It is evident that private housing construction, and the market in general, did not have clear equalising effects. In reality the market as such does not exist. Only different forms of markets exist. The early housing market of state-socialist economies (if it can be called a market at all) can be considered a market only in a very limited sense of the term, as it was subordinated to the redistributive system and was deeply interwoven with the characteristics of reciprocity.

It also appears that East-European reformists were very naive when (starting from the observation that the slowly developing market economy creates new types of social inequalities and a different hierarchy from the one characteristic of the redistributive economy) they constructed different models of the equalising effects of a market economy. It becomes even more evident nowadays that both redistributive and market allocations follow the logic of the fundamental power and interest relations of the given society and thus it cannot be stated that market allocation is more or less egalitarian than centralised redistribution. The only thing which can be stated quite safely is that, in addition to the fairly similar social effects, centralised redistribution is less efficient as far as the economy in its narrow sense is concerned.

Chapter 11

Home ownership and family wealth in Japan

Yosuke Hirayama and Kazuo Hayakawa

INTRODUCTION

Home ownership is the basic factor in the family's concept of wealth in Japan. Land prices in that country have increased greatly since the end of World War II. The rate of land-price increase has been overwhelming compared with that in other developed countries. It has surpassed the price-rise of goods as well as increases in the level of incomes, and the acquisition of a house and land ownership involve the acquisition of important financial assets. However, ownership of a home in Japan not only provides an asset for the present household but also secures one for the next generation which will inherit it, and involves the buildup of wealth for the family across generations.

The improvement in the housing conditions of the Japanese people since the end of World War II has been made possible by home ownership. However, it is now widely acknowledged that despite Japan being a 'developed nation', housing conditions remain on the whole very poor. Dwellings are small in area, are built at a very high density, often with an inferior environment. They also have high rents and numerous other problems (Hayakawa 1983). The quality of rental housing is particularly poor and for renting families to be able to improve their housing conditions, home ownership remains the only option.

In Europe, public housing and/or the supply of social housing stands with home ownership as a central pillar in housing policy and there is a comprehensive approach to setting housing standards, for housing subsidy systems, for low interest loans, and so on. In contrast, in Japan, housing policy is based on the idea that housing is the individual's responsibility, a personal problem and one that depends solely on the private market. Low-interest loans to those who try to own their own home are a central feature of the government's housing policy. Only a tiny amount of public housing is supplied directly, and there is no subsidy for the construction of private rental housing nor for rents. In this context land prices have risen steadily and people continue to seek to own their home in order to improve their housing conditions and to acquire wealth.

At the end of the 1980s the Nakasone administration relaxed regulations on investment in land and related matters and as a result land prices increased rapidly and housing problems were exacerbated. The Japanese government, as in the past, continued to push home ownership as the central element of its approach to housing, but due to the high cost of housing and land, the ability to purchase housing declined to a significant extent. The overall effect has been the emergence of a wide gap between the wealth of those families that already own a home and those that do not.

In this chapter, we will discuss the development of the sense of home ownership in Japan, as well as the role of home ownership in the wealth of the family. We will also discuss the current housing crisis in relation both to home ownership and to family wealth.

A HISTORICAL OVERVIEW OF HOME OWNERSHIP IN JAPAN

Before World War II, the rate of home ownership in Japan was very low. Almost all households rented private housing. The real-estate market and the house-construction industry which supplies homes to be owned had not yet been formed. In each part of the country small land owners provided rental housing on a small scale and people lived in rented housing irrespective of their income level. In 1941, the rate of home ownership in Tokyo was a little over 20 per cent while in Osaka it was below 10 per cent.

Home ownership developed after the war. During the Pacific War, much of the housing in Japan's large cities was destroyed. In Western Japan, air raids destroyed an enormous part of the housing stock, 93 per cent of the existing housing units in the city of Hiroshima, 78 per cent in Okayama and 59 per cent in Osaka. It was under these conditions that people started to build houses themselves and gradually home ownership began to take root. During the war, in 1939 and 1940, the government had introduced a system of Rent Regulation which involved holding housing and land rents at a low level. As a result, incentives to provide rented housing decreased and the private housing market stagnated. The rent for existing housing became almost the same as the land property tax. As a result, a large amount of prewar rental housing was sold to sitting tenants who became home owners.

Postwar housing policy took shape with the 1946 Public Housing Act, the 1950 Housing Loan Act and the 1955 Housing Corporation Act (Building Centre of Japan, 1987). These three laws are called the 'three pillars' of housing policy in Japan. Local government received Central Government subsidies to supply low-cost public rental housing directly to low-income families. The Housing Corporation supplied public rental housing and housing for sale directly to middle-income workers. The Housing Loan Association had the role of providing low-interest loans for home ownership to those at more than the middle-income level. From the beginning, the emphasis was on supplying mortgages, and this is a major factor in the expansion of the supply of owner-occupied housing (Hayakawa 1990).

In the 1960s, the housing-construction industry began to grow, and housing supply expanded gradually as the private real estate and house-building industries grew. The demand for home ownership increased as incomes increased, and a large private housing market developed. Private loan bodies which had previously given loans primarily to industry began to give loans for private housing. Loan conditions improved, the trust-support system was organised, and home ownership advanced.

In the 1970s the supply of housing for home owners expanded greatly. In 1973, the oil embargo caused a sudden decline in the Japanese economy, but policies related to home ownership were given a central place in improving the nation's economy. In 1975, housing loans were relied upon to improve the economy, and the supply of new mortgaged housing expanded greatly in the last half of the 1970s. In 1976, a system of financing for the purchase of existing housing, and in 1977 a system of savings for housing investment were set up advancing the organisation of home-ownership-related systems even further. Of the 'three pillars' in Japan's postwar housing policy, the housing loan pillar was emphasised from the start, and after the 1970s it was given even greater emphasis, including housing policy even more towards home ownership. In contrast, the supply of public housing decreased conspicuously, and its role in housing policy became an ever-decreasing one.

The Central Government issued its 'First Housing Construction Five-Year Plan' in 1966. Looking at its content and results, we can confirm clearly its strong bias towards the provision of mortgages and encouragement of home ownership. This is clear from the targets for the public and private sectors in terms of the total number of housing units built. The respective proportions of housing for purchase and public housing were as follows: in the first 5-year plan period (1966–70), 16.1 per cent to 6.6 per cent, in the second period (1971–5), 14.3 per cent to 6.2 per cent, in the third (1976–80), 22.1 per cent to 5.2 per cent, and in the fourth period (1981–5), 28.6 per cent to 4.2 per cent. Furthermore, when the actual number of units built is compared with those planned ('plan achievement rate') was 100.7 per cent, 121.5 per cent, 134.1 per cent and 111.7 per cent, respectively, for housing for purchase in the first to fourth 5-year-plan period, while for public housing it was 101.3 per cent, 76.0 per cent, 73.8 per cent and 72.0 per cent, respectively. House-purchase/housing-construction plans expanded and the actual units constructed exceeded the number planned. In contrast, the construction of public housing declined and did not even achieve the numbers planned. This trend has continued since.

By 1988, home ownership had grown to 61.4 per cent of households. This is a relatively high standard compared to other developed nations except England where it was 66.2 per cent (in 1987) and the United States where it was 63.5 per cent (in 1985). However, looking at the changes in the number of housing units in Japan by type of ownership (Table 11.1), we find that the rate of home ownership is no longer increasing, but is holding steady at around 60 per cent. Housing loan conditions have been reformed in response to the rapid rise in general land and housing costs. To meet this rise in housing and land prices, loans for home ownership have expanded and this has enabled the high rate of home ownership to be maintained.

HOME OWNERSHIP AS THE FORMATION OF ASSETS

In Japan, people seek home ownership as a means of building up family assets. After World War II the price of land increased dramatically and much more rapidly than the increase in income

Table 11.1 The ratio of housing units by tenure

	Owned houses	Public rented houses	Private rented houses	Company houses
1963	64.3	4.6	15.3	7.0
1968	60.3	5.8	27.0	6.9
1973	59.2	6.9	27.5	6.4
1978	60.4	7.6	26.1	5.7
1983	62.3	7.5	24.3	5.3
1988	61.3	7.5	25.9	4.1

Sources: Statistics Bureau, Management and Coordination Agency, Housing Survey of Japan

or the price of goods (Table 11.2). An index of price changes (with 1955 as 100) shows that by 1988 the index for incomes had grown to 1,982. It was 526 for the price of consumer goods but was 5,360 for land prices in urban areas and was 15,468 for land prices in the six largest cities. Thus, for those who were able to buy a home or land, the rate of asset formation had been advantageous compared with other forms of saving, making it a good hedge against inflation. The rate of land-price rise is head and shoulders above that in other developed nations, making the strong tendency towards home ownership for asset formation perhaps a unique characteristic of Japan.

According to the 1988 Housing Survey statistics, 32 per cent of home owners got their wealth by inheriting housing and land. This rate is expected to increase in the future. The reasons for this are as follows:

1 After the end of World War II there was great movement of the population and especially of the agrarian population to the city. Many of these households had to buy land and housing in the city. In contrast, at present, population movement has subsided relatively and the rate of land and housing inheritance has increased. From the 1950s and through the 1960s, the rate of migrants from smaller to larger city regions was about 35 per cent, but in the 1970s this figure dropped to 20 per cent, this being short-distance moves within the large city regions or to the hinterland of smaller cities.

2 The birth rate has declined, so the rate at which children inherit their parents' land and house has increased. The birth rate

Table 11.2 Land price index and other economic indications

	1955	1960	1965	1970	1975	1980	1985	1986	1987	1988
Land price index of six large cities	100	303	1,033	1,832	3,836	5,844	7,817	8,571	10,885	15,468
Land price index of the whole nation's built-up area	100	280	768	1,395	2,691	3,231	4,177	4,296	4,529	5,360
GNP index	100	183	371	829	1,678	2,703	3,541	3,690	4,113	–
Income index	100	132	215	408	962	1,406	1,735	1,782	1,894	1,982
Consumer price index	100	108	145	189	325	446	511	514	521	526

Sources: Japan Real Estate Institute, Economic Planning Agency, the Ministry of Labor, Statistics Bureau, Management and Coordination Agency

in Japan is low compared with other developed countries. In 1990 it was 9.9 per 1,000 population compared with 16.6 per 1,000 in the US, 13.6 per 1,000 in England and the same in France. In the pre-war era when birth rates were high, the eldest son would inherit the land and house, but when there were not many children there was a higher possibility of each inheriting land and housing. According to a 1983 Comprehensive Research and Development Agency survey, 20.6 per cent of all those surveyed replied that 'I will inherit a house from my parents, and I want to live there'. This figure was 34.9 per cent for those without brothers and sisters. Looking at them according to age, the younger they were, the higher this percentage became and it was 39.6 per cent for those in their twenties, a reflection of the fact that in recent years, the younger people are, the fewer brothers and sisters they have.

3   As will be mentioned later, land and housing price rises were more rapid in the latter half of the 1980s than ever before, making the purchase of newly built homes next to impossible. Today, the only way the young can own their own home is to inherit it from their parents.

Furthermore, the number of cases in which parents and their children's families live under the same roof jointly owning a home and thus contributing to the formation of family assets is increasing. In 1980, the Housing Loan Association instituted the 'two-generation housing loan' (a loan inheritance system) to deal with this trend. Prior to the development of this system, when a person 60 years old or older went to get a loan from the Loan Association, they were given only a short period in which to repay it. However, with the 'two-generation housing loan', the children continue to bear the burden of loan repayment making it possible to obtain a longer repayment period. Private loan organisations now also use this system to expand the scope of housing loans. In this way, the trend toward the joint ownership of land and housing by more than one generation as a way to transmit wealth is increasing.

HOME OWNERSHIP AS A MEANS OF SOCIAL SECURITY

Japan is going to become the first 'society of elderly people' in history. As of 1991, 12.5 per cent of the population was 65 or older, lower than the 17.8 per cent in Sweden and 15.6 per cent in England and Denmark. However, by the year 2005, the percentage of elderly people in Japan will be greater than in other countries. The Japanese Welfare Ministry estimates that by 2020, 25 per cent of Japan's population will be over 65. In the light of this, home ownership is beginning to have a significance as a means of social security for the elderly. Compared to the countries of Europe, Japan's standard of social security is still low. In 1985, the percentage of GNP devoted to social security in Denmark was 29.8 per cent, in France it was 30.1 per cent, and in England it was 27.8 per cent, while in Japan it was only 11.3 per cent. Against a background of lagging pensions and social means of covering medical and other such expenses, people use home ownership to accumulate wealth that can be used when they reach their later years. In this sense, home ownership in Japan has the character of being a substitute means of social security.

In 1981, the city of Musashino in Tokyo Prefecture began a Basic Social Security System for the elderly. Under it, home ownership can be used by the elderly as an asset to obtain welfare services. Under this system, the elderly can use their home as collateral in order to receive welfare payments or to pay for social welfare home helps, food services and other kinds of assistance. After the elderly person passes away, the inheritor makes a payment for the services used at cost-plus-interest, or the welfare company may use its right to sell securities to obtain payment for services rendered. Since this service applies only to the elderly who are home owners, there has been controversy about the justice of its use, however the system clearly reflects the social-security-substitute nature of home ownership in Japan.

In recent times, the family in Japan has become nuclear and small. However, when compared to that in the West, it remains strongly Asian in nature as can be seen in the desire of the elderly to live with their children in the absence or insufficiency of social security. There are many elderly people who see living with their children as a way to take care of their daily living expenses, to help cover costs, and to provide themselves with peace of mind. According to the 1985 National Census of Japan, 69.3 per cent of those over 65 years of age live with their children, an over-whelmingly high figure when compared to that in the West. In an opinion survey in 1982, 56 per cent of those who replied said 'we think it is good for parents to live with their children'. This figure was 66 per cent and 73 per cent for those replying who were in their sixties and over 70 years old, respectively. Home ownership is a prerequisite for the realisation of this very strong living-together tendency. As will be mentioned later, rental housing in Japan is very small, making extended family residence extremely difficult. According to a 1988 Housing Statistics Survey, the proportion of those over 65 years of age who lived with their children in rented housing was 47 per cent compared to 76 per cent who lived in owner-occupied housing.

THE GAP BETWEEN HOME OWNERS AND NON-OWNERS

We have thus far seen the importance of home ownership in Japan as a means of social security for the elderly as well as a way to accumulate family wealth. However, this does not mean that everyone can own their own home, and there is a gap between the haves and have-nots in home ownership. If we look at the percentage of home-owning families by income level, we find that in 1988 the proportion of home owners was 45.6 per cent of those with an income of up to 2 million yen annually (approximately US $38,500–$54,000) and 85 per cent in the income bracket above 7 million yen per year (over US $54,000). Those in the higher income brackets are able to purchase a home and with it further increase their assets, while in contrast those in the lower income brackets have difficulties in becoming home owners and are placed in a disadvantageous position when it comes to creating assets.

Home ownership gives the elderly a stable living and provides a greater possibility of living together with their children. However, those elderly who have been unable to purchase their own home live in private rental housing not only with little possibility of living with their house-renting children but also without being able to secure stable housing conditions. In Japan, those who run private rental housing have a strong tendency to avoid renting to the elderly. According to the 1985 Housing Statistics Survey, in the five years between 1979 and 1983, the national percentage of those who gave 'eviction' as the reason for having to move was 9.5 per cent compared to 24.0 per cent of households where the head was 65 years old or older. So, we see that for the elderly in private rental housing, housing was a particularly unstable factor in their life.

In Japan, there is a great gap in housing quality when owned and rented housing are compared. The average floor area in owned housing is 116.8 square metres as compared to only 46.4 square metres in public rental housing and 40.8 square metres in private rental housing, a difference of nearly three times (as of 1988). Even publicly rented housing is very small. The Japanese government has a minimum-housing-standard index for density. While only 2.7 per cent of owned housing is below this standard, 27.4 per cent of public and 20.4 per cent of private rental housing are below it. This indicates the poor quality of rental housing in Japan. This difference holds true even when compared to housing sizes overseas. The ratio of owner-housing floor area to rented-housing floor area in the US is 1.37 times, in England it is 1.17 times, and in France it is 1.42 times, but in Japan it is 2.64 times.

Japanese housing policy is strongly inclined toward home ownership with public housing being of low quality and supplied in only small quantities. There is no policy for even supplying good-quality private rental housing, and there is no housing allowance system. The supply of housing is in large part left to the market mechanism and to the individual's own resources. A look at the way the housing budget for the fiscal year 1991 is made up reveals that the per capita allocation for public housing, Housing Corporation and mortgage housing is 35,000 yen (US $270), 11,000 yen (US $85), and 110,000 yen (US $850), respectively. It is clear here that the income strata which is most able to purchase housing is the one receiving the greatest government investment. In the meantime, land-price rises are unchecked and social-security provision continues to lag. In this context, home ownership has a very important meaning in every aspect of life in Japan. It also gives rise to an inevitable gap between home owners and non-owners.

FAMILY, WEALTH, HOME OWNERSHIP AND THE HOUSING CRISIS

The price of land in Japan rose rapidly after World War II, but in the latter half of the 1980s the rate of increase far surpassed previous experience. The recorded annual land-price rise in Japan's six largest cities in 1987 was 27 per cent, and in 1988 it was 42 per cent (see Table 11.2). The maximum rise in 1987 compared to the year before was 79 per cent in Tokyo, 67 per cent in Osaka, 60 per cent in Yokohama, 56 per cent in Kyoto and 53 per cent in Nagoya. The main cause of this abnormal rise in land price was the relaxation of land and housing price controls during the Nakasone administration (1982–7). Land and housing in Japan has always been heavily dependent on the private market, but this relaxation of controls made the supply of both land and housing absolutely dependent on market principles. In 1983, many types of zoning controls were relaxed, and in 1984 the sale of public land began. The land and rent control system was abandoned in 1986, and in 1991 the Housing Rental Law was changed weakening the rights of tenants. In the 1980s, interest rates were extremely low, so when controls were relaxed, excess capital flowed into land and housing, and land prices rose drastically (Hayakawa and Hirayama 1991).

Of course, housing prices rose too. In 1988, the average price of a condominium in the Tokyo region was 47,500,000 yen (about US $350,000), some 6.9 times the average annual income, and the price of a detached single house was 50,850,000 yen (about US $390,000) or 7.4 times the average annual income. The price of 100 square metres of housing land in the Tokyo Metropolitan Area was over 130 million yen (about US $1 million) and that of a 60 square metres condominium apartment was over 80,000,000 yen (about US $615,000) in 1989. The possibility of an individual owning his/her own home decreased conspicuously. For example, according to calculations of the Economic Planning Agency the average cost of a detached single home on a site of 103 square metres and with a total floor area of 123 square metres in the Tokyo Prefecture in 1987 was 81,530,000 yen (about US $625,000). The average wage earner would have to pay 5,990,000 yen (about US$46,000) down and pay back the rest with a loan (interest rate 4.45 per cent–6.12 per cent) of 557,607 yen (about US $4,300) per month. This is 123 per cent of the average monthly income. If daily living costs are included, monthly expenses would be 194 per cent of the monthly income. These figures in other prefectures are not as high as in Tokyo but are still high at 118 per cent in Osaka, 118 per cent in Kanagawa and 112 per cent in Hyogo.

At the beginning of the 1990s, land prices stopped rising and stabilised at a very high level leaving the price of land and housing still very high. Previously mentioned housing problems, such as the small size of dwellings, their high density, dilapidation and so on persist, but now it is 'affordability' which has emerged as the most serious problem.

One of the reasons for the emphasis on supplying homes for purchase in Japan's housing policy is 'filtering'. By giving subsidies to households in the above-middle-income bracket who are able to purchase their own homes, these households will be enabled to move out of their present quarters leaving them available for those in lower income groups to move into. This 'filtering' to the low income strata should result in the phased improvement of housing conditions. However, due to the high price of land, for all intents and purposes, 'filtering' does not work.

According to the Housing Demand Survey, the proportion of home owners who had purchased their houses in the five years before the year of the survey was 10 per cent, but in 1988 was 6.5 per cent, a drop of 3.5 per cent. In the Tokyo region the drop was 4.3 per cent, while in the Osaka Metropolitan Area there was a decrease of 4.7 per cent, in other words the rate of home purchasers in Japan's large cities declined significantly. Furthermore, the percentage of home owners who had moved into their own home in 1983 was 40.3 per cent, but in 1988 it had fallen to 30.7 per cent. In contrast, the percentage that moved into rental housing increased from 58.0 per cent to 62.8 per cent. A new stratum is being formed, one made up of those who are unable to purchase their own home so they have no choice but to move into the rental housing market.

The same survey shows that the percentage of those with 'concrete plans to improve their housing conditions in the future' or who 'are thinking of doing so' was 45.8 per cent in 1969, 38.1 per cent in 1978 and 31.4 per cent in 1988, a definite declining tendency. This trend was particularly strong in house-renting households. A look at the contents of their plans reveals that from 1978 to 1988, those who planned to buy their own homes decreased from 80.7 per cent to 69.0 per cent, and those who planned to move into rental housing increased from 14.1 per cent to 19.7 per cent. Of those households in their own homes which had no improvement plans, 46.7 per cent said 'We are satisfied with our present housing' compared to 38.9 per cent of renters who said, 'We do not have money so we have given up on home ownership.'

THE EXPANSION OF INEQUALITY

The Japanese have a strong drive to own their own homes, but it has become very difficult to do so and a large gap has developed in the assets of those who are home owners and those who are not. This gap existed before, but the high price of land has made it even larger. For instance, let's look at the published value of land for each household of the five income strata having the greatest assets. The value of the holdings of the fifth strata increased 1.8 times in the 1985–7 period and reached 98,640,000 yen (about US $760,000) in 1987. This was 9.0 times the value of the third strata and 59.8 times that of the second strata. In the Tokyo metropolitan area, the value of the land assets of the fifth strata was over 200 million yen (about US $1.54 million) per household. A look at the JINI-index (Japan Inequality Index), which shows the amount of inequality, indicates that the distribution of flow income acquired was about 0.2 compared to the distribution of stock assets which surpassed 0.6. The economic conditions of life in Japan today are governed by land and housing holdings, and the gap in assets is even larger. Even if the gap in income is corrected, nothing will change as long as the ownership gap does not.

While it is difficult to acquire new land or housing, the assets of land and home owners continue to increase in value. When a home-owning family sells its home and land, it is able to buy even better-quality housing that has a higher asset value. Also, it can use its holdings as collateral to receive loans with which to purchase a second house. The ratio of home-owning families living in one house and owning a second is 4 per cent in the 3 million yen (about US $23,000/year) or less income bracket, and 6.3 per cent in the 3 to 5 million yen (about US $23,000–$38,500/year) income bracket, while in the 10 to 15 million yen (about US $77,000–$115,000/year) bracket, this figure jumps to 23.3 per cent, and in the income bracket about 15 million yen (about US $115,000/year) it was 38.8 per cent in 1988. There are many types of 'second homes' including villas, rental housing and housing for parents and relatives, but it goes without saying that these holdings play a major role in asset formation. Many second-home owners or those families wishing to be second-home owners live in large cities. According to the 1988 Housing Demand Survey, the percentage of those replying that they 'already own', 'plan to own' or 'hope to own' a second home averaged 23.9 per cent nationally, while it was 32.8 per cent in the Tokyo metropolitan area. The possibility of even further asset formation from land and home ownership in the large cities is expected to increase.

INEQUALITY ACROSS GENERATIONS

Today's asset formation by home ownership is different in character from that in the past. Before the skyrocketing land and housing prices, it was those with a high income who would purchase their own home, while those with a low income could not. Prior to the recent increase in land prices, home ownership or non-ownership gave rise to great differences in the way people accumulated wealth. It also resulted in major differences in the quality of life, peace of mind for the elderly and life as a whole. However, today, it is difficult to purchase your own home. Social inequalities are not a result of income level, individual effort or even schooling, but relate to when a home was purchased.

For the young who are thinking about buying a home, it will be much harder to do so as a means of wealth accumulation, even if they have a high income and work hard, than it was for their home-owning parents. From 1983 to 1988, the rate of home ownership in Japan dropped only 1 percentage point from 62.4 per cent to 61.4 per cent, but the drop was greater in the younger generations at 6.9 percentage points for those 30–34 years of age and 3.6 percentage points for those 35–9 years old. This rate was even higher for younger people in the large cities, for instance 8.9 percentage points for 30–34-year-old group and 6.7 percentage points for 35–9-year-olds in the Tokyo Region. According to an opinion survey conducted by the Tokyo Prefecture government in 1987, 37.8 per cent of all those replying said 'we do not think we will ever be able to be home owners'. The percentage in their twenties who replied this way was 52.2 per cent, and it was 50.2 per cent for those in their thirties.

The response was different for those in the same age groups whose parents are home owners. As mentioned earlier, due to the stabilisation of population movements and the low birth rate, the possibility of the young inheriting their parents' home is great. If their parents' home is large, the young may live with their parents even before inheritance. These young people will be able to get out of their small high-rent quarters and their parents will have peace of mind in their old age. The central product of the housing industry in Japan today is the prefabricated two-generation home, planned on the presumption that parents will live with their children. Sales have increased rapidly in recent years with the rebuilding of existing owned houses. The ratio of two-generation houses to single-family detached houses supplied by private home-building companies in 1991 was estimated at over 40 per cent for the whole of Japan and about 50 per cent for Tokyo (*Asahi Newspaper*, 23 January 1992). In contrast, when parents do not own their own home, it will be very difficult for the young to become home owners in the future.

Furthermore, it is now almost impossible for the young to purchase their own home without financial help from their parents. The 1988 Housing Statistics Survey reflects this with a place for the name of the home owner as one of the items to be filled in. A very high 92.6 per cent of respondents filled this in. Some 1.8 per cent gave 'the name of parent with whom the respondent is living', and only 3.4 per cent gave a name other than that parent. However, the percentages of heads of the households that were 30–34 years old giving these replies were 4.7 per cent and 16.4 per cent, respectively. In the Tokyo Metropolitan area the percentages for this age group were 4.8 per cent and 20.7 per cent, respectively. Particularly in the large cities, a certain portion of the young who owned their own home did so with financial assistance from their parents. It can be conjectured that not a small number of those young adults who signed themselves as the home owner also got financial assistance from their parents.

Thus, the possibility of young adults owning their own home is largely controlled by whether their parents are land and home owners as well as by whether they receive financial help from their parents. The financial assets parents acquired by owning a home have meaning, not only for them, but across generations as family wealth and as the basis for new wealth formation.

CONCLUSIONS

The gap in incomes has been narrowed in postwar Japan, and the road to a society of equality has been travelled by the establishment of legally generated democratic laws. However, with the high land prices of the last half of the 1980s, a decisive gap has emerged between those who own land and their own home and those that do not, giving rise to new social inequality. The result has been the appearance of social problems, such as a decline in the desire to work.

The formation of great family wealth has come to be based on home ownership, but this wealth is not the true size of one's wealth nor one's real wealth. The owned home has a certain average floor area, but the relative gap in this is very large. For instance, condominiums which appeared in the 1970s are quite small. This is the same phenomenon as when we say 'Japan is an "economic giant", but the quality of the people's life is low'.

Japan's postwar housing policy has been centred on home ownership, which, against a background of continually rising land prices and inadequacies in the country's social-security system, has taken on the character of wealth formation and a substitute for social security. As a result, home ownership, instead of housing reforms, has become like a goal in itself. If one does purchase a home, even if it is small, unsafe and inconveniently located, one will tend to feel mentally satisfied. The low standard of housing in Japan when compared to that in the West led to the world-famous 'rabbit hutch' expression in the EC. The accumulation of individual family wealth by home ownership has led to contradictions, such as 'capsule hotel' housing and disorders which do not point towards comfortable urban housing nor to the formation of wealth for the entire society.

Chapter 12

Family networks, reciprocity and housing wealth

Adrian Franklin

INTRODUCTION

Given the ubiquitous view of family decline and domestic privatism accompanied by the near-universal commodification of housing, it might seem odd to associate family networks with housing wealth. In Britain the more popular image is one of sovereign individual consumers dealing mainly through contract with a host of legal and financial companies, making strategic housing-investment decisions and winning unusually large returns to their capital – on their own. In formal terms this is precisely what appears to happen, particularly if the data used are the snapshot survey or yearly return. But the process and organisation of accumulation remains hidden. This imagery goes uncontested partly as a result of disciplinary boundaries and taboos. Housing finance, for example, remains 'culture free' and family studies tend to focus on poverty and inequality rather more than on equity and wealth. But there is sufficient evidence to indicate the growing functional significance of family involvement in accumulation processes as well as the disposal of housing wealth. In order to understand these processes we have to understand the cultural and organisational nature of kinship and informal networks.

A recent contribution to this slow realisation comes from an unusual quarter. By way of introducing his *A Nation of Home Owners*, Peter Saunders (1990) provides us with a fascinating biographical account of his own family's growing wealth in housing, and the housing wealth which he stands to inherit as a result. It is unusual for Saunders to give any credibility to anecdote or salience to kinship. His urban sociology gives the distinct impression that kinship and family networks count for very little. Clearly he has had a change of heart. His family biography, which works very well within the book, is mainly there to illustrate the historic growth and significance of owner-occupation. But the subtext is clear enough: that the family as an institution is rendered equally important by virtue of the fact that housing wealth is usually given to kin upon the death of an owner. Even allowing for the equity release and leakage of older owner-occupiers, this transfer is still very significant. In addition, housing capital and equity is a resource which living relatives can use to assist kin in all sorts of ways. In order to keep abreast of social class structure and reproduction within nations of home owners therefore, it becomes increasingly important to understand the changing nature of rules and practices which relate to this transmission. But Saunders' anecdote also suggests two further truths. The first is that familial involvement and reciprocity in British housing has changed and the second is that the advent of widespread housing wealth was relatively sudden. It makes sense therefore to ask how families were involved in housing before and how well and in what ways families coped with these new opportunities and responsibilities. More particularly, how did previous familial norms and practices develop in changing conditions? To understand emerging housing practices associated with material assistance and reciprocity one needs to understand how they are transformations of previous practices.

But the significance of family networks and wealth is not confined to the restructuring of social class and life chances: it has wider ramifications in the organisation of housing opportunities. As the state and the private-rented sectors have shrunk, the majority of private individuals and families do not only hold housing wealth. In various ways they have begun to take on housing provision roles which in Britain were carried out more or less exclusively in the recent past by institutions external to the family: feudal, private and state landlords as well as banks and building societies. Although formal title to housing wealth is held individually or in marital or *de facto* domestic partnerships we are now becoming aware of the significance of wider familial links to both housing practices and the patterns of ownership career. Moreover there are many respects and instances where private owners do not operate as isolated individual consumers or merely with naked self-interest. To a significant degree many people are inextricably locked into the moral community of kinship.

The particular contribution that social anthropologists can make to this debate is at the conceptual, historical and comparative levels. Anthropologists working in European countries have also worked in the context of changing cultural practices particularly in the field of kinship and property. An historical approach has therefore become imperative and normative within this discipline: an outcome predicted by Evans-Pritchard (1962), the instigator of a European social anthropology, in the 1950s. This paper aims to provide an overview of these historical changes in Britain and to make some modest international comparisons. Before that, the first section aims to clarify the concepts that are being used. It will be argued that the concept of 'family' is too imprecise in almost any context and that particular care must be taken to specify different kinship terms, groupings, and practices. Secondly, it considers a conceptual typology of the economics of kinship and housing wealth. It is suggested that this typology is useful in showing how and why kinship is central to two out of the four discernible sub-economies involved in the generation and distribution of housing wealth.

Using this conceptual framework the second section examines the broad historical changes in relations between family structures, reciprocity and housing wealth. For the purpose of exposition the past is divided into three periods: traditional, modern and postmodern. The reason for doing this is, crudely, the common association of familial centrality in traditional societies, the displacement of family in modernity, and areas of refamilisation in postmodernity (giving back responsibility and obligation to assist to the informal, largely kinship sector). Although it is possible to present family change in these terms one must not lose sight of cultural variations across space and cultural continuities across time: the former emphasising locality effects (Savage *et al.* 1987), the latter emphasising the tendency to draw on informal cultural repertoires in changing circumstances and the uniquely enduring nature of kinship relations. The main argument of this chapter is that the social relations of kinship and friendship are increasingly interwoven in the accumulation and distribution of housing wealth, and that as modernist bureaucratic welfare solutions to mass housing provision collapse such networks are more or less obliged to step in. It is possible to amplify the positive aspects of this market freedom and the rallying of the family and network but the downside appears to be an alarming number of people without any social support at all.

WHAT DO WE MEAN BY 'FAMILY'?

From a social anthropological perspective it is important to add further clarification to one of the main terms used in this collection. 'The family' is a highly imprecise term even in those societies where it is a used and taken for granted reality. In the English language it can be used to refer to:

1 a nuclear family (parents and their unmarried or co-residing children)
2 a domestic group (members of the same enduring household – including cohabiting extended families and other composite groups)
3 a kinship core (an ego-centred grouping of several spatially scattered households usually comprising a married couple, their parents, their children and to a lesser extent, their siblings). In England this is often referred to as 'the dispersed extended family' (Willmott 1987b). It is a term which is designed to acknowledge both the significance and the spatial specificity of kinship ties.
4 a kindred group (an ego-centred grouping where kinship is reckoned beyond the categories of the kinship core and typically includes cousins, e.g. father's and mother's siblings' children, more distant cousins and affines and more generations – indeed it can be referred to as the existing kin universe of known and unknown living kin).

In addition to these relationships, which are based on descent and marriage, there are kin-like or pseudo-kin relationships which are based on a range of other criteria. In the formal case of godparenthood the criteria may be patronage (creating a patron for children and possibly parents too), alliance (cementing links between unrelated groups) or friendship (cementing and formalising relations with trusted significant non-kin). In some cases actual kin are selected for godparenthood (reaffirming specific kin ties). But there are other, informal cases of pseudo-kinship where non-kin act as if they were kin, modelling behaviour on specific types of kin tie or in other cases extending kinship terminology to non-kin. English children are for example often encouraged to refer to their parents' close friends as if they were their parents' siblings. This example falls halfway between formal pseudo-kin such as godparents and the day-to-day community neighbourhood ties where, according to Oliver Harris (1982), close neighbour-friends operationalise kin-like moral expectations and reciprocal obligations. Certainly in the past, non-kin in such relations have routinely parented orphaned children (Chayter 1980). Such discussions inevitably question the distinction between friendship and kinship. Other anthropologists working in non-European contexts have made similar points (Wallman, 1974).

It is always important therefore to specify the precise group and relationship being referred to, and to appreciate the normative obligations and exchanges which are made within and between each category of kin. Generally speaking social anthropologists use the term kinship rather than family, and tend to be better at making the important residential and kin-categorical distinctions than housing sociologists. In the case of Britain, for example, specific reciprocities and obligations in housing link different categories of kin, and as we shall see this happened in the past in a range of different ways. Thus all studies of kinship behaviour have identified the kinship core as the key unit of responsibility. As a kinship group they are distinguished from others by being composed of current and former domestic groups, a nexus of parent–child relations typified by a high degree of normative responsibility for life chances, health and care. To date there are few studies, contemporary or comparative, which point to the normative functions that different kin-relationships have. Responsibility for housing in broad terms (ensuring that the appropriate kin are appropriately housed) is arguably in the remit of kinship cores in England and elsewhere in Europe, Australia, and the US, although the degree to which this responsibility may fall to categories of kin outside the core may vary (Finch 1989). What is appropriate housing, and how kin ensure it for themselves will vary from culture to culture, and different kin categories will have different roles and expectations over the lifecourse. The notion of normative responsibility may vary from, say, adult children in low-income British families seeing through an application for state housing on behalf of an elderly parent, to an affluent elderly parent making the gift of a downpayment on a house to a grandchild. More research clearly needs to be done in this area given the restructuring of housing relations in Britain and elsewhere. A particular interest in cases such as those above is whether and how the gift is ever reciprocated.

THE ECONOMICS OF KINSHIP, RECIPROCITY AND HOUSING WEALTH

In discussing the relationship between kinship, reciprocity and housing wealth then, we are by and large in the terrain of exchange and gift. Exchange might be defined as reciprocities of various kinds which take place over a range of time scales, and between individuals and groups with precise socially defined relations and obligations to one another.

However we need to specify this terrain further by distinguishing different economic spheres in which housing wealth and kinship articulate. A useful distinction is offered by Davis (1972). He argues that in Britain and in many other areas four different sub-economies should be distinguished: the market economy ('governed by laws of commercial trading, employment, labour relations and so on'), the redistributive economy ('governed by laws of taxation and welfare and state expenditure'), the domestic economy ('governed by family law', 'customs and expectations, . . . and includes all productive [and consumer] activities not mediated by the market') and the gift economy ('governed by rules of reciprocity, and includes all those transactions which we call giving a present, making a gift and so on'). The relationship between kinship and housing wealth straddles the domestic and the gift sub-economies and in turn has significance for both the market and redistributive sub-economies.

Matters of inheritance of housing wealth can be subsumed under the domestic sub-economy. Although the boundary between domestic and gift sub-economies is not always clear, the domestic sub-economy tends to be more formalised either in laws relating to different categories of kinship transaction or in terms of normative custom/expectations governing relations between kin. This is more so in Italy and Greece where for example the notion of 'family' property is active, than in England where the testator has more or less complete freedom of choice in bequeathing property. There is a developed literature on the structure and social implications of different forms of inheritance systems although this is largely confined to the social anthropology of the north shore of the Mediterranean and the Alps (Davis 1972). It would seem profitable to extend this kind of analysis to housing wealth in other countries, especially where 'traditional' housing patterns are changing. The Mediterranean material, for example, looks at how and when patrimony is divided, and investigates and compares systems where property is divided prior to death (usually on marriage although this translates, basically, to new 'legitimate' household formation) and where it is divided upon the death of an owner. It also describes and distinguishes how property is divided among children (equally, unequally, dividing the principal property or not, working out equal divisions of property and working out comparable divisions of value). The literature on reciprocity tends to associate the moral nature of close kin ties with 'generalised exchange' (where immediate reciprocation is not required) and more distant relations with 'restricted exchange' (where immediate reciprocation is required) (Bloch 1975). Indeed generalised exchange tends to be a feature of 'close' trustful and dependent relations irrespective of whether they are kin or not (Wallman 1974). We shall see that one of the features of reciprocity and housing wealth is that it tends to be conducted between various categories of close relations and that it tends to be generalised. However the pattern of generalisation in Britain varies between the generalised exchange of housing wealth from the old to the young (the young generation receive from their elders and reciprocate to their juniors) and other exchanges, to flow from givers (of various ages) to receiver and back in an ongoing or according-to-need basis. A very similar pattern was found in Australia (Kendig 1982).

Siblings in Britain appear very rarely to give back significant or equal amounts of wealth to parents or grandparents – for housing or any other reasons. There are some custom practices involving the rehousing of frail parents near their children but this appears rarely to involve a reciprocation of housing wealth. According to Finch (1989), most British parents wish to and in fact do manage to remain financially independent of their children irrespective of their changing fortunes and relative incomes. Indeed the common parental practice of boosting the income of relatively poor young adult children is not followed by any demand to have it repaid in their own retirement. What is more characteristic of grandparents is a concern to assist yet more junior kin such as grandchildren, nephews and nieces.

The active production of housing wealth within kinship and other 'close social' networks (kindreds in the British sense) is another area of activity on which recent studies have shed some light (e.g. Pahl 1984, Warde *et al.* 1989). Such wealth-enhancing reciprocal activities include informal collective improvements to property, the exchange of advice and encouragement on housing strategies, and the sharing of important information. Studies to date have simply recorded transactions on a 'who does what' and 'how frequently' basis. However we need to know not only who they do it for but why and how the exchanges come into being. There are also the questions to do with the development and articulation of 'taste in housing' and 'housing career'. In previous papers (Franklin 1990, 1986) I have suggested that housing practices are the outcome of cultural distinctions and articulated on the ground by small networks of friends and kin. Taste and career may be similar expressions – functions of similar cultures and networks. In Britain this area of social activity and its role in wealth creation cannot be underestimated. It is largely but not exclusively conducted outside the kinship core, through siblings, cousins, affines and pseudo-kin (which might include close friends and neighbours). We know very little about the moral and cultural basis of this production and reciprocity at this level of society and there is a case for more research in this direction (Allan 1989).

Although patterns of gift-giving, exchange and reciprocity are far from informal or random – indeed they tend to follow a structured timetable (birthdays, 21st birthday, engagement, wedding gifts) – they allow room for individual discretion and their flexibility is an important aspect. Parents, children, grand-parents and grandchildren may make gifts amongst themselves which may either originate from housing wealth or be intended to enhance, amongst other things, the housing wealth or opportu-nities of the recipient. Such gifts may be given as cash, free rental, or property and although they may later be calculated as part of a patrimonial share, in many cases they are distinguished from inheritance, and in many places gifts are distinguished from other property transfers for taxation purposes. Gifts of housing wealth may be a relatively new type of gift in mature industrial countries, a response to changes in access and ownership. Housing gifts for example are a means of resolving the contradiction between high house values and the low earning power of newly formed households. As the costs of equipping a modern house fall within the budgets of many new households, their gift needs are often for housing wealth itself. This gift and the greater significance it accords kinship demonstrate both the latent powers and roles that stem from its unique moral (obligations to care for kin) and cultural (local patterns of behaviour, norms and expectations) qualities. It also signifies the crisis of both the market and redistributive housing spheres. This will be explored more below.

The anthropology of housing and kinship is therefore composed of a diverse range of patterns of domestic and gift relations and in recent times we have witnessed processes of defamilisation (reducing the economic role/functions/obligations of the kinship core) and refamilisation (kinship cores regain economic roles, functions and obligations) depending on very specific historic-spatial movements of market prices, privatisation and socialisation.

HOUSING PRACTICES

It is now possible to draw this conceptual analysis together and to outline the broad content of housing practices. I would define these as normative cultural approaches to the content, access, exchange and disposal of housing that are normally identifiable or evident in patterned ways in any cultural milieu. This concept mainly derives from an ethnographic approach to housing and identifies the cultural specificities of housing behaviour among a clearly defined, culturally coherent group. Thus it may be specific to a rural peasant village (Pitt-Rivers' (1974) work on Alcala, Spain for example illustrates how cultural practices vary between contiguous villages in a single province), a region (e.g. southern Italy), an ethnic group, or a social class or class subculture (a level of distinction in practice reflecting subcultural forms of stratification, of the sort identified by Bourdieu). Although some housing practices are rulebound, many will in fact turn out to be variations on a normative or current theme; they are flexible, open to innovation, prone to external change (market change and government policy especially) and prone to fashion. Whilst they are blurred by individual contingencies, a broad pattern of practice can usually be discerned. Like other cultural phenomena however they are self-evident, taken-for-granted practices (often taken for granted by researchers too) and as a result, they are often not researched in sufficient detail. This has certainly been the case in industrial societies, although some of the best examples of attention to detail in research have come from the social anthropology of Europe, particularly in the northern Mediterranean region.

Housing practices are fashioned by custom, by legal codes, by market conditions, by the state and by other cultural norms such as rules and norms of kinship. There are at least five broad areas of housing practices that can be distinguished and are worth setting out here: these are residency, household formation, reciprocities in housing, tenure preferences/options and housing taste.

Residency refers to norms or preferences of location; where people typically locate their housing relative to others. In anthropology this norm-bound activity is usually included in marriage rules but in fact it refers mainly to the housing location of legitimate new domestic partnerships/households and their subsequent housing career. There is a sub-terminology associated with this: patrilocality (residence near husband's parents or in their settlement), matrilocality (residence with wife's parents), natolocal (residence in ego's birth settlement or with parents), neolocal (new separate residence). But there will be other location norms. For example it will be argued below that in modern Britain one of the key criteria in housing location is to be near friends. The operation of such norms and rules has important implications for the structuration of neighbourhoods, villages, suburbs and other social-spatial entities. It also has obvious implications for patterns of reciprocity. In the anthropological record there has been a tendency to set out residency norms as if they were always followed, whereas in fact they are often merely ideals. Indeed in most societies there are a number of options available to people, each of which is operationalised in particular contexts.

The process of household formation is also governed by norms and rules that influence housing practices. Practices vary widely across Europe and include at one extreme, the Croatian zadruga (a corporate landowning group of related men and their wives living on one farmstead) in which new households simply extend the already large corporate group; the extended families of rural Greece (sons and their wives live in their father's home until he dies); and the new household formed on marriage in southern Italy. The pattern and timing of household formation is thus crucial to the process of endowing new households with the necessary form of housing wealth. In the case of the zadruga a new household may require the collective building of extra rooms. In rural southern Italy a poor man is one who has large numbers of daughters and few sons. In order to maintain honour and prestige, parents should be able to provide housing for each daughter on marriage.

A third broad area of housing practices concerns reciprocity and assistance. Globally, constructing – and indeed maintaining – permanent housing is too large a task for every household to conduct for itself. In this sense housing is like other common collective ventures such as fencing, road building, or irrigation. Throughout the world, this work is traditionally the province of kinship and neighbouring. However the process of modernisation tends to commodify or socialise these activities, which are nevertheless often managed informally or traditionally to a significant degree. Housing is a particularly apt example of this since it is intricately woven into domestic, kinship and cultural concerns. Patterns of reciprocity (who helps whom with what tasks), are the key questions here. In addition we need to know the conditions of reciprocity: are they generalised (provision given according to need and not repaid immediately, if at all) or restricted (provision given on condition of short-term repayment)? Anthropologists have found that patterns of reciprocity often reflect the significance of different kin and non-kin relationships. In the sphere of housing there are four areas of reciprocity which are significant: exchange of labour, exchange of skilled tasks, loan of equipment, sharing of information. The literature is particularly weak in this area.

Tenure preferences/options and housing tasks are important areas to investigate if only because they do not correspond to income levels or social class as some analysts suggest. New values may arise in response to changing market conditions, to political commitments, to new labour-market conditions affecting specific groups in society. The distribution of tenure preferences has clear implications for kinship and housing wealth.

Aspects of taste include design, location, functionality, status (housing as a positional good), interiors and age. People tend to know what they want in advance of building or purchase. In traditional rural areas there are everywhere traditions of vernacular architecture: tried and tested local design themes. In cities of some maturity, architectural diversity is more common though it is by no means clear who, at any income level, prefers a particular type of house. We know from housing-search behaviour, for example, that in the British market people tend to search known areas or areas friends have moved into (Short 1976).

Having sketched out a conceptual schema for these practices and relationships we can now provide an illustration of them at work and as they change over time. The material will relate mainly to Britain.

HOUSING PRACTICES IN THE FOUR PERIODS OF TRADITIONAL BRITAIN

The historical anthropology of housing wealth and kinship in Britain should start in what is commonly called the traditional period. In Britain the history and archaeology of housing and the social relations in which it was produced and consumed is very complete – as far back as when hunter and gatherer peoples first inhabited the island after the last ice age some 10,000 years BC. Within this traditional period before industrialism and urbanisation four distinct periods can be discerned. The very early periods are included in order to show the cultural continuities in terms of housing practices and in particular the continuing role of both kinship cores and local social networks. The early hunters and gatherers – of the first period – were highly mobile, making small, temporary shelters rather than inhabiting caves on a long-term basis (Darvill 1987). They were small shelters for single nuclear families and recorded camp sites show that most of them consisted of only one to two nuclear families. Housing was neither a wealth item nor a product of anything more than a few hours' domestic family labour. Among some groups, residence was organised on a winter base-camp–summer mobile-camp cycle. The winter camps were more elaborate and enduring and were intended for collective ritual and social occasions. The archaeological record is quite clear however on the generally enduring nature of both nuclear family homes and isolated one-family homesteads over most of the traditional period (Taylor 1983).

This pattern survived subsequent social transformations, from small tribal structures to princely kingdoms and to the centralised kingdoms in existence at the time of early Roman Britain. It also spanned both hunting and agricultural modes of production. With a larger, settled agricultural population whether engaged in animal husbandry, arable farming or both, came a more sedentary settlement structure where houses were placed in the centre of individual family holdings rather than in a nucleated settlement (village). This forms the second period dating from roughly 4,000 years BC taking in what we think of as the Neolithic period. These homes were more elaborate than the mobile hunters' shelter, and it is estimated that some form of collective effort was made to set out each structure, to form the walls and to thatch them. Homes dating from this period were made of entirely organic materials and lasted on average 25 years, this being the time it took for load-bearing posts to rot in unlined holes and become dangerous. New homes were then rebuilt nearby, as the old structure fell into disuse or was used as storage or stabling. Housing was built by households who organised its production for their needs probably through generalised reciprocity in local, but scattered, communities. A structure of interlinked gift and counter-gift of house-building labour among local social networks served to ensure that new and more mature households were adequately housed. Any one nuclear household would require no more than 2 houses to be built in this way, one of which would have been built on marriage. Thus with this style of house in this period, housing wealth was widely and evenly distributed and was not passed down through generations but produced and exchanged as housing labour within generations (or closely overlapping generations). What is almost certain is that kin and neighbours were at the core of this form of reciprocity. Individual households needed external help to produce a house and were in turn obliged to help others. In this way this period is characterised by gener-alised gift exchanges of house-building labour as the sole mode of housing provision. Hence in this second period housing wealth was produced by both domestic and gift relations.

In the subsequent period a variety of changes were apparent. Footings, lower walls, and entire dwellings constructed from stone are increasingly evident on isolated farmsteads and in the earliest nuclear village from the tenth century AD on. In all cases the buildings were more durable and were a fixed and inheritable part of any farm or property. The economy was dominated by a mix of both market and redistributive (feudal) mechanisms (Homans 1941; Macfarlane 1978). The free yeomanry and traders continued to rely heavily on the domestic and gift sub-economy in housing wealth – the domestic economy acquiring sophisticated and fixed customary law relating to property and inheritance in many localities. There is also evidence of much trading in land and houses, and of geographical mobility over the lifecycle, such that individuals tended not to stay in their natal residence or village after early adulthood if not before. Most new households were set up away from natal districts and would have bought or rented housing from savings and parental cash gifts. Throughout most of England primogeniture ensured that only one sibling inherited the parental farming property: other children were set up in trade and assisted in a variety of ways prior to marriage, and to a much lesser extent upon marriage itself and in setting up a household elsewhere. English parents tended to invest patrimonial shares in cultural capital, in securing both career, education and standing in advantageous social networks. The process of socialisation into freestanding adult status was a long one. The English married late by European standards and seldom required the elaborate home-building support characteristic of European peasant or urban households (Macfarlane 1986; Davis 1977). In this period, therefore, with a greater division of labour, kinship-driven bifurcation into farming or artisan careers and the emergence of a class structure, different patterns of sub-economy responsible for housing wealth emerged. Among the farming sector there was a decline in social network or gift economy and a consolidation of domestic responsibility through inheritance – mainly within the kinship core. Among the artisan class living away from their natal home the domestic property component was less but it was converted into purchasing power in the market through *inter-vivos* gifts of cultural capital (education, apprenticeship). The third period then is characterised by the growth of domestic economy for housing among one broad group, and a similar growth in the market for another. Many farm-labouring households by contrast rented from small landlords or lived in tied accommodation. However there is evidence that whether by right or by customary practice, rights to jobs and the housing that went with them were in many places inheritable. In effect the mode of transmission of housing rights was of little consequence: specific families had claim to specific domestic properties and to general rights to housing for their children in particular estates (Strathern 1981). This feudal form of redistributive sub-economy was unevenly spread and highly variable in quality.

From the fifteenth century AD onwards there is evidence of crisis and conflict in rural tied housing (Marx 1976; Taylor 1983) and this played no small part in the growth of pauperism. Equally the small farmer of the twelfth to fourteenth century AD had by then come under threat from rising land values and the spread of sheep pasturage. As farm holdings became concentrated in fewer hands the domestic mode of transmission in domestic property among the yeomanry gave way to dependency on wage labour and the market for rented housing in labour-market centres. Together with a further decline in the vestiges of the feudal-housing sector, Britain became a nation of home renters and the market closed off most other sub-economic roles in housing. This then is the emerging dominant sub-economy for housing at the end of the fourth period. It is important to remember however that other economic relations carried on and were perhaps more highly valued. First home ownership and the inheritance of domestic property, the preserve of the rural gentry and the bourgeoisie, were of course valued and coveted by those excluded from it. Ownership *per se* may be one important value but domestic control and assistance were arguably as highly valued (Englander 1983). Second, among the landowning classes, vestiges of redistributive values persisted in the guise of paternalism and this group was involved in influencing the eventual form of social housing in Britain.

The traditional period foreshadows many aspects of housing practices which are familiar today and which are associated with modernity and postmodernity. The historical context demonstrates the function of kinship within rival modes of housing organisation and indicates that domestic and gift sub-economies survive in vestigial family practices and less precisely as cultural ambitions.

Most social anthropological research focuses on non-industrial societies and we might expect there to be a rich tradition of comparative material at our disposal. In fact there is very little.

The British, European and Australasian traditions concentrate more on social relations than material culture; the US tradition by contrast, emphasises the latter at the expense of the former. Although housing practice as defined here spans social relations and material culture, housing remains an under-researched area (but see the work of Amos Rapoport). This can partly be explained by the ephemerality and absence of value attached to housing in many areas of the world. Followers of structuralist approaches to gender would not be surprised to learn that women tend to be responsible for the building of ephemeral shelters throughout much of the world (house building subsumed under 'the domestic'), and that men tend to involve themselves where housing has implications for exchange, patronage, wealth and prestige. The literature is strong on patterns of residence, juxta-position of dwellings and the social organisation of collective house building and the exchange of labour. What is of interest to us here is how traditional and custom practice is transformed through modernisation practices throughout the world.

HOUSING PRACTICES IN MODERNITY: BRITAIN AND ELSEWHERE

In Britain throughout the early modern period there is evidence of the unpopularity of the private landlord (Englander 1983). The market was unable to deliver a profitable alternative to private renting, and private renting was unable to deliver mass housing-provision of adequate quality. Industrial and rural paternalism were models for experimental thought in alternative, 'redistri-butive' housing, but neither of these were as far-reaching as the eventual form of subsidised mass social housing. Elsewhere in Europe similar problems existed and the different responses adopted had an impact on the role of kinship in housing practices. In French cities the private rented apartment system reduced the role of kin to nothing more than suppliers of information and influence. However apartments and houses were bought as investment goods and eventually such wealth was bequeathed to children. Social or state housing was an approach embraced more by Scandinavian countries and Britain, and it extended an already reduced role of the family in housing, replacing land-lordism with a 'housing' bureaucracy. Cheaper land and materials in Australia and the USA favoured the owner-occupied solution

and were substantially supported by central and state governments. In the rural fringes of modernising nations there was
continuity of local custom and housing practices, and modified
versions of the former as kinship networks have managed the
process of social mobility and semi-urbanisation (some members
of the network move into city labour markets, others remain on
the land, but the distribution of people in space remains a family-
network matter to a great extent).

One of the early social concerns raised in conjunction with
increased redistributive welfare in British housing, was over the
alleged loss of the 'responsible' family. This anticipated a decline
in long-enshrined duties to provide financial support. There is
very little evidence to show that the family ever fully shied away
from supporting kin. Rather, welfare provision made their efforts
more effective and even (see Klein 1965). The welfare state was
never a complete substitution for the family and, indeed, it
was never intended to be. The family proved reluctant to give up
its role as the only unconditional carer. An early example of this
is revealed in Peter Willmott's (1963) study of Dagenham. After
forty years a rehoused inner-city community from London's East
End more or less completely recomposed their pattern of intense
kinship and neighbourhood links in a newly built council estate.
Neighbourhood and kinship networks operated on the basis
of generalised reciprocity. In this system, gifts of goods and
services are not repaid immediately but they are given as if from
a common pool of goodwill and public generosity and are
returned only when they are apparently needed, if at all. Within
families a similar ethos applied to those kin outside the kinship
core. Kinship cores were expected to support individuals in times
of need and did so. Simply because the state became the provider
of mass housing did not mean that the family would not take
over housing roles wherever required in the future. All the
evidence shows that it did.

Alongside the modern welfare state was a growth in the
numbers who could and wanted to afford to be purchasers of
domestic property. It became highly respectable to hold mortgage
debt in Britain. Partly as a response to negative experiences of
alternative tenures and partly as the fulfilment of widely shared
aspirations of domestic independence, privacy and autonomy,
this trend opened up a new market for private dwellings.

In early post-1945 Britain, housing services became highly

professionalised. DIY renovation and repairs were costly and rarer, and styles and tastes were longer-lasting (combining domestic furniture from the 1930s, 40s, 50s, and 60s was normal, if unsightly) (Morley 1990). The market was less easy to play for gain (house-price inflation was low and mortgageable houses for the first-time buyer were more limited), and very few were likely to inherit housing wealth. Although DIY has a long history, stretching back to the 1940s and before, it remained a relatively minor industry until the 1970s. Materials were expensive, tools were more expensive still, and the 'handy man' was in fact the skilled artisan working at home, on the home. Do-it-yourself magazines carried designs and patterns that only the artisan could follow. Dependence on professional domestic services rendered owner-occupation yet more expensive and served to restrict it.

All of these factors restricted the role that kinship could play in the creation and management of housing wealth. The few studies carried out in these early days suggest that among the very poor sections of the working class, kin were still important in securing nearby private rented accommodation for children (Young and Willmott 1957), but that among the skilled working class and lower-middle class the take-up of council housing tended to divide households sooner and place a greater distance between them (Stacey *et al.* 1975). Perhaps they were prepared to do this since the telephone and personal and public transport maintained adequate contact and reduced travel-to-visit times (Goldthorpe *et al.* 1969).

It needs to be remembered that the main mood of the time was a working-class victory against landlordism, slums and over-crowding. The quality of the resulting provision (e.g. the early cottage developments of the interwar years) overwhelmed many of the first tenants (Jevons and Madge 1946).

The earliest studies relevant to this hail from the end of the 1960s when the notion of embourgeoisiement was being taken seriously by sociologists (Barker 1972; Bell 1968; Atkinson and Harrison 1978). According to Atkinson and Harrison (1978) the pool of inheritable money available in 1968 was very little – only 10 per cent of individuals had £5,000 or more. Most individuals inherited either nothing or very little. Moreover at this time such small amounts made very little impact on the mature lifecycle stage of recipient's lives. Equally it is estimated that the small sums would have made very little difference to relationships and behaviour between the generations (Allan 1982).

Of far greater significance was *inter vivos* inheritance or gifts between living relatives (Finch 1989). According to Bell's (1968) study of stable middle-class families, parents provided very significant gifts of money and goods throughout their children's early adulthood, extending into their early years as parents. There are several significant points to note. First, the sorts of gifts made were often indirect (e.g. in the form of grandchildren's clothes) but the intention was clear enough. Their children's costs, particularly housing costs were greatest and income least at this time in their lifecycle. Such gifts at the margin were often crucial or at least a major financial relief. Second, parents were at a stage in the lifecycle when they were most able to afford such gifts. Their housing costs were relatively low, and their income at its maximum. Third, the size of transfers was not calculated nor was it repaid. Fourth, on average the young always receive more than the old, in other words wealth is continuously being passed down through the generations. And fifth, from Bell's and Barker's accounts, the effect of this transfer is to create a sense of closeness between two households which might otherwise drift apart and to maintain standards of living within families. Barker (1972) argues from her Welsh study, that mothers in particular 'spoiled' their married children in this way – their motive being to continue an important involvement in their lives at a time when they may sense a less direct need for it.

Barker's study was not restricted to middle-class families but her findings showed a similar middle-class pattern. Research conducted since the 1960s appears to confirm this pattern elsewhere in Britain (Wilson 1987; Quereshi and Simons 1987), as well as in Australia (Stivens 1981) and the USA (Hill 1970). Not all of this research is based on middle-class data although it strongly suggests that parents are at least attempting to keep their children in the manner to which they are accustomed. To what extent this *inter vivos* transfer of wealth was practised more widely (across space and social class) will remain unknown unless biographical and oral history is able to recover the information. It will be argued, however, that in the next period where owner-occupation became a mass phenomenon house purchase provides the rationale for increasing parental involvement in a range of gifts to their children including *inter vivos* inheritance. It may also have set in motion a complex set of exchanges between kin and quasi-kin that were hitherto merely latent propensities to assist.

Postwar Australia was expanding and affluent. Housing practices which were well established by the mid-1930s were set to continue more or less unchanged in this period. In contrast to kin-centred southern Europe, or even the newly stabilised kinship cores in Britain (see Franklin 1986), Australians were still characterised by their migrant experience, family networks were less dense, and individuals were less reliant on kinship assistance. From the early colonial period when Australia was a predominantly male society, the institution of mateship (strong moral imperative for groups of men to provide mutual emotional and practical assistance) functioned in many ways as a substitute kindred (Ward 1958; Conway 1985). By 1945 Australia was more demographically balanced but the institution of mateship was still active (Oxley 1978), and intimately woven into housing practices. Since the nineteenth century Australian towns gradually expanded through suburban sub-division, and the pattern of newly married couples building their own homes on the edge of town (one of the cheapest options) became established and entrenched. This provided the basis for considerable cooperation between mates in building, extension and maintenance. Research into community ties in Australian cities reveals tight clusters of friends in particular suburbs, particularly among the middle-to-low income groups (Martin 1985). The now classic weatherboard house on a quarter-acre block is the ubiquitous Australian dream house and is found, with some minor local variations, in all six capital cities.

Modernisation in rural Greece by contrast involved far greater continuities in kin ties and housing-support practices. On the one hand a substantial number of people continued to farm family holdings, and housing wealth was circulated in the traditional way (Sanders 1953; Friedl 1970; Herzfeld 1980). On the other, most Greek families were involved in moving children through education, into an urban career, and establishing an urban base. With a growing urban 'side' or base to Greek rural families, the movement of subsequent generations into town occupations was made even easier, and as visiting became more regularised, young people were as likely to meet an urban spouse as a rural spouse. The blurring of urban and rural communities through socially mobile kinship networks created difficulties in the normal transmission of property from one generation to the next. For example in Vasilika land was traditionally given as a dowry, but as more and more daughters married town husbands this proved inflexible – as well as less attractive to the would-be town husband. From the 1950s therefore, farmers spent their savings (or sold land) to build houses – often over a long period – for their daughters in Athens.

POSTMODERN HOUSING PRACTICES

From the general conditions of postmodernity (Harvey 1989) or more properly perhaps, postmodernising conditions (Crook, Pakulski and Waters 1991), one is able also to sketch out some general postmodernising housing characteristics and tendencies:

1 the reduction in state production and management of housing – though *not* an end to state subsidy;
2 the state continues to be needed to subsidise and encourage housing for smaller groups of low-income households;
3 more choice in housing; a freer market; easier access, more flexible housing finance;
4 proliferation of choice in rented housing provision and management types, including both tenant management co-ops and private management companies;
5 flexible housing careers, choice of tenure;
6 housing development of wide range of market niches but including gentrified, nostalgic and pastiched 'quartiers' such as inner-city terrace, dockland waterfront, rural village new-build, studio and loft-land, and neo-modern;
7 small development and in-fill rather than mega estate;
8 restructuring of house-price regions;
9 greater flexibility in relations between home and work (rise of computer-based home working and decentralised production);
10 general growth and wider spread of private housing wealth including more flexible forms of equity release and usage;
11 decline in prominence of professionalised housing maintenance and repair services and the growth of DIY, system build, personalisation of living space;
12 fewer restrictions on 'alternative' types of household and household formation;
13 commodification of former state housing.

Postmodernisation by definition involves a diversification of experiences, niches, markets, and subcultural variations out of what was once easily characterised by simpler divisions of society in class and tenure. In this section it is argued that kinship practices which preceded modernity and never fully disappeared, have returned in recent years, particularly in areas where housing has been recommodified, or where owner-occupation expanded at the expense of other tenures. This refamilisation of housing roles has no single cause, but the decline in the state, the commodification of state housing, the spread of ownership opportunities and certain labour-market conditions all promote it.

The housing practices of both middle and working classes have merged in some areas and remained distinctive in others. Clearly the experience of owner-occupation is a major area of convergence, though the cultural aspects of it as class practice are clearly very different. And as others have commented, those cultural differences may outweigh any tenurial similarities (Forrest and Murie 1989).

What follows is a preliminary investigation of some aspects of changes in the postmodern period. Continuing our primary focus on Britain, the first section considers changes in the kinship core, in respect of both low and higher income groups. Three aspects will be considered: low-income owner-occupation, high-income owner-occupation and tenant purchase of state housing. Secondly we will explore changes in the housing practices of siblings, friends and social networks. Two areas are particularly noteworthy and will be dealt with separately: first, borrowing and helping (new patterns of generalised exchange); and second, the provisioning of role models and information (new patterns of social support).

Low-Income Owner-Occupation

The majority of low-income couples able to purchase a home independently do so either because they live in a low-priced region or because they have bought a property which needs extensive renovation. The removal of British building society rules preventing loans on older (pre-1918) and poor-quality homes enabled many low-income families to make substantial gains through investing their own trade skills into their own home (Merrett 1982). Any property showing a gap between current market value and potential market value provided an opportunity for entry to the lower rungs of the housing market. There is now substantial evidence that working-class families use family labour and trade skills to this end (Pahl 1984; Warde *et al.* 1989).

The working-class-recession studies in Britain (Pahl 1984; Warde *et al.* 1989; Willmott 1987; Wallman 1982) in which data on all sorts of exchanges within families were gathered, did not ask about *inter vivos* money and other significant gifts. Willmott is able to show that working-class people are most likely to approach close kin for a loan of up to £50, suggesting that it is commonplace, but the frequency and the actual values were not recorded. The degree to which young couples intent on purchase receive gifts or loans from within the kinship core is unknown but the obvious working hypothesis is that it is most common in high-price regions. Building on the work of Barker, it may be that parents are keen to provide this service in order to keep their children 'close by'. One obvious solution to the problem of house prices which have risen beyond the reach of young low-income couples is to move to a low-price region. To many parents this might be a less appealing solution than to offer the couple financial assistance themselves. Parents have several options open to them: they can divide savings among children, or failing that parents who are still working can remortgage their own property to release the capital required. This phenomenon of 'staying close' when pressures threaten to break up kinship cores was also found in a study of Consett (Franklin 1990a; Forrest 1987) following the closure of the dominant employer, British Steel.

Staying close need not involve staying in one locality, however. In a study of kinship in London, R.G.A. Williams (1983) found that family cores tended to move out to new locations together: parents and siblings following an initial sibling relocation. The housing and wealth implications of this are clear enough. It is a solution (again) to external pressures to move for housing and work-related purposes. There are many reasons why entire kinship cores will want to move, other than a desire to stay together: these include better employment possibilities, cheaper housing, and equity release (e.g. to set up a business).

Strategies to maintain communal ties in the face of development and rising land and property prices are now a global problem from coastal North Carolina (Peck and Lepie 1989) to

Tonga (Urbanowicz 1989). Indeed as tourism has expanded beyond highly stylised modern 'packages' to postmodern 'diversities', more and more of these low-price regions are becoming inflated beyond local financial means, first by being 'opened up' by tourists and then by a second wave of retiree colonists.

High-Income Owner-Occupation

Middle-class children in Britain are more likely to receive gifts of money, if not property itself, at the start-up stage of their adult housing careers and this may come from more than one familial source. Parents tend to help children most with putting downpayments together while grandparents may leave them substantial inheritances around the time they are starting a family and perhaps looking for a larger family property. They may receive substantial parcels of property on the death of their parents at late middle age, foreshadowing a move to a more prestigious home. They may be just as dependent on kinship assistance as working-class children in satisfying their taste in housing but they are less likely to come under pressure to 'stay close'. Indeed, there is in middle-class culture a strong ethos to encourage travel, independence and exploration (Firth 1970; Bell 1968; Goldthorpe *et al.* 1968).

Middle-class kinship cores are more geographically mobile and wider spaced – often outside easy visiting and provision of care. Combined with their relative longevity, middle-class parents may be more likely to trade in housing equity for health care than their working-class counterparts.

Two very different housing strategies are beginning to emerge inside kinship cores. The first, related most to low-income groups, sees housing wealth as a means of keeping kinship cores together in a localised mutual dependence. The second, characteristic more of middle-class groups, is a strategy where housing wealth is used to maintain independence and spatial separation. In both, however, housing wealth and family organisation reproduces cultural difference and residential segregation.

Siblings, Friends and Networks 1: Borrowing and Helping

As we have seen, friendships have always been particularly strong in Britain, and it is arguable that they have come to fill the place occupied elsewhere by larger localised kindreds. These significant non-kinship core relationships also tend to have a strong moral foundation which gives rise to expectations to help on a day-to-day basis, to cooperate on joint projects, and to assist in times of crisis. The nature of exchange is generalised and no criteria for assistance is specified. However, over time the nature of required help has changed, and we are arguing here that with the decline of the state housing infrastructure, the decline of the professional monopoly of housing provision, management and maintenance, the growth of owner-occupation and the declining costs of DIY, many of these functions are now worked out within friendship and kinship networks. While very substantial help has remained the remit of kinship cores, many of the smaller – but arguably no less substantial – exchanges are normally undertaken in friendship networks. This process is governed by at least three key factors:

1 the pattern of settlement – people typically live among non-kin in their immediate neighbourhood, and many move far away from their kin cores (Short 1976);
2 life stage/cycle – grandparents are less likely to know about DIY than young couples who are also renovating houses nearby;
3 subculture/taste – taste may vary within kin cores but similarity or sharing of taste style and subculture is one criteria of friendship (Allan 1989).

Meaningful relations between non-core kin are in fact frequently little more than friendships (see Wallman 1974). These together with other friendships formed at school, in neighbourhoods and at work provide a significant resource to most people. In Britain friendship is beginning to be recognised as a more significant social phenomenon with far-reaching material, emotional and cultural significance (Willmott 1987; Allan 1989; Hollinger and Haller 1990). This significance may also have grown in recent years (see Willmott 1987).

In terms of help with house maintenance Willmott found that friends were the main source in over 50 per cent of his sample, whereas only one third turned to relatives. Moreover, the significance of friends for such help did not vary by social class. Although domestic labour and paid market-sector labour feature most in terms of labour used for home improvement and renovation, the communal sector (friends and neighbours) features prominently. For example, Pahl (1984) in a study of the Isle of Sheppey in the south of England found that the communal sector featured strongly in significant renovation tasks: 50 per cent used communal labour for putting in attics, 12 per cent for plastering, 11 per cent for glazing, 10 per cent for building extensions. Such labour was used far more for housing-related tasks than for work on cars or childcare. Since the majority of Pahl's sample would be among the first in their family to purchase their own home, this degree of exchange between friends is relatively new. An identical study conducted in Lancashire in 1988 (Warde *et al.* 1989) found significantly less exchange of this kind, which shows that the South may be, contrary to popular opinion, more 'friendly' or 'generous' than the North. However, none of these studies have had friend-ship in prime focus, and the degree of follow-up to survey questions is disappointing in this area. Thus we know very little about why and when such services are rendered, how they are reciprocated, and how choices and recruitments are made.

Such findings are not peculiar to Britain. Friendships appear to be a very Anglo-Saxon phenomenon with Australians and North Americans claiming to have the largest number of friends (Hollinger and Haller 1990). In the study of seven countries however Hollinger and Haller found that friends were the single largest source of assistance for household and sickness-related problems other than co-partners. More significantly, almost 20 per cent of the sample used friends (parents accounted for only 12 per cent) for assistance with emotional problems and for 'big decision' making. Such a finding squares with another claim being made here that friends feature perhaps more prominently in terms of information and the formation of taste and style. In terms of housing wealth they may not be the most significant material providers but they play no small part as providers of inspiration and role models. This is again no great surprise, but it has yet to be fully realised and researched.

Siblings, Friends and Networks 2: Role Models and Information

In a study of working-class housing-decision-making in Bristol, Short (1976) indicated that not only were friends the most often consulted group, they were often the main source of ideas. Moreover it was clear that people wanted to live among their friends: to be near friends for example was one of the most significant reasons given for moving; being near friends was the single biggest criterion in housing searches; and only those areas where friends lived were routinely searched. In Willmott's (1987) study, he found that 54 per cent of working-class respondents' friends were within ten minutes' travel time away and a further 27 per cent were between 10 and 30 minutes away. Middle-class respondents' friends were more widely dispersed: 38 per cent within 10 minutes and 33 per cent between 10 and 30 minutes. Nonetheless, it would appear that people like to live near their friends. Comparing the proximity of friends and relatives, Willmott found that whereas 42 per cent of friends were living within 10 minutes, only 22 per cent of core relatives lived so close. Similar evidence can be found for the USA (Fischer 1982). Again this seems to corroborate our claim that core family are important for major issues while friends are most important for routine day-to-day issues and sociability. Kin can be kept at some distance, but close friends need to be on hand.

In making a decision to buy a house friends may be extremely significant. In the first place there is the decision to buy a first home or not. Biographical interviews conducted by the author in Bristol indicated that friendship networks are influential in setting up housing-career trajectories (a progression through the market in terms of stages and strategic purchases) and in setting up parameters of choice (style of housing, size, location, age and so on). Almost every respondent reported having an influential friend in a network who 'pioneered' entry into owner-occupation, and who (again through friendship networks) devised some strategic plans and adopted points of style. Respondents reported that the precise timing of their entry had to do with an association with a pioneer. Some had already considered house purchase, but only vaguely, while others had not given it any thought at all. In the British context, the timing of entry has little to do with establishing an income and mortgage commensurate with a desirable form of housing. Since entry conditions are always changing (what is a desirable house, location; changing rates of interest; changing mortgage deals; changing tax breaks, etc.), potential 'entrants' are unlikely to be in possession of perfect and full market knowledge. And they need both accurate and reliable knowledge and, because it is the single biggest financial decision in their life, some encouragement. 'Pioneer' friends are perfect mediators in this process: they can be trusted, they have all the necessary experience, they have enthusiasm (they also need to justify their own decision) and the pleasure of being envied and emulated. This relates back to the data, noted above, on friendships and 'big decisions'.

For obvious reasons these decisions relate directly to housing wealth. Indeed, some of the key strategies were directly concerned with wealth creation. Research in this area should look back on this period and investigate different strategies. During the pre-building boom of the 1980s, for example, conversion strategies were profitable; during the boom itself several strategies emerged: restoration of popular 'period' homes was one, holding title to as much housing value as possible was another.

All cultures and subcultures involve assumptions about housing: design, size, style, career and so on. Here the operation of friendship networks serves to multiply and diversify the housing locations individuals occupy in their lifetime and the sequence and timing of changes. In modernity a small, modest dwelling may have been all most people aspired to, and indeed it may have served people throughout most of their life. In postmodernity there is no limit to housing careers, and there is less pressure to narrow choices.

All this has a bearing on the privatism debate which emerged during the 1980s (see Franklin 1989a). During these years the collective communal fabric of social identity was held to be undermined (Saunders 1990; Marshall *et al.* 1988). Replacing it was a more privatised, self-contained social identity focused on the family and centred in the privately owned home and garden. The power, control and ontological security which was lost in the public fields of politics and workplace were restored to male workers – if not to their female partners – in this haven in a hostile world. The analysis presented here indicates that this privatised solution did not emerge. Instead, the modernist social relations of housing (the bureaucratic solution for 'mass' provision) were recomposed within a diverse mix of market transactions and informal networks. Although housing in this new postmodern form became more significant, it distinguished groups, belongings and subcultures rather than individuals or individual status.

Following Bourdieu therefore, much could and should be made of the cultural capital, the social groups, the tastes, and the distinctions involved in housing in Britain – and elsewhere. In the case of British housing practices and the adult subcultures that articulate them, it is very unlikely that distinctions would naturally break into broad groupings based simply on class and cultural capital – hence they do not belong to the somewhat tired sociology of stratification. That may have featured more in modernity, but postmodernising conditions allow for much more flexibility, design and identity to be expressed through housing by larger numbers of unstratified, different groups.

CONCLUSION

This paper has argued that kinship and social networks are increasingly involved, through a variety of reciprocal arrangements, in the creation and transmission of housing wealth. Through an historical examination of the involvements of kin and kin-like networks in housing provisions it is possible to view this trend in terms of a return to a former function of the family and local social network. Indeed it is argued that the propensity to assist and to engage in generalised exchange in this area was modified in modernity as the state took over roles which were formerly performed by kin and later by market provision. Housing provision, management and maintenance were increasingly professionalised by the state and informal social involvement was minimal. Indeed, family assistance in modernity appeared to be most concerned with the provision and rapid replacement of the new modern complement of domestic furnishing.

In dealing with such complex arrangements within and between families we have argued that a more precise conceptual framework is required. It was suggested that precise kinship relations and groups are always specified and that further research should seek to understand the developing nature of these social relations and exchanges. It was also argued that we need to distinguish a typology of exchanges and spheres of exchange which relate to such relationships and emerging new arrangements in housing. More research is required into the nature of gift giving, the moral nature of exchange and reciprocity, and the emergence of new forms of 'domestic custom' in relation to the transmission of housing wealth. Such new customs and practices it is suggested will be mediated by class, location and labour market.

Also emerging from the intense period of privatisation are sub-class adult networks based on taste and shared subculture, which establish common housing practices and perform important reference and advisory functions. Their agency lies not only in advice and reference but in their interpretation of the housing market and how it will be shaped and incorporated into (their) new cultural repertoires.

Chapter 13

Shifting paradigms
The sociology of housing, the sociology of the family, and the crisis of modernity

Antonio Tosi

INTRODUCTION

A distinctive feature of the sociology of family since the 1970s has been the 'discovery' of the theoretical importance of family networks in contemporary urban society (see Konig 1976; Segalen 1981). On the basis of a growing body of empirical evidence, the presence in our societies of a variety of family structures (including extended family forms) and the persistent supportive role of kinship relations have been emphasised, and opposed to what were current opinions in the conventional sociology of the family. Ample documentation has been provided on the precise nature of these family ties, and on the role of exchange of goods and services, which takes place on a family-network level, showing their importance on both material and cultural levels.[1]

This 'discovery' is significant because it has called into question conventional sociological ideas on the relationship between family and modernisation. The discovery of family networks has above all questioned the functionalist theory of the industrialisation–family relationship, stressing the ideological nature of the opposition between household and network. This reflection is part of a fertile debate on the kind of family structures prevalent in Western Europe. Since the studies of the Cambridge Group (see Wall *et al.* 1983), serious criticisms and empirical refutations have scotched the prevailing opinion among sociologists that, in the past, families were of a 'multiple structure' kind and that they had traversed what Durkheim called a process of progressive contraction. According to this report, which Goode (quoted in Saraceno 1988, 26) dubbed 'the family of western nostalgia', industrialisation had played a vital role, almost a watershed, fostering the emergence of the neo-local, nuclear family in capitalist, industrialised Western Europe. In fact, it was shown on the one hand that during the various centuries prior to industrialisation the nuclear family was already the structural family model in several countries in northern Europe; while on the other, it was shown that the transformations which altered the family situation were neither linear nor univocal, and that the outcome was a certain variance of forms, according to places and social groups, rather than standardisation of family structures.

The crux came with the discovery of the importance of kinship. While industrialisation was long considered to be the virtually exclusive cause of the diffusion of the nuclear-family type of domestic group, it was also considered responsible for the waning social impact of kinship. As has already been observed (Saraceno 1988), rather than supply information on what really transpired in family relations, this interpretation of social change (which found its most systematic explanation in the functionalist theory of the family) supplied information on the forms of representation and self-representation of contemporary western society – particularly applicable to the 1940s and 1950s, i.e. 'a faith in the universalism of reason and the equality of opportunity on the market, where individuals could freely meet and exchange goods and political choices alike' (ibid., 38). In this perspective, family ties seemed a contradiction, owing to their somewhat irrational and undemocratic particularism. Furthermore, they were seen as something residual, typical to less socially and politically 'evolved' classes and regions. It was seen as 'backward' to be bogged down by kinship ties, a situation that was described not only as 'disfunctional' with regard to economic efficiency, but 'immoral' in terms of democratic evolution and personal liberty (e.g. Banfield 1958).

This outlook began to be questioned in the mid-1960s. Various studies showed that, in certain circumstances, kinship networks were far from idle in terms of economic–social resources or as a source of control; actually they proved to be an important agent of mediation. Little by little a new picture emerged with the household in the centre of a dense network of relationships and exchange between relatives or related households. The idea of network – a common reference in the sociology of the family since the 1970s – appropriately suggested exchange taking place in many directions, an intersecting of relations and exchange that was not always direct or linear, enhanced by a general system of support or protection. Furthermore it signalled the inherent dynamism, not dictated exclusively by any strict, ascribed code but by an interplay of needs and personal choices, which the flexibility of these networks was most suited to fulfil (Hill and Konig 1970). Accordingly, ideological attitudes towards networks began to change.

This change was possible because during this very period there had been a shift in the debate on modernisation and modernity. This rethink marked the need to interpret the transition to post-industrial forms of society. It also signalled the emphasis of many social theories on the 'crisis in modernity', and not least a widespread crisis in the theories of modernisation and the theoretical paradigms influenced by the ideologies of modernity. The family-networks issue expressed this theoretical shift in the sociology of the family, which in turn contributed significantly to the critique of theories of modernisation. Relative to family itself, it was asserted that 'modernity is not monolithic. There are as many ways of being modern as there are separate cultures experiencing it' (Pitkin 1985, 206).

As it turned out, the crisis in paradigms of modernity was linked to a general theoretical upheaval in the social sciences that reverberated through various fields of social theory and research. The new interest in 'informal' phenomena, of which exchanges within family networks are an important feature, played a decisive part in that reappraisal. In general terms, it heralded a shift in theoretical paradigms which expressed two converging crises affecting social sciences: the crisis in modernisation theory, and the crisis in the positivistic tradition (Tosi 1991a). The shift involved the various fields of social research, and prompted a substantial overhaul of ideas and methods. Consequently, housing theory was also affected, where various attempts at revision borrowed the tools supplied by the 'new sociologies' spawned by the crisis – as when one tries to construct actor-oriented, or 'individual-based' (Kemeny 1986) approaches to housing research, or perspectives which are more sensitive to the variances in markets and needs (Tosi 1991a).

As for housing, the crisis in the very systems of reference – the cultural models, the policy models, the models of provision – and the crisis in the relative theoretical paradigms sparked what might be defined as a case of real theoretical 'deconstruction' of the field. On the basis of their common bond with the crisis in the theories of modernisation, it seems feasible to tie in the debate arising from the new sociology of the family with the attempts at reconstruction under way in the field of housing. On both sides, the theoretical crisis calls into question the fundamental issue of links between house and family as defined in the models emerging from modernisation. In the light of this, an aspect of family housing practices comes to the fore: provision within the family network system.

HOUSING AND FAMILY NETWORKS

At the crossroads between the sociology of the family and the sociology of housing, an innovating body of research has grown on this idea. So far, much attention has been paid to the economic and financial aspects of the problem and to the effectiveness of this kind of informal provision in creating housing opportunities. However, even in order to recognise the economic aspects of these processes, a broader approach is required which covers the various implications of reference to family, and relates this area of research to relevant aspects of the general housing debate.

The point will be clear if we consider the role that extended family networks – and their local bases – have in a number of housing strategies. Substantial empirical evidence is now available which illustrates a variety of setups that exist among the housing practices of households belonging to the same family network. The strategies that link them are created through the exchange of goods and services between households, and in many cases they have a spatial factor, or they set up spatial associations between the households.[2]

Housing as a family enterprise: mobilising a family network

One of the primary forms of linkage in the housing practices of related households lies in the exchange of goods and services, which takes place on a family level. Some of these take the form of a free-flowing mutual exchange of self-help activities between different households. Other forms of exchange crop up in crucial moments in the lifecycle of a household, such as for weddings, or when someone looks for a new job or moves house (Cuturello 1987). To a great extent, these exchanges can be grouped under

the heading 'intergenerational transfers', with particular reference to the handing down of material wealth, coming variously
in the form of financial aid, gifts, or inheritances (see Kessler
1979, 33–4).

The steady increase in these intergenerational transfers has
been documented in a number of countries. In France, for
instance, the amount of donations or gifts between family
members increased twofold between 1945 and 1985. There has
been a marked rise in 'non-ritualised' gifts, i.e. those that have
no real link with family events; furthermore, these transfers
are becoming more and more evenly spread throughout the
human lifespan (Gotman 1986). The gradual increase in the years
a person is expected to live has influenced the models for intergenerational transfers. Instead of post-mortem transfers, help
and donations constitute a sort of 'anticipated inheritance', aimed
at providing the household with resources in crucial moments
of its lifecycle (Cuturello and Godard 1980). Alongside this rise
in intergenerational transfers there has been a basic increase in
family assets, largely through home ownership (especially in the
middle-to-lower income brackets).

As is to be expected, the inter-generational transfers pave
the way generously to home ownership. In France 28 per cent of
owners have had family backing in their purchase (Cuturello
1987). Thirteen per cent of the semi- and unskilled working
class achieved home ownership either through inheritance or
donation (Gotman 1988). In Italy 23 per cent of owner families
received their home through inheritances, gifts, or dowry.
(Another substantial number of families become home owners
with financial help that originates in family transfers, either
directly or indirectly.) In an area of settled and widespread
urbanisation like Lombardy, 21 per cent of owner families gained
their home through inheritance or gift, and 27 per cent received
financial assistance from their parents for the purchase or
construction of a home (Tosi 1987, 1991b).

This correlation between intergenerational transfers and home
ownership does not mean that the transfer of assets and property
is a straightforward 'translation' or 'reflection' of family relationships (see Gotman 1988, 177). In most cases, ownership comes
about as a result of active mobilisation of the family network:
it is a fully-fledged 'family enterprise' which mobilises the family
network in order to produce the necessary resources (see Cuturello

1987). This mobilisation takes place within the complex system of exchanges that form the informal economy pivoting on the family. Given the importance of the enterprise, the network called on in this case is an extensive one, and goes far beyond the inner circle of parents and their married children, involving the extended family network and on occasion the friendship network.

Research carried out in the Veneto region and the Nice area provides ample clues to this form of mobilisation. The resources supplied directly by parents are always the main ones. In the Nice area, this form of anticipated inheritance has a fundamental role in determining the solvency of households (Cuturello and Godard 1980). For those households who go in for self-construction, mobilising the family network is essential for achieving ownership (Cuturello 1987). In the communities studied in the Veneto region, family help is nearly always decisive. In many cases the parents manage to provide almost all the resources required. Furthermore, in all the cases reported, ownership is achieved through an active strategy that 'pools' the many kinds of resources the family network is able to round up. These include financial resources, but also the plot of land for building the new house – something that is common among families of farming origin. In addition there is also the essential manual labour that various family members and relatives may be able to provide in the course of realisation (Baggio and Donato 1986).

The analysis of this assemblage of resources offers a challenge to basic assumptions implied in housing policies – the idea of an isolated household that presents itself on the market with its own resources; and the notion of 'solvency', understood simply as a unit of financial data (see Cuturello and Godard 1980). Actually the solvency of a household cannot be treated separately from the many complex social processes set in motion. It is 'pieced together', and is the result of mobilising a broader network, with both financial and non-financial resources that spread out in many directions (Tosi 1987).

It is obvious, however, that this recourse to the family network cannot be read simply as a strategy for increasing resources on an economic-rational basis. A closer look at the processes of mobilisation points to other meanings and purposes behind the said exchanges. One of the indications that emerges in the research carried out by Cuturello on self-help practices concerns the 'social position' of the exchanges. First, most transfers pass through a sort of vertical mobilisation that passes from ascendants to descendants. More than two-thirds of the individuals who contribute are either ascendants or descendants, while less than one-third are collateral relatives. (This is one example of a general historical process of reinforcement of the direct line within the kin network (Cuturello 1987, 150–3).) Secondly, there is a kind of division of labour according to the position a member occupies within the kinship, and hence to the generation to which the member belongs. 'The ascendants guarantee the financing, while the contemporaries of the household (the collaterals) and the new generations (the children) act as a complementary workforce – the strong correlation between the position in the kinship and the belonging to a particular generation entails a fairly rigid division of roles' (ibid., 154–5). Finally, we can note an interaction between the strategies employed – the moment of the lifecycle in which a household takes on the enterprise – and the gender of the family line that brings the necessary financial aid. Two-thirds of the households that adopt active strategies have a network of financial assistance that comes exclusively from the husband's family. In contrast, nearly all the 'passive' households (characterised by a later access to home ownership) have a network of financial aid coming from the wife's family. Whatever the explanations may be for this phenomenon (see Cuturello 1987, 156ff), it nevertheless denotes a gender division of mutual aid, and confirms the general character brought to light by the analysis – the aid varies according to the position an individual occupies in the scheme of family relationships. This would suggest that relationships behind the exchange count at least as much as the nature and level of the resources exchanged.

An aspect of analogous importance is evident in research on the Veneto region. In this case it would appear that another sphere of the network comes up with the resources, namely the local or community sphere. A complex web of informal relationships based on extended family and community is involved not only in the production of the necessary resources, but in all the aspects and phases of the process of home ownership. Even the planning and execution of the labour take place within this network. Relationships of all kinds – relatives, co-workers, friends, neighbours – frequently overlap, and the same applies to professional and market assistance, which is often played out in the context of informal relations (see Baggio and Donato 1986;

Dal Dosso 1982). Home ownership turns out to be a local-specific strategy, that unfolds within a framework of community relations, and among extended family networks (Tosi 1987). Once more, in this case as above we can assume that the social relations between those participating count as much as the functional contents of the services provided.

The two examples suggest that, in addition to generating a 'real' economy, the exchanges connected with home ownership have a function that we could call 'symbolic'. The development of primary socialities and identity processes are the most evident aspects of this, and those particularly linked to the family and local character of the resources put to use. In the two examples these functions are both evident and considerable because other factors concur – a structure of small communities, and the predominance of self-provision processes. In their symbolic capacity, the practices described express forms of rationality that differ from the conventional ones. 'They are practices which fall outside a budget logic.' This questions one of the basic attitudes in housing policy; the evidence of informal mechanisms used to create solvency 'opens serious breaches in the theories of social order based on statistical indicators, which draw on a typical consumer, considered as someone interchangeable and oriented to economic rationality' (Cuturello and Godard 1980, 62).

Family homes: homes within extended family relations

The material and symbolic significance of the exchanges within family networks are also important outside the contexts already mentioned: this becomes clear if we look at the processes of inheritance related to the home. Despite the transformations under way in the functions and models of transmission, the strictly hereditary ones have remained a substantial contribution (see for instance Kessler 1979; Hamnett 1984; Forrest and Murie 1989). From research on the Veneto region and Nice it would appear that inheritances provide a vital source of access to ownership. This ties in with what regional and national data have revealed. For instance in Lombardy 17 per cent of home ownership comes from inheritances (Tosi 1991b).

Inheritance can influence access to ownership in a variety of ways. By analysing the ways that 'tie' the residential paths of individual households with those of their extended families,

Gotman has pinpointed five different types of path linked to inheritance, and these are: (a) paths directly linked to the widowing of either of the parents – the consequent closing of the distance of parents to their children, with their coming to live close by; (b) cases in which inheritance triggers access to ownership of the main home, or allows for the purchase of a more suitable home for the household; (c) cases in which inheritance brings about a second home, making purchase possible, or allows the re-use of the parents' house as a second home; (d) cases in which inheritance passes on to children, or an inherited dwelling is reserved in their name, or a home is bought for them with money from an inheritance; (e) and finally the straightforward case of the re-occupation of an inherited dwelling as a household's main home (Gotman 1988, 178).

It is commonly considered that more than just patrimonial resources pass through this particular kind of relationship (see for example Cuturello and Godard 1980; Henretta 1984). Gotman (1988, 14) stresses the 'model' character that such transmission still has in the 'wage-earning society': 'where there are squanderers they take a stand against this norm, which they are aware of transgressing'. Only a 'symbolic family economy' can do justice to the complexity of the strategies of inheritance: 'strategies aimed at building up capital that will guarantee material livelihood, but which also symbolize a certain kind of family' (Gotman 1985, 16). This is evident in the specific status that inherited houses may assume. In many cases, they cannot be dispensed with: they are not 'ordinary capital', but 'the object of investments on a long-term basis', for the children; 'a house for the future generations, for family reunions, something that remains in the family' (ibid., 20). Extreme implications of this can be observed in the case of 'poor people who inherit from even poorer parents': the inherited property is 'added' to their own but not integrated with it. It 'serves as a reserve, either for themselves or their own children, not a means to exploit. It is something untouchable, rather than a capital asset. Although these families have debts, no one draws on the inherited capital to pay them off or to improve their standard of living. The inheritance in these cases can in some cases be a costly affair, rather than any real advantage' (ibid., 21).

In both cases the inherited house holds a special status that derives from its position within ascendant–descendant relations – the house is 'within' the family (Gotman 1985). Somehow the dwelling 'belongs' to the family, as a succession of generations. And being located within the family, the house is in some way 'removed' from the market.

These exchanges and transfers within the family network shed much light on a particular kind of dwelling – the family home. The family home is the place of the extended family, and represents the most important spatial reference-point for its symbolic functions. The definition, as the above cases show, can actually be inverted – the family network is the 'place' of the dwelling, a system to which the dwelling 'pertains' or 'belongs'. This can have various implications. If for instance a family network has an important role in the process of constructing identity (Segalen 1981), and the family home is its focus and symbol, the theme of 'house and identity' in many cases should be redefined in reference to the family home.

Proximity to family: home is where the family is

The residential practices of households belonging to the same family network can be linked up irrespective of the distance between the households. But there are strategies in which the space and place of the relations are fundamental ingredients. Proximity is a resource in itself, on both a material and a symbolic level, and can therefore be significant in the economic and symbolic functioning of the family network. Research into the persistence of extended family relations in urban societies underlines the astonishing closeness of the various households, especially between married children and their parents' home. The phenomenon has been well documented throughout industrialised countries (e.g. Konig 1976; Segalen 1981; Gaunt 1988; Tosi 1991b).

Residential proximity is the most well-known spatial means through which the strategies of various households are linked together. The impact of proximity changes somewhat when the strategy includes the local system in which family relations come to be set up. While in the city proximity to relatives may not imply any particular participation or identification with the local area, in smaller towns and villages the local system and place is often involved – 'with' the family network – in the residential strategy of the household. In these situations there is often an accentuated integration between family network and community network.

We have already mentioned that in the case of the Veneto region, the local character of the informal network determines the entire process of ownership access, so that in those communities the operation is both determined by the family network and is locally specific. Proximity is at the same time a question of integration in the family network and in the local system. The overlapping of the two networks reinforces the consistency of the system of production of resources, highlights the symbolic dimension of the networks, and the significance of the social position of the acts that generate ownership.

In these communities the links between family networks and the local system are largely generated around the informal economy and self-provision practices. The intense system of exchanges that develops on a local basis and through family networks is a real economy and at the same time a factor of the symbolic and identity processes. For example, research on a small manufacturing town in the Meuse valley found that self-provisioning – 'the production of goods and services outside the field of market production' –

> presupposes an intense degree of sociality, which these practices help to maintain and develop. This sociality is one of the main features on which the identification processes rely, one of the bases of social identity. Self-provisioning, sociality, and identity appear to be very closely bound to relations of inter-dependence, in which they are at once the condition and consequence of each other.
>
> (Pinçon 1986, 629)

Housing is one of the central elements of this informal economy. First of all the house is the place and, to some extent, the condition of self-provisioning and of the informal circuits that are structured around family networks and the sociality of the village or small town. 'On the basis of the networks of kinship, exchanges take place through the vegetable gardens, the freezers, the houses. Through the maintenance of the vegetable gardens the entire sociality of the family is held together' (Segalen 1980, 43). 'The freezer is a tool of exchange' (Auffray *et al.* 1980, 206). Above all, the construction of the house is a critical moment in the informal economy, and is a vital occasion for intense mutual help, that draws first and foremost on the relatives.

Parents, brothers, sisters, and in-laws all flock to help lay the foundations, build the support walls, install the electrical circuits and plumbing. Irrespective of whether they work downtown or in the country, the relatives are called on for their contribution each weekend or during their annual holidays. This help – based on reciprocity relationships – is entirely free, ready to be given back the moment another relative is in need of aid in building his or her new home, or there is need of other mutual assistance within the family. The construction of the house signals a moment in which family relationships reach a peak, and on such occasions the network draws both on close relatives, and on collateral relations and similar – anyone who lives within a radius of thirty kilometres or so. The more far-reaching kinship radius is mobilized to give adequate backing to the household, which takes up or resumes residence in the town, as if to justify its decision and encourage the social reproduction of the model.

(Segalen 1980, 46)

Two-home families: connecting places and families

Relationships with the local society and with the local and family network can turn out to be far more complex than the traditional image of a small community would first suggest. This kind of sociality can be cultivated by members of the community who in fact live outside it, as in the case of emigrants who retain close ties with their place of origin. Spatial schemes organised on two homes and two places of residence are a common occurrence, and tend to instil specific linkage practices between the two places in question.

Segalen (1980) describes an example of two generations of inhabitants of a Breton village. One of the groups is made up of emigrants who moved away in the 1950s, and became gendarmes or employees in administration in Nantes, Quimper, or Paris. When their parents retired, they shared out their land among all their children, on a strictly egalitarian basis. Each of them was thus in a position to build a second home, where they could come and spend their holidays and long weekends. These houses contribute to the perpetuation of the kin relations – brothers and sisters who had emigrated had their homes built on nearby plots, and often close to other relatives. Such practices as the upkeep of the garden plots during the summer bind together family sociability.

> The emigrant in the city often has an impoverished social life, limited to relations with people from work; in the smaller town or village it is very easy to fall back in with relatives and old friendships, even after some time. On his re-entry in the village, he resumes his place in the heart of the village society. For these emigrants the social identification and way of life are held together by the presence of relatives in the village sociality. This is symbolised by the home, built in true Breton style. In total contrast with the city dwelling (often rented), the home is the focus of the investment of both affections and material livelihood.
>
> (Segalen 1980, 43–4)

Today young people, the second group considered, are more and more on the look-out for a job that will enable them to stay in the vicinity, or at least within 150 kilometres. If they stray further, it is usually with the intention of returning as soon as possible, and their hope is to build. 'This drive to "build" is an obsession with the young – their desire to see a house thrust up from the ground, which is the clearest sign that they have definitively taken root' (ibid., 45). In the meanwhile, those who work reasonably close at hand have relations that prove much denser than those of their emigrant counterparts.

> The young household spends each weekend at the parental home. The use of the city is pared down to a minimum. The city is where the young couple earns its livelihood; that is where they sleep, put their children through school, but they don't have their cultural consumptions there. All their free time, all their tension is brought back to their parent's house in the village or district.
>
> (ibid., 43–4)

In this case too, the 'home' is where the extended family is – the family and the local network continue to perform their material and symbolic functions. But this takes place also through spatial practices, which link up the two houses and their territories – relations are kept up through a sort of intermittent proximity, the functions and meaning behind the rapport with the 'family home' are developed through a combination of proximity and distance.

In a similar situation in Maienne, there is speculation as to the existence of a 'sociality that lies along the seam of the two environments – town and country' (Auffray *et al.* 1980, 194). Grafted on to this sociality is a set of opposing identities, determined by a markedly positive rapport with the place of origin. At the end of the week 'they leave the place in which their only definition is in terms of their work, a workforce on a labour market, and go and invest their energies where they are recognised as socially different' (ibid., 201). 'All kinds of cultural expectations crystallise around the relatives who stayed behind in the village, and there is a growing sense of an identity that exists neither where they work, nor where they live, but where they were born, where they were socialized' (Segalen 1980, 42).

The process is situated within a 'globality of rural and urban environments', which traces an outline of the family territory: 'the city is no more than a specification of this territory, a precinct imposed by work, and frequently also by accommodation needs, while the country is quite another form of habitat – it typifies family ties, and activities that are not governed by market laws' (Auffray *et al.* 1980, 206).

> There exists a sort of specialisation of habitats – the urban habitat is the focus for the household production, the village the locus for realising desires, and for appeasing the imagination. The family relationships in the five days spent in the city are bounded to the conjugal 'cell', while in the country, two days a week are spent in a far wider family sociality.
>
> (Segalen 1980, 45)

SYMBOLIC ECONOMY, ANALYTICAL CATEGORIES AND THE SOCIAL CONSTRUCTION OF HOUSING

What we must underline is that a number of housing practices can be interpreted only by referring to the networks in which they are developed. This extension could directly affect conventional images which have been current in the sociology of housing. In many instances, the topic 'house and family' itself should be redefined by substituting the second term for 'family network', or 'extended family', or 'intergenerational relations', or 'kin', or 'family circle' etc.

For example, the importance of intergenerational transfers leads to questions regarding the possibility of the housing situation's being hereditary, particularly that of ownership. Bequeathing of estate is the most obvious aspect of the hereditary determination of the housing situation. But the analysis of transfers seems to indicate that what can be so defined is something slightly more complex. Some enquiries show that ownership status can be correlated to the owner status of parents, while no relation exists with their social status (Tosi 1987; Henretta 1984). By analysing the distribution of property throughout the extended family network, Gotman (1988, 178–9) hypothesises that there are 'family residential statuses' – 'the combined occurrence of ownership status within the same family is not a casual factor, nor does it come from the socio-economic status of its members, but in fact results from the spreading from within the family of a certain relationship they have with home-ownership'. It seems to be a case of transmission of advantages formed from estate resources, and at the same time it appears to involve an 'owner model'. Finally, a variety of skills and residential preferences are likewise handed down from the source family, together with ways of relating to a given local area and so on. In the case of the Veneto region, transfers of resources leading to home ownership and the transmission of cultural models tend to combine to create a number of quasi-ascribed housing situations (Tosi 1987).

To a large extent, redefinitions are connected with representing family and local networks as aspects of 'informal' systems. A critical point is the strategies which develop around the informal economy of the family. These may be interpreted only with reference to the cultural or symbolic implications of network exchanges. Many informal housing practices appear to be closely interconnected with the development of primary socialities and identity processes. Then, their distance from the logic of formal production becomes evident, and the critical relevance that informal processes can assume is suggested – as they can contribute to the creation of oppositive identities (fostered by the local-family networks), and support (for their self-provisioning contents) the autonomous generation of use value.

Moreover, the fact that the practices we face are both anomalous and widespread throws some doubt on many of the analytical categories on which the analysis of housing needs and housing construction is currently based. In our case, the reference to the family networks has enabled us to question an assortment of categories currently adopted in the analysis of housing processes and in policy-making. The image of a family as an isolated entity (frequently implied in policy definitions), hinders the understanding of housing practices and needs, both in terms of levels and systems of resources and in terms of the forms of rationality involved.

As for the first aspect, the impossibility of conceptualising housing resources independently from the network in which they are produced and exchanged implies obvious criteria for analysing the processes of social stratification connected with the house. We have seen that intergenerational transfers have a strong influence on the opportunities of ownership. In general, family resources and the quality and extensiveness of social and kinship networks are important factors in determining the ability to compete in the housing market (Forrest 1988). From the point of view of housing policies, it is doubtful that redistributive policies can be applied with success when there is no control over the systems of resources in which the family moves, or of the relative transfers.[3]

The second aspect draws attention to the cultural or symbolic implications of network exchanges. The importance of the social relations between those participating in exchange suggests that specific 'rules' are implied. Since they tend to structure exchanges according to principles that differ from those of the market, these rules give rise to what (from the market point of view) is termed 'distortion'. From the point of view of those benefitting from networks, these are local rules, which refer to the symbolic (as well as economic) advantages of participation in the networks – advantages that turn out to be a necessary key in explaining these practices, as they are part of a symbolic economy. They are not, however, comprehensible in terms of conventional rationality.

Inasmuch as they are determined by the social relations that subsist between those involved, exchanges within family-local networks display a specific 'regulatory principle' – that differs from those related to market exchanges and public production: they draw on those 'reciprocity rules', which Polanyi (1944/75, 1977) identified as one of the three forms that are fundamental for economic integration.

Unlike those that take place on the market, the transactions that take place on this basis are an expression of social obligations. The economic content is not sufficient to explain the meaning of the relationship. The social relations between those taking part in the transaction are at least as important as the transaction itself.

The movement of goods and services derives from expectations or requirements imposed by a particular parental set-up, by the community, by the circle of friends.

The family, or a kinship, is the prototype of this reciprocity system.

(Polanyi 1977, 35ff)

A systematic consideration of informal practices would help reveal the shortcomings of the formal housing processes, and the failings of analytical frameworks referring to state and market rationality principles. As for policy issues, these remarks converge with criticisms of the 'institutional' and 'unitary' perspectives, which have been established in the bureaucratic-professional approaches to social needs, implying a reductionist view with respect to the forms of rationality of users (see Tosi 1991a). As for analytical issues, attention to informal processes could deeply affect theoretical attitudes in the field of housing studies. Recognising that informal practices are likely to be structural elements throughout postindustrial societies would imply a systematic consideration of regulatory principles, and rationality patterns, which differs from those on which established housing approaches have been based.

To emphasise the heuristic importance of the analysis of family networks does not however imply any a priori and abstractly positive attitude regarding their role. In fact, two of the main foci of the debate on informal processes are their ambivalence – for their redistributive implications as much as for the type of solidarity implied, and the impossibility of generalising about their effects independently from the context in which they occur (Mingione 1991). As for family and local networks, ambivalence is suggested by the contrasting definitions offered in the debate: on the one hand, integration of resources and support for the reproduction of social inequality and processes of social polarisation (see e.g. Forrest 1988; Mingione 1991);[4] on the other, reference for the creation of oppositive identities, premise for the autonomous generation of use values, and material support for neo-familism, reproduction of asymmetrical family relations etc. (see e.g. Godard 1985; Saraceno 1988).[5]

Lastly, analysis of family and local networks leads to the debate on modernity. This is evident when family and local networks are analysed as specific kinds of informal processes. The importance (or growth) of informal practices in industrialised societies has been a major reference for the theoretical renewal of these decades, and this category has played a crucial role in the debate about the 'crisis of modernity' and modernisation theory, and the reconceptualisation of modern society.[6] With reference to non-housing issues, the interpretation of informal practices in terms of rules of reciprocity has been widely used in the debate on the crisis of modernity and of the paradigms inspired by the ideology of modernisation. The crucial point is the presence in modern societies of large areas (i.e. informal activities) and of organisational principles (e.g. those founded on reciprocity) of a pre-non-modern character – both being structural, i.e. non-residual and not reducible to other organisational principles. What is more, with regard to the pre-non-modern social relationships in our society we can speak not only in terms of persistence, but also of 'enlarged reproduction' (Gallino 1982).

This remark is in keeping with the criticism of the traditional paradigms of development and modernisation. As has been observed elsewhere in reference to the interpretations tendered by Polanyi, it was the very growth of the market (while it undermined the traditional fabric) that sparked off new and limiting socialities in the market. This was veiled by an assumption of 'industrial tendency' (Mingione 1991), and by recourse to evaluative schemes of a unilinear nature, prevalent in development theory. In viewing development as a progressive expansion of a dominant organisational state, these theories were inadequate to deal with the simultaneous presence of other states, except as residues of obsolete social formations. The transition to forms of advanced industrial societies or postindustrial societies has accentuated the inadequacy of this kind of theoretical schema, as it has implied new evidence of informal logic in society. But it is the notion of modern society itself which is at issue. The co-presence of modern and non-modern principles challenges any monolithic representation of modernity (Pitkin 1985, 206). In fact, the need to adopt more open theoretical schemes capable of handling the combined presence of various organisational principles, or the peaceful coexistence of different social formations, becomes evident from the processes under way, namely those processes which denote the crisis of modernity as the transition to a postindustrial society. One of the prominent features is the sheer variety of behaviour that has emerged from the crisis of modernity and of the industrial models of social organisation, manifested by the appearance of numerous alternative paths, strategies, and forms of rationality – a situation that shows up the dire inadequacy of interpretations based on a single regulatory principle, and likewise the shortcomings of dualistic models founded on the dichotomy of modern/postmodern, and so forth (Negri 1986). Another feature concerns the processes of social 'de-differentiation' and 'de-regulation' as they denote the transition towards a postindustrial reality. The increasing importance of processes which are conforming to reciprocity principles suggests that economy goes back to being 'embedded' (to use one of Polanyi's terms) in a non-economic context, shedding its institutional component. Again, the logic behind the 'rational' action interacts with the different rationality behind 'non-logical' actions (Polanyi 1977). Furthermore, informalisation reflects an 'escape from universalism'. Social relations become structured in a particularistic fashion in order to best exploit the sum of the economic and extra-economic advantages in the exchange of resources (Gallino 1982). Clearly, informal housing practices belong to this category of processes, and the interpretative framework brought about by the debate about the 'crisis of the modernity' is also applicable to the housing field.

MODERN MODELS IN HOUSING: RETHINKING ANOMALOUS PRACTICES

The heuristic interest of the role of family networks in housing may be assessed from different points of view. As already mentioned, the relationships between social stratification and housing processes need to be reconceptualised in this perspective, and this could entail a redefinition of the redistributive implications of housing policies.

Again, a number of practical implications for housing planning and design could be derived from recognition of the role of family networks (Gaunt 1988), and this could question the prevailing models of conventional provision. Beyond these suggestions, however, a shift of theoretical paradigms of housing studies can be perceived, whose implications may be far-reaching. As in other fields of research, consideration of informal processes – and reference to 'informal' as a theoretical category – have proved to be powerful factors in challenging the current theoretical frameworks. This is even clearer if we consider that an analogous interpretative shift signals a specific crisis in this field, involving what we may call the 'modern model' in housing. Also in this respect, the informal processes – the network provision being its most remarkable aspect – are evidence of the crisis, as well as illustration of its 'reasons' and of the sense in which theoretical paradigms could be redefined.

From this point of view, what are called into question are the unitarism and centralism which have been typical of the 'modern tradition' of housing. Speaking of our housing norms as modern means emphasis on the relationships between our ideas on housing and the main constituting processes of modern society. As remarked by many authors, the idea of the home as a specific place that lends itself to the appropriation of the family unit can be connected with processes of structural differentiation and rationalisation established with modernisation: in more concrete terms, with the development of the distinction between public and private spheres, the transformation of family structure, the diffusion of the distinction between workplace (and time) and non-workplace (and time) (see Ariès and Duby 1986). These processes heralded the completion of the process of functional reduction and autonomisation of the living space. The home became a place of reproduction and consumption, living became a separate function, with a value of its own. The functional and cultural transformation coincided with the propagation of the spatial arrangement we are all familiar with – a layout that not only establishes the distinction between the workplace and the living space, but which assigns functional distinctions within the dwelling (Rybczynski 1986; Ariès and Duby eds 1986; Rapoport 1969).

The diffusion of the model is consistent with universalistic orientations, and with the basic concepts regarding the rationalisation of everyday life, as envisaged by the 'modern project'. We can assume that the critical problems of modern housing have been largely determined by the arrival of these models. They are implied by rationalisation and universalistic 'normalising' assumptions, and by the application of the principles of division of labour to housing processes – and hence by the social and administrative distance that arose between housing producers and users, and by the mediating role performed by the various technical, cultural, and political systems that were assigned the task of guaranteeing the universal suitability of the model. Housing behaviour in our societies is strongly determined by the cultural and spatial principles of the model. The homogeneity of the cultural references is indicative of the success of the modern model. The relative variations in practices are equally interesting. They betoken the various hurdles encountered by the diffusion of modern housing culture, and the precariousness of the integration achieved on this basis (Rakoff 1977). In fact, the diffusion over time of these models has been slow, and fraught with obstacles (Ion 1980; Ward 1985; Kaufmann 1988). The variance reminds us that modern models have never achieved a complete success. Informal practices are remarkable indicators of this. As relying on unconventional resources or keeping to unconventional rules, they are manifestly anomalous – they diverge from dominant housing norms, and specifically from the modern model. Now, for a number of reasons, research on informal housing invites a reconsideration of the anomalous character of these practices. In a context of crisis involving housing cultural models and policies, housing conditions and provision, anomalous practices may assume a new strategic relevance, both in practical and theoretical terms.

Particularly notable in this regard are those self-provision and self-organisation dimensions which are implied in the term 'self-help housing', and which are widely present in the network practices we have described. Relatively autonomous from institutional normative determination, these practices are markedly anomalous as regards the spatial schemes, the systems of value involved, and the provision patterns. As with other anomalous practices, anomaly has been closely linked to their irrelevance in the current representations in housing policies and studies. Nevertheless they are widespread; and, like other anomalous practices, deviation from norms can enlighten the precariousness of the dominant models, and inform us about distinctive patterns of behaviour that pass through the whole society (Kaufmann 1988).[7] If analysed from an anthropological viewpoint, many informal practices seem to evince a kind of reinterpretation – the norms are rewritten in family vernacular, as particularly evident with the spatial norms set by the modern model. Non-conformity evidences the complex difficulties in adhering to the cultural model. For instance, the fact that these houses are usually provided with large 'non-residential' areas implies that important multifunctional spaces are re-established in the dwelling: unarticulated spaces – available for a number of activities, particularly for those which the modern model has expelled from the residential sphere. Thus, a dualism results between these spaces, characterised by multifunctionality, and spaces that carry out the modern model. As suggested by various studies on self-help (see for example Dal Dosso 1982), the two kinds of space are carefully separated – the latter being a 'ruled' space, namely a space in which the principles of the modern model are in force. The distance from the modern model may also appear from conflicts between space arrangements and living practices. Good evidence on this point comes from a research on self-managed changes of the traditional habitat in a rural region in France (Bonnin *et al.* 1981). One interesting example is the bedroom. The evaluative process observed corresponds to the realisation of the 'model': from an initial promiscuity (the whole family sleeping in the same space) a final point is achieved in which a specific space is assigned to each gender and age category. This evolution is related to a basic value in the modern model: the emergence and internalisation of the idea of intimacy.

> But the internalization of the new model is not accompanied by acquiescence to the notion of intimacy. It results in a number of contradictions between modernist speech and previous practices; many properly separated rooms have no use, and children sleep with parents. Clearly, the adoption of the architectural significant of intimacy, the separate space, taken as a sign of modernity, is disjoined from its signified.
>
> (ibid., 20)

In fact, the modern spatial model can come about 'without the practices being affected, either directly or deeply. There is no passive interiorizing of the models proposed by global society, nor are the local models destroyed' (ibid., 7).

In this case, the working of specific rules constitutes a clear distance from the modern model. Reinterpretative practices signal working difficulties of the modern project: we can observe a replacement of 'the ambiguity of the old multifunctional space, meaningful for its relationship with experienced living practices, with a system of mono-functional spaces, meant as clear and universal, and manageable through the tools of public intervention' (ibid., 21). A different aspect of this distance is directly implied by the process of production. Self-help practices signal a concrete rebuttal of one of the general assumptions of formal production (public or private), that points to the irrelevance of the ways of producing and supplying homes. For either type of production, it is implicitly assumed that questions of 'sense' regard use of the home, while the way it is produced means little to the inhabitants. Self-help housing practices tend to give weight to the link that 'must' exist between production and use, and testify as to how the production of housing is actually connected with the logic of use. The eventual significance of the produced object is not independent from the way it is produced. Thus the location of production within the local/family networks discussed earlier in this chapter, determines the importance of housing both as an object and as a process. The critical distance from the modern model appearing in these practices involves both the rational-universalistic logic of the model, and the specialised-heteronomous character of the modern provision. 'Housing as a process' – a keynote in criticisms of mass housing (see Tosi 1990) – summarises the sense of this distance. It also suggests that the opposition between informal practices and conventional models could constitute a major locus of re-definition of theoretical paradigms of housing. Most informal practices refer to specific 'patterns' of housing experience, whose qualifying features are the evaluative and flexible character of the house, the initiative and competence of dwellers, and the pertinence of housing to extended family and local systems, on which we have commented before. Elements of pre-existent housing cultures, these traits have been systematically repressed throughout the development of modernity (Tosi 1990). Now the opposition between these patterns and the modern processes of housing production is reproposed in different terms by the new social presence of informal practices. The opposition is pervasive, and regards a whole series of features of a structural nature.

Drawing on what are now stock observations in criticisms of conventional housing, the situation is briefly thus: modern production pivots on housing as an 'object' (a 'product'); informal practices, by reconquering processual dimensions, reinstate (to use the formula that conveys the sense of many proposals in these past few years) 'housing as an act'. Formal production is tied to a certain model of 'end-user' who is seen simply as a passive consumer; informal practice infers and demonstrates the dweller's action as a 'planning' and 'rational' action.

Modern mediations in housing production (sustained by the bureaucratic-professional definitions) entail separated and hierarchised competences and professionalisation of construction and provision; informal housing may involve the competence of the dweller, and in the self-management of the building process the various moments of house building are reunited. These perspectives also affect spatial schemes and the cultural experience of housing. One of the immediate general effects is the frequent importance, in informal production, of the local character of construction and living: not the restricted sphere of the home, but rapport with an environment, often a specific relationship with a given place. This is counter to that general disregard for the site which characterises standard bureaucratic-professional housing-production practices (De Carlo 1984). Another outcome is the creation of an evaluative logic to housing, in direct opposition to the image of the home as a finished, definite, non-changing object (see Franck 1985). As has been observed, the revival of flexibility can be related to the crisis in the ideal model of the single-family home (Pahl 1989). Furthermore, it is linked to the discovery of the persistence, or revitalisation, of family networks. As with traditional practices, it is often a question of adaptation to changes in needs in an extended family network (Pitkin 1985).[8] Beyond the historical friction between traditional housing cultures and the modern project, informalisation – inasmuch as the 'crisis of modernity' has tendered a new social space to informal practices – means the reappearance of the 'reasons' for these patterns. As a result, the status of informal practices changes. So far, these practices have generally been viewed as a persistence or residue of traditional behaviour criteria and organisational principles. These definitions cannot be maintained in a context in which there are multiple signs of crisis in the cultural models brought about by modernisation (see e.g.

Perrinjacquet 1986; Franck 1985; Pahl 1989), and this is coupled with a crisis in the models of housing provision, a breakdown of policy models, and new signs of hardship and exclusion. This framework adds to the interest of informal/anomalous practices as 'reinterpretative' practices. Now they are likely to invite questions about the historical consistency of the modern model. On one hand it is clear that their inconsistency with prevailing housing norms urges the introduction of different theoretical schemes. All the various definitions provided by the general debate on the crisis of modernisation may apply: anomalous practices may reveal the persistence of traditional principles in modern society; the combination of modern and non-modern principles is a structural condition of modern society; the 'refunctionalizing' of non-modern elements is a crucial component in the transition to a postindustrial society.

On the other hand, informal/anomalous practices appear as indicators of possible directions of change, and their significance is likely to increase.[9] This significance has been enhanced by the crisis of the ruling principles of the 'modern tradition' of housing – unitarism and centralism, together with what they have entailed in terms of standardisation, rigidity of solutions and eteronomy of decisions – a structural difficulty in recognising variety of needs, and refusal to admit the competence and 'autonomy' of dwellers (see Tosi 1991a). The overall crisis of conventional housing-provision models – which has particularly involved mass housing – has led to rediscovery of the variety of housing possibilities, and – at the same time – of the importance of the experiences and abilities of the people concerned. Correspondingly, an element closely connected with modern housing models is increasingly appearing as a problem, namely the 'distance' between dwellers and the producers of dwellings. In this framework, informal housing increasingly appears as evidence of the possible departure from that *homo castrensis* – 'housed man' – that has been viewed as the model of the modern reduction of housing (Illich 1986), and self-help has turned to a metaphor of reappropriation of housing.

NOTES

1   The term 'family network' will be employed here as a general term to refer to the various systems involving a plurality of related house-

holds. It is not necessary, for our discussion, to work out the different types suggested by the different terms established in the sociology and anthropology of family (see e.g. Segalen 1981). However, in the reported examples the relationships are often wider than bi-generational systems, and in some cases they correspond to extended family relationships in the strict sense.

2   The point is developed here with reference to France and Italy, where substantial research evidence in this perspective is available. The importance of informal practices in other industrialised countries is however supported by most references in this chapter. For other European countries, see also Turpijn 1988. In order that the extent of these practices is not attributed to traditional factors, the examples I have chosen mainly refer to urban areas, or areas under intense development, or areas in which the traditional structures have been subjected to extensive modernisation. The research drawn on here concerns housing conditions and family relations in the Lombardy region (Tosi 1991b); self-help housing and access to home ownership in a selection of communities in the region of Nice (Cuturello and Godard 1980; Cuturello 1987), and in the Veneto region (Dal Dosso 1982, and Baggio and Donato 1986, revisited by Tosi 1987); relations with native communities in an area of Brittany (Segalen 1980); hereditary transmissions in certain urban situations in France (Gotman 1985, 1988).

3   The problem faced is a more general one, and concerns the relationship between the wealth-producing aspects of home ownership, intergenerational transfers, and social stratification (cf. Forrest 1988; Forrest and Murie 1989). In the United Kingdom it has been argued that 'hereditary owner-classes' can emerge, and that at present a 'social polarization' is taking place 'based on property ownership' (Hamnett 1984).

4   As for the relationship between hereditary transmission and social stratification effects, it does not seem to be a case of a straightforward 'reproduction of inequality'. The outcome tends to be rather more complex. Intergenerational transfers generally seem to catalyse different redistributive effects according to the segments of the class system involved, to the segments of market, to the territorial context, etc. (cf. Kessler 1979; Forrest and Murie 1989).

5   Similar remarks can be made for housing culture and models. For instance, ambivalence can be observed as regards such values as intimacy and privacy, and the diffusion of domesticity. The attitudes of the working class have swung between refusal and deep identification with the 'intimacy ethos'. As has been suggested, both attitudes may reflect 'subordinate statuses' (Kaufmann 1988). But practices induced by the diffusion of these values are not merely expressive of subalternity. To some extent, they elaborate specific principles that need to be defined in positive terms (Ariès and Duby eds 1986), and are partly independent from the dominant models (Kaufmann 1988).

6   'Informal' has been used as a contrast category, aimed at critically

highlighting 'underground' processes, as something in interaction with the formal processes governed by the state and by the market. It implies rejection of the institutional reduction of social needs, and of uni-dimensional definitions of social practices. One prominent feature which is emphasised is the sheer variety of behaviour that has emerged from the crisis of modernity and of industrial growth (cf. Tosi 1991a).

7 For want of a better term, I have labelled these processes 'self-help housing'. Here the term aims to stress the 'autonomous' nature of the processes – the recourse to non-institutional factors, and the content of self-organisation inherent in the production process. A fair dose of informal elements (in terms of contexts and resources utilised) does not imply, however, what is often associated with the idea of 'informal sector': illegality, self-construction etc. Nor is the informality of the process a totally determining factor. As we have repeatedly observed, informal practices tend to be a widespread process that mingles with a great variety of other, formal processes. The analytical interest of self-help housing is to highlight these interrelations, the complex links between formal and informal factors. On the importance of self-help housing practices in European countries, see e.g. Cuturello 1987; Turpijn 1988; Ward 1985; Harms 1988.

8 Pahl suggests some relationships between the different factors we have mentioned: the new reasons for evaluative housing, the replacement of a standardised norm of a single-family home by a demand for a variety of housing forms, the new importance of local and family networks, and the increase in self-provisioning activities. One reason for more variety is that 'people may prefer to adapt and extend their present house rather than spending more time earning money in employment in order to move to a dwelling that is already suited to their new needs'. This relates to lifestyles that are determined (rather than by position in the occupational hierarchy) by the particular milieu in which these families live.

> Thus the man on Sheppey who has bought his council house and who has knocked the wall down between his front and back room has done so in order to hold large family parties for his sons and daughters and his grandchildren, as well as the children of his siblings who live nearby. It is the proximity of kin that has stimulated his work on his house which, in turn has provided him with a sense of identity and a considerable burden of self-provisioning work.
>
> (Pahl 1989, 79–80)

9 Without overrating the alternative nature of self-help housing, we can observe that elements such as self-management and flexibility can now be upgraded from mere evidence of a crisis to viable projects.

> One could imagine a form of house building which was specifically designed for people to enlarge, change or develop the existing structure. Rather than attempting to provide a whole range of

housing designs and arrangement to cope with every conceivable type of household structure, houses would be built more simply, but with the foundations and services able to cope with expansion.

In Post-Fordist society the 'Boxes, little boxes and they all look the same' of Pete Seeger's song a quarter of a century ago are giving way to a world of extensions, conversions and alterations. No developer could possibly keep up with the variations in needs and aspirations of different household structures and types and the way they split, reform, dissolve and coalesce through the life course as values, lovers and material circumstances change.

Developers should give up the struggle and allow self-build groups and community architects to take over.

(Pahl 1989, 80)

Chapter 14

Informal allocation of housing wealth in Swedish social renting

Jim Kemeny

INTRODUCTION: THE HOUSING-WEALTH DEBATE AND SOCIAL RENTING

Housing wealth has been a peculiarly anglo-saxon preoccupation in the last few years, stimulated by the rising cost of housing in many countries and the rapid expansion of owner-occupation in England during the 1980s. The knee-jerk response to this has been to study the extent to which one particular tenure – owner-occupation – generates wealth without explicit analyses of wealth accumulation in other forms of housing, such as public renting, or asking questions about the wider relationship between housing and wealth. Indeed, the whole approach of such research, by focusing exclusively on wealth in owner-occupation, implicitly treats owner-occupation as if it were the only form of tenure in which housing wealth existed. The result of this has been that housing wealth is equated with owner-occupation and the wealth generated in social-rental housing is ignored. For the fact of the matter is that housing wealth is not tenure-specific. There is nothing unique to owner-occupation in this respect. In all housing, housing wealth is generated by the process of house-price inflation which increases the gap between outstanding loan and current market value. In both social renting and owner-occupation the wealth is made use of through the lower housing costs associated with the growing imputed rental value of the dwelling. In both owner-occupation and social renting the owner may realise the capital value tied up in the housing through remortgaging or through sale with vacant possession. The main difference between these two forms of tenure lies in the fact that capital realisation in owner-occupation is exclusively made for private-consumption purposes, whereas the wealth accumulated in social-rental housing is more flexible because while it, too, can be accessed privately by various measures, it can also be easily accessed for satisfying collective-consumption needs. Given the ideologically-charged nature of the policy debates in Britain and other anglo-saxon societies over tenure, the preoccupation in English-language research with housing wealth and owner-occupation plays directly into the hands of political ideologues who wish to foster and spread the belief that owner-occupation generates wealth while social renting does not.

It is largely as a result of this that data on the generation of wealth in social-rental housing is almost completely non-existent, despite the fact that the social construction of such data would be a relatively simple matter. An important dimension of the attempt to define housing wealth exclusively as owner-occupied housing wealth is to deny that social-rental housing generates wealth. There is therefore no concept of the imputed rental value of the social-rental housing stock, nor any concept of the net asset value of social-rental housing that can be used as security for loans. The only ideologically allowable recognition of wealth in social renting is when it is sold into owner-occupation. But then, perversely, the resulting wealth realisation is attributed not to social renting but to the fact that social-rental housing has been converted into owner-occupied housing. By some intellectual sleight of hand, then, social-rental housing is defined as not being a repository for housing wealth, but should it be sold into owner-occupation it suddenly and miraculously becomes so. The reasons for this perversion cannot be gone into here, other than a tradition of not realising the wealth in social-rental housing for either private consumption or infrastructural investment, but using it instead to keep loan costs, and so rents in general, as low as possible.

In this paper I wish to challenge the belief that there is no wealth realisation in social-rental housing by showing how the wealth accumulated in social rental housing in Sweden is made use of and transferred from household to household. Integral to this is an understanding of the complex relationship between different forms of allocation of resources, notably those of market, state, and informal processes. I therefore propose to begin with a discussion of the relationship between state, market and informal allocation before moving on to consider the particular manner in which these relationships have developed generally and historically in the case of Sweden. I then evaluate the extent of wealth generation in Swedish social renting, and show how informal processes of allocation play a major part in the Swedish rental system.

THE MYTH OF 'THE FREE MARKET'

The last decade or so has seen the re-emergence into respectability of the concept of 'the free market', following generations of disrepute resulting from some of the appalling consequences of the industrial revolution. The peculiarly strong hold that *laissez-faire* had on social sciences in the nineteenth century derived from the ideological dominance of a combination of a patriarchal 'rational man' ideology and Social Darwinism at a time when the social sciences were still in their infancy. The concept of a 'free' market, in which untrammelled competition results in the balancing of demand and supply, assumes that markets are detached from the impact of social and political institutions and from social relationships, whether in terms of class, ethnicity, gender or other dimensions of social structure, but most particularly from the state and from legislative and political intervention.

The idea that economic institutions are somehow free-floating entities unaffected by the social, political and legal structures of which they are a part derives from an old pre-sociological concept of human association that sees human behaviour in terms of rationality and a model of 'economic man' with its roots in the early nineteenth century. It finds expression in classical sociology in the work of Emile Durkheim, Max Weber and other sociologists who saw the emergence of the market as a product of industrialisation that was driven by the process of social differentiation. Max Weber, for example, in *Economy and Society* argued that the factory system emerged out of the less differentiated household economy to constitute a separate institutional sphere. In the same way, bureaucracy was seen by Weber as a 'modern' institution, epitomising 'rational' behaviour, in which, ideal typically, administration as a specific task is institutionalised and detached from such extraneous 'social' influences such as friendship loyalties, charismatic leadership, and family and kinship obligations.

If pressed to explain the continuing universal importance of informal allocation and state allocation in markets, the proponents of 'the free market' would therefore argue that markets contain imperfections because they are still affected by 'social' influences of one sort or another and therefore remain somehow underdeveloped because they have not become sufficiently differentiated out from the wider social structure into specialised economic institutions. This is the traditional view, for example, of the existence of nepotism and corruption in Third-World societies. The solution to dealing with such 'imperfections' in markets is therefore to increase exertions to purge the market of all 'extraneous' influences, and it is this that explains, to some extent at least, the vehemence with which free-market proponents insist that the state withdraw from market activities. Yet paradoxically, few, if any, free marketeers would go so far as to argue that state involvement in markets can be totally eliminated: for example by repealing all legislation that impinges however remotely and indirectly on market behaviour. This fact alone is sufficient to raise serious doubts about the validity of the market-autonomy thesis.

The increasing ideological dominance of the ideal-type concept of a free market has resulted in a growing awareness of the distinction between market and other forms of allocation, such as administrative allocation by the state and allocation through informal networks. Indeed, this collection of papers is but the latest example of such awareness. For most of the postwar period, when state involvement in markets was taken for granted, this conceptual distinction remained unclear, the lack of clarity reflecting the fact that the theory that lay behind state and market interactions remained unarticulated. However, now that there is interest in distinguishing between the different forms of allocation there is a danger that the artificial distinction between 'free markets' on the one hand and social structure on the other will become further entrenched and legitimated. For although the market–state–household distinction based on the ideal-type concept of a free market has some limited heuristic value, it is liable to foster a misconception of the relationship between markets and social structure that unfortunately has a long tradition of legitimacy in the social sciences.

The concept of the 'free' market has come under increasing conceptual and theoretical attack by sociologists and political scientists since the late 1980s. Political scientists, such as Bowles and Gintis (1990), argue that markets can never be understood without reference to the exercise of power, both in its narrower political sense and in more general social terms. Sociologists tend to focus on the importance of informal relationships as a key enabling dimension of the functioning of markets. Silver (1990), for example, argues that friendship is not merely an extraneous social factor that intrudes on and distorts market processes but on the contrary underlies them, since it provides the basis for the spread of information about prices and quality without which markets would be much more ineffective. Granovetter (1973, 1983) argues that 'weak ties' perform an essential informational function in enabling markets to operate at all. In short, the very functioning of a market is fundamentally dependent upon – and therefore cannot operate without – the existence of active networks of informal information based in the final analysis on relationships, friendships, gossip and rumour and mutual backscratching. This in turn is generated by informal relationships, between the insiders of different institutions in the give and take of news and information in informal settings such as bars and restaurants, and mediated by news-culling through networks of friends and relatives.

More recently, Granovetter (1985) launched a frontal assault on the assumption that economic institutions such as markets can be analysed or understood without the social structures of which they are a part. He coined the term 'embeddedness' to sensitise analysis to the fact that markets are inextricably part of society and that the structuring of the market is directly formed by the values, power relationships, and institutional arrangements of that society, both in terms of the social institutions out of which markets originally emerged and in terms of existing institutions with which market organisation co-exists and operates. What this means in practice is that markets are essentially cultural phenomena, and that the norms and standards of behaviour that govern them are to a large extent a reflection of the particular pattern of social relationships that have emerged in the social structures within which markets are located. Markets cannot exist without the dense network of informal relationships that both constitute the information sources that enable markets to function and provide the moral codes – including, for example, the need for bribery and nepotism – upon which transactions are based.

The argument that markets cannot be understood without reference to either power as pointed out by political scientists or informal networks as pointed out by sociologists means, if it is to be taken seriously, that it is impossible to separate different forms of allocation from one another. Markets are always governed by some sort of state intervention, even if this only takes the form of the legislation of standardised measures (weight, volume etc.), a state-produced and regulated currency, and basic laws such as the law of contract, consumer rights, guarantees, and standards of advertising. By the same token, markets are always characterised by a considerable element of informally obtained information through weak ties. Indeed, markets can hardly be conceived of without this in some considerable measure. It is therefore misleading to contrast 'markets' to state allocative systems on the one hand and informal allocative systems on the other. Rather, these three must be understood as variants of each other in which the 'mix' of the three constituent parts varies.

In this paper I want to examine access to housing in terms of the interaction between households, state agencies and markets in a rich industrialised society which possesses both strong informal and kinship networks and powerful and well-developed local and central state agencies. Sweden has experienced urbanisation in very recent times, particularly during the early postwar period. The state has played a somewhat mixed role in the allocation of housing to households, being heavily involved in aspects of the allocation of rental housing and involved in certain aspects of the allocation of owner-occupied housing. Informal processes of allocation have, on the other hand, always been a major aspect of Swedish culture, and informal networks of allocation continue to play a significant part in the functioning of the housing market in a number of important respects. By way of providing a background I discuss the cultural and historical factors which have formed the relationship between state, market and household in modern Sweden. I then consider the various housing-allocation systems in Sweden, and the extent to which the housing market is embedded in a social structure with strong informal networks and state institutions. I then draw some general conclusions about the nature of the embeddedness of Sweden's housing market in social structure and its consequences for the distribution of housing wealth.

STATE, HOUSEHOLD AND MARKET IN SWEDEN

The development of state and household in Sweden differed radically from that in most of the rest of Europe. Unaffected by Roman Empire colonisation, the raiding and trading era of Swedish viking society that followed the collapse of Rome preserved a pre-feudal clan-like social structure with a strong independent land-owning and arms-bearing peasantry and a weak nobility well into the fourteenth century. This in turn constituted the basis for strong local representation through the institution of the *ting*. The belated trend in Sweden towards feudalism during the fourteenth and fifteenth centuries never resulted in a fully-developed feudal nobility based on extensive serfdom. This in turn facilitated the relatively unimpeded emergence of a powerful centralised state under the Renaissance monarchs of the Vasa Dynasty in the sixteenth and seventeenth centuries. Thus, for example, using the nationalised church and its extensive local patronage, Sweden was the first country in Europe to develop a national population register for the more efficient administration of taxation and military conscription, and this was an important factor in the emergence of Sweden as a major European power during the seventeenth and eighteenth centuries.

This combination of circumstances resulted in the development of strong central and local government and the emergence of a large independent peasantry without the mediation of a powerful nobility. Strong centralised political institutions and an independent and close-knit kinship structure within a well-developed local community network and strong local political traditions became defining characteristics of Swedish social structure. These in turn constituted the basis for a particular relationship between the political institutions of the state and informal local and kinship/clan structures.

Sweden's modern development has been deeply affected by the manner in which state and household have developed and interacted with each other over the centuries. The emergence of a welfare state in Sweden cannot be understood as the product of a strong social democratic movement. On the contrary, social democracy built upon a vibrant tradition of local popular movements and employed the resources of an already well-developed state apparatus complete with its traditions of thorough investigation, extensive consultation, and centralised decision-making at both the national and local levels. The existence of on the one hand vociferous local popular movements and on the other a powerful central state therefore long predate the rise of social democracy in Sweden and provided the political and social conditions for its success.

In addition to these political and quasi-political preconditions at the local and national levels, household and kinship networks constituted a continuing and to some extent integrating thread throughout the early period of Swedish industrialisation. The early and middle phases of the industrialisation process remained remarkably rural in nature and took place without large-scale migrations to growing urban conurbations as had been the case in England and many other countries which lacked a superabundance of water power but possessed significant coal reserves on or near which the conurbations developed. In Sweden, by contrast, iron works and machine factories were typically set up in villages with access to abundant water power and which grew into small one-industry towns with a locally-recruited population, some of which, such as the steel giant Sandviken and the white goods manufacturer Husqvarna ultimately became the homes of multinational corporations, though still remaining small towns. To this day, industry – and particularly heavy industry – remains widely dispersed, with many small mill-towns and even mill-villages surviving as intact communities, though today using grid-drawn electric power. As a result, there is in Sweden no equivalent to the huge concentrations of steel mills and other heavy industry in massive conurbations such as the West Midlands, South Yorkshire, The Rhur, or North-east France.

This pattern of what might best be termed 'rural' industrialisation was only broken after the Second World War when urbanisation began to take place on a large scale. Modern sociology derives its models of industrialism from the experiences of early industrialising societies in which the urban population has long forgotten its rural origins of several generations back, and in which geographical mobility has considerably dispersed the original rural-based wider kinship structures. In countries with a long history of urbanisation, such as Britain, local community studies were, even by the early postwar period, already based to a considerable extent on the existence of long-established *urban* kinship networks and how these are disrupted by postwar suburbanisation (Willmott and Young 1957, 1960). It is easy to forget that large towns in Sweden are remarkably modern phenomena barely predating the Second World War, and that many middle-aged Swedes still have extensive family and kinship connections in the rural areas from which their parents or grandparents migrated. It is, for example, still not uncommon today for urban-dwelling Swedes to inherit the family country house or cottage and use it as a second home (or if that is not possible to acquire a second home in the area of origin) to be near grandparents, aunts, uncles and other members of their family of origin who did not migrate to the towns. The Swedish second-home phenomenon therefore has considerable importance as a means of retaining family ties to the countryside, and to that extent differs markedly from the social organisation and the meaning of second homes in most western countries.

The strength of ties to the land among modern urban Swedes is reflected in numerous attitude surveys in which living in the country in a small cottage is seen as the ideal, particularly living close to friends and relatives (for a review of the literature see Folkesdotter 1985, 31), and more popularly, romanticised in the widely popular 'children of Bullerby' stories of Astrid Lindgren centring on children living in a small village and able to drop in to granny for home-made fruit juice and buns. This desire to return to the family bosom is a theme of some importance in Swedish housing research, which has shown that the desire is not infrequently realised (ibid., 20). Indeed, a surprisingly high percentage of first and second homes – up to 80 per cent in some study areas – are made over to relatives rather than sold on the market (Folkesdotter, 1986).

But informal and family ties are not only country-based. They are also found in urban areas. A large-scale interview survey of kinship-network activity among married or previously married middle-aged women in Stockholm and Gävle (Gaunt 1987, 211) found that about half in Stockholm and two-thirds in Gävle had at least one close relative within 5 km and in Gävle – the thirteenth largest urban area in Sweden – fully 90 per cent had one relative within 50 km. This clearly shows the influence of the pattern of 'rural industrialisation' and the local nature of urbanisation. But it would seem that patterns of socialisation have also reflected deeper cultural values that go back to the pre-feudal social formations of traditional Swedish society. Swedish research into urban lifestyles has tended to stress the importance of both kinship and informal (non-kinship) networks for care and social support, and Hanssen (1978) uses the term *clan* to describe this network of relatives and local contacts. There is also a whole field of social research in Swedish urban sociology which is concerned almost exclusively with the nurturing of local social networks that has had a major impact on Swedish urban and neighbourhood planning. Indeed, one of the major political concerns in the early postwar period was how to preserve primary group relationships in the face of massive urbanisation that was then starting to take place, both to enable the strong popular movements to continue to play a central political role under social democratic hegemony and to counteract personal isolation (for a discussion see Kemeny 1992a, 136–7).

All this points to the special position of informal networks in Swedish social organisation. What is of particular interest in this paper is the way in which these play a part in access to housing in a society which also possesses strong state-allocation institutions. It has already been noted in passing that in rural areas the informal transfer of housing to locals is a major form of access and that second homes have a special significance in this context. I now want to look more closely at the allocation of Swedish housing in two areas where state allocation and informal allocation are particularly important to delineate their main characteristics and draw some general conclusions about how they affect the distribution of housing wealth. The areas for analysis cover the most important allocation processes in the rental market: allocation via the housing exchanges run by local government and the informal allocation of private rental housing. I will begin with an evaluation of the amount of wealth generated by social rental housing.

WEALTH GENERATION IN SWEDISH SOCIAL RENTING

In this section I propose to crudely estimate the amount of wealth in Swedish social rental housing to provide an indication of the amount of wealth that is available for allocation. The estimate is based on the annual reports of a social-rental housing company, which, according to all the major indices, is very representative of social-rental housing in the country as a whole. The company,

Gavlegårdarna in the town of Gävle, founded at the end of the First World War, was one of the first social-rental housing companies in Sweden.

Data was collected for every year from 1945 to 1985 inclusive, on the total outstanding debt and the number of dwellings. The total outstanding debt was then divided by the number of dwellings to obtain average outstanding debt per dwelling per year. This is summarised in Table 14.1.

To obtain a general indication of the growing gap between outstanding debt and new debt, I divided the increase in total debt in a given year by the increase in the number of dwellings in that year (Table 14.2).

The figures for average debt per new dwelling are roughly comparable to figures published for the whole of Sweden in the Yearbook of Housing and Building Statistics, especially bearing in mind the approximate nature of the debt data in Gavlegårdarna's accounts as discussed earlier. The national data begin in 1965 when the average production cost of a flat was 70,300 kr., somewhat more that the average debt on a new Gavlegårdarna dwelling. In 1974 it rose to 101,700 kr., in 1985 to 460,700 kr.

These figures show that average debt per dwelling in the social-rental stock remained close to average new construction costs until the mid-1970s as a result of very heavy front-end loading while the stock expanded rapidly. However, since the end of the so-called Million Programme from 1965 to 1974 when 100,000 new dwellings were built a year nationally, new production has fallen, while prices have risen, rapidly increasing the gap between outstanding and new debt per dwelling.

If we conservatively estimate the average ratio of outstanding debt per dwelling to new debt per new or renovated dwelling at 4:1, then it can be seen that in 1985 the difference between existing and new debt amounts to some 300,000 kr., or an asset value net of debt of about £30,000 per dwelling. The income from this wealth in terms of reduced housing costs – the imputed rental income – assuming a rate of return of 5 per cent amounts to about £1,500 per year per household, this being a rough estimate of the difference between the element of the market rent required to provide a commercial return on the capital value of the dwelling to a profit-seeking landlord and the return required to cover debt-servicing.

Table 14.1 Gavlegårdarna's stock and average
outstanding debt 1945–85

Year	No. of dwellings	Average debt per dwelling (Sw. kr.)
1945	345	12327
1950	929	17417
1955	1645	25312
1960	2534	32618
1965	3475	39175
1970	6059	44073
1975	8160	56880
1980	8648	71158
1985	9667	101696

Table 14.2 Average outstanding debt and average newbuild debt
per dwelling, Sw. kr., selected years

Year	No. dwgs built	Average debt per dwg	Average debt per new dwg	Ratio of new to debt
1947	206	13367	13693	1.02:1
1959	211	32875	34062	1.04:1
1964	225	37543	65234	1.74:1
1967	565	44561	57954	1.30:1
1969	622	48902	56302	1.21:1
1973	560	56720	58430	1.03:1
1974	188	57854	112626	1.95:1
1976	082	57943	163779	2.83:1
1980	262	71158	251614	3.54:1
1985	184	101696	414291	4.07:1

But average outstanding debt conceals wide variations between dwellings of different ages. Thus, for example, in Table 14.1 it can be seen that the outstanding debt on a dwelling built in 1945 is little more than a tenth that of a dwelling built in 1985. Clearly there will therefore be substantial differences in the amounts of net wealth in social-rental housing of different ages and with different levels of modernisation investment in them.

It is here that the allocation process of social-rental housing becomes of vital importance in determining who lives in dwellings possessing the greatest amounts of net wealth. This is because rents in Swedish social-rental housing follow closely the cost – and hence debt – structure of individual buildings. Use-value rent pooling still has only a marginal – if increasing – importance in determining rents. This means that the wealth of social-rental housing in the form of the imputed rental value created by the falling real value of the outstanding debt on older housing accrues mostly to the tenants of older housing and is not redistributed in any major way and shared out with the tenants of newer housing. Access to older, low-rent, social-rental housing is therefore a major means of gaining access to, and enjoying the benefits of, the accumulated wealth in social-rental housing. It is to the issue of how such access is gained that we may now turn.

RENTAL HOUSING ALLOCATION IN SWEDEN

Rental housing in Sweden comprises almost exclusively apartment flats as distinct from one- or two-family houses or terraced houses, and has been under some form of rent regulation for the whole of the postwar period (for a good general overview of the Swedish housing system see Anas *et al.* 1985). During this time, demand for rental housing has been high, and for most of the postwar period, despite high rates of newbuild by cost-rental housing companies, demand has outstripped supply. This has been particularly so for older, and largely privately-owned, rental housing, since rent regulation operates in such a manner as to tie rents to individual historic costs. This means that, unless extensive investment in modernisation has taken place, the rents of older flats are lower than those of new flats of a comparable size.

The low ratios of outstanding debt to current newbuild costs that we have seen in the previous section are now beginning to emerge on a substantial scale, together with the cost-rent principle underlying rent-setting; and the continuing close link between the historic costs of individual buildings and rents means that the net wealth value of older dwellings to tenants is substantial: a net wealth which provides an income for tenants in the form of high imputed rent. The effect of this has been to skew demand towards older flats with lower rents, which in turn has created a heavy demand for older, largely inner-urban flats in preference to newer, largely outer suburban flats. The other characteristic of the Swedish housing stock that is worth noting in this context is that the bulk of new construction during the postwar period has been undertaken by cost-rental housing companies. The general pattern is therefore that the inner-urban stock comprises largely privately-owned, predominantly old, low-rise apartment blocks with low rents, while the outer sub-urban stock tends to be made up of newer high-rise apartment blocks owned by cost-rental housing companies and with high rents. For most of the postwar period demand for housing has been so high that it has never been problematic to rent out the latter kind of flat, though there have been two periods – the late 1970s and the early 1990s – when there have been vacancies in the newer stock, both coinciding with economic downturns and rising unemployment.

Access to these two kinds of rental housing has tended to vary quite considerably. The overarching aim of Swedish rental policy has been to integrate private renting with 'public' rental (or more accurately, housing produced by cost-rental housing companies). To this end, a rent harmonisation policy has been striven for, though so far with only minimal success (for a discussion see Kemeny 1992b). Equally problematic has been the attempt to ensure that the allocation of all rental housing takes place through the housing exchanges set up by most local authorities. These operate a queue for allocation purposes based on length of time registered with the exchange, together with indicated preferences of housing area/suburb, size of flat and amount of rent willing to be paid. The demand for a centrally situated low-rent flat in the housing exchanges can be so great as to produce queues with waiting times of heroic lengths – 40 years or more – and, as with access to some private schools in Britain, it is not uncommon for newborn babies to be registered in the local-rental housing waiting list.

Due to the continuing failure to attain full rent harmonisation between low-debt and high-debt housing, the housing exchanges have singularly failed to ensure that vacancies reflecting a broad range of housing are channelled through their own operations. The cost-rental companies have been the main producers of newbuild during the postwar period and newbuild has almost always been allocated through the housing exchanges. Older cost-rental flats and private rental flats are much less universally available through the exchanges, in large part because tenants have considerable rights to transfer their rental contract or privately organise a direct swap of flats. The flats built or renovated in the 1970s, 1980s and early 1990s that the housing exchanges tend to receive are those which are in particularly unattractive areas, notably in the large high-rise developments of the late 1960s and early 1970s. Access to the more attractive older and low-rent stock by the housing exchanges is even less common, and tends to be restricted to the occasional vacancy arising from the death of a tenant living alone.

Access to vacancies by the housing exchanges is further limited by the reluctance of many private landlords to make their vacancies available to the housing exchanges. They often find it more convenient to handle the transfer of tenancy themselves informally – in those cases where the outgoing tenants do not do so – which gives them greater control over who the next tenant will be. This has been a source of political conflict and has resulted in legislation to try to increase the proportion of private rentals being allocated through the exchanges. As the law stands now, private landlords must register a certain proportion of their vacancies with the local housing exchange, though this law is impossible to enforce, and functions more in the nature of general pressure on private landlords to use the housing exchanges more.

The predominant forms of transfer in the rental market are therefore (1) the housing exchanges which are run by local authorities and which tend to handle the bulk of newbuild and less attractive 'recent-build' and (2) a range of informal allocation methods which tend to cover the older, low-rent and often centrally located housing stock in which most of the net wealth of the rental-housing stock is found. Here, then, we have side by side a state allocation system, managed by the local authorities and buttressed by laws, and an informal allocation system of considerable complexity also buttressed and ordered by laws.

The existence of rent regulation therefore operates to divide allocation into an informal sector where personal contacts – and occasionally black-market key money – are of paramount importance in obtaining a low-rent flat and a formal market by means of a local public-housing exchange through which mostly newbuild and less attractive flats with high rents are allocated. The specific form that rent regulation has taken in Sweden therefore results in very particular kinds of allocation in which market (price) allocation plays a secondary role to informal and state allocation.

This contrasts with the rental sectors in Britain, North America and Australasia where (predominantly) state allocation in public housing is found alongside (predominantly) market allocation in private renting and where informal rental-housing allocation mechanisms are only weakly developed except in minor niche markets.

What has effectively happened is that the informal sector has appropriated the bulk of low-rent social-rental housing in both private and cost-rental stocks, while state allocation through the housing exchanges has been left to the part of the stock where wealth accumulation has been least. It is therefore through informal processes that the lion's share of rental housing wealth is allocated. Obtaining a flat through the housing exchange normally only enables households to get their foot on the bottom of the housing ladder in anticipation that inflation will reduce the value of their rent as wealth accumulation increases the imputed rental value of the dwelling.

In practice the distinction between the informal and state allocation processes are not as clearcut as this. State allocation through the housing exchange is mediated by subtle and complex informal processes, while the informal allocation process is buttressed by legislation and judicial practice. This becomes apparent when we consider the two dominant forms of allocation in turn.

1 Housing exchanges

Studies of housing exchanges in Sweden have been greatly neglected. There is no equivalent to the detailed observation and interview studies of public-rental allocation that exists, for example, in Britain (Henderson and Karn 1987). At best, studies of housing exchanges in Sweden are limited to broad overviews of the process and analyses of legislation and reform (for examples see Wiktorin 1980; Wiktorin and Kemeny 1981; Wiktorin 1982a, 1982b). Housing exchanges typically operate a queue system according primarily to the length of time a person has been registered in the queue. The first-come-first-served principle is, of course, an essential element in the workings of a market, and queue systems, for examples at sales or in the futures markets, are standard market rationing techniques. The other market rationing mechanism that operates through housing exchanges is that of price (despite rent regulation), since larger flats command a higher rent. Applicants fill in an application form which indicates their preference for size, rent, and location. But because rent regulation distorts demand towards older and cheaper flats there is a tendency for the larger flats to remain unlet for longer and for these to be offered rather than the more sought-after smaller flats by the housing exchange when an applicant reaches the top of the queue. To put it another way, applicants who have indicated their willingness to accept a large flat in an unpopular area are more likely to receive a quick offer than those who want a small flat in a popular area.

But these market characteristics are considerably modified by a priority system in which certain cases are classified as being in urgent need. The rules vary from one local authority to another but normally included are single parents and immigrants to the local government area both from abroad and other parts of Sweden. Here again we need to be careful in defining the priority system of allocation as bureaucratic and non-market in nature, since private companies and individuals often operate a priority system that overrides market considerations and allocate resources on the basis of perceived need. But if we consider this narrowly, then it does seem to comprise a clear example of a politically-defined set of criteria for access that is aimed at benefitting certain social groups.

The discretion allowed to the personnel of the housing exchanges to withhold flats from the queue for certain special-priority cases transforms the functioning of the housing exchange from a purely mechanical queue mechanism to a highly discretionary system. It gives the personnel considerable power to allocate or not. So the priority system also strengthens the informal allocative mechanisms in the housing exchange, by encouraging applicants to press personnel to allocate them a flat when officially there would appear not to be any available. For, of course, if a priority system is in operation there always have to be flats available that are being withheld from the queue 'just in case' an urgent applicant appears. The degree of ambiguity that this introduces into housing-exchange allocation encourages entrepreneurial aggression and stubbornness among a proportion at least of the streetwise and less shy applicants for housing. 'Nagging' strategies, strategies that facilitate 'fraternisation' with the staff, the 'sad story' and other inventive forms of interaction with housing-exchange personnel become the common currency of gossip among the habituees of the housing exchange.

Housing exchanges therefore exhibit complex combinations of market, state, and informal allocation, which combine in different ways in different aspects of their social organisation. Indeed, one might accurately define and describe the workings of housing exchanges in terms of the interaction between these three forms of social organisation.

2 Informal allocation

The allocation of much private-rental housing is heavily determined by informal allocation processes. It is above all in the private-rental stock that the greatest housing wealth has accumulated, and where the greatest benefits of housing wealth in the form of high imputed rental values may be enjoyed. Yet informal access to such housing is a subject that has until recently been barely investigated. However, there is a recent interview survey of a sample of private-rental households in inner Stockholm. Such housing has low rents and high levels of wealth accumulation, as well as often possessing extremely attractive locational advantages. In their study, Sikjiö and Borgegård (1991) found that the most common means of access to such flats was by the direct bilateral exchange (swapping) of flats (45 per cent), while the next most common means was by means of personal contacts through the person's social network (26 per cent) with housing-exchange allocation third (19 per cent). Other ways (10 per cent) also included informal access, for example by moving in with a partner who already had such a flat (6 per cent). Altogether then about half of flats were obtained by swapping, a third by various social-network means, and a fifth through the housing exchange. This, of course, understates the importance of social networks, since a proportion of swapping is based on informal contacts rather than on advertising in the newspapers or at the housing exchange.

However, the data understate the importance of informal contacts in another, more important, sense. Clearly, the most important means of obtaining an inner-city flat is to already have a flat with a high exchange value (that is, a flat with a high imputed rental value) and to swap it for another, though presumably some of those who swapped would have done so from a high imputed rental value flat outside the inner city. This therefore leaves unanswered the question of how initial access was obtained to an inner-city flat by those in the sample who swapped one inner-city flat for another together with those who obtained an inner-city flat by swapping it for a high imputed rental value flat outside the inner city. It is likely that an answer to this question would further increase the importance of social networks in access to inner city flats to perhaps the principle means of access.

Nevertheless a substantial minority of inner-city flats were obtained through the housing exchange. Many of these are likely to be newly built flats following the substantial slum clearances of the 1950s and 1960s, or heavily renovated flats with high rents, particularly under the extensive programme of renovation that took place in the 1980s (the so-called ROT plan). Such high-debt inner-city flats embody relatively modest levels of wealth accumulation, though still being substantially more attractive in locational terms than comparable high-rent new flats in outer suburban areas, and particularly the large-scale high-rise 'concrete jungle' developments. But a proportion of inner-city flats allocated by the housing exchange must have been flats with relatively high imputed rental value: vacancies in older cost-rental housing-company stock, together with at least some flats made available by private landlords as a result of legal and social pressure. State allocation therefore plays a significant secondary role in this part of the rental market.

The strength of informal allocation processes is buttressed by laws governing security of tenure and housing succession that heavily favour the retention of rental flats in families and their passing on to friends and relatives. Tenants enjoy high levels of security of tenure. They can pass on the tenancy to anyone of their choice and though landlords can in theory veto this they rarely do so. Many tenants will pass on a tenancy to friends or relatives or even illegally sell the tenancy (i.e. sell its imputed rental value). But a tenant also has the *right* to pass the tenancy on to a relative who has been living in the flat, even against the landlord's will. The relative need not even be particularly close. Just how distant the relative can be has not been fully tested. However, there is a well-known case in which a man passed his tenancy on to a niece who had lived in to take care of him during illness but who did not have enough income to pay the rent after he left, as she was a student. The landlord took the case to the Housing Court to obtain an eviction but the niece was granted the tenancy when another relative stood as guarantor for her rent.

The full extent of the role of informal allocation processes in Swedish housing remains to be researched. The importance of direct swapping of dwellings as a means of moving has already been indicated. It has for long been illegal to sell a rental contract and so a 'grey' market has grown up in which sums change hands informally ('I will turn this rental contract over to you if you buy this mirror here for 100,000 kronor') or in which tenants swap rental contracts with owner-occupiers for a substantial reduction in the price of the owner-occupied house. It has only recently been made legal to swap a rental flat for an owner-occupied house and for the tenant to obtain a discount on the house price to reflect the imputed rental value and the locational value of the flat. That is, the tenant may realise the capital value of the flat through an indirect sale, even though the rental contract itself cannot be legally sold. However, swapping can take complex forms, involving well-developed informal contacts. Thus, for example, there is only anecdotal evidence on the existence of 'exchange chains' involving complex sets of exchanges, often set up by well-connected estate agents. These can be highly convoluted: a simple illustration being say between a tenant (A) in inner Stockholm who wants a house for sale in outer Gothenburg the owner of which (B) wants to buy a terraced inner-suburban house in Malmö, while a third person in Malmö (C) owns such a house but wants to swap it for an inner-Stockholm flat. So B swaps first with C and then with A. However, it is precisely the opaqueness of informal allocation that makes it difficult to identify and hard to research. It is perhaps for this reason that housing research has neglected informal processes of allocation and placed so much emphasis on studies of state and market forms of allocation, with the result that the importance of informal allocation has been grossly underestimated.

STATE, MARKET AND INFORMAL ALLOCATION OF RENTAL-HOUSING WEALTH: 'THE ETERNAL TRIANGLE'

Access to housing wealth cannot be understood narrowly as a phenomenon of owner-occupation as has tended to be the case in housing studies. Rental housing in industrialised societies accounts for anything from a quarter to three quarters of the housing stock and incorporates considerable net asset values which accrue to tenants in different ways and to different extents, depending on the structuring of the rental market and strategic government policies towards the rental market. The allocation of this housing wealth has been neglected in the housing literature in the wake of the ideologically-driven obsession with owner-occupation in anglo-saxon societies. A particularly regrettable *lacuna* is the failure to conduct economic analyses of the impact of discounted public rental sales on the transfer of rental-housing wealth from the bulk of tenants who do not buy to the smaller number who do buy. The reduction in imputed rental income to remaining tenants can be measured as a direct result of the capital subsidy to buying tenants that is the difference between market value and discounted value. In the wake of large-scale discounted sales of public-rental housing in many countries we need to know much more about how these impact on the extraction of wealth from public-rental housing.

The Swedish rental market provides an interesting case study in the allocation of rental-housing wealth because of the central role that informal processes of allocation play in Swedish housing across all tenures, both in the existence of extensive networks of informal exchange and familial allocation and in a strongly entrenched informal dimension to the allocation processes of both state and market forms. The three dimensions are particularly evident in Sweden due to that country's strong state-allocation institutions and its well-developed informal allocation mechanisms. Yet the informal allocation process is almost certainly greatly underestimated in other countries which appear on the surface to have a much more 'market-like' allocation system as well as those where state allocation is well developed. All forms of allocation have elements of all three types of allocation that are intimately intertwined with one another and even constitute each other to a great extent. The ideal-type market of neo-liberalists, or the Weberian ideal type of bureaucracy in which informal processes are purged from analysis and treated as dysfunctional social residues are models that dominate studies of housing allocation. Much of this is founded on an idealised version of reality in which the importance of corruption and nepotism is played down. These abstract and unrealistic models of economics and political science need to be abandoned in favour of more sociologically nuanced models which give a substantial – some would argue central – place to informal allocation processes in their own right. Applying such models to the study of the allocation of housing wealth – in all forms of housing, including rental housing – will ultimately revolutionise our understanding of the significance of all forms of housing – not just owner-occupation – for the distribution of housing wealth.

Chapter 15

Points of departure

Ray Forrest and Alan Murie

In the introduction to this text we set out the intention of broadening existing debates around issues of housing and wealth. The aim was to broaden the debates in two particular ways. First, to show that in different cultural settings superficially similar processes and relationships can have quite different nuances and implications. A second aim was to broaden the focus of current debates beyond a dominant preoccupation, at least in mainstream housing studies, with the measurement of monetary gains in home ownership. This was to be achieved through drawing on a range of disciplinary perspectives and in consciously linking processes of wealth accumulation in housing to issues such as reciprocity, informal exchange and kinship networks and to demonstrate that changing forms of housing provision had broader sociological implications beyond the potential macro effects on the distribution of personal wealth.

The aspiration was to begin to make new links between debates focused around the growth of individual home ownership and wider debates within the sociology of the family, economic sociology and social anthropology. Inevitably and intentionally, the different chapters pursue different aspects reflecting a variety of disciplinary points of departure and cultural contexts. Some chapters, including our own, are situated firmly within the mainstream of current housing debates but equally recognise and refer to a literature which lies beyond and which must be increasingly engaged. Other contributions more immediately locate the issue of housing and wealth within a perspective which sees the family, kinship and informal exchange as a central feature of housing provision. One of the general theoretical points to emerge is that housing markets are embedded within specific cultural and institutional contexts. Kemeny makes this point very firmly when he argues against the analytical separation of market, state and informal spheres. And this view of housing markets as culturally specific and operating in distinctive ways relates to a growing literature concerned with reasserting the importance of informal processes and reciprocity in contemporary economic life. Drawing on this general literature (e.g. Granovetter 1985; Mingione 1991; Sayer and Walker 1992) the implication for housing debates is for a greater recognition of informal elements in analyses of housing opportunities and housing histories. In conceptualising the different structures of housing provision in different nation states (Ball *et al.* 1990), more attention should be paid to their embeddedness in specific social relations. The general tendency in housing studies has been to work with an implicit model of atomised households operating in a market increasingly disembedded from processes of negotiation, informalisation and reciprocity. Perhaps para-doxically, the potential for greater accumulation of personal wealth through the growth of mass, individual home ownership has resurrected interest in the sociological dimensions of gifts and exchange within social and kinship networks and the culturally specific dimensions of these exchanges.

While some authors in this volume have correctly pointed to different conceptions of wealth which encompass collective forms of housing provision and the mobilisation of informal resources, the primary focus has been on home ownership. The preference expressed by households (albeit socially constructed) and supported by governments in the late twentieth century appears to be for home ownership and the growth of that sector in various forms has been apparent in all of the countries discussed here. It is a growth at the expense, initially, of other forms of private ownership – private landlordism and tied accommodation. More recently it has been at the expense of state housing. Home ownership has been sponsored and, indeed, subsidised in some countries and periods, and some growth, most obviously relating to privatisations of state housing, has occurred in an environment where the risks associated with the market have not existed and where reasons for buying relate to calculations about housing costs rather than ontological security or an overriding desire to own rather than rent the place in which you live. While policy and supply-side developments have affected the growth of home ownership it is also evident that much of the growth reflects autonomous individual effort. Considerable attention is given in the housing literature to the tradition of self help and sweat equity as a driving element in home ownership, and Ladanyi's contribution in this collection demonstrates the importance of such factors in an environment which was initially unfriendly to it. A balanced view of the growth of home ownership acknowledges the importance of self help, of individual choice and action and also the way in which home ownership is situated in the wider economy and will reflect the actions of the state, property owners and financial institutions in creating that economy and determining the forms in which housing is produced and consumed. These elements differ between countries and caution against the error of associating home ownership with some universal set of attributes or implications about their social significance.

Attention to the different origins and nature of home owner- ship in different countries is an important common element in the papers in this book. The ideological association in modern times between home ownership and the private market has led to an equation with individual market processes. Most of the contributors demonstrate the error of this association. As has been emphasised above, markets do not operate in a vacuum but within an institutional and social structure which is more complex than theoretical economic models. Rather than home ownership being equated with private individualised processes in which income, occupation and affordability determine access, the papers in this book catalogue, in different ways for different periods and places, the importance of other factors. The papers by Tosi and Franklin offer deeper theoretical accounts of relationships which are identified elsewhere. These relate particularly to family, kinship and friends, gift relationships and reciprocity and to housing practices which embrace all of these. The discussion of home ownership in southern Europe and Japan suggests that home ownership can involve a dwelling created and regarded as a family or collective asset. One consequence is that it is not widely exchanged through the market, and financial and other institutions have not developed as a result. These family or collective elements in home ownership have been less widely recognised in some other countries including the USA and the UK. However, these aspects are apparent from in-depth interviews and qualitative research. The paucity of evidence from survey-based quantitative research may owe more to problems of design and implementation.

The recognition of family and reciprocal arrangements then has an importance for debates which have developed about wealth and accumulation in housing. If home ownership is not seen simply as individual wealth then its impact on patterns of wealth distribution and through this on social structure and inequality is more difficult to assess. This, in itself, is an important conclusion which raises questions about the appropriateness of some of the debate. It is all too easy to equate housing wealth with home ownership and with personal wealth. Not all housing wealth is in home ownership. Rights associated with other tenures have an accumulative value, people may own more than one house and multiple ownership by private landlords continues to affect the distribution of wealth. Social housing represents collective wealth and much wealth associated with family and kinship may not be appropriately treated as personal wealth. These are important conceptual and definitional questions and the temptation to neglect them in the enthusiasm to move on to measurement can contribute to the neglect of fundamental issues and spurious assessments of social inequalities.

Even when formulated in narrower terms, however, the role of housing in personal wealth is often difficult to assess. National data on aggregate personal wealth generally includes housing but data on the distribution and composition of personal wealth are less easily obtained. Properties are often burdened with debt and movements in property values mean that accurate data are not easy to obtain and analyses have tended to refer to estates passing at death. This has added to the interest in inheritance of housing property. In addition to these data there has been an active debate about rates of accumulation of wealth through housing. The reason for this interest and the interest in inheritance is the contention that accumulation through home ownership has changed patterns of social inequality and social stratification. It is argued that wealth accumulation through home ownership is now sufficient to outweigh gains made through wages and salaries, consequently having the potential to change patterns of inequality associated with the labour market. The debate about this is outlined in the papers by Choko and Forrest and Murie. Reference to rates of return has been used to indicate that gains from home ownership do not follow the same pattern as those associated with employment. However, lifetime patterns suggest that absolute gains do conform. While home ownership results in some redistribution between people with similar lifetime incomes and occupations it seems likely that gains will reinforce differences between different occupational class groups.

The evidence on inheritance has an additional significance for this debate. Increased longevity means that property is generally inherited by people late in their working lives. As a result, inheritance of housing wealth occurs too late to alter patterns of stratification during people's working lives. It is more likely to affect inequalities in old age. In this context the erosion of forms of social security, both formal and informal, is important as it is evident from various contributions that there is increasing pressure to draw on housing resources to compensate. The awareness of personal wealth holdings associated with home ownership may affect both government and household decisions about incomes in older age and it cannot be assumed that past patterns of inheritance, transfer and residential mobility in older age will apply in the future.

In conclusion, the papers in this book demonstrate the importance and diversity of the links between housing and family wealth. If we are to build a stronger appreciation of those links we need to start with clear concepts and definitions and to avoid certain automatic links. The point of departure for debate should recognise the importance of family, kinship and informal aspects of housing provision, and acknowledge continuities associated with place and differences associated with cohort effects and changes over time. It should reassess the importance of housing practices and *inter vivos* transfers as well as the importance of housing in social security and in coping strategies of households in an uncertain social and economic environment. Housing processes have a role in reducing inequalities or reinforcing them but the extent to which they do this and how they do it cannot be taken for granted. An understanding of housing as wealth requires careful analysis within specific contexts of time and place and the avoidance of ethnocentric and time-specific generalisations.

Bibliography

Agnew, J. (1982) 'Home ownership and identity in capitalist societies'. In James S. Duncan (ed.) *Housing and Identity. Cross-cultural Perspectives*. New York: Holmes and Meier, pp. 60–97.

Allan, G. (1982) 'Property and family solidarity'. In P. Hollowell (ed.) *Property and Social Relations*. London: Heinemann.

Allan, G. (1989) *Friendship: Developing a Sociological Perspective*. London: Harvester.

Anas, A., Jirlow, U., Gustafsson, J., Hårsman, B. and Anderson, P. (1974) *Passages from Antiquity to Feudalism*. London: Verso.

Anas, A., Jirlow, U., Gustafsson, J., Hårsman, B. and Snickars, F. (1985) *Scandinavian Housing and Planning Research* 2, 3–4, pp. 169–87.

Anderton, N. and Lloyd, C. (1991) *Housing Australia: An Analysis of the 1986 Census*. Canberra: AGPS.

Anselme, M. (1988a) 'L'accession au parc HLM. Les filières d'accès au logement locatif social'. In *Transformation de la famille et Habitat*, INED, Direction Régionale de l'Equipement d'Ile-de-France, Ministère de l'Equipement, June 1988, Paris, Travaux et Documents, Cahier 120, pp. 325–32.

Anselme, M. (1988b) 'Les réseaux familiaux dans le parc HLM'. In *Transformation de la famille et Habitat*, INED, Direction Régionale de l'Equipement d'Ile-de-France, Ministère de l'Equipement, June 1988, Paris, Travaux et Documents, Cahier 120, pp. 181–5.

Ariès, P. and Duby, G. (eds) (1986) *Histoire de la vie privée*, vols 2–4. Paris: Editions du Seuil.

Atkinson, A. B. (1975) *The Economics of Inequality*. Oxford: Clarendon Press.

Atkinson, A. B. and Harrison, A. M. (1978) *Distribution of Personal Wealth in Britain*. Cambridge: Cambridge University Press.

Attali, J. (1988) *Au propre et au figuré. Une histoire de la propriété*. Paris: Fayard.

Auffray, D., Baudoin, T., Collin, M. and Guillerm, A. (1980) *Feux et lieux. Histoire d'une famille et d'un pays face à la société industrielle*. Paris: Galilée.

Babeau, A. (1988) *Le patrimoine aujourd'hui*. Paris: Nathan.

Badcock, B. (1989a) 'Homeownership and the accumulation of real wealth', *Environment and Planning D: Society and Space* 7, pp. 69–91.

Badcock, B. (1989b) 'The role of housing expenditure in state development: South Australia, 1936–88', *International Journal of Urban and Regional Research* 13, pp. 436–61.

Badcock, B. (1992) 'Adelaide's heart transplant, 1970–88: 2. The "transfer" of value within the housing market', *Environment and Planning A* 24, pp. 323–39.

Baggio, L. and Donato, P. (1986) *Modalità di accesso alla casa in proprietà*, graduation thesis, Facoltà di Architettura, Venice.

Bagwell, S. (1993) 'The windfall awaiting. The new inheritors', *The Australian Financial Review*, 15 April, p. 12.

Baker, H. (1979) *Chinese Family and Kinship*. London: Macmillan.

Ball, M. (1983) *Housing Policy and Economic Power: The Political Economy of Owner Occupation*. London: Methuen.

Ball, M., Harloe, M. and Martens, M. (1988) *Housing and Social Change in Europe and the USA*. London: Routledge.

Baltas, N. K. and Drougas, V. T. (1980) *Empirical Analysis of Saving Behaviour and the Demand for Deposits in the Private Sector*. Athens (in Greek).

Banfield, E. C. (1958) *The Moral Basis of a Backward Society*. Glencoe: Free Press.

Bank, H. S. (1992) 'Outlook for the residential property market', *Hang Seng Economic Monthly*, May.

Barker, D. L. (1972) 'Young people and their homes: spoiling and keeping close in a South Wales town', *Sociological Review*, 20, 4, pp. 569–90.

Bartlett, F. (1990) 'Big bucks in the small market', *Asian Property*, Nov., pp. 7–11.

Becker, G. (1984) *A Treatise on the Family*. Cambridge, Mass.: Harvard University Press.

Beer, A. (1989) 'Owner-occupation and profit: the creation and capture of value through Canberra's residential property market', doctoral thesis presented to the Australian National University, Canberra.

Bell, C. (1968) *Middle-class Families*. London: Routledge and Kegan Paul.

Bentham, G. (1986) 'Socio-tenural polarisation in the United Kingdom, 1953–83: the income evidence', *Urban Studies*, 23, 157–62.

Berry, F. (1974) *Housing: The Great British Failure*. London: C. Knight.

Bianchi, M. S., Reynolds, F. and Daphney, S. (1982) 'Racial inequalities in housing: an examination of recent trends', *Demography*, 19, 1, pp. 37–51.

Bloch, M. (1975) 'The long term and the short term: the economic and political significance of the morality of kinship', in J. Goody (ed.) *The Character of Kinship*. Cambridge: Cambridge University Press.

Blöss, T. (1986) 'L'accession à la propriété du logement: vers de nouvelles solidarités entre générations?', *Revue française des affaires sociales*, 3, pp. 107–20.

Blöss, T. (1989) 'Jeunes Maghrebins des quartiers nords de Marseille, une génération charnière'. In *Familles et Patrimoines*, Les Annales de la Recherche Urbaine, 41, Mars-Avril, pp. 59–66.

Blöss, T. and Godard, F. (1990) 'Décohabitation juvénile: Stratégies juvéniles et conjoncture de l'existence' in *Stratégies résidentielles*, INED, Plan Construction, Congrès et Colloques 2, pp. 205–22.

Bonnin, P., Perrot, M. and de la Soudière, M. (1981) 'Habiter et se déplacer en Margeride', *Ethnologie française*, 1, pp. 7–32.

Bonvalet, C. (1988) with A. Bringé and B. Riandey) *Cycle de vie et changements urbains en Région Parisienne: Histoire résidentielle d'une génération*, Rapport de recherche INED, Caisse Nationale des Allocations Familiales, Direction Régionale de l'Equipement d'Ile-de-France, Ministère de l'Equipement, 250 pp.

Bonvalet, C. (1990) 'Accession à la propriété et cycle de vie', in *Stratégies résidentielles*, INED, Plan Construction, Congrès et Colloques 2, pp. 129–37.

Bonvalet, C. (1991) 'La famille et la marchée du logement: une logique cachée'. In M. Segalen (ed.) *Jeux de famille*. Paris: Presses du CNRS.

Bonvalet, C. (1992) 'Transformation de l'habitat: évolution de la structure des ménages en France.' Paper presented to the 5th International Research Conference on Housing, Montreal, 7–10 July.

Bonvalet, C. and Lelievre, E. (1989) 'Mobilité en France et à Paris depuis 1945: bilan résidentiel d'une génération', *Population*, 3, pp. 531–60.

Bonvalet, C., Gotman, A. *et al.* (1991) *Statuts residentielles: approche intergénérationale*, rapport de recherche, Ministère de L'Equipement, September.

Bourdieu, P. and Saint-Martin, M. (1990) 'Le sens de la propriété', *Actes de la recherche en sciences sociales*, 81/82, pp. 52–64.

Bowles, S. and Gintis, H. (1990) 'Contested exchange: new microfoundations for the political economy of capitalism', *Politics and Society* (June) 18, 2, pp. 165–222.

Bradbury, J. (1990) 'Housing Policy and Home Ownership in Mining Towns: Quebec, Canada', *International Journal of Urban and Regional Research* 9, 1, pp. 1–14.

British Market Research Bureau (1976), *Housing Consumer Survey*, NEDO.

Builder Magazine (1988) '88 Candidates Forum', January, pp. 209–22.

Building Centre of Japan (1987) *A Quick Look at Housing in Japan* (2nd edn).

Building Societies Association (1985) 'Trends in personal sector wealth', *BSA Bulletin* 144, October, pp. 16–19.

Burke, T. and Hayward, D. (1992) 'Australian housing at the crossroads?', *Built Environment* 18, pp. 199–213.

Burke, T., Hancock, L. and Newton, P. (1984) *A Roof over their Heads: Housing Issues and Families in Australia*, Institute of Families Studies Monograph No. 4, Melbourne.

Canceil, G. (1990) 'Le revenu des menages', *Données Sociales*, INSEE.

Cass, B. (1991) *The Housing Needs of Women and Children*, National Housing Strategy Discussion Paper. Canberra: AGPS.

Census and Statistics Department (1972) *Hong Kong Population and Housing Census: 1971*, Main Report. Hong Kong: Government Printer.

Central Statistical Office (1988, 1993) *Social Trends*. London: HMSO.

Chandler, D. (1977) 'Urban renewal in Auckland' in C. Bush and C. Scott (eds) *Auckland at Full Stretch*. Auckland: Auckland City Council and University of Auckland Board of Urban Studies.

Chayter, M. (1980) 'Household and kinship: Ryton in the late 16th and early 17th centuries', *History Workshop*, 10, pp. 25–60.

Chevan, A. (1989) 'The growth of home ownership: 1940–1980', *Demography*, 26, 2, pp. 249–66.

Choko, M. (1980) *Crises du logement à Montréal (1860–1939)*. Montreal: Éditions Saint-Martin.

Choko, M. and Dansereau, F. (1987) 'Restauration résidentielle et copropriété au centre-ville de Montréal'. Montreal: INRS-Urbanisation, Études et documents 53.

Clayton Research Associates Ltd. (1992) *Homeownership as an Investment*. The Canadian Home Builders' Association.

Coleman, L. and Watson, S. (1987): *Women over Sixty. A Study of the Housing, Economic and Social Circumstances of Older Women*, Australian Institute of Urban Studies Pub. No. 130, Canberra.

Commonwealth of Australia (1990) *The Treasury Economic Round-up*, Summer. Canberra: AGPS.

Conway, R. (1985) *The Great Australian Stupor*. Melbourne: Macmillan.

Courson, J. P. and Saboulin, M. de (1985) 'Ménages, familles: vers de nouveaux modes de vie?', *Economie et Statistique*, 175, March.

Cribier, F. (1989) (with M. L. Duffau and A. Kych) 'La cohabitation au temps de la retraite', *Rapport de recherche* CNRS, I, II.

Crook, S., Pakulski, J. and Waters, M. (1991) *Postmodernisation Change in Advanced Societies*. London: Sage Publications.

Crothers, C. (1984) 'The role of the private sector over the post war period'. In C. Wilkes and I. Shirley (eds) *In the Public Interest*. Auckland: Benton Ross.

Cuturello P. (1987) 'Les nouveaux "Castors": des solidarités collectives aux solidarités familiales. Les pratiques d'auto-construction des ménages accédant à la propriété en maison individuelle'. Nice: GERM-CERCOM.

Cuturello, P. (1988) 'Entraide familiale'. In *Transformation de la famille et Habitat*, INED, Direction Régionale de l'Equipement d'Ile-de-France, Ministère de l'Equipement, June 1988, Paris, Travaux et Documents, Cahier 120, pp. 149–68.

Cuturello, P. (1989) 'Itinéraires résidentiels: statuts du logement, activité féminine et patrimoine'. In *Itinéraires féminins. Les calendriers familiaux professionnels et résidentiels de deux générations de jeunes femmes dans les Alpes-Maritimes*, Rapport de recherches du GERM-CERCOM, September, pp. 485–547.

Cuturello, P. (1990) 'Statut du logement et réseau familial'. In *Stratégies résidentielles*, INED, Plan Construction, Congrès et Colloques 2, pp. 195–202.

Cuturello, P. and Godard, F. (1980) *Familles mobilisées. Accession à la propriété du logement et notion d'effort des ménages*. Nice: GERM.

Cuturello, P. and Godard, F. (1982) *Familles mobilisées*. Paris: Plan Construction, p. 282.

Dal Dosso, A. (1982) 'Casabrutta, le trasformazioni del paesaggio veneto', *Spazio e società*, 19, pp. 94–109.

Darvill, T. (1987) *Prehistoric Britain*. London: Batsford.

Daumard, A. (1987) *Les bourgeois et la bourgeoisie en France depuis 1815*. Paris: Aubier.

Daunton, M. (1987) *A Property-owning Democracy?* London: Faber.

Davis, J. (1972) 'Gifts and the UK economy'. In *Man*, 7, 3, pp. 408–29.

Davis, J. (1973a) *Land and Family in Pisticci*. London: Athlone Press.

Davis, J. (1973b) 'Forms and Norms: the economy of social relations'. In *Man*, 8, 2, pp. 159–76.

Davis, J. (1977) *People of the Mediterranean*. London: Routledge and Kegan Paul.

De Carlo, G. (1984) Preface to *The Scope of Social Architecture*, ed. C. R. Hatch. New York: Van Nostrand Reinholt.

DelliBovi, Alfred A. (1991) 'Where there's HOPE . . .', La Follette Lecture, University of Wisconsin-Madison, 11 April.

Department of the Environment (1977a), Cmnd 6851, *Housing Policy: A Consultative Document*. London: HMSO.

Department of the Environment (1977b), Cmnd 6851, *Housing Policy*, Technical Volume 1. London: HMSO.

Department of the Environment (1993a), *Housing in England*. London: HMSO.

Department of the Environment (1993b) *English House Condition Survey, 1991*. London: HMSO.

DEPOS (Public Corporation for Housing and Urban Development) (1989, 1990) *Conditions and Trends in the Housing Market of Large Urban Centers: 1988 Survey*, I (1989) and II (1990). Athens: mimeo (in Greek).

DEPOS (1989) *Current Trends and Problems in the Housing Sector, 1987–1988*. Athens: mimeo (in Greek).

Dilnot, A. W. (1990) 'The distribution and composition of personal sector wealth in Australia', *Australian Economic Review*, 1st Quarter, pp. 33–40.

Divay, G. and Richard, L. (1981) 'L'aide gouvernementale au logement et sa distribution sociale'. Montreal: INRS-Urbanisation, Études et documents 26.

Doling, J. and Lehtinen, J. (1992) 'Developments in home ownership markets: a comparative study of Britain and Finland.' Paper presented to the 5th International Research Conference on Housing, Montreal, 7–10 July.

Doling, J., Karn, V. and Stafford, B. (1986) 'The impact of unemployment on home ownership', *Housing Studies*, 1, 1: pp. 49–59.

Doucet, M. and Weaver, J. (1991) *Housing the North American City*. Montreal and Kingston: McGill-Queen's University Press.

Dubois, R. (1989) *Enrichissez-vous avec l'immobilier*. Montreal: La Presse.

Dunleavy, P. (1980) *Urban Political Analysis*. London: Macmillan.

Dunleavy, P. (1986) 'The growth of sectoral cleavages and the stabilization of state expenditures', *Society and Space* 4, pp. 129–44.

Dupuis, A. (1989) *Consumption Sectors*, MA thesis, University of Canterbury.

Dupuis, A. (1991) 'Financial gains from owner occupation: the New Zealand case 1970–88', *Housing Studies* 7, pp. 27–44.

Edel, M. (1981) 'Home ownership and working class unity', *International Journal of Urban and Regional Research*, 6, 2, pp. 205–22.

Edel, M., Sklar, E. D. and Luria, D. (1984) *Shaky Palaces: Homeownership and Social Mobility in Boston's Suburbanization*. New York: Columbia University Press.

Emmanuel, D. (1979) *Categories of Households Outside the System of Housing Assistance*. Athens (in Greek).

Emmanuel, D. (1981) *The Growth of Speculative Building in Greece: Modes of Housing Production and Socioeconomic Change 1950–1974*. Athens.

Emmanuel, D. (1987a) *Building Activity in Greece: Determinant Factors and Model for Predictions*. Athens: mimeo (in Greek).

Emmanuel, D. (1987b) 'Housing problems of young people in urban areas: the case of Greece'. Unpublished report for the International Study on the Housing Problems of Young People, SAUS, University of Bristol.

Emmanuel, D. (1990) 'Trends in housing markets and finance and subsidy systems in the 1980s: the case of Greece', *Urban Studies* 27, 6, pp. 931–50.

Engels, F. (1975) *The Housing Question*. 1887. Moscow: Progress Publishers.

Englander, D. (1983) *Landlord and Tenant in Urban Britain*. Oxford: Clarendon Press.

Evans-Pritchard, E. E. (1962) *Essays in Social Anthropology*. London: Faber.

Farkas, E. János and Vajda, Zsuzsa (1990) 'Lakáshelyzet: állami es maganlakssok' [Housing conditions: state and private housing]. In Andorka, Rudolf *et al.* (eds) *Tarsadalmi riport* [Social report]. Budapest: Tárki.

Federal National Mortgage Association (1992) *National Housing Survey*. Washington, D.C.

Ferge, Zsuzsa (1986) 'Zsörtölödö megjegyzések Szelényi Iván es Manchin Róbert Banulmányához', [Comments on the study of Szelényi and Manchin], *Medvetánc*, 2–3.

Festy, P. (1990) 'Statut d'occupation du dernier domicile conjugal et mobilité résidentielle à partir de la séparation'. In *Transformation de la Famille et Habitat*, INED, Direction Régionale de l'Equipement d'Ile-de-France, Ministère de l'Equipement, June 1988, Paris, Travaux et Documents, Cahier 120, pp. 95–106.

Festy, P. (1991) 'Mobilité résidentielle des femmes séparées: une étape dans le cycle de vie familiale'. In *Stratégies résidentielles*, INED, Plan Construction, Congrès et Colloques 2, pp. 231–52.

Finch J. (1989) *Family Obligations and Social Change*. Oxford: Basil Blackwell.

Finch, J. (1994) 'Inheritance and financial transfers in families'. In A. Walker (ed.) *The New Generational Contract*. London: Harvester Wheatsheaf.

Finch, J. and Hayes, L. (1994) 'Inheritance, death and the concept of the home', *Sociology* (forthcoming).

Fischer, C. S (1982) *To Dwell Among Friends*. Chicago: University of Chicago Press.

Folkesdotter, G. (1985) *Housing construction and rural settlement: a descriptive bibliography*. Swedish Institute for Building Research Bulletin M85:23, Gävle.

Folkesdotter, G. (1986) 'Housing market in a rural area', paper presented at the International Research Conference on Housing Policy, Gävle.

Forrest, R. (1983) 'The meaning of homeownership', *Society and Space* 1, pp. 205–16.

Forrest, R. (1987) 'Spatial mobility, tenure mobility and emerging social divisions in the UK housing market', *Environment and Planning* A, 19, pp. 1611–30.

Forrest, R. (1988) 'Between state and market. Privatisation, family resources and aspects of early household formation in European housing systems'. Workshop entitled 'Housing Between State and Market', Dubrovnik, September.

Forrest, R. and Murie, A. (1987a) 'Social polarization and housing tenure polarization', paper presented at the Sixth Urban Change and Conflict Conference, University of Kent.

Forrest, R. and Murie, A. (1987b) 'The affluent home owner: labour market position and the shaping of housing histories', *The Sociological Review*, 35, 2, pp. 370–403.

Forrest, R. and Murie, A. (1988) 'The affluent home owner: labour market position and the shaping of housing histories'. In N. Thrift and P. Williams (eds) *Class and Space*. London: Routledge.

Forrest, R. and Murie, A. (1989a) 'Differential accumulation: wealth, inheritance and housing policy reconsidered', *Policy and Politics* 17, 1, pp. 25–39.

Forrest, R. and Murie, A. (1989b) 'Housing markets, labour markets and housing histories'. In C. Hamnett and J. Allen (eds) *Housing Markets and Labour Markets*. London: Unwin Hyman.

Forrest, R. and Murie, A. (1993) *New Homes for Home Owners*. London: HMSO (DoE).

Forrest, R., Kennet, P. and Leather, P. (1994) 'Coping strategies among home owners with negative equity'. Mimeo.

Forrest, R., Murie, A. and Williams, P. (1990) *Home Ownership. Differentiation and Fragmentation*. London: Unwin Hyman.

Franck K. H. (1985) 'Small spaces, shared spaces and spaces that grow', *International Conference on Housing*, Amsterdam, June.

Franklin, A. (1986) 'Owner occupation, privatism, and ontological security: a critical reformulation'. Bristol: School for Advanced Urban Studies, University of Bristol.

Franklin, A. (1989a) 'Working class privatism: An historical case study of Bedminster, Bristol', *Society and Space* 7, pp. 93–113.

Franklin, A. (1989b) 'Labour mobility and housing provision in South and East England', unpublished project paper, School for Advanced Urban Studies, University of Bristol.

Franklin, A. (1990) 'Variations in marital relations and the implications for women's experience of the home'. In T. Putnam and C. Newton,

Household Choices. London: Futures Publications.

Franklin, A. (forthcoming) 'Housing practices in Bristol: distinction, taste and social network', research paper in preparation: Department of Sociology, University of Tasmania.

Friedl, E. (1970) 'The family in a Greek village: dowry and inheritance; formal structure'. In C. C. Harris (ed.) *Readings in Kinship in Urban Society.* New York: Pergamon.

Froszteg, M. and Holmans, A. (1993) 'Inheritance of house property', *Economic Trends* 481. London: HMSO.

Gaboriault, R. (1989) 'Le financement de la propriété résidentielle', *Actualité Immobilière*, 13, 3, pp. 18–29.

Gallino, L. (1982) 'Doppio lavoro ed economia informale. Verso la futura società pre-moderna'. In *Occupati e bioccupati.* Bologna: Il Mulino.

Gaunt, L. (1987) *The family circle: housing, contacts and care.* Swedish Institute for Building Research, Bulletin M:9, Gävle (in Swedish).

Gaunt, L. (1988) 'The family circle: challenge for planning', International Conference on Housing, Policy and Urban Innovation, Amsterdam, June–July.

Gerth, H. and Mills, C. (eds) (1948) *From Max Weber.* London: Routledge and Kegan Paul.

Giddens, A. (1990) *The Consequences of Modernity.* Cambridge: Polity Press.

Glick, P. and Sung-lin, Lin (1986) 'More young adults are living with their parents: who are they?', *Journal of Marriage and the Family* 48, pp. 107–12.

Godard, F. (1985) 'How do ways of life change?'. In N. Redclift and E. Mingione, *Beyond Employment.* Oxford: Basil Blackwell, pp. 317–37.

Godard, F. and Blöss, T. (1988) 'La décohabitation des jeunes'. In *Transformation de la famille et habitat*, INED, Direction Régionale de l'Equipement d'Ile-de-France, Ministère de l'Equipement, June, Paris, Travaux et Documents, Cahier 120, pp. 31–55.

Godbout, J. and Blais, S. (1983) 'L'accessibilité financière au logement neuf'. Montreal: INRS-Urbanisation.

Gokalp, C. (1978) 'Le réseau familial', *Population* 6, pp. 1077–94.

Goldthorpe, J. H., Lockwood, D., Beckhofer, F. and Platt, J. (1968) *The Affluent Worker.* Cambridge: Cambridge University Press.

Gorz, André (1967) *Le socialisme difficile.* Paris: Editions du Seuil.

Gotman, A. (1985) 'Les biens de famille', *Informations sociales* 6, pp. 15–21.

Gotman, A. (1988) 'Le logement comme patrimoine familial.' In Catherine Bonvalet and Pierre Merlin (eds) *Transformation de la famille et habitat.* Presses universitaires de France, pp. 169–80.

Gotman, A. (1988c) *Hériter*, Paris: PUF.

Gotman, A. (1989) 'Familles, Générations, Patrimoines'. In *Familles et Patrimoines*, Les Annales de la Récherche Urbaine, 41, Mars–Avril, pp. 87–96.

Grafmeyer, Y. (1990) 'Solidarités intergénérationnelles dans l'accession au parc locatif privé lyonnais'. In *Stratégies résidentielles*, INED, Plan Construction, Congrès et Colloques 2, pp. 183–94.

Granovetter, M. (1973) 'The strength of weak ties', *American Journal of*

Sociology 78, pp.1360–80.

Granovetter, M. (1983) 'The strength of weak ties revisited'. In Randall Collins (ed.) *Sociological Theory*. San Francisco: Jossey-Bass, pp. 201–33.

Granovetter, M. (1985) 'Economic action and social structure: the problem of embeddedness', *American Journal of Sociology* 91, 3, November, pp. 481–510.

Guerrand, R. H. (1967) *Les origines du logement social en France*. Paris: Les éditions ouvrières.

Habermas, J. (1981) *Theorie des kommunikativen Handelns*. Frankfurt: Suhrkamp.

Haddon, R. A. (1970) 'Minority in a welfare state society', *New Atlantis* 2, 74, March, pp. 452–99.

Hall, P. (1989) 'Arcadia for some. The strange story of autonomous housing', Housing Studies, 4, 3, pp. 149–54.

Hall, R. R., Raper, C., Thorns, D. C. and Willmott, W. E. (1982) 'Torrens Certificate of Title', Social Sciences Research Fund Technical Paper No 1. Wellington.

Hamnett, C. (1984) 'Housing the two nations: socio-tenural polarisation in England and Wales, 1961–81', *Urban Studies* 43, pp. 387–405.

Hamnett, C. (1989a) 'The owner-occupied housing market in Britain in the 1970s and 1980s'. J. Lewis and A. Townsend (eds) *North South Divide: Regional Change in Britain in the 1980s*. London: Paul Chapman.

Hamnett, C. (1989b) 'Cycling Across the Gap', *Housing Review*, May–June, pp. 83–5.

Hamnett, C. (1989c) 'Consumption and class in contemporary Britain'. In C. Hamnett, L. McDowell and P. Sarre (eds), *The Changing Social Structure*. London: Sage, pp. 200–43.

Hamnett, C. (1992a), 'The Geography of Housing Wealth and Inheritance in Britain', *The Geographical Journal* 158, 3, pp. 307–21.

Hamnett, C. (1992b) *Inheritance in Britain: the Disappearing Millions* London: PPP Lifetime.

Hamnett, C., Harmer, M. and Williams, P. (1989) 'Housing Inheritance and Wealth: A Pilot Study', Economic Social Research Council.

Hamnett, C., Harmer, M. and Williams, P. (1991) *Safe as Houses. Housing Inheritance in Britain*. London: Paul Chapman.

Hancock, J. (1980) 'The apartment house in urban America'. In Anthony D. King (ed) *Buildings and Society*. London: Routledge and Kegan Paul, pp. 151–89.

Hang Seng Bank (1992) 'Outlook for the Residential Property Market', *Hang Seng Economic Monthly*, May.

Hanssen, B. (1978) *Family, household, and relative: a longitudinal study of environment and group activity in a Stockholm suburb, 1957 and 1972*. Stockholm: Gidlunds.

Haraszti, M. (1989) *Darabbér*. Worker in a worker's state. Budapest: Teka.

Harbury, C. D. and Hitchens, D. W. A. (1979) *Inheritance and Wealth Inequality in Britain*, London: Allen and Unwin.

Harloe, M. (1989) 'Between the state and the market?', International Conference on Self-Government and Social Protection in the Urban

Settlement, Moscow, September.

Harms, H. (1988) 'Self-help housing, crisis, and structural transformation', *Trialog*, 18, 3, pp. 40–2.

Harris, O. (1982) 'Households and their boundaries', *History Workshop Journal* 13.

Harris, R. and Hamnett, C. (1987) 'The myth of the promised land: the social diffusion of home ownership in Britain and North America', *Annals of the Association of American Geographers*, 77, 2, pp. 173–90.

Harris, R. and Weaver, J. (1994) 'House and home in Canadian cities, 1850–1950'.

Harvey, D. (1978) 'Labor, capital, and class struggle around the built environment in advanced capitalist societies'. In Kevin R. Cox (ed) *Urbanization and Conflict in Market Societies*. Chicago: Mearoufa.

Harvey, D. (1989) *The Condition of Postmodernity*. Oxford: Basil Blackwell.

Haumont, N. (1976) *Les locataires*. Paris: Institut de sociologie urbaine.

Hayakawa, K. (1983) 'Housing poverty in Japan', *Ekistics* 50 (298), pp. 4–9.

Hayakawa, K. (1990) 'Japan'. In W. V. Vliet (ed.) *International Handbook of Housing Policies and Practices*, pp. 671–94.

Hayakawa, K. and Hirayama, Y. (1990) 'The impact of the Minkatsu policy on Japanese housing and land use', *Society and Space* 9, pp. 151–64.

Hayakawa, K. and Yosuke, H. (1990) 'Housing and related inequalities in Japanese society'. Paper presented to the XIth World Congress of the Sociological Association, Madrid, July 9–13.

Henderson, J. and Karn, V. (1987) *Race, Class and State Housing*. Aldershot: Gower.

Henretta, J. (1984) 'Parental status and child's homeownership', *American Sociological Review* 49, pp. 131–40.

Henretta, J. (1987) 'Family transitions, housing market context, and first home purchased by young married households', *Social Forces* 66, pp. 520–36.

Herzfeld, M. (1980) 'Social tension and inheritance by lot in three Greek villages', *Anthropological Quarterly* 53, 2, pp. 91–8.

Heseltine, M. (1979) *House of Commons Debates* 15.5.79, Col. 80. London: HMSO.

Heskin, Allen David (1981) 'The History of Tenants in the United States, Struggle and Ideology', *International Journal of Urban and Regional Research* 5, 2, pp. 178–204.

Héthy, Lajos and Makó, Osaba (1972) *Munkásmagatartások es a gazdasagi szervezet* [Workers' behaviour and economic organization] Kiadd, Budapest: Akademia.

Hill, R. (1970) *Family Development in Three Generations*, Cambridge, Mass.: Schenkman.

Hill, R. and Konig, R. (eds) (1970), *Family in East and West. Socialization Processes and Kinship Ties*. The Hague: Mouton.

Hogan, D., Eggebeen, D., and Clogg, C. (1993) 'The structure of intergenerational exchanges in American families', *American Journal of Sociology* 98, 6, pp. 1428–57.

Hohm, C. (1984) 'Housing aspirations and fertility', *Sociology and Social*

Research 68, 3, pp. 350–63.

Hohm, C. (1985) 'The financial commitment to homeownership: attitudes of future homebuyers', *Social Science Journal* 22, pp. 47–55.

Hollinger, F. and Haller, M. (1990) 'Kinship and social networks in modern societies: a cross cultural comparison among seven nations', *European Sociological Review* 6, 2, pp. 103–24.

Holloway, T. (1991) 'The role of homeownership and home price appreciation in the accumulation and distribution of household sector wealth', *Business Economics*, April, pp. 38–44.

Holmans, A. (1991) *Estimates of Housing Equity withdrawal in the United Kingdom*, Government Economic Services Working Paper. London: Department of the Environment.

Homans, G. C. (1941) *English Villagers of the Thirteenth Century*. Cambridge, Mass.: Harvard University Press.

Hong, L. K. (1970) 'The Chinese family in a modern industrial setting', unpublished Ph.D. thesis, University of Notre Dame.

Hong Kong Bank (1992) 'The Hong Kong property market', Hong Kong Bank Economic Report, May.

Horowitz, C. (1990) 'Washington's continuing fiction: a national housing shortage', *Backgrounder No. 783*, Washington, D.C.: The Heritage Foundation.

Houdeville, L. (1969) *Pour une civilisation de l'habitat*. Paris: Éditions ouvrières.

Hoyt, H. (1966) *According to Hoyt*. Washington D.C.: Homer Hoyt.

Hughes, J. (1991) 'Clashing demographics: homeownership and affordability dilemmas', *Housing Policy Debate* 2, 4, pp. 1215–50.

Hulchanski, J. D. (1988) 'New forms of owning and renting.' In CMHC, *Housing Progress in Canada since 1945*, unpublished. Vancouver: University of British Columbia, p. 20.

Ibbotson, R. and Siegel, L. (1984) 'Real estate returns: A comparison with other investments', *Journal of the American Real Estate and Urban Economics Association* 12, 3, pp. 219–42.

Illich, I. (1986) 'Dwelling', *Development*, 4, pp. 15–25.

Inland Revenue (1990), *Inland Revenue Statistics*, London: HMSO.

Ion, J. (1980) 'Détermination historique et sociale des pratiques d'habitat', *Vie quotidienne en milieu urbain*. Paris: Centre de Recherche d'Urbanisme, pp. 63–71.

James, L. (1991) 'Housing and social welfare'. In S.K. Lau *et al.* (eds) *Indicators of Social Development: Hong Kong 1988*. Hong Kong: Hong Kong Institute of Asia-Pacific Studies.

Jevons, R. and Madge, J. (1946) 'Housing estates: a study of Bristol Corporation policy and practice between the wars', Reconstruction and Research Group: University of Bristol.

Johnson, B. M. (1971) *Household Behaviour: Consumption, Income and Wealth*. London.

Joint Center for Housing Studies of Harvard University (1990, 1991) *The State of the Nation's Housing*, Cambridge, Mass.

Kaufmann, J.-C. (1985) *Les accédants à la propriété en difficultés financières*. AUDIAR.

Kaufmann, J.-C. (1988) *La chaleur du foyer. Analyse du repli domestique.* Paris: Meridiens Klincksieck.

Kemény, István (1972) 'A Magyar munkásosztály rétegzodése' [Stratification of the Hungarian Working class], *Szociologia* 1, pp. 30–48.

Kemény, István and Kozák, Gyula (1971) *A Csepel Vas - es Fémmövek munkásai* [Workers of the Csepel Metal Works], Budapest: Tarsadalomtudományi Intézet.

Kemeny, J. (1980) 'The South Australian Housing Trust: a socio-economic case study of public housing', *Australian Journal of Social Issues* 15, 2, May, pp. 108–34.

Kemeny, J. (1981a) 'The cost of selling public rental housing: Victoria and South Australia compared', *Australian Journal of Social Issues* 16, 4, November, pp. 297–312.

Kemeny, J. (1981b) *The Myth of Home Ownership.* London: Routledge and Kegan Paul.

Kemeny, J. (1983) *The Great Australian Nightmare. A Critique of the Home-ownership Ideology.* Melbourne: Georgian House.

Kemeny, J. (1986) 'Ideological hegemony in housing research: towards an individual-based alternative', International Research Conference on Housing Policies, Gävle, June.

Kemeny, J. (1992a) *Housing and Social Theory.* London: Routledge.

Kemeny, J. (1992b) 'The significance of Swedish rental housing: from dualism to unitary renting in comparative perspective', *Swedish Institute for Building Research*, Working Paper, January, Gävle.

Kendig, H. L. (1982) 'The cumulation of inequality: housing in old age', Seminar Paper presented at the Australian National University, Research School of Social Science, 20 October.

Kendig, H., Paris, C. and Anderton, N. (1987) *Towards Fair Shares in Australian Housing.* Canberra: Highland Press.

Kessler, D. (1979) 'Aides, donations, héritages', *Economie et statistique* 107, pp. 31–51.

Kessler, D. and Masson, A. (1979) 'Transmission, accumulation et immo-bilité intergénérationnelle des patrimoines', *Consommation*, 3–4.

Khawaja, M. (1985) 'Trends and differentials in fertility'. In *ESCAP Population of New Zealand*, Country Monograph Series Vol. 1. New York: United Nations, pp. 152–77.

Kilmartin, L. (1988) 'Housing: an Antipodean perspective.' Keynote address to the conference 'Housing Policy and Urban Innovation', Amsterdam, June 27–July 1.

Klein, V. (1965) *Samples from English Cultures*, Vol. 1. London: Routledge and Kegan Paul.

Konig, R. (1976) 'Soziologie der Familie', In *Handbuchh der empirischen Sozialforschung*, vol. 7. Stuttgart: Enke, pp. 1–217.

Konrád, György and Szelényi, Iván (1971) 'A késleltetett városfajlödés tásadalmi konfliktusai [Social conflicts of delayed urbanization], *Valoság* 12, pp. 19–35. In English, A. A. Brown *et al.* (eds) (1974), *Urban and social economics in market and planned economies*, Vol. 1, *France*. New York, pp. 206–26.

Koopman-Boyden, P. G. (1992) *The Impact of New Zealand's Ageing Society.*

Koutsouveli, P. (1985) *Determinants of the Saving Behaviour of Individuals in Greece.* Athens (in Greek).

Kouveli, A. and Kotzamanis, V. (1988) *Preliminaries to the Question of Rental Housing,* Athens: National Center of Social Research, mimeo (in Greek).

Krohn, R. and Duff, H. (1971) 'The other housing economy: self-renewal in a central Montreal neighborhood'. Unpublished.

Kuttner, R. (1987) 'The patrimony society', *The New Republic* 3773, pp. 18–21.

Ladányi, János (1975) 'Fogyasztoi arak és szociálpolitika', *Valoság* 12, pp. 16–29. In English: 'Consumer prices and social policy', Paper presented at the 9th World Congress of Sociology, Uppsala, Sweden, August 1978.

Ladányi, János (1976) 'A gazdasági mechanizmus változásai, Központi és vállalati szociális juttatások, szociálpolitika [Changes of the economic mechanism, central and entrepreneurial social benefits, social policy]. *Valoság* 9, pp. 33–46.

Ladányi, János (1977) 'Községakbon élé munkások' [Workers living in villages], *Szociológia* 1, pp. 28–41.

Le Bras, H. and Gore, C. (1985) *Géographie physique et sociale de la famille dans la France actuelle,* Centre nationale recherches sociales (CNRS) A. T. P. Famille.

Le logement en France (1987) *Histoire d'une marchandise impossible.* Paris: Presses de la Fondation Nationale des Sciences Politiques.

Le Wita, B. (1984) 'La mémoire familiale des Parisiens appartenant aux classes moyennes', *Ethnologie Française,* 14.

Leather, P. (1990) 'The potential and implications of home equity release in old age', *Housing Studies* 5, pp. 3–13.

Lee, J. (1991) 'Housing and Social Welfare'. In S.K. Lau *et al.* (eds) *Indicators of Social Development: Hong Kong 1988.* Hong Kong Institute of Asia-Pacific Studies.

LePlay, F. (1864) *La réforme sociale.* 2 vols.

Leroy-Beaulieu, P. (1896) *Traité théorique et pratique d'économie politique.* Paris: Guillaumin.

Lin, W. L. *et al.* (1989) *Dao You Ke Zhi Lu* [The Road to Accommodation]. Taipei: Nan Fang (in Chinese).

Linneman, P. and Wachter, S. (1989) 'The impacts of borrowing constraints on home-ownership'. *AREUEA Journal* 17, 4, pp. 389–402.

Lloyds Bank (1993) 'Inheritances – all our futures', *Lloyds Bank Economic Bulletin,* 176, August.

Long, J. E. and Caudill, S. B. (1992) 'Racial differences in homeownership and housing wealth, 1970–1986', *Economic Inquiry,* 30, 1, pp. 83–100.

Lowe, S. G. (1992) 'Home ownership, wealth and welfare: new connections'. In A. Corden, E. Robertson and K. Tolley (eds) *Meeting Needs in an Affluent Society.* Aldershot: Avebury.

Lui, T. (1971) 'Residential patterns and family networks (I)', *International Journal of Sociology of the Family,* 2, pp. 23–41.

Lui, T. (1981) 'The implications of differential rates of capital gain from owner occupation for the formation and development of housing classes', *International Journal of Urban and Regional Research*, 5, pp. 205–30.

Lui, T. (1989) 'The impact of homeownership and capital gains upon class and consumption sectors', *Society and Space*, 7, pp. 293–312.

Lui, T. (1991) 'Housing and social welfare', in S.K. Lau *et al.* (eds), *Indicators of Social Development: Hong Kong 1988*. Hong Kong: Hong Kong Institute of Asia-Pacific Studies.

Lui, T. 1992 'Reinstating class', Occasional Paper, Social Sciences Research Centre, University of Hong Kong.

McDonald, P. (1986) *Setting up: property and income distribution and divorce*. Melbourne: Australian Institute of Family Studies.

McDonald, P. (1990) 'The 1990s: social and economic change affecting families', *Family Matters* 26, pp. 13–18.

Macfarlane, A. (1978) *The Origins of English Individualism*, Oxford: Basil Blackwell.

Macfarlane, A. (1986) *Marriage and Love in England, 1300–1840*, Oxford: Basil Blackwell.

Maclennan, D. *et al.* (1994) 'Reports from the Housing and the Macro Economy Programme', Joseph Rowntree Foundation.

Mahar, C. (1984) 'Government housing policy: the impact on consumers'. In C. Wilkes and I. Shirley, *In the Public Interest*. Auckland: Benton Ross.

Maison, D. (1990) 'Rapport à l'espace urbain et stratégies résidentielles en Région parisienne', Colloque de l'AIDELF de Rabat, Mai.

Maison, D. (1992) 'Pionniers de l'accession.' Paper presented to the 5th International Research Conference on Housing, Montreal, 7–10 July 1992.

Mallet, S. (1963) *La nouvelle classe ouvriers*. Paris: Editions du Seuil.

Maloutas, T. and Economou, D. (1988) 'Welfare state: the "model" and its Greek version'. In Maloutas and Economou (eds) *Development Problems of the Welfare State in Greece*. Athens (in Greek), pp. 13–56.

Maloutas, T. (1990a) 'Statut d'occupation, mode d'acquisition du logement et choix de localisation résidentielle à Athènes.' Paper presented to the 4th International Research Conference on Housing, Paris, 3–6.

Maloutas, T. (1990b) *Athens, Housing, Family: An Analysis of Postwar Housing Practices*. Athens (in Greek).

Marglin, S. A. (1984) *Growth, Distribution, and Prices*. Cambridge, Mass.

Márkus, István (1991) *Az ismeretlen föszereplö* [The unknown hero] Budapest: Szépirodalmi Könyvkiadó.

Marpasat, M. (1991) 'Les échanges au sein de la famille: héritage, aides financières, garde des enfants et visite aux grandparents', *Economie et Statistiques* 239, January.

Martin, J. (1985) 'Suburbia, community and network'. In S. Encel and M. Berry, *Selected Readings in Australian Society*. Melbourne: Longman Cheshire.

Marx, K. (1976) *Capital Vol. l*. Harmondsworth: Penguin.

Marshall, G., Newby, H., Rose, D. and Vogter, C. (1988) *Social Class in Modern Britain*. London: Hutchinson.

Masson, A. (1990) 'Logement et comportements patrimoniaux: modèles micro-économiques du cycle de vie'. In *Stratégies Résidentielles*, INED, Plan Construction, Congrès et Colloques 2, pp. 139–55.

Massot, A. (1989) 'Les acquéreurs de logements à Paris en 1988', Chambre interdépartementale des Notaires de Paris, December.

Massot, A. (1990) 'Qui achète des logements à Paris?' *Cahiers de l'Aurif*, 93, pp. 81–88.

Merrett, S. (1982) *Owner occupation in Britain*. London: Routledge and Kegan Paul.

Minc, A. (1991) 'Si la gauche était au pouvoir . . .' *Le Nouvel Observateur*.

Mingione, E. (1991) *Fragmented Societies: A Sociology of Economic Life Beyond the Market Paradigm*. Oxford: Basil Blackwell.

Ministry of Housing (Netherlands)(1991) *Statistics on Housing in the European Community*. The Hague.

Mitchell, B. (1993) 'Nation to inherit new wealthy class', *The Sunday Age*, 25 April, p. 14.

Mitchell, R. (1969) *Levels of Emotional Strain in Southeast Asian Cities*. Taipei: The Orient Cultural Service.

Mitchell, R. E. (1971) 'Residential patterns and family networks', *International Journal of Sociology of the Family* 2, pp. 23–41.

Morley, C. (1990) 'Home makers and design advice in the post-war period'. In T. Putnam and C. Newton, *Household Choices*. London: Futures Publications.

Mullings, B. (1992) 'Ageing and the extraction of equity from housing assets'. Paper presented to the 5th International Research Conference on Housing, Montreal.

Munro, M. and Maclennan, D. (1987) 'Intra-urban changes in housing prices: Glasgow 1972–83', *Housing Studies*, 2, 2, pp. 65–81.

Munro, M. (1988) 'Housing wealth and inheritance', *Journal of Social Policy*, 17, 4, pp. 417–36.

Murie, A. (1974) *Household movement and housing choice*, CURS, University of Birmingham.

Murie, A. (1975) *The Sale of Council Houses: A Study in Social Policy*, Occasional Paper No. 35, CURS, University of Birmingham.

Murie, A. (1983) *Housing Inequality and Deprivation*. London: Heinemann.

Murie, A. (1991) 'Divisions of home ownership housing tenure and social change', *Environment and Planning* A, 23, 3, pp. 349–70.

Murie, A. and Forrest, R. (1980a) *Housing Market Processes and the Inner City*. SSRC: School Publishing House.

Murie, A. and Forrest, R. (1980b) 'Wealth, inheritance and housing policy', *Policy and Politics* 8, pp. 1–19.

Myers, D. (1985) 'Wives' earnings and rising costs of homeownership', *Social Science Quarterly*, 66, pp. 319–29.

Naisbitt, J. (1984) *Megatrends. Ten New Directions Forming Our Lives*. London: Futura Books-MacDonald.

Nasar, S. (1992) 'The 1980s: a very good time for the very rich', *The New York Times*, pp. A–1, C–13.

National Housing Commission (1988) *Housing in New Zealand.* Wellington: N.H.C.

National Housing Strategy (1991) *Australian Housing: the demographic, economic and social environment,* Issues Paper l. Canberra: Department of Community Services and Health.

Negri, N. (1986) 'Instabilità e discontinuità nelle formazioni sociali metropolitane', *Sociologia urbana e rurale,* 8, pp. 141–8.

Nelson, K. and Khadduri, J. (1992) 'To whom shall limited housing resources be directed?', *Housing, Policy Debate,* 2, 2, pp. 1–56.

Neutze, M. and Kendig, H. L (1991) 'Achievement of home ownership among post-war Australian cohorts', *Housing Studies* 6, pp. 3–14.

New Zealand Planning Council (NZPC) (1990) *Who Gets What. The Distribution of Income and Wealth in New Zealand.* Wellington: NZPC.

OECD (1991) *Historical Statistics 1960–1989.* Paris.

Office of Population Censuses and Surveys (OPCS) (1978) *General Household Survey 1976.* London: HMSO.

Oxley, H. G. (1978) *Mateship in Local Organisation.* St Lucia: Queensland University Press.

Pahl, R. E. (1975) *Whose City?* (2nd edn). Harmondsworth: Penguin.

Pahl, R. E. (1984) *Divisions of Labour.* Oxford: Basil Blackwell.

Pahl, R. E. (1989) 'Housing, work and life style', *Tijdschrift voor Economische en Sociale Geografie,* 80, 2, pp. 75–81.

Pastor, M. H. (1992) 'Concentration of wealth through ownership', CMHC, Research and Development Highlights, Socio-economic Series, no. 8. Unpublished.

Pats, B. (1987) 'Variables affecting college seniors' expectations about returning home', *Journal of College Student Personnel,* 28, pp. 246–52.

Payne, S. (1990) *Estate Duty Data and FTS Use for Constructing Estimates of Wealth.* Wellington: New Zealand Planning Council.

Peck, J. G. and Lepie, A. S. (1989) 'Tourism and development in three North Carolina coastal towns'. In V.I. Smith (ed.) *Hosts and Guests: The Anthropology of Tourism* (2nd edn). Philadelphia: University of Pennsylvania Press.

Peraldi, M. (1989) 'Lien familial et lien civil en cité HLM'. In *Familles et Patrimoines,* Les Annales de la Recherche Urbaine, 41, Mars–Avril, pp. 104–11.

Peraldi, M. and Spinousa, N. (1990) Les accédants à la propriété en difficulté dans les Bouches-du-Rhône. Mimeo.

Perrinjaquet, R. (1986) *La dynamique socio-spatiale de l'habiter.* Lausanne: IREC.

Phillips, K. (1990) *The Politics of Rich and Poor. Wealth and the American Electorate in the Reagan Aftermath.* New York: Random House.

Pickvance, C. and Pickvance, K. (1993) 'The role of family help in the housing decisions of young people'. Mimeo.

Pinçon, D. (1988) *Du logement pour tous aux maisons en tous genres.* Paris: Ministère de l'Équipement et du Logement, Plan construction et architecture.

Pinçon, M. (1986) 'Autoproduction, sociabilité et identité dans une petite ville ouvrière', *Revue Française de Sociologie,* 28.

Pitkin, D. S. (1985) *The House that Giacomo Built. History of an Italian Family, 1898–1978*. New York: Cambridge University Press.

Pitrou, A. (1976) 'Le soutien familial dans la société urbaine', *Revue Française de Sociologie*, XVIII, 177, pp. 47–84.

Pitrou, A. (1978) *Vivre sans famille*. Toulouse: Privat, 235 pp.

Pitt-Rivers, J. A. (1974) *The People of the Sierra*, Chicago: University of Chicago Press.

Polanyi, K. (1944/75) *The Great Transformation*, Boston: Beacon Press.

Polanyi, K. (1977) *The Livelihood of Man*, ed. H. W. Pearson. New York: Academic Press.

Pollakowski, H., Stegman, M. and Rohe, W. (1991) 'Rates of return on housing of low- and moderate-income homeowners', *AREUEA Journal* 19, 3, pp. 417–25.

Potter, P. and Drevermann, M. (1988) 'Home ownership, foreclosure and compulsory auction in the Federal Republic of Germany', *Housing Studies* 3, 2, pp. 94–104.

Pratt, G. (1986a) 'Housing consumption sectors and political response in urban Canada', *Society and Space* 4, pp. 165–82.

Pratt, G. (1986b) 'Housing tenure and social cleavages in urban Canada', *Annals of the Association of American Geographers* 76, pp. 366–80.

Quercia, R. and Rohe, W. (1992) 'Housing adjustments among older home owners', *Urban Affairs Quarterly* 28, 1.

Quereshi, H. and Simons, K. (1987) 'Resources within families: caring for elderly people'. In J. Brannen and G. Wilson (eds) *Give and Take in Families*. London: Allen and Unwin.

Rakoff, R. M. (1977) 'Ideology in everyday life: the meaning of the house', *Politics and Society* 7, pp. 85–104.

Rapoport, A. (1969) *Housing Form and Culture*. Englewood Cliffs: Prentice-Hall.

Raspberry, W. (1990) 'Kemp at HUD paving path out of dependency', *Raleigh News and Observer*.

Raymond, H. *et al.* (1966) *L'habitat pavillonnaire*. Paris: Centre de recherche d'urbanisme, 1966.

Reserve Bank (1990) *Reserve Bank of Australia Bulletin*. Canberra.

Reserve Bank of New Zealand (1986) *Reserve Bank Bulletin 49* (8). Wellington.

Rex, J. and Moore, R. (1967) *Race, Community and Conflict: A Study of Sparkbrook*. Oxford: Oxford University Press.

Richards, L. (1990) *Nobody's Home. Dreams and Realities in a New Suburb*. Melbourne: Oxford University Press.

Robins, A. (1990) *Household Distribution of Material and Financial Assets*. Wellington: New Zealand Planning Council.

Rohe, W. M. and Stegman, M. (1990) *Public Housing Homeownership Demonstration Assessment*. Washington DC: US Department of Housing and Urban Development, April.

Roistacher, E. and Young, J. S. (1979) 'Two earner families in the housing market', *Policy Studies Journal*, 8, 2, pp. 227–40.

Roper, B. (1991) 'From welfare state to free market: explaining the transition', *New Zealand Sociology*, 6, 1, pp. 38–63.

Rosen, S. (1976) *Mei Foo Sun Chuen: Middle-Class Chinese Families in Transition*. Taipei: The Orient Cultural Service.

Rossi, A. and Rossi, P. (1990) *Of Human Bonding: Parent Child Relations Across the Life Course*, New York: De Gruyter.

Roussel, L. and Bourguignon, O. (1976) 'La famille après le mariage des enfants', Paris, PUF/INED, *Travaux et Documents*, cahier 78, 258 pp.

Royal Commission on the Distribution of Income and Wealth (1977) Cmnd 6999, *Third Report on the Standing Reference*, London: HMSO.

Rudel, Thomas K. (1987) 'Housing price inflation, family growth and the move from rented to owner occupied housing', *Urban Studies*, 24, 4, pp. 258–67.

Rybczynski, W. (1986) *Home. A Short History of an Idea*. New York: Penguin.

Salaff, J. (1981) *Working Daughters of Hong Kong*. Cambridge: Cambridge University Press.

Salt, J. and Coleman, D. (1992) *The British Population*. Oxford: Oxford University Press.

Sanders, I. T. (1953) 'Village social organisation in Greece', *Rural Sociology*, 18, 1, pp. 366–75.

Saraceno, C. (1988) *Sociologia della famiglia*. Bologna: Il Mulino.

Saunders, P. (1977) 'Housing tenure and class interests'. Brighton: University of Sussex, Urban and Regional Studies, Working Paper 6.

Saunders, P. (1978) 'Domestic property and social class', *International Journal of Urban and Regional Research*, 2, pp. 233–51.

Saunders, P. (1984) 'Beyond housing classes', *International Journal of Urban and Regional Research*, 8, pp. 202–27.

Saunders, P. (1986) *Social Theory and the Urban Question* (2nd edn). London: Hutchinson.

Saunders, P. (1990) *A Nation of Home Owners*. London: Unwin Hyman.

Saunders, P. and Harris, C. (1988) *Home Ownership and Capital Gains*. Working Paper 64, University of Sussex.

Savage, M., Barlow, J., Duncan, S. and Saunders, P. (1987) 'Locality Research: the Sussex programme on economic restructuring, social change and the locality', *The Quarterly Journal of Social Affairs* 3, 1, pp. 27–51.

Sayer, A. and Walker, R. (1992) *The New Social Economy*. Oxford: Basil Blackwell.

Schellenberg, K. (1987) 'The persistence of the home-ownership norm and the implications of mortgage debt', *Journal of Urban Affairs*, 9, 4, p. 355–66.

Schwartz, D. C., Ferlauto, R. C. and Hoffman, D. N. (1988) *A New Housing Policy for America. Recapturing the American Dream.* Philadelphia: Temple University Press.

Segalen, M. (1980) '"Faire construire". Résistances et contre-pouvoirs familiaux en Bretagne', *Economie et Humanisme*, 251, pp. 40–50.

Segalen, M. (1981) *Sociologie de la Famille* (2nd edn). Paris: A. Colin.

Segalen, M. (1990) (with F. Bekus) *Nanterriens: les familles dans la ville.*

Toulouse: Presses universitaires du Mirail.

Segalen, M. and Bekus, F. (1989) 'S'installer dans une ville. Nanterre 1900–1980'. In *Familles et Patrimoines*, Les Annales de la Recherche Urbaine, 41, Mars–Avril, pp. 51–8.

Seward, J., Delaney, C. and Smith, M. (1992) 'An empirical analysis of housing price appreciation in a market stratified by size and value of the housing stock', *The Journal of Real Estate*, 7, 2, pp. 195–205.

Shear, W., Wachter, S. and Weicher, J. 'Housing as an asset in the 1980s and 1990s', mimeo, undated.

Short, J. R. (1982) *Housing in Britain*. London: Methuen.

Short, J. R. (1976) *Aspects of residential mobility in Bristol*, PhD thesis, University of Bristol.

Sik, Endre (1988) 'Az "örök" Kaléka, Gondolat Könyvkiado, Budapest'. In English, 'Reciprocal exchange of labour in Hungary'. In Raymond Pahl (ed.) *On Work*. Oxford: Basil Blackwell.

Sikjiö, O. and Borgegård, L. (1991) 'Households in action - on access to housing in a regulated private rental market', *Scandinavian Housing and Planning Research* 8, 1 (February), pp. 1–11.

Silver, A. (1990) 'Friendship in Commercial Society: eighteenth century social theory and modern sociology', *American Journal of Sociology* 95, 6 (May), pp. 1475–504.

Smith, B. and Teserak, W. (1991) 'House prices and regional real estate cycles: market adjustments in Houston', *AREUEA Journal*, 19, 3, pp. 396–416.

Smith, B. N. and Thorns, D. C. (1979) *Constraints, Choices and Housing Environments*. Wellington: National Housing Commission.

Smith, S. J. (1990) 'Income, housing wealth and gender inequality', *Urban Studies* 27, pp. 67–88.

Snickars, F. (1985) *Scandinavian Housing and Planning Research* 2, 3–4 (Aug./Nov.), pp. 169–87.

Snively, S. (1981) *Housing: the Capacity to Buy*. Wellington: National Housing Commission.

South Australian Department of Lands (n.d.) State Accumulated Sales Report, microfiche.

Spinousa, N. (1991) *La propriété différée*. Marseille: CERFISE mimeo.

Stacey, M., Batstone, E., Bell, C. and Murcott, A. (1975) *Power, Persistence and Change*. London: Routledge and Kegan Paul.

Steele, M. (1988) 'The demand for home ownership'. In CMHC, *Housing Progress in Canada Since 1945*. Toronto: University of Toronto Press. Unpublished.

Stegman, Michael A. (1991) 'The limits of privatization'. In *More Housing, More Fairly*, Report of the Twentieth Century Task Force on Affordable Housing. New York.

Steinbach, Carol F. (1991) 'Housing the haves', *National Journal*, June 29, pp. 1615–19.

Stimson, R. J. (1988) 'Housing tenure and costs in Australia'. Paper presented to the 3rd International Research Conference on Housing, Amsterdam.

Stivens, M. (1981) 'Women, kinship and capitalist development'. In K. Young, C. Wokowitcz and R. McCullagh (eds) *Of Marriage and the*

Market. London: Routledge and Kegan Paul.

Strathern, M. (1981) *Kinship at the Core: an Anthropology of Elmdon Essex*. Cambridge: Cambridge University Press.

Stretton, H. (1974) *Housing and Government*. Adelaide: Australian Broadcasting Commission.

Stroombergen, A. and Koy, K. (1987) *Housing: the Capacity to Buy*. Wellington: National Housing Commission.

Szelényi, Iván (1972) 'Lakásrendszer és társadalmi struktura' [Social structure and housing], *Szociológia* 1, pp. 49–74.

Szelényi, Iván (1983) *Urban Inequalities under State Socialism*. Oxford: Oxford University Press.

Szelényi, Iván and Manchin, Robert (1986) Szociálpolitika az államszocilaitmushan, *Medvetano* 2–3, pp. 69–111. In English, 'Social policy under state socialism'. In G. L. Esping-Anderson and M. R. Rainwater (eds) (1987) *Stagnation and Renewal in Social Policy*, White Plains, N.Y.: Sharpe.

Taffin, C. (1987) 'L'accession à tout prix'. *Économie et statistique*, 202, pp. 5–15.

Taylor, C. (1983) *Village and farmstead*. London: George Philip.

Teserak, W. and Smith, B. (1991) 'House prices and regional real estate cycles: market adjustments in Houston', *AREUEA Journal* 19, 3, pp. 396–416.

Thatcher, M. (1979) *House of Commons Debates*, 15.5.79, Col. 80. London: HMSO.

Thomas, T. (1990) 'The inheritance windfall', *Business Review Weekly* 12, pp. 44–9.

Thorns, D. C. (1981a) 'Housing policies and the influence of the growth of owner-occupation in a social and political change.' Paper presented to the conference 'Comparative urban research', Essen, October 3–5.

Thorns, D. C. (1981b) 'The implications of differential rates of capital gain from owner-occupation for the formation and development of housing classes', *International Journal of Urban and Regional Research* 5, pp. 205–30.

Thorns, D. C. (1982) 'Industrial restructuring and change in the labour and property markets in Britain', *Environment and Planning* 14, pp. 745–63.

Thorns, D. C. (1989a) 'The production of homelessness. From individual failure to system inadequacies', *Housing Studies* 4, 4, pp. 253–66.

Thorns, D. C. (1989b) 'The impact of homeownership and capital gains upon class and consumption sectors', *Society and Space* 7, pp. 293–312.

Thorns, D. C. (1992) *Fragmenting Societies? A Comparative Analysis of Regional and Urban Development*. London: Routledge.

Topalov, C. (1981) *Tous propriétaires! Propriété du logement et classes sociales en France depuis 1950*. Paris: Centre de sociologie urbaine.

Topalov, C. (1987) *Le logement en France. Histoire d'une marchandaise impossible*. Paris: Presses de la Fondation Nationale des Sciences Politiques.

Topley, M. (1969) 'The role of savings and wealth among Hong Kong Chinese', in Ian C. Jarvie and Joseph Agassi (eds) *Hong Kong: A Society in Transition*. New York: Frederick A. Praeger Publishers.

Tosi, A. (1987) 'La produzione della casa in proprietà. Pratiche familiari, informale, politiche', *Sociologia e ricerca sociale*, 22, pp. 7–24.

Tosi, A. (1990) 'Pratiche abitative anomale'. In A. Magnaghi (ed.) *Il territorio dell'abitare*. Milan: Franco Angeli, pp. 357–94.

Tosi, A. (1991a) 'Urban Theory and the Treatment of Differences. Administrative Practices, Social Sciences, and the Difficulties of Specifics', *International Journal of Urban and Regional Research*, 15, 4, pp. 594–609.

Tosi, A. (1991b), 'Condizioni e processi abitativi'. In *Social Survey in Lombardia*. Milan: Franco Angeli-IReR, pp. 239–79.

Toulemon, L. and Villeneuve-Gokalp, C. (1988) 'Les vacances des enfants', *Population* 6, pp. 1065–87.

Treasury (New Zealand) (1984) *Economic Management*. Wellington: Government Printer.

Trout, K. (1979) 'Construction de logements et crise économique. Quelques éléments d'analyse', *Critiques de l'économie politique*, 9.

Troy, P. N. (1991) *The benefits of owner-occupation*. Urban Research Program Working Paper 22, No. 29. Canberra: ANU.

Tsoughiopoulos, G. (1981) *The Greek Urban Centre*. Athens (in Greek).

Turner, J. F. C. (1976) *Housing by People*. London: Marion Boyards.

Turpijn, W. (1988) 'Self-help housing in West Europe', *Trialog* 3, pp. 36–42.

Urbanowicz, C. F. (1989) 'Tourism in Tonga revisited: continued troubled times'. In V. I. Smith (ed.) *Hosts and Guests: The Anthropology of Tourism* (2nd edn). Philadelphia: University of Pennsylvania Press.

US Bureau of the Census (1990) 'Marital status and living arrangements', *Current Population Reports*, Series P-60, No. 450. Washington, DC.

US Bureau of the Census (1991a) 'Trends in relative income: 1964 to 1989', *Current Population Reports, Consumer Income*, Series P-60, No. 177. Washington, DC.

US Bureau of the Census (1991b) 'Who can afford to buy a house?', *Current Housing Reports*, Series H121/91–1, Washington, DC.

US Bureau of the Census (1991c) 'Housing characteristics of recent movers: 1989', *Current Housing Reports*, Series H121/91–2. Washington, DC.

US Bureau of the Census (1992) 'Housing in America: 1989–1990', *Current Housing Reports*, Series H123/91–1. Washington, DC.

US Department of Housing and Urban Development (1989) *HOPE, Home Ownership for People Everywhere*. Washington, DC.

US Department of Housing and Urban Development (1991) *Housing Discrimination Study, Synthesis*, Washington, DC.

Verret, Michel (1979) *L'ouvrier français. L'espace ouvrier*. Paris: Armand Colin.

Vervaeke, M. (1990a) 'Les réseaux d'accès au logement'. Paris, IRESCO, séminaire LASMAS, February.

Vervaeke, M. (1990b) 'Ségrégation sociale: l'accès au logement dans un espace régional connaissant une désindustrialisation.' Paper presented to the conference 'Housing Debates–Urban Challenges'. Paris, July 3–6.

Vitt, L. A. (1990) 'The social psychology of homeownership in US society'. Paper presented to the conference 'Housing Debates–Urban Challenges', Paris, July 3–6.

Vitt, L. A. (1992) 'Homeownership, well-being, class and politics in US society'. Paper presented to the 5th International Research Conference on Housing, Montreal, 7–10 July.

Walden, Michael L. (1987) 'Effects of housing codes on local housing markets'. *AREUEA Journal* 15, 2, pp. 13–31.

Wall, R., Robin, J., Laslett, P. (1983) *Family Forms in Historic Europe.* Cambridge: Cambridge University Press.

Wallace, J. and Faure, A. (1991) *Hong Kong Property Market Review: Sectoral Analysis.* London: Baring Securities.

Wallman, S. (1974) 'Kinship, a-kinship and anti-kinship'. In E. Leyton (ed.) *The Compact*, Newfoundland social and economic papers 3. Memorial University of Newfoundland.

Wallman, S. (1982) *Living in South London.* London: Gower.

Ward, C. (1985) *When We Build Again.* London and Sydney: Pluto Press.

Ward, R. (1958) *The Australian Legend.* Melbourne: Oxford University Press.

Warde, A., Soothill, K., Shapiro, D. and Papantonakou, A. (1989) 'Divisions of labour in North-West England', WP 38, Lancaster Regionalism Group, University of Lancaster.

Weicher, J. C. (1992) 'FHA reform: balancing public purpose and financial soundness', *Journal of Real Estate Finance and Economics* 5, pp. 133–50.

Welfeld, I. (1988) *Where We Live: A Social History of American Housing.* New York: Simon and Schuster.

Wieman, E. (1990) 'The millionaire's market', *Asian Property*, Feb., pp. 11–13.

Wiktorin, M. (1980) 'Housing exchanges in Swedish housing policy'. Paper presented at the Conference on Housing and the State in Sweden and Britain, Sussex University (October).

Wiktorin, M. (1982a) 'Housing policy and disadvantaged groups in Sweden', *International Journal of Urban and Regional Research* 6, 2, pp. 246–55.

Wiktorin, M. (1982b) 'Housing allocation and queueing principles in Sweden'. Paper prepared for the Swedish–Hungarian research exchange (September).

Wiktorin, M. and Kemeny, J. (1981) 'Housing allocation and the Swedish rental market'. In Jim Kemeny (ed.) *Swedish Rental Housing: Policies and Problems.* Centre for Urban and Regional Studies, Occasional Paper 4 (New Series), Birmingham University.

Williams, N. J. (1988) 'Housing tenure, political attitudes and voting behaviour.' Paper presented to the conference 'Housing Policy and Urban Innovation', Amsterdam.

Williams, P. (1984) 'The politics of property: home ownership in Australia'. In J. Halligan and C. Paris (eds) *Australian Urban Politics.* Melbourne: Longman Cheshire, pp. 167–92.

Williams, R. G. A. (1983) 'Kinship and migration strategies among settled Londoners; two responses to population pressure', *British*

Journal of Sociology, 34, 3, pp. 386–415.

Willmott, P. (1963) *The Evolution of a Community – a Study of Dagenham after Forty Years*. London: Routledge and Kegan Paul.

Willmott, P. (1987a) *Friendship Networks and Social Support*. London: Policy Studies Institute.

Willmott, P. (1987b) 'Kinship and urban communities: past and present', the ninth H. J. Dyos Memorial Lecture, Victorian Studies Centre, University of Leicester.

Willmott, P. and Young, M. (1957) *Family and Kinship in East London*. London: Routledge and Kegan Paul.

Willmott, P. and Young, M. (1960) *Family and Class in a London Suburb*. London: Routledge and Kegan Paul.

Wilson, G. (1987) 'Women's work: the role of grandmothers in inter-generational transfers', *Sociological Review*, 35, 4, pp. 703–20.

Wong, T. W. P. and Lui, T. L. (1992a) 'From one brand of politics to one brand of political culture', Occasional Paper No. 10, Hong Kong Institute of Asia-Pacific Studies.

Wong, T. P. and Lui, T. L. (1992b) *Reinstating Class*, Occasional Paper, Social Sciences Research Centre, University of Hong Kong.

Wood, G. A. (1990) 'The tax treatment of housing: economic issues and reform measures', *Urban Studies* 27, 6, pp. 809–30.

Woodward, S. and Weicher, J. (1989) 'Goring the wrong ox: a defense of the mortgage interest deduction', *National Tax Journal* XLII, 3, pp. 301–13.

Wulff, M. G. (1982) 'The two-income household: relative contribution of earnings to housing costs', *Urban Studies* 19, pp. 343–50.

Yates, J. (1991) *Australia's Owner-occupied Housing Wealth and its Impact upon Income Distribution*, Social Policy Research Centre Reports and Proceedings No 92, Sydney.

Young, M. and Willmott, P. (1957) *Family and Kinship in East London*. Harmondsworth: Penguin.

Index